LIBERALISM UNMASKED

Men did not love Rome because she was great. She was great because they had loved her.

— G.K. Chesterton, *Orthodoxy*

Who fears the wolf should never enter the forest.

— Fyodor Dostoyevsky, *The Gambler*

For Europe. The Promethean fire of mankind.

For America. The last bastion of freedom.

For my people. The most beloved possession I have.

To my dad. I never would have started this project, nor finished, without your encouragement. For that I am truly grateful. This book is little more than a record of our conversations together from the time I was young.

To my mom. Your determination and resolve have always been inspirational to me. A reminder of what can be achieved with little more than hope and steely-eyed grit. I never would have been able to spend my winters in Paris, taking those long walks alone at night, if it was not for you keeping the bike shop open. I'll never forget that.

RICHARD HOUCK

ARKTOS
LONDON 2018

Printed in the United Kingdom.

ISBN	978-1-912079-31-5 (Paperback) 978-1-912079-30-8 (Ebook)
EDITOR	John Bruce Leonard
COVER	Tor Westman
LAYOUT	Daniel Friberg

Arktos.com fb.com/Arktos @arktosmedia arktosmedia

CONTENTS

ACT I: KNOW THY ENEMY

ACT II: FIGHTING THE BATTLES

ACT III: WINNING THE WAR

About the Cover

The image on the cover is an allusion to the classic cult film, *They Live*. The glasses serve as an allegory to this book, and the struggles of Nada, are akin to those seeing the truth.

My goal was to write a book that serves as the glasses from *They Live*. A simple yet powerful tool to see Liberalism unmasked, for the pathological madness it is and to see the international Left without the facade.

They Live was before my time. My parents introduced me to classic books, music, and films throughout my childhood. My dad suggested we watch *They Live* many years ago, when I was still quite young. From the first viewing, it became one of my all time favorite movies. Not too long ago, I was fortunate enough to see the film on the big screen. A local cinema was playing 80s cult and horror classics during the month of October for Halloween, it was truly an experience. For those few fleeting hours, it felt as if I were back in a better time. I felt a sort of hiraeth that evening, a grief, nostalgia, and homesickness for a time and place that I had never seen myself.

In *They Live*, a hostile race of aliens has subtly enslaved humanity through control of the mass media and the banking system. Through control of the media, the hostile invaders were able to control the population by inducing a sort of semi-conscious state, turning humans into unthinking, unquestioning, unmotivated, zombie-like cattle. Those who wore the special sunglasses were able to see the veiled messages, and the aliens without their masks. What are seen as benign commercials, ads, and billboards to most people, with the glasses, now read as haunting instructions to the human race;

Obey authority. Consume. No imagination. Submit. Conform. Watch TV. No independent thought. Stay asleep.

When you put on the glasses, you can see for the first time, the nature of our reality. Our world is somewhat of a pseudo-reality, a simulacrum, mere shadows along the cave walls. Seeing past the thin facade and the true nature of Liberalism without its mask, is often a lonely journey.

In the film there is a fight scene, one of the longest fight scenes in film history. The unnamed main character, referred only to as Nada in the final credits, played by the late Rowdy Roddy Piper, is trying to convince his friend, Frank, to put on the sunglasses. The fight scene is one of the longest in film for a reason, it serves to illuminate the struggle of trying to get others to see what you can see. At one point in the fight Nada yells to Frank, "I'm trying to save you and your family's life!" Despite his good intentions, Nada was met with hostility and aggression. Just as many of us who speak the truth in this modern world are met with hostility and aggression, merely for wanting to show people the truth, and perhaps, save their lives. We are the only one's trying to save civilization, and for that, we are hated.

Those who can see, those wearing the glasses, are at first shocked, then horrified, saddened, and ultimately, furious. They feel alone, they wonder if they are going crazy, then begin wondering how many others out there can see, and start to wonder if they are the only ones left.

Once the alien race and their willing human accomplices that are bought and sold, realize others see them for what they truly are, they have the police hunt them down. For it is far too dangerous to allow "ones who can see", to walk among them. They live, while we are meant to stay asleep.

If the film, those who wear the glasses too long, that is if you spend too long looking directly at the truth, began to feel ill. Wearing the glasses too long causes you to feel like "a knife turning in your head." I felt the same way writing this book. And I know many others felt the same level of horror, sadness, and rage, upon realizing the truth as well. The truth is a heavy cross to bear. I don't like what I see one bit. Not one bit.

It's far easier to take the glasses off, take the blue pill, and to go back to sleep. And that's exactly what they want. And that's exactly why I'll never take the glasses off again.

Put on the glasses, and welcome to the party, pal. The world needs a wake up call, it's time to phone it in.

I have come here to chew bubblegum and fight for Western
Civilization. And I'm all out of bubblegum.

Act I:

Know Thy Enemy

I

Introduction

I never intended to write a book on politics. I am a simple man, from a small, beautiful town, that has been tucked away and forgotten. I spend the evenings riding my bicycle through the woods, and passing time with those for whom I care deeply.

To be honest, I was never all that interested in politics. Certainly not interested enough to write a book about the subject.

But something changed. Not within me, at least not at first. But in the world around me. The America that I knew and loved was slowly fading. I know every generation has similar sentiments. That things aren't the way they used to be, in the "good old days."

The harsh reality is that the America my parents grew up in is not the one I am going to inherit. National debt is at an all time high, consumer debt is piling up, race relations are the worst they have been since the 1960s, if not before, with a particularly anti-white bent, and it seems the bi-partisan appetite for war has grown insatiable.

When I first became aware of these changes, I began to pay much more attention to national news, world news, politics, and I looked through history for insight. I wanted to know how we got here, and who was behind the dumpster fire. What I began to see were cowardly Republicans, helpless conservatives, and mentally ill Liberals, hell-bent on destroying everything I held dear.

I can't recall when it happened exactly; I used to be very much a live-and-let-live type of man. I always thought people were *entitled* to their own political opinions, and I never really gave the matter much more thought than that. I really don't recall the moment something changed within me. Maybe it was gradual, and then all at once. Much like how fall collapses into winter. First the leaves begin to change color, falling slowly, one by one, until the trees are bare. Letting go of all they held onto so tightly all summer long. Then one morning you wake up to snow covering the forest.

Maybe mine was a similar path. When I began researching this book, I came across many things that kept me awake at night. I found news reports that have been largely kept out of the mainstream media. Stories of murder, torture, molestation, and gang rapes being committed against my people by hostile invaders. I listened to first-hand accounts of people I know who have been personally affected by these crimes. With each revelation, I was slowly changing. I could feel it in my bones. And one morning, I woke up a grim man with a hard heart. It's not what I set out to become, but it's what I needed to become to tell this story.

I remember a Clinical Psychology class I took. The professor was talking about personality disorders one day. She said that when there are no biochemical, substance, or environmental factors that explain irrational behavior, no logic to it, no way to reason with the person, it is likely he is suffering from some sort of mental illness.

Take the psychopath who feels no remorse, no matter whom he hurts. Or the schizophrenic, who is convinced the mountain of cans and egg cartons in his shopping cart will power the rocket ship he built to go to another star system. You cannot explain their thinking with logic or reason or facts, because their thinking is not based in reality. Such people are simply insane. Simply mentally ill. Similarly, Liberals cannot be understood through logic and reason. But Liberalism itself can be understood as a pathological neurosis.

I thought back to all the historical atrocities levied by the Left in the name of "progress." I thought of their current obsession with open borders and their fanatical dedication to "equality." Nothing explained why. *Why* would Germany, France, and Sweden continue to allow foreigners into their land when the native population is being victimized at such an alarming rate? *Why* would the Left be so determined to strip away basic American freedoms, such as free speech and the right to arms? How could anybody justify the slaughter of the unborn with such callous disregard for life? I was asking these questions on the assumption that Liberals were rational, logical, and concerned with some sort of morality. What I realized was that Liberals are not like the rest of us. They are sick. They are depraved. They are the largest population of mental patients in the world.

This is a heavy charge to which I've laid claim. I am going to make my case, first by outlining and explaining the characteristics of the Liberal sickness, then by providing evidence of their characteristics in action, and hopefully before the end by showing that the only way to subscribe to the Left is by denouncing basic human rights, ignoring objective truths, and denying verifiable facts.

This book opens with a brief history and overview of Liberalism. Part I includes my diagnostic theory, and the rationale for my claim that Liberalism is a diagnosable personality disorder, as modeled on the *Diagnostic and Statistical Manual of Mental Disorders.*

In Act II we disarm Liberal arguments and claims, while at the same time providing robust critiques and counter-arguments. Across nine primary topics, dozens of arguments from the Left are deconstructed via logic and data. Act II also illustrates the observable manifestations of Liberal sickness. Act III brings us full circle, back to where we started. Offering ways to get back on track, and find our way back home.

Liberals are always and inherently fighting from uneven ground. There is a reason so many Liberals believe in postmodernism, relativism, moral nihilism, and a subjective reality of truth. They need to believe in ideologies that allow for flexibility when it comes to truth, facts, and reality; otherwise their entire house of cards collapses at the first level.

The truth will always stand on two legs. Lies stand on but one.

So if you would, take a walk with me on the wild side, into the heart of darkness, as we critically examine the sickness known as Liberalism.

II

Liberalism: Diagnostic Criteria of a Mental Illness

A. The condition is marked by at least two symptoms from Cluster I and two symptoms from Cluster II, with an additional symptom from either cluster.

Cluster I

1. Deceitfulness, indicated by repeated lying, grand exaggerations, or omission of contrary information, with the purpose of advancing their chosen narrative and discrediting others.

2. Irritability or aggressiveness towards anybody that questions or opposes their views. Coupled with the inability to recognize their own hypocrisy, double standards, and doublethink.

3. Inability to adjust views when presented with information contrary to their own beliefs.

4. Frequent projection of their own traits onto others.

5. Difficulty in dealing with a loss of control or power, or a strong desire for control and power.

Cluster II

6. Appeals to altered and redefined definitions of words, or relies on fictitious terms for argumentation.

7. Consistent feelings of having been victimized or wronged, without any actual harm being done. Seen also to play the victim after attacking others.

8. Intense sense of righteousness or moral superiority.

9. The inability to recognize the negative outcomes of their own actions. Often places the blame on others.

10. Intense guilt or self-hatred, often manifests as hatred towards one's larger group identity.

B. The condition must be persistent for more than 6 months.
C. Its occurrence is marked by adult onset.
D. The disturbance causes distress to the person or others in family, social, work, or educational areas of functioning.
E. The sufferer insists the condition will continue to persist and will often refuse help.

Symptoms in Cluster I deal primarily with the psychological traits and defensiveness of Liberals. Deception, cognitive rigidity, and neuroticism. We also see anti-social traits making their appearance, low levels of agreeableness, a desire for control, and projection.

1. Deceitfulness, indicated by repeated lying, grand exaggerations, or omission of contrary information, with the purpose of advancing their chosen narrative and discrediting others.

The very basis of Liberalism is to operate under the cover of lies. In their redefinition of words, their agenda-driven narratives in press coverage, and their total failure to acknowledge reasonable counter-arguments, Liberal deceit surrounds us. The hundreds of hoax hate crimes following the 2016 election showcase the Liberal propensity for deception. Only a mentally ill person would burn down his own church, vandalize his own house, and falsify police reports, all to defame his political opposition.

Deception and Liberal lies have proliferated in every aspect of society. A research paper published in the *American Journal of Political Science* entitled, "Correlation Not Causation: The Relationship between Personality Traits and Political Ideologies," "found" that Liberals exhibit more socially desirable traits, while conservatives are more likely to be authoritarian, hostile, manipulative, neurotic, and overall more psychotic. Three years following the paper's original publication, a correction was issued after researchers in Denmark detected a mistake.[1] The original researchers had "accidentally" reversed the scoring of their data: the findings actually revealed that *conservatives* are the ones who exhibit more socially desirable traits, while Liberals were more authoritarian, psychotic, hostile, manipulative, and neurotic. When contacted about the "mistake," author of the study, Brad Verhulst, insisted the error was "quite minor" in nature.[2]

What a beautiful twist of fate! What an incredibly complicated method of projection! Liberals, who claim the Right is a hateful group of liars, prove *themselves* time and time again to be the true enemies of honesty and integrity.

2. *Irritability or aggressiveness towards anybody that questions or opposes their views. Coupled with the inability to recognize their own hypocrisy, double standards, and doublethink.*

---

1 Ronald Bailey. "Liberals, Not conservatives, Express More Psychoticism" Reason.com. June 10, 2016. http://reason.com/blog/2016/06/10/Liberals-not-conservatives-express-more. [http://archive.is/iee0g]

2 Elizabeth Harrington. "Error Linking conservatives With Psychoticism 'Quite Minor'" Washington Free Beacon. June 10, 2016. http://freebeacon.com/issues/researcher-error-scientific-paper-falsely-linking-conservatives-psychoticism-quite-minor/. [http://archive.li/A8C0n]

We've seen extreme violence from the Left for over a century. Everything from the killing fields of Khmer Rouge to the Antifa Berkeley riots in "protest" of conservative speakers. The principle is always the same. Liberals simply are not able to tolerate anybody that dares to question their dogmatic beliefs.

For years the Left has portrayed the Right as intolerant and closed-minded. Psychologist Mark Brandt began putting this portrayal to the test. What Brandt found was that in fact Liberals, every bit as much as conservatives, are discriminatory and intolerant of those with opposing views.[3]

Liberal irritability and aggression arise from the extreme negative emotional and mental state caused by cognitive dissonance, exacerbated by a set of dogmatic beliefs unrelated to reality and an inability to recognize their own hypocrisy, double standards, and doublethink — all stemming from cognitive rigidity.

3. *Inability to adjust views when presented with information contrary to their own beliefs.*

While debating a Liberal friend on the ethics and practicality of an "assault rifle" ban, she made a very interesting comment. "Nothing you can say," she said to me, "will make me change my mind." It did not matter to her that more people are killed every year with baseball bats than with rifles. She wanted rifles to be banned. This line of thinking is incredibly pervasive in the Liberal mind. Cognitive rigidity, the inability to adjust one's views to reality, is, at the very least, a sign of poor executive function.

Liberals, when presented with data contrary to their beliefs, such as comparisons of crime statistics between races, or rates of welfare use among migrants, will often double down on their position. They will attack the data with superfluous claims, or attempt to discredit the author or the research. No matter how robust it is, it is never enough to satisfy them. They will claim the data is wrong, out-dated, or racist; they will say it does

3 Matthew Hutson. "Why Liberals Aren't as Tolerant as They Think" POLITICO. May 09, 2017. https://www.politico.com/magazine/story/2017/05/09/why-liberals-arent-as-tolerant-as-they-think-215114. [http://archive.li/408yD]

not have enough reviews or citations. Instead of accepting the reality of the information, they force their way down the same deluded path.

4. Frequent projection of their own traits onto others.

Liberals never tire of claiming that the Right is violent, racist, and hateful. Yet the vast majority of riots and assaults originate with Liberals. Most of the people beaten during protests have been beaten by Liberals. Their violent disdain for anybody with opposing views highlights exactly how hateful they truly are. But they do not see this in themselves; they prefer to project their own behaviors and traits onto their opponents, and they seldom miss an opportunity to do so.

While the Liberal advocates rights for one group, they have no scruples in trampling on the rights of another. They hold a double standard for nearly every position they take, freely employing doublethink to reduce the resulting cognitive dissonance.

Look in any Liberal group or subgroup, and you'll find it is fraught with contradiction, hypocrisy, and incessant double standards. This is true in all realms of Liberalism: the Left is entirely devoid of moral principles, and lacks the ability to cut its ideals to fit reality. Instead, every issue is warped, twisted, and mangled, to fit nicely into their dogmatic Procrustean bed.

And this is precisely what they accuse their opponents of doing.

5. Difficulty in dealing with a loss of power or control, or a strong desire for more power and control.

Behind nearly every Liberal issue is the desire for control. Liberals want to control our money via taxes; they want more control and regulations over firearms and our healthcare; they want to control our education through government-mandated curricula (Common Core); they want to control what information we have access to, what we can say, think, and do.

When Liberals lose power, they threaten to kill the president, they fund re-counts, they threaten to kill Electors if they do not switch their vote. They riot, they destroy buildings, they spend all their time frantically vying for impeachments. In short, they become totally unhinged. They recently lost in a fair election. Yet they have been entirely unable to cope with the defeat. Sure signs of a maniacal illness. People with narcissistic personality disorder, histrionic personality disorder, antisocial personality disorder, and authoritarian personalities, all typically struggle with the loss of control. Just as those with the mental illness of Liberalism.

Symptoms in Cluster II of Liberalism deal primarily with the loss of contact to reality. Irrational guilt, feeling victimized, and psychosis, are readily apparent in Cluster II.

6. Appeals to altered and redefined definitions of words, or relies on fictitious terms for argumentation.

Similar to Orwellian "Newspeak," Liberals are constantly redefining words to mean something different, or creating new words to advance their narrative.

- Cis-gendered
- Cultural appropriation
- Micro-aggression
- Politically correct
- Social justice
- Systemic racism
- The patriarchy
- Toxic masculinity
- Toxic whiteness
- Wage gap
- White privilege

The list is endless. All are words created by the Left in an effort to demonize one group, while portraying the other as the victim.

Similarly, the Left never ceases to redefine words that already exist. Racism is no longer defined by the Left to describe different treatment of people irrationally based on race. Racism is now defined as a power and privilege that only whites can possess, which makes whites the only group that can be racist. Liberals reframe and redefine nearly all issues in this way. Abortion is now referred to as "women's rights," a child is now referred to as a "fetus," and the act of infanticide is now called a "choice."

The Left redefines words every few years or so to fit their current political agenda. But that is not how language functions; only in the warped mind of a Liberal does this incessant manipulation of language and definitions pass as legitimate.

7. Consistent feelings of having been victimized or wronged, without any actual harm being done. Seen also to play the victim after attacking others.

We see this manifested in events like the Women's March in D.C on January 21st, 2017. Hundreds of thousands of Liberals marching for their endangered "rights." I checked: there are exactly *zero* rights that men have, and women do not. There have been exactly *zero* rights taken away from women — or anybody else, for that matter. Yet there they were in D.C., playing the victim.

This victim mentality is yet another trait that appears to correlate highly with Liberalism. Persistent feelings of victimization arise partly from the Liberal narrative itself and form a crucial element of their ploy to gain support.

White privilege theory tells all non-whites they are being constantly victimized by systemic racism, whether they realize it or not. Feminist theory tells women they are victims of the patriarchy, which subjects them to lower wages and unfair treatment. Liberals espouse these theories for several reasons. First, it enables them to blame a despised out-group (white men). Second, Liberals are able to garner support from their willing proles by promising to protect them from the evils of white supremacy and patriarchal oppression.

All of these theories are derived from the Frankfurt School teachings of Critical Theory, often referred to as Cultural Marxism. Where classical Marxism posited that the working class was being unfairly oppressed by the capitalist class, Cultural Marxism employs the same oppressor-oppressed paradigm, but frames it in terms of race, sexuality, and gender. Instead of telling the workers they are being held down by the capitalists, Cultural Marxism or Critical Theory simply switched from an idea of socioeconomic class warfare, towards one of race, sexuality, and gender, telling non-whites and women they are being oppressed by straight white men.

Confirmation bias and availability heuristics play important roles in Liberals seeing racism and sexism in everything, everywhere. People tend to find what they're looking for.

If you are always told that you are the victim, told that everybody is racist and out to get you, you will start to attribute everything to racism. The more that society and the media blame everything on racism and sexism, the more racism and sexism become your go-to explanation for everybody else's behavior. People then start to make attribution errors by assuming that *everything* done by certain people is due to racist or sexist motivations.

When non-whites or women feel they have been wronged, they will assume it must originate in racism or sexism. We saw this in the way Liberals blamed sexism for two-time presidential loser Hillary Clinton's failure to make it to the White House. Despite the fact that she was one of the largest corporate shills and most corrupt candidates we have ever seen, Liberals still think it was sexism that defeated her. Not a rap sheet of scandals a mile long: it was the fact that she was belonged to the wrong sex.

When people are frequently told they are victims, they start to develop a confirmation bias to that idea. The bias assures them that nothing *they* do is the problem, that they are nothing but helpless cogs in a machine designed to oppress them. And all that is left for them to do at that point is to "rage against the machine."

Liberals always cry out in pain as they strike you.

8. Intense sense of righteousness or moral superiority.

The self-righteous superiority complex arises when people believe they possess greater moral virtue than others. Liberals see other views as ignorant, ill-informed, and inferior. The self-righteous person becomes highly intolerant toward those who do not share his views. Virtually all Liberals have the impression that they consistently take the moral high ground.

Liberals declare their superiority without ever having demonstrated a single successful policy. Liberals demand that everybody else capitulate to their will without ever feeling the need to prove that they are justified or deserving of such adulation. They turn every issue into a moral issue — while having precisely zero moral standards themselves.

9. The inability to recognize the negative outcomes of their own actions. Often places the blame on others.

Liberal projection is caused in part by their inability to claim blame or responsibility for actions or policies. Liberals never take responsibility for their failures. Falsifiable Liberal theories such as white privilege and the wage gap provide perfect examples of their constant attempt to find scapegoats to blame their failures on.

When once-great cities become stricken with crime, poverty, and hopelessness thanks to local Liberal governments and demographic changes, Liberals refuse to change their policies or take the blame for these ills. When inner-city schools are organized to provide terrible educations, they never look to themselves, the creators of those policies, as the root cause.

When Liberal immigration policies lead to a rise in crime and terrorism, they continue on as if nothing were the matter. Then they blame all these phenomena on "intolerance." Their solution to Muslim terrorism is therefore to invite more Muslims into the country. The Left appears to be entirely devoid of any ability for self-reflection and critical evaluation.

If Liberals had even a shred of human decency, even the dimmest ability for self-reflection, they would be embarrassed to publicly admit their own Liberalism. If society were not so decadent and warped, openly admitting one's support of mass migration, infanticide, forced taxation, censorship, and feminism, would be met with hostile derision, not accepted and lauded.

10. Intense guilt or self-hatred, often manifests as hatred towards one's larger group identity.

Commonly known as "white guilt" and ethnomasochism. These arise from the cognitive dissonance that comes from a white person believing in the theory of white privilege. Liberals struggle to reconcile these opposing views, one which says all whites are inherently benefiting from this all-powerful white privilege and therefore inherently morally corrupt, the other which says that these same whites are good people for believing these things. The result is a warped hatred of one's self and one's group identity. To escape from this conundrum, many Liberals want to see the demise of what they call "white supremacy" so that they no longer have to feel the perceived burden of being "privileged."

Ideally, they would move to another country where they would be in the minority. But that's a discussion for another day.

Further Field Observations

Self-deception plays a prominent role in several mental-health conditions. Self-deception is seen in borderline personality disorder, narcissistic personality disorder, and histrionic personality disorder. Nearly all Liberal narratives require the believer to reconcile the difference between factual reality and the Liberal view by lying to themselves about the nature of reality.

Political Correctness causes yet more anxiety, depression, and mental dysfunction. To be out of touch with reality is the foundation of mental illness. The suggestion that race is a social construct, that there are more than two genders, or that biological sex has zero influence on behavior, for example, takes one down a path that leads away from reality. The purpose of these blatant affronts to reality is deceive those who believe them, and to humiliate anyone who does not voluntarily remain silent. To accept beliefs that one knows are obvious lies, is nothing other than admiring the Emperor's New Clothes.

Promoting white privilege while ignoring the relationship between single parenthood rates, IQ, and race on the one hand, to life outcomes in terms of education, crime, and earning potential on the other, leads the believer *away* from reality. Believing in systemic racism and the oppression of non-whites by whites, while ignoring the fact that blacks victimize whites at a rate twenty-seven times higher than whites victimize blacks, promotes a disconnection from reality.

Preaching that guns are the cause of violence, when we see from the data that some groups of people are simply more prone to violence than others, leads one *away* from objective truth and reality.

Espousing the politically correct slogan that "Islam is a religion of peace" while blasphemy, apostasy, adultery, and homosexuality, are all punishable by death in Muslim nations, is an affront to reality. Since September of 2001, there have been over 28,000 Islamic terror attacks worldwide;[4] that is nearly five terrorist attacks every day. And they are the *peaceful* ones.

Hearing that "diversity is our greatest strength" over and over leads the believer further away from reality and deeper into mental illness. In *reality*, diversity has been empirically shown to cause nothing but lower trust, lower social capital, lower happiness, and a lower quality of life.

The Liberal mind is caught between reality and its own dogma. A cognitive Scylla and Charybdis.

It appears that most Liberals process information using peripheral route elaboration, meaning they go with what "feels right" emotionally, instead of critically evaluating all information and opposing views. Evaluation based upon emotion leads one to be more easily persuaded and manipulated. This is why we so often see former Liberals turning to the Right, yet seldom see the contrary. The further you dive into each political issue, the more you realize that the facts are consistently on the side of the Right and rarely, if ever, on that of the Left. Liberalism is a form of emotional and cognitive immaturity, a sort of prolonged arrested development. The truth is hard. It is brutal, it is ugly, it is unforgiving. Learning the truth, knowing the truth, and speaking the truth, are all difficult propositions. It is much easier to believe comforting lies — and this in my opinion is the primary appeal of Liberalism for so many.

Perhaps Liberalism, rather than being an immature ideology, is really a form of submission. A sort of egalitarian plague, infecting the soft minds of the weak and the docile. It is a world view for those lacking in moral strength, spiritual toughness, and wild hearts. Liberalism as a political

---

4 Brigitte Gabriel. "Committed to Denial: Since 9/11, Some 28,000 Terrorist Attacks Worldwide." Breitbart. June 14, 2016. www.breitbart.com/big-government/2016/06/14/committed-denial-since-911-28000-terrorist-attacks-worldwide/. [http://archive.is/6gd4s]

project is not designed to tackle the harsh realities we are facing today, and its purveyors are even less equipped to do so.

People do not arrive at the ideology of Liberalism via research, truth, and critical thinking. They arrive at Liberalism through lies, dogmatic indoctrination, and the brainwashing brought by endless propaganda. The truth is with *us*. And it always will be.

The mental illness colloquially known as Liberalism indicates one of two things about its host. Either the person in question is consistently so out of touch with reality that he has developed a vast web of lies which he must continually tell himself in order to reconcile his cognitive dissonance. Or he is so cognitively rigid he is unwilling to change his views in light of new information, a state aggravated by a heavy confirmation bias and a strong dose of self-deception. I'm not sure if the loss of touch with reality comes first, and self-deception is the method by which Liberals ease the negative state caused by their cognitive dissonance, or if the extreme cognitive dissonance from holding views that are not grounded in reality leads to heightened levels of psychosis and a loss of touch with reality.

In a way, this is the old chicken or egg conundrum. And for now, I do not think it particularly matters. The end result is that the violence we see from the Left, the cognitive rigidity, the guilt, the projections, the righteousness, and the lies — all of it is a result of the Liberal's fundamental removal from reality.

One way or another, Liberalism is a mental illness.

III

Liberalism in Theory & Practice

Liberalism With the Mask Off

Modern Liberalism is based on lies.

Through this book I frequently use the terms "Right-wing," "Left-wing," "Liberal," and "conservative." As these terms have all taken on a variety of meanings and definitions, it is important they be defined both in their historical context, and in their modern usage.

The terms "liberal" and "conservative" have meant many different things in different times and places. These two terms are incredibly context-dependent: a Liberal in the United States in 2017 is a different animal than a liberal in Europe in 2017, and radically different from a liberal during the Age of Enlightenment.

Conservative is a word that has also undergone many iterations. What it meant to be a conservative during the French Revolution is equivalent to what we would have called a Loyalist or Tory in the American Revolution.

Conservatism in Europe once meant conserving the order of monarchies. From the earliest usages in the United States, meanwhile, conservatism has meant conserving the Republic, the Constitution; it is founded on individual liberties on the one hand, and on pragmatism on the other. Although the Right-wing and Left-wing distinction can carry across nations as well, Liberal and conservative mean two wildly different things to an American and to a European or an Australian.

What we call conservatism in America today is closer to the Classical Liberal views which arose in the Age of Enlightenment, and to our own during the American Revolution. It includes belief in small governments, economic freedom, minimal taxation, and expansive civil liberties. Conservatives are fighting to conserve these values and our people, which are the founding values and founding stock of our nation, even as the Left is entirely hell-bent on destroying them.

What is now referred to as Classical Liberalism has its origins in the Age of Enlightenment. The "Classical" was added to the term "Liberalism" to distinguish it from Social Liberalism, which is nothing but Marxism with a 21st-century name. Social Liberalism is what we know as modern Liberalism, in which evils like political correctness and social justice abound.

Classical Liberalism is the idea that we are free to be, say, and do what we want, so long as our actions do not interfere with the freedoms or rights of others, or damage society at large. That nobody should have the right or power to rule over us. That government should be small, and should exist only to serve the people. That markets should be mostly free to provide goods and services, regulated when necessary to protect the citizens or environment. According to Classical Liberalism, every transaction should be voluntary.

The idea of progressivism, like many modern values related to Classical Liberalism, rose to popularity in the Age of Enlightenment. The idea of progressivism was simple: it amounted to the view that we can improve the human condition. The Age of Enlightenment, or Age of Reason, was in many ways merely a return to the classical ideals known in ancient Greece and Rome. The reemergence of such ideas as constitutional governments, the separation of church and state, human progress, civil liberty, as well as the revolt against the Divine Right of Kings, all came *en vogue* once more during the Enlightenment.

In American politics, the term "progressive" was once used to describe policies which aimed to reform industry, to protect citizens, and to safeguard the future of our lands. The great Theodore Roosevelt passed the Antiquities Act, establishing the presidential authority to set aside protected lands for all to enjoy unto futurity. The one and only decent thing Woodrow Wilson would do, was to follow suit in expanding what Roosevelt had begun, by establishing the National Park Service Organic Act.

Prior to these Acts, lands that are now revered the world over were being ravaged. Native American ruins were destroyed, great redwood groves were being devastated for lumber, petrified forests were ransacked, and waste was dumped freely into the waters. As was quite clear to conservationist John Muir, these precious lands needed to be protected. Muir urged his friend Teddy Roosevelt to ensure that these unique lands would continue beyond their lives. No greater legacy could have been established.

During the true progressive era, Roosevelt and Taft took on the monopolies for their unfair treatment of consumers. They oversaw the breaking up of over one hundred trusts, and continued seeking laws to benefit the citizens by pushing for the Pure Food and Drug Act and establishing the earliest acts of conservationism in our nation's history.

The United States also saw the introduction of regulations on industry and labor. Progressivism was in many ways nonpartisan. There were progressives in both political parties, and looking back, it is evident that a series of good decisions were made which truly favored the American people. It was a different era. President Roosevelt and Taft were not men beholden to their corporate or foreign masters. They were looking out for the people that had elected them, as it should be. A long-forgotten tradition in politics.

Historically, the term "progressivism" in the United States was used to describe reforms aimed at helping the common American, protecting them from unscrupulous business practices and from those looking to profit off what John Muir and Teddy Roosevelt felt were national treasures.

The modern uses of the terms "Liberal" and "progressive" are nothing more than marketing gimmicks employed by the Left to give themselves a fresh new image. The terms began to be applied to Democrats sometime in the New Deal Era. By "progress" and "Liberalism," Franklin D. Roosevelt actually meant an unprecedented expansion of the federal government, the creation of the socialist welfare state, and massive wealth redistribution. Franklin D. Roosevelt spoke of the "freedom from want," which he saw as both liberating and progressive.[1]

1 Eric Alterman. "How Classical Liberalism Morphed Into New Deal Liberalism" Center for American Progress. April 26, 2012. https://www.americanprogress.org/issues/general/news/2012/04/26/11379/think-again-how-classical-Liberalism-morphed-into-new-deal-Liberalism/.

The historical meanings of Liberalism and progressivism would forever be changed in the United States from that point on. These terms were blatantly stolen from Classical Liberals—men like Thomas Paine and John Locke, and the true progressives like Teddy Roosevelt. What modern day Liberals and progressives stand for could not be further from the ideals of those great characters. Modern-day Leftists are nothing but thieves, as they reveal, quite appropriately, even in the names they use to describe themselves: the two terms have been appropriated from their true historical uses and made to describe the massive welfare state, open borders, the slaughter of unborn babies, and increased government intervention in all aspects of our lives.

Throughout the remainder of the book I will use the terms "Liberal" and "progressive" as they are used in modern colloquial language. I also use "Leftist" and the "Left-wing" to refer to Liberal ideologies and people.

I use the term "conservative" and "Right," on the other hand, in reference to the people that believe in upholding the ideals and values this nation was founded on. And in reference more broadly to those who oppose modern Liberalism and progressives.

Right-wing and Left-wing are terms that have maintained a bit more consistency through history. It is again helpful if we establish some historical context and thence a working definition of these terms, for they are used heavily throughout this book. It is also imperative to understand that those we know as Liberals today in America have historically manipulated these terms for political gain. They continue to manipulate these terms even today, rewriting much of their own history.

Right-wing and Left-wing are terms originating in the French Revolution, and they indicated little more than who was sitting where. Those members of the National Assembly who sided with the King sat on one side of the room, while those supporting the revolution sat on the other side. The terms "Right-wing" and "Left-wing" have applied to different movements throughout history, but their usage has maintained a level of uniformity the world over.

Contemporary Left-wing ideals can be easily traced to communism. Like most modern Liberal ideals, their roots are in Marx, the Bolshevik party, the NKVD, and the KPD. Leftists all over the world are preachers of social justice, egalitarianism, forced financial equality, and (their hallmark feature) a massive government that the people serve. Leftist claim to be the party of Classical Liberalism and civil liberties, but as we can clearly see, they are in favor of anything *but* individual liberty.

At the beginning, Right-wing views were considered to be those opposing the communist Left, views based on conserving the beauty, order, and people of a nation. Right-wing philosophy is associated with Classical Liberalism, nationalism, the belief in certain inalienable individual liberties, and a government that exists to serve the people.

The absurdity of the American Left calling themselves Liberal is apparent in the differences of philosophy between the Modern Liberals and Classical Liberals. Classical Liberals believe in a small government and low, voluntary, taxation. Modern Liberalism is predicated on a massive State and oppressive taxation, enforced through the threat of violence. While Classical Liberals held individual liberty in high esteem, Modern Liberals routinely sacrifice individual rights to appease the collective. While Classical Liberals viewed freedom of speech, association, religion, thought, firearm ownership, and property ownership to be worthy values, the Modern Liberal rejects all these tenets.

When I speak of "individualism" throughout this book, I am using it in the traditionalist, European, almost aristocratic sense of the term associated with mastery and discipline. The sort of individualism that fosters creativity, high art, order, and a concern with our shared cultural destiny. Those individuals a little bit ahead of the rest, those who push humanity a little further, the aristocrats of the soul. Not the rootless, atomized, deracinated, selfish, plebeian, narcissistic, individualism of the modern era that Liberalism promotes — an individualism based on empty hedonism and hostile disregard for order and beauty.

Similarly, when I speak of "collectivism," I am using the Marxist definition which seeks to create a forced equality and imbue the State with power. One can support individual liberties while still believing in a cohesive group identity and working together to preserve those liberties from hostile influence. These are not mutually exclusive ideas. Working as a group is not the same as a Marxist-collectivist ideology. The West has been unique in its ability to combine a strong national identity with profound freedoms for individuals within that group.

The Social Liberal of today advocates for "hate speech" laws, strict gun control, routine confiscation of property and labor through taxation, and even forced association through mass migration and open-border policies. Modern Liberals feel they have an inherent *right* to other people's labor and property. Perhaps the most glaring difference between Modern Liberals and Classical Liberals is their views of the State. Classical Liberals view the State as something that works only for the people, something that should be allowed minimal interference, while Modern Liberals regularly seek to utilize the State to force others to succumb to their will. Individual rights to property, speech, association, are all damned in the collectivist framework of Modern Liberalism.

I think of the Left-Right spectrum as being arranged on the basis of the size of government and its involvement in people's lives. Massive, overreaching governments based on communist principles are universally Left-wing. It is well agreed upon that communism is a Left-wing ideology, and all subsequent political movements based upon communism are thus also Left-wing.

Political ideologies that favor smaller governments which exists to serve the people, protect them, and otherwise let them be, are Right-wing. Leftists political theorists have sought to over-complicate the dynamic in an effort to rewrite history and disguise their motives. Although historical examples of Right-wing governments that have grown large and powerful do exist, they have generally become that way as a reaction to Leftist attacks. The underlying principles of a concern and protection for their own people remained despite their reaching high magnitudes.

When a group wants to use the State to force their ideology on others, that is classic Leftism, for it necessitates a large government enforcing its will, and limits the individual liberties of citizens.

This idea of liberty was posited in opposition to the monarchs of Europe, who appealed to the Divine Right of Kings and believed that God had bestowed power upon them to rule over their subjects. John Locke arrived on the scene and declared that something had gone horribly awry. God would never make man in His image only to be ruled by another; the Divine Rights are a lie. To make a long story short, the idea caught on with a few people on a distant continent; they grabbed their muskets and declared their independence from Great Britain. And here we are today, once again, fighting tyranny.

Through the remainder of the book, I use "Left-wing" to describe policies and practices that support a large state, favor collective rights over individual rights, or seek to impose the will of a few on the whole of society through the apparatus of the State.

"Right-wing" will be used to describe policies and practices that foster more individual freedoms, while limiting the power of the collective and the State. There is also a demarcation between Left and Right in terms of nationalism. Where the Left favors globalism, open borders, and mass migration, the Right is concerned first and foremost with the well-being of its own people and self-determination.

When referencing other nations and politics outside of the USA, I also use Right-wing and Left-wing, as those terms still mean more or less the same thing across the pond.

The names and key figures have changed throughout history, yet the underlying principles and conflicts have remained constant. There are factions of people who want to impose their will upon others. In some cases theirs has been a religious will, an economic vision, or a perverse view of justice. And as long as there have been societies, there have been others who fight for the rights of the individual and for personal liberties, opposing the collectivist mob rule. Our side has always fought for the individual, the health of our people, and the triumph of will.

There is a good reason the American Left has fought so hard to call themselves Liberals and progressives, taking on the good name of better men that came before them. The Democratic party, the party that claims to be and always to have been progressive and Liberal, has a storied past which is nothing short of demonic.

Let's take a quick look at the "Liberal" and "progressive" legacy of the American Left. Here are their programs:

- The Revenue Act of 1913, which established the income tax.
- The Federal Reserve Act, which established a central bank.
- The New Deal, which created the welfare state.
- The removal of the US from the gold standard.

- The National Firearms Act.
- The Great Society, which expanded the welfare state.
- The Hart-Celler Immigration Act of 1965.

And here is a brief history of war mongering in the United States:

- World War I — 1.6 years — Woodrow Wilson (Democrat)
- World War II — 3.7 years — Franklin D. Roosevelt (Democrat)
- Korean War — 3.1 years — Harry Truman (Democrat)
- Vietnam War — 8.1 years –
  Johnson, 4 years (Democrat)
  Nixon, 4 years (Republican)
- Persian Gulf War — 0.5 years — Bush Sr. (Republican)
- War on Terror, including Iraq & Afghanistan –
  Bush Jr. 8 years (Republican)
  Obama 8 years (Democrat)[2]

Looking back through our history, it can be seen that Republicans have been in the minority when it comes to military interventions. The body count for the American Democratic party is staggering. It is one of the deadliest ideologies in all of human history. Second only perhaps to communism.

Of the 32.5 years the US has spent in major wars during the twentieth century to date, Democrats have been in office for twenty of those years. Nixon inherited a war, and the Bushes are nothing but neoconservatives.

Democrats have initiated involvement in all but the two of these wars, for which the Bushes are responsible. Of the years spent at war, Democrats have been in office for 63 percent of that time.

Which is no surprise. The bellicosity we see from the American Left is strikingly similar to that of the Trotskyite tradition. Under president Woodrow Wilson, a foreign policy known as Liberal internationalism was instituted, according to which sovereign nations should intervene through military invasion and aid in the affairs of other sovereign nations

2 "U.S. Participation in Major Wars." Fox News. November 25, 2016. www.foxnews.com/printer_friendly_wires/2006Nov25/0,4675,USWarsHowLong,00.html. [http://archive.li/Avpoz]

in an effort to spread the so-called values of Liberalism. The theory was that if nations the world over are operating under similar ideals, peace will be achieved through globalism, with the necessary consequence of undermining the sovereignty of nations. Leon Trotsky advanced the idea of "permanent revolution," which has very similar ideological underpinnings to Liberal internationalism. Trotsky theorized that the cause of communism in one country would be greatly benefited by other nations operating on a similar ideology; disparate segments of society could draw support from others, and revolution in one nation would aid and inspire revolution in another. By solidifying the establishment of communism on a broader stage, the revolution in one nation would thus become "permanent" and secured. In precisely the same way that Wilson saw the spread of Liberal values being aided by global Liberalism, Trotsky believed that communism would be promoted by global communism.

Foreign invasions and communist revolutions, of course, tend to be rather violent. Both Liberal internationalism and permanent revolution theory require the erosion of sovereignty; just as Liberal internationalism opposes isolationism and non-interventionism, Trotsky's theory of permanent revolution was in opposition to Stalin's vision of national communism or "socialism in one country."

In contemporary times we see these philosophical expressions being displayed in nation-building at the behest of neoconservative Trotskyites, who claim that their goal is to "spread democracy and freedom" through the Middle East. This of course, sounds oddly familiar. Neoconservative military intervention and Liberal "humanitarian" aid are two sides of the same coin, one that very easily traces back to Liberal internationalism and permanent revolution theory.

The Democratic party, especially in its most modern incarnation, is little more than the American branch of the Communist party. The parallels are striking: the obsession with forced egalitarianism; the policing of speech and thoughts; heavy wealth redistribution through taxation; the advocating of policies that destroy the family unit; a severe disdain for the right to bear arms. All are qualities shared by modern Liberals and communists alike. Those on the Left are the rightful ideological heirs to the throne of Bolshevism.

With that said, it is important to note that the US in no way whatsoever has a real Right-wing party. The current Republican party serves little function other than gate-keeping, giving people the illusion they are voting Right, when instead we get nothing but Trotskyites who support globalized trade deals that hurt American workers, spark off endless wars, and promote population replacement through mass migration. No semblance of protectionism, isolationism, or nationalism is to be found in the official GOP program. The only reason any of these sentiments have a voice in current US politics is because a political outsider entered the arena, and because dissidents are forcing the crimes of the establishment into the light.

The modern Left is not entirely bad. Mentally ill, certainly, and blindly following an evil ideology — but not all bad. It does have a few good positions, and I must give them credit where it's due. Liberals have been against corporate welfare and bailouts, they are interested in protecting the environment, wildlife, and animal rights. I think the average rank-and-file Liberal may have a handful of good intentions. But as always — the road to Hell is paved with good intentions.

With that said, the support of wildlife and environmentalism has its origins in Classical Liberalism and the Right. As does hostility towards corporations. Isolationism is another classic form of Right-wing nationalism. Every admirable issue espoused by social Liberals originates on the Right.

Republican governor Gifford Pinchot, ardent advocate of forest conservation, was the first chief of the United States Forest Service. The Forest Service itself was an offshoot of Teddy Roosevelt's Boone and Crockett Club, the oldest wildlife and habitat conservation organization in the US. The Boone and Crocket Club eliminated commercial hunting and helped to create the National Park Service and the Wildlife Refuge.

Henry David Thoreau, a tax resister who argued for civil disobedience against an unjust government, was an early advocate of environmentalism. The same men who fought against taxation, also fought to preserve wildlife and nature. John Locke argued that cruelty to animals was morally wrong, and Rousseau felt that humans are morally bound to do no harm to our fellow creatures on account of our shared sentience. Years later, Thomas Jefferson would craft much of our Declaration of Independence based on the works of Locke and Rousseau.

I once viewed my own political philosophy as somewhat out of place in the modern world, as it did not fit in well with any contemporary ideology. Only later would I realize that my views place me in a long line of those who came before me. These views surfaced in the West again during the Enlightenment, and have been held by many great men.

While looking at lists of "Liberal" accomplishments, I notice they take credit for the majority of things the Republicans have fought for. They cannot simply decide now that defending nature and animal conservation was *their* idea. Those were the ideals of Classical Liberalism, which has no relation to Modern Liberalism as we know it today.

The Democratic regime claims to be the party of the people, yet the Democratic party has done nothing for the people, except see to it that the middle class has been all but eviscerated through open borders, crippling taxation, and globalist trade policies that smother US workers. The American Left has taken credit for all the work accomplished by the very people who opposed them. They have lied to entire generations, manipulating them into believing that theirs is the party of the common man.

I should not be surprised that the Democratic party has made such an effort to erase history. Every communist regime has done precisely the same. From Lenin to Mao, the Left has censored speech, rewritten the past, manipulated the media. Anything deemed politically incorrect, anybody that might threaten the narrative, is silenced.

Same old game, different players. The Left must censor history and outlaw the truth, for these things have always been their downfall.

My hope is that through my work and the work of others like me, the Liberal empire of lies will be dismantled, brick by brick.

> For nothing is hidden that shall not be revealed, and nothing is secret that will not be made known.
>
> — Matthew 10:26

What is Liberalism?

The heart of Liberalism is nothing more than an insatiable desire for control. Liberals want to control our healthcare, our education, what we can say, the news we watch; they want to control our money, our guns, and, ultimately, our freedom.

Liberalism is anti-gun, anti-family, anti-free speech, anti-Constitution, and anti-free thinking. It supports degeneracy in all forms, globalism in the form of mass migration, heavy taxation to fund socialist efforts; it is pro-war, pro-Sharia, and pro-violence. Liberals oppose all efforts to preserve individual liberty. Liberals favor all ways to exert more control over the population.

Why have we seen so much outrage and violence since the 2016 election? Because Liberals in America have lost the one thing they care about most. Power.

Liberalism is communism. And every time communist have taken control, they have slaughtered the people who opposed them.

Every communist regime through history has done the same things upon seizing power. They have killed the free thinkers who oppose them. They have severed ties to history, religion, and culture. They have erased and rewritten history. They have torn down old monuments, and erected new ones in their likeness. They have renamed entire cities and streets to accommodate their view of the past. We see this same pattern playing out everywhere Liberalism takes hold. Modern Liberals are the same in nearly every respect to their communist forebears.

Liberals have the same values as the old Loyalists to the king. They want the State to have the utmost authority, the power to rule over everyone with impunity. In the same sense that Loyalists did not mind being subservient to the king, Liberals do not mind being subjects of the State.

The moral philosophy of Liberalism is one of collective consequentialism. Liberals believe in totalitarian collectivism, in which everybody in a society is forced to sacrifice his individual liberties for some "greater good." Generally this means taking away rights and resources from one group and keeping these for themselves.

And moral goodness is simply defined as what is "good"—for Liberals. It matters not how much property and liberty it deprives people of, how many atrocities they are subjected to. So long as the action aims at furthering the Liberal agenda, the action was justified, "good," and "progressive."

The Liberal State augments its power in many ways. One is by destroying families. After the Bolshevik Revolution in Russia, the new regime immediately instituted fast, no-fault divorces, and rampant abortions.[3] When the family unit is destroyed, the State assumes the empty space. Higher rates of single mothers, more children from broken homes, and more unemployed men increase the number of dependents relying on the State. We see the same degeneracy coming from the modern Feminism that Liberals feverishly push on young men and women. Encouragement of promiscuity, abortion, and meaningless jobs over family, are all means to undermine the family unit, which is perhaps one of the greatest antidotes to State power.

The State gains power by disarming its citizens. Before the Great Purge, before the Great Leap Forward, before the Killing Fields, before the Holodomor, governments first had to ensure citizens were not well armed, either though strict gun control, confiscations, or scarcity. Liberals today pushing for more and more firearm restrictions are employing a one-hundred-year-old Left-wing tactic to seize more power.

Creating social chaos is another common stratagem for gaining power. Through perpetuating lies and presenting a false view of reality, the Left incites hatred for other groups among citizens, primarily by demonizing whites. Increasing the "diversity" in an area is another method to destroy social capital and trust. We also see this in the way Feminists seek to pit women against men through the lies of the wage gap and the glass ceiling.

Endless wars are another tool of social chaos. The constant threat of war and terrorism is a way to keep a population docile and controlled. The terrorism threat is so high in Europe that people are afraid to leave their homes, and many simply no longer do.

Passing laws to limit free speech is another hallmark Liberal agenda which seeks to limit the power of their subjects. Such limitations on open discussion creates another pretext for jailing dissidents.

Liberals are interested in one thing: total control through mob rule. From the early days of the Bolshevik Party to American Democrats in 2017, there has never been an exception. Liberals advocate for mob rule

---

3 A Woman Resident In Russia . "The Russian Effort to Abolish Marriage" The Atlantic. July, 1926. https://www.theatlantic.com/magazine/archive/1926/07/the-russian-effort-to-abolish-marriage/306295/. [http://archive.li/Lgi8o]

under the guise of democracy, using terms like "Democratic Socialism" and "progressive Democrat" so conceal their motives. Allow me then to to reveal these: "Democratic Socialism" simply means promising the majority of people in a nation the resources of the minority, so that the majority votes to steal from the minority, convincing itself that the theft was justified because it was done "democratically." And modern "democracy" is no different.

The mob rule mentality of Liberals is captured perfectly in their obsession with the popular vote from the 2016 election. They cannot get over the fact that America still has the remnants of a system that protects the few from the many. They are outraged that despite their efforts to import well over fifty million new Democrat voters (and their children) through mass migration, enough people still rejected their demagoguery to hold them at bay a while longer.

The United States was designed as a Constitutional Republic and not a direct democracy for very specific reasons. The rights of the individual are endowed by the Constitution. The Republic was meant to consist of those voted into office by the people, those entrusted to uphold the liberties granted by the Constitution.

Liberals are constantly promoting "democracy," which is simply a system in which the minority of people in a society are forced to comply with the wishes or whims of the majority. We were never supposed to have a system in which the 51 percent could vote to levy taxes on the remaining 49 percent, or in which the simple majority could elect a number of Liberals sufficient to limit our liberties. The closer we move towards a direct democracy, the further we move from a Constitutional Republic.

A Constitutional Republic ensures that the collective and the many could not rule over the individual and the few. Democracy always devolves into mob rule, so soon as the 51 percent realize they can vote to eat the remaining 49 percent. The purpose of our Constitution and Bill of Rights was to place certain ideas — the right to life, liberty, property, the right to bear arms, free expression — out of reach of elected officials, and beyond the reach of the 51 percent. No election can touch these rights.

Democracy has very little if anything at all to do with freedom. It is only a polite version of mob rule and collectivism, in which individual rights and property may be stripped away for the "common good."

Hans-Hermann Hoppe has written that "Democracy has nothing to do with freedom. Democracy is a soft variant of communism, and rarely in the history of ideas has it been taken for anything else."[4]

Liberals are of the opinion that we must obey them, or else they will have the State violate our rights to property and liberty. The Left is of the opinion that even if Liberals rally enough support, and vote for a system in which we must obey them, they are some how morally legitimated in forcing everyone else to concede, even if it means the erosion of our rights or the confiscation of our property.

Two infamous quotes from Hillary Clinton, are perfect examples;

> "We're going to take things away from you on behalf of the common good."[5]

> "We must stop thinking of the individual and start thinking about what is best for society." [6]

These quotes sound very much like they were taken from a page of Orwell's *1984*:

"It had long been realized that the only secure basis for oligarchy is collectivism."

Really, this all makes perfect sense. Right-leaning political thought emphasizes the importance of the individual and the family unit. The Left is a hive of groupthink and collectivism. In a way, it is more of a cult that wants Big Brother to take care of everything.

Groupthink is the ordinary *modus operandi* for the Left. There is little critical thought from the Left; if there were, they wouldn't be Liberal. They are all willing followers; they seek to de-individualize their members, and instill the proper, politically correct, hive-minded values. Exactly like a cult.

---

4 Hans-Hermann Hoppe. "The Paradox of Imperialism" Mises Institute. June 04, 2013. https://mises.org/library/paradox-imperialism. [http://archive.li/iEdKN]

5 Thomas DiLorenzo. "The Problem with Hillary Clinton" Breitbart. July 07, 2016. http://www.breitbart.com/big-government/2016/07/07/problem-hillary-clinton/. [http://archive.li/ta0QC]

6 Deroy Murdock. "Hillary Clinton, Socialist Still" National Review. October 09, 2007. http://www.nationalreview.com/article/222433/hillary-clinton-socialist-still -deroy-murdock.

I noticed during the last couple of years that Liberals are using their children more and more to advance their agenda. We saw this in commercials sponsored by a Liberal political action committee, in which children were featured yelling "Fuck you, you racist fucks!"[7] During the Women's March in D.C., children were photographed holding signs filled with political propaganda. The continued exploitation of children as seen from the Left is a very bizarre and disturbing trend.

What is Neoconservatism?

Neoconservatives are nothing more than Liberals masquerading as Republicans. This is a clever way to infiltrate the Republican party under the guise of conservatism. Irving Kristol, a Jewish journalist who is considered "the godfather of neoconservatism" started the movement that would later become the predominant "conservative" ideology in American politics.[8] There is very little, if anything, the purveyors of this brand of "conservatism" are interested in conserving. Neoconservatism is marked by incredibly hawkish foreign policy and intervention, coupled with a merchant theory of economics, in which GDP is seen as the highest economic good.

George Bush Sr. pushing for the New World Order was not conservative. Bush Jr. and his cabal of advisers spending trillions and costing thousands upon thousands of the lives of our own soldiers, and hundreds of thousands of innocent lives of Middle Easterners, was not conservative.

The Neo-Con-Artists that advocated for the Iraq War on entirely false premises are not conservatives. As with the founding of neoconservativism, the majority of those pushing for the Iraq War were Jewish.[9] There

---

7 Joel Pollak. "Video--Latino Kids Blast Donald Trump: 'F*ck you, racist f*ck!'" Breitbart. November 04, 2015. http://www.breitbart.com/big-government/2015/11/04/video-latino-kids-blast-donald-trump-fck-you-racist-fck/. [http://archive.is/OrWrN]

8 Barry Gewen. "Irving Kristol, Godfather of Modern Conservatism, Dies at 89." The New York Times. September 18, 2009. www.nytimes.com/2009/09/19/us/politics/19kristol.html?pagewanted=all. [http://archive.li/4ta3K]

9 Ari Shavit. "White man's burden" Haaretz.com. April 22, 2010. http://www.haaretz.com/israel-news/white-man-s-burden-1.14110. [http://archive.li/3bWXQ]

is nothing conservative or Right-wing about endless interventionalism.[10] Nor is the fact that the neocon camp largely backed Hillary Clinton, a sign of any sort of Right-wing ideology.[11]

"Republicans" like Lindsey Graham, John McCain & Co. who want amnesty for illegal immigrants are not conservative.[12] [13] Granting amnesty to eleven million people (a *low* estimate) who are in the US illegally would cost the US tax payers over six trillion dollars. These illegal immigrants will be a net burden to Americans for their entire lives.[14] All these "Republicans" are doing is demonstrating that they are really crypto-Liberals who support our replacement. All of these politicians have had a high number of neocon advisors.

John Kasich, Republican Governor of Ohio, welcoming countless Somalis into the state, Somalis who are overwhelmingly on welfare that *we* must pay for, is not conservative.[15] [16]

---

10 Robert Parry. "The Iraq War, The Neocons and America's Chalabi Legacy of Lies" Global Research. November 6, 2015. https://www.globalresearch.ca/the-iraq-war-the-neocons-and-americas-chalabi-legacy-of-lies/5487105. [http://archive.li/VAM62]

11 Rania Khalek. "Robert Kagan and Other Neocons Are Backing Hillary Clinton" The Intercept. July 25, 2016. https://theintercept.com/2016/07/25/robert-kagan-and-other-neocons-back-hillary-clinton/. [http://archive.li/BX3p4]

12 Katie McHugh. "Lindsey Graham Allies with Democrats to Continue Obama's 2012 Amnesty" Breitbart. December 12, 2016. http://www.breitbart.com/big-government/2016/12/12/lindsey-graham-allies-with-democrats-to-continue-obamas-2012-amnesty/. [http://archive.li/y7I4W]

13 Tom Tancredo. "John McCain the Poster Boy for Establishment Illegal Immigration Dishonesty" Breitbart. July 23, 2016. http://www.breitbart.com/2016-presidential-race/2016/07/23/john-mccain-poster-boy-establishment-illegal-immigration-dishonesty/. [http://archive.li/fxP7Q]

14 Jim DeMint and Robert Rector. "Amnesty for illegal immigrants will cost America" The Washington Post. May 06, 2013. https://www.washingtonpost.com/opinions/amnesty-for-illegal-immigrants-will-cost-america/2013/05/06/e5d19afc-b661-11e2-b94c-b684dda07add_story.html?utm_term=.b91372546b7c.

15 Christian Datoc. "OHIO STATE ATTACK: Twitter EXPLODES On John Kasich For Opening State's Borders To Refugees" The Daily Caller. November 28, 2016. http://dailycaller.com/2016/11/28/ohio-state-attack-twitter-explodes-on-john-kasich-for-opening-states-borders-to-refugees/. [http://archive.is/Yq34c]

16 Kimberly Smith. "Ohio Gov. Kasich Gets Destroyed on Twitter for What He Did Before Ohio State Attack" conservative Tribune. November 29, 2016. http://

In an interview, Paul Ryan proclaimed he would not support restrictions on Muslim migration. He said that limiting Muslims is un-American, and not who we are.[17] There is nothing conservative about unfettered migration of a people that openly admits murder as a justifiable penalty for those who insult their religion.

It is important to understand that many people within the GOP and Republican party have no semblance of conservative or Right-leaning views. They remind me of the *1984* character, Emmanuel Goldstein: they are nothing but controlled opposition, who exist to give the illusion that there is some choice other than voting for open-border, collectivist, Liberal lunatics. Or perhaps they are willing gatekeepers serving a similar function.

The people we elected to stop the regressive policies of the Democratic machine have betrayed us for their thirty pieces of silver. Most neocons are no better than the most ardent Liberal, and many are worse. In the last twenty years in America, the political spectrum has moved so far to the Left that Bill Clinton's presidency makes most modern "conservatives" look like members of the Bolshevik inner circle.

Prominent neocons such as John Podhoretz, Bill Kristol, David Frum, Ben Shapiro, Jennifer Rubin, and Jonah Goldberg, are all opponents of any semblance of an America First policy. They favor mass migration, foreign wars, foreign aid, and seem to wholly embrace the fact that White Europeans are becoming a minority in our own homelands, all while they support incredibly strict immigration policies for their own homeland of Israel.

When I speak of conservatism throughout this book, I refer to the more classic sense, a people with an actual desire to conserve something other than a few dollars in their wallet. I speak of those of us who wish to conserve and secure our cultures, our identities, our natural world, and above all else, our people.

In American politics, we do not really have a true Right-wing political party, and it has been this way for the better part of a century, perhaps

---

conservativetribune.com/kasich-twitter-did-ohio-attack/. [http://archive.li/ZjFTe]

17 Jay Newton-Small. "Speaker Paul Ryan Condemns Donald Trump's Ban on Muslims" Time. December 8, 2015. http://time.com/4140558/paul-ryan-donald-trump-muslims/. [http://archive.li/MNJKU]

longer. We really have one party with two factions, a far Left-wing party based on the cultural Marxist teachings of the Frankfurt School that is concerned with social issues and mass migration. And another Left-wing party, the neoconservatives, who are concerned with foreign intervention and the economy, who are also supportive of mass migration and population replacement. Neither are nationalists in nature, nor do they concern themselves with such trifles as whether or not their policies are good for Americans.

Neoconservatives are nothing more than Trotskyite Leftists, equally deserving of the ice-pick.

Western Tradition

American values, the Western tradition, and Right-wing political views are at heart quite similar. The idea of a free and self-governing people dates back to the Romans and Ancient Greeks. These values were once again ignited during the European Age of Reason.

The idea of small governments that serve the people is a cornerstone of the American value system. With it comes the necessity of the freedom to keep and bear arms. Arms are paramount to the maintenance of liberty.

American, Western, and Right-wing views embrace the individual and family unit. We believe in the freedom to say, do, and be whatever one would like in one's pursuit of happiness, so long as others and our shared cultures are not damaged. These values should instill a sense of national pride in one's homeland, one's people, and one's heritage. These things should be protected and revered.

At the core of conservatism is the pragmatic desire to ensure these values are maintained through the generations.

American Values bestow liberty to each and every individual in a society. Liberal values are collectivist in nature and aim to place group welfare over that of the individual. Although the Right is concerned with the well-being of their people, the route to achieve a strong society is vastly different. These two sets of values cannot coexist in one nation. Fundamentally, Western, American, and Right-wing values are diametrically opposed to the collectivist nature of Liberal and Left-wing values. Most political quarrels between the Left and Right stem from a failure to understand that these are not simply two different political ideologies. They are different cultures entirely.

How can two groups coexist when one is supporting mass migration, censorship, gun restrictions, "hate speech" laws, open borders, and higher taxation? The very truths the Right holds as self-evident, are the very things the Left wishes to destroy.

It all ultimately comes down to something exceedingly simple: the difference between the ideal Liberal state of collectivism versus the essence of American and Western identity, self-reliance and self-determination.

Some of us still believe in the heroic nature of the individual struggling against all odds. It is a deeply rooted Western tradition for one man to go forth alone, to struggle, and overcome. Although it remains true that no man is an island, we still hold a truly remarkable regard for the triumph of will.

The Left will never understand this. They come from a different culture entirely. When the children of men still looked longingly into the heavens in envy of the free and soaring birds, it was two humble sons of Ohio who would teach the world to fly. Collectivism is not what enabled two of Ohio's finest to soar above the world; it was self-determination, an iron will, and their own fearless struggle.

Collectivism did not make Tesla the master of electricity. Nor did collectivism ever write a single novel, symphony, or treatise. All of these things were accomplished by societies that had granted prolific freedoms, allowing its citizens to go forth into the darkness and conquer the night.

The Occident rose from the brilliant Promethean flame that illuminated humankind: *per aspera ad astra.* The desire to struggle, to dare greatly, to overcome and conquer, is the essence of the soul of Western tradition.

Behold a Pale Horse: The Four Horsemen of the Apocalyptic Left

There are four values that the international Left incessantly advocates: egalitarianism, diversity, progress, and tolerance. Each one is an ignoble distortion of reality.

1. Egalitarianism

Egalitarianism is nothing but the Liberal perversion of equality. Egalitarianism seeks to take the ideals of equality under the law, turn them upside down, and extend them to financial and social outcomes, enforced by the law and the State.

The differences between equality and egalitarianism derive from the differences between equality of opportunity and equality of outcome. Liberals believe that effort should be nearly irrelevant, that there are no inherent differences between people, and that everybody should have virtually the same outcome no matter what. But people living in the real world understand that different outcomes in terms of success and life-trajectory are based on a myriad of factors.

Marx urged erasing inequality through socialism, eliminating social and class inequality through the elimination of financial inequality. The problem with this premise is that it implies that people are only unequal financially because of some rigged system which ensures that some of them will never succeed, while granting success to others through no effort of their own. Liberals entirely disregard that individual who struggles, who fails, and who builds the resolve to try again. And again. And again. So that one day he may eventually overcome all trials and emerge as something far greater than what he was when he started. The Liberal position here is perhaps best exemplified by the statement made by Barack Obama in regard to success: "If you've got a business, you didn't build that. Somebody else made that happen."[18]

The Liberal bastardization of equality called "equality of outcome" looks not at the efforts, but the results, to decide if something is fair or not. I once had a class that discussed the psychology of stereotypes, racism, and prejudice, which offered the number of Fortune 500 CEOs and congressmen as evidence of racial and sexual inequality. The argument was that if there were true equality, there would be more women and non-whites running Fortune 500 companies and in key political positions. By

---

18 Aaron Blake. "Obama's 'You didn't build that' problem" The Washington Post. July 18, 2012. https://www.washingtonpost.com/blogs/the-fix/post/obamas-you-didnt-build-that-problem/2012/07/18/gJQAJxyotW_blog.html?utm_term=.0c6fe006611b.

this view, in order to achieve true social justice, we need more women and non-whites in key positions of business and Congress. This is where the notion of equality goes off the rails. Liberals never consider that the people presently running those companies might just happen to be the best suited for the job. Maybe these people went to the best schools and achieved the best grades because they worked the longest hours and persevered through all adversity. That never enters the Liberal mind.

Liberals can look to the NFL, in which the players are around 70 percent black, and conclude simply that the best players made the team. Yet when looking at the fact that around 70 percent of head coaches of the teams are white, they assume that this percentage must be sign of racism and inequality.[19] This is a classic example of the doublethink so commonly seen among Liberals, that strange ability to hold two contradictory views, while only applying their standard rule to one of them.

Liberals look at data showing that whites and Asians earn more money than blacks and Hispanics, and they see only a problem that needs to be fixed. They think that because some groups outperform others in certain areas, there *must* be systemic oppression. Never mind the fact that whites and Asians have lower rates of crime, lower rates of single parenthood, and higher rates of education than blacks and Hispanics; Liberals still see the results as unfair. The Left now attributes any difference in outcome to factors beyond a person's control, something that must be remedied. And the common remedy is taking away the effort, opportunity, or property of one person, to give it to another.

Liberals proclaim that anything which does not perfectly mirror the demographic makeup of society is racist or sexist, or proves that the system is rigged in favor of one group, the group of white men. In their warped minds, everybody, from every background, is identical and equal. Liberals live in a world of relativism and subjectivity, in which everybody is equally amazing and special in their own ways. And that's all wonderful—but in the real world, we all have different sets of skills and make different life decisions, and these things lead to different outcomes.

---

19 Jason Reid and Jane McManus. "The NFL's racial divide" The Undefeated. May 09, 2017. https://theundefeated.com/features/the-nfls-racial-divide/. [http://archive.li/ARuic]

Egalitarianism, like socialism and communism, is an ideology for losers and for the dredges of society. It seeks to pull the strongest and most productive members of a society down to the lowly ranks of the least productive and laziest. All ideologies that are rooted in forced equality are little more than cultural crabs-in-a-barrel: the lowest members are forever able to keep the best from reaching higher.

Equality as it is understood by the Right means that we all deserve what we earn through our own efforts. Liberals believe equality means everybody should end in a similar material position. Liberals feel that resources should be redistributed to lessen any and all material inequality, regardless of individual effort and decisions.

"Politically correct" and "social justice" are two egalitarian terms that need to be eradicated, as they are both morally corrupt and logically incoherent. Truth, honesty, and justice are all being subverted by this Liberal obsession with political correctness and social justice. When you take ideals that are inherently good — the ideals of justice and correctness, truth and honesty — and you alter them, they are warped into an inherently perverse sense of justice or truth.

When you add a modifier to the words "correct" or "justice," you entirely alter their meaning. *Justice* refers to objective moral correctness; it indicates that each person receives what he rightfully deserves. *Correct* means to be objectively truthful. It's that simple. Anybody who insists on political correctness or social justice is inherently a liar advocating for severe injustices. This idea is perhaps best exemplified by a former Khmer Rouge leader, Khieu Samphan, who, while on trial for crimes against humanity, told the court he was only fighting for "social justice."[20]

The modifiers to these words are of communist origins. They refer not to righteous or epistemological truths, but to the "proper" way of doing and saying things under the new regime, in which the collective will supersedes individual justice. In egalitarian thought, the collective is taken to be inherently more important than any individual, and the individual is sacrificed to the false god of the collective whenever necessary.

---

20 Afp. "Top Khmer Rouge leader tells court he fought for 'social justice'." Daily Mail Online. February 18, 2016. www.dailymail.co.uk/wires/afp/article-3452925/Top-Khmer-Rouge-leader-tells-court-fought-social-justice.html. [http://archive.li/QslTT]

What I have found, and what I hope to convey in these pages, is that there is no difference at all between the modern Liberals inhabiting the Democrat party and the members of any of the communist regimes we have ever seen the world over. They all work from exactly the same playbook, every single time.

Liberals use the term "politically correct" to regulate what facts they deem acceptable for discussion. It is factually correct for me to say that black men commit homicide at a rate far higher than any other group in America; however, it is not *politically correct* of me to say it. This essentially distorts reality and prevents us from having productive discussions or creating effective policies to solve problems. If there were no stigma associated with facts having to do with race, we could have open discussions regarding these questions. We could look at the plight of inner cities, the impact of unemployment and single motherhood on crime, and we could work towards a better country for everybody. Yet because it is not considered "politically correct" to acknowledge any differences between people or groups, society is prevented from seeking resolutions.

Political correctness is costing lives. When people bring up gun violence and deaths, they don't mention that the majority of young white men killed with guns are suicides. Or that the majority of young black men killed with guns are killed by other young black men. Political correctness has kept issues like gun control in the media without allowing us to discuss the real and deep troubles among young white men and young black men.

Not only in the realm of firearm deaths is political correctness literally killing us, but we are seeing the same horrific effects in terms of migration and crime. All over Europe migrants are robbing, assaulting, and raping native Europeans, but few people will stand up and openly proclaim the issue, the violence continues on. For it is not seen as *politically correct* to draw the correlation between steeply increasing rape rates, and the number of foreign men flooding into Europe. Even more taboo is the discussion of who opened the gates to the Saracen hordes.

The equality between men and women means that persons of both genders have an equal, inherent, and intrinsic basic value. It does not mean that all people are going to be equal from birth until death. You *start out* equal — meaning with the same rights and the same protections under the law. From there, it's up to you. Liberals seem to have gotten the idea that human equality means readjusting our entire society at the end of the year so that everybody gets the same trophy, the same salary. Equality does *not* mean that if you do not achieve your goals, whatever these may be, you get to blame all those who were able to reach theirs.

I will never be the CEO of a Fortune 500 company, race the Monaco Grand Prix, or ride in the Tour de France. This acceptance of reality is beyond the Liberal realm of understanding. I would really like to race Monaco at least once or ride a Grand Tour through Europe—but it just isn't on the cards for me. That doesn't mean I was somehow cheated somewhere in my life.

Egalitarianism forces equality by undermining individual effort. It means nothing but taking positions away from those who rightfully earned them, and giving them to those who did not. It means high taxation on those who have toiled and struggled their lives away to earn a good living for their family, and giving this stolen money to those who have done nothing. It means theft in the name of equality.

By nature people are inherently unequal, a simple concept the Left will not admit. Egalitarianism is the false god worshiped by secular Liberals. It is a destructive dogma, an evil that distorts actual equality and destroys societies from within. Every country in the world that has attempted to force equality onto its people, has ended in the ruins of starvation and decay.

2. Diversity

"Diversity is our greatest strength," is the favorite mantra of the international Left the world over. It is used as a call for mass migration and an excuse to permit the invasion and destruction of cultures, in the name of supposedly great benefits. But never is a single shred of evidence raised in defense of this platitude.

In reality, Liberals do not believe in true diversity—diversity of thoughts and of ideas. The Liberal, multicultural utopia is one in which everybody has different skin color, but thinks exactly the same. Even the Liberal concept of diversity itself is a perversion.

Liberals have lately been claiming that diversity is a core American value. As if our most treasured and central value as a nation could possibly be allowing millions of foreigners that have no connection to our history or values to come here and collect welfare.

Diversity is not what built this nation and made it into the envy of the world. What built this nation was European people coming together, putting their differences aside and working towards a common goal. The value of freedom and hard work is what brought people together. They worked towards a few common American goals to create something special. And now Liberals want to pretend that importing hordes of foreigners who have no intention of integrating, or even working for that matter, is somehow going to enrich our culture. By every measure, increased diversity lowers trust, erodes social capital, and ultimately weakens society.

Diversity is not an asset, but a weakness, one which destroys societies. Multiculturalism is a failed experiment.

We have seen the outcomes throughout Europe and the US. We know what decades of diversity and multiculturalism do to a nation and its people. Certain cultures and ethnicities may simply never get along, and there's nothing wrong with that. Forcing multiculturalism benefits nobody but a select few in the upper echelons of society, whose wealth and status shelters them from all its horrific consequences.

If the visible outcomes of European "enrichment" programs are not enough to convince you of the devastating harm that diversity does to societies, there's more. Robert Putnam, Harvard professor, researcher, author of *Bowling Alone*, and renowned expert on social capital, made an extensive study of diversity. His study put the phrase "diversity is our greatest strength" scientifically to the test.

"Social capital" indicates the relationships between people in a culture or society. It refers to the level of trust, cooperation, norms, values, civic engagement, friendships, quality of life, and the like. Researching social capital within communities, Putnam embarked on a monumental feat of data collection. Putnam collected data from 30,000 people across neighborhoods in forty-one United States cities. Participants were interviewed on numerous topics relating to social capital in their local communities.

What Putnam found in his now infamous study was the last thing he, or most Liberals, ever expected.[21]

Since the 1950s, sociologists have been putting forth the theory of Contact Hypothesis — the idea, simply put, that the best way to improve relationships between different groups is merely to bring them to interact with each other. And in many ways, this idea has its merits — assuming the interactions with the other groups are positive. What Putnam found was not only that increased diversity in societies leads to lower levels of trust between different out-groups, but also that people in diverse societies became less trusting overall, even towards their own in-group.

Putnam found that as diversity increases, so does social isolation: people living in diverse areas stay in more and spend more time alone, watching TV by themselves. As diversity increases, trust levels decrease. Trust not only of each other, but of the local government, the local news, and the media. As diversity increases, fewer community members register to vote, fewer give to charity, and fewer work on community projects. Diversity lowers social cohesion; people in diverse societies are less inclined to work together.

Is it any wonder? The greatest of societies have been created and built by a common group of people working towards a common goal, something greater than themselves. Diversity makes this unified effort all but impossible.

Perhaps the saddest and most damning finding from Putnam's study: as diversity increases, people report having fewer close friends, they report lower ratings of happiness, and a lower quality of life overall.

In areas that were less diverse and more racially homogeneous, all the negative effects of diversity disappear. The least diverse areas of the country, even when one controls for other factors, engage in more community involvement; their members are more trusting of each other and spend more time with others, and more time outdoors generally. The most homogeneous cities have the highest levels of trust among members of the community. Happiness, quality of life, numbers of close friends per

---

21 Robert D. Putnam. "E Pluribus Unum: Diversity and Community in the Twenty-first Century The 2006 Johan Skytte Prize Lecture" Scandinavian Political Studies 30, no. 2 (2007): 137-74. doi:10.1111/j.1467-9477.2007.00176.x.

individual, all increase in areas that are less diverse and more ethnically homogeneous.

Professor Tatu Vanhanen of the University of Helsinki conducted a study that investigated the relationship between conflict and ethnic diversity.[22] Professor Vanhanen found a very high correlation (.726) between the amount of conflict in an area and the amount of diversity. His study ranges from almost entirely homogeneous areas, with little to no conflict (South Korea and Japan), all the way to the exceptionally diverse and war-torn nations of Bosnia and Sudan.

Another analysis done on diversity found that life satisfaction, national wealth, and life expectancy are negatively correlated to increased ethnic diversity; these qualities all decline in the 130 nations studied as their level of diversity increases.[23] The safest, happiest, nations in Europe, Iceland, Poland, Slovenia, all happen to be the *least* diverse.[24]

But set the science aside. Ask yourself: has increased diversity made you happier? Safer? Healthier? Has it made *your* life any better or more enriching? Has it at any point benefited any of the recipients of this "enrichment"? The next time you're stuck in a three hour long TSA line at the airport, you can undoubtedly thank diversity and tolerance for the delay.

Diversity, by all measures, weakens society, lowers trust, destroys social capital, damages happiness, and degrades quality of life. Far from being our "strength," it leads to fragmentation and mutual mistrust, making all cohesion or social unity impossible.

---

22 Tatu Vanhanen. Ethnic conflicts explained by ethnic nepotism. Stamford: Jai Press, 1999.

23 Ryan Faulk. "What Diverse Countries Really Look Like" The Alternative Hypothesis. November 30, 2016. http://thealternativehypothesis.org/index.php/2016/11/30/what-diverse-countries-really-look-like/. [http://archive.li/xsvah]

24 "Europe's safest countries 2017" PolishWiFi. April 02, 2017. http://www.polishwifi.com/en/blog/0/10/europe percentE2 percent80 percent99s-safest-countries-2017.html.

3. Progress

Freedom once implied certain unalienable rights. The right to speech, press, worship, and to property. The freedom to pursue one's own happiness. There is an essential quality common to all of these rights; they do not require anything from anybody else. I can say whatever I like without needing anyone's participation. Nobody even has to listen to my ravings for me to have that freedom. These rights do not require any sort of limiting principle; they are passive in nature, and ask nothing of anyone.

You can faithfully pursue your happiness, whatever that may be, so long as you do not impede on another person's freedom or harm society. These freedoms and rights in a certain sense exist almost naturally: if you do not impede another person's rights or harm society at large, then you are for that very reason acting in a virtuous and just manner. All that needs be done to maintain these freedoms is to ensure that whenever anyone's rights are infringed, there is a system in place to deal with such transgressions. In our case, this is the court system; and even here, the accused has a *right* to a fair and quick trial.

This was the status quo in the United States for the better part of its history. Then Franklin Roosevelt in his 1941 State of the Union Address declared the "freedom from want," which would forever turn the passive nature of rights upside down in the United States. To declare that all people have the right to a certain standard of living, as FDR did, is to open the floodgates to constant and incessant "progress" with no limiting factor. There is always going to be some new arbitrary crusade, some manufactured battle to fight. To declare that coverage of basic living expenses is a "right," is also to declare that some other person must be obligated to provide that right. Which of course violates the property rights of the provider.

FDR with his New Deal did nothing less than introduce socialism into the United States. He created a system that forces workers to pay for others. Had welfare programs been created using excise taxes alone, I would be in support of them, as many people legitimately need help: people born disabled or mentally retarded, or those who become disabled through war or accidents, or others yet who are simply down on their luck. I have great compassion for people in need of a helping hand, and I want there to be help for them when they need it.

However, once the federal income tax was implemented and the New Deal kicked off, we found ourselves beneath a system which could seize more and more from the workers, giving it freely away. All under the banner of "progress" and the "right" to a certain standard of living. FDR and the New Deal introduced an enormous and illimitable system of wealth redistribution. Today the welfare state has swollen to the point that the number of people who feed off the system is almost the same as the number of those who contribute to it.

Unless we establish some sort of limiting factor, the entitlement system will continue to spiral out of control. The Left will continue to push for more and more new programs and expansions of existing programs, until the workers are no better off than those receiving the benefits of their labor. Liberals want thereby to force economic equality on us. They truly believe it is unfair for somebody to possess more than others. Their solution to this "injustice" was the federal income tax and the welfare state. If there were no federal income tax, no deficit spending, and the welfare state were only funded by voluntary excise taxes or bonds, then the system would be forced to cut redundancy and limit aid to those who truly need help.

And many people truly do need help. We need places that care for those who cannot care for themselves. It's wonderful that we have programs, for example, to assist the parents of disabled children. However, there is also an incredible amount of waste, and there are too many incentives to take advantage of such generous programs.

We could easily cut spending to these programs overnight. For example, 90 percent of immigrants coming from more than ten specific nations are presently on welfare. Over 50 percent of immigrant households generally are on welfare. These people did not pay into the system, they do not contribute to our culture, they share no history or values with us. There is no reason to force working Americans to pay for them to come here and freeload. Indeed, it is entirely devoid of morality to force this on them.

The Leftist obsession with progress needs to be curtailed. It is important for us to understand that no matter how much we give, they will try to take more. The Left will never heed any limiting principle unless we institute one for them.

Allowing the income tax to be levied, departing from the gold standard, and utilizing deficit spending, have all ensured government can continue to grow until its enormous weight cripples the very citizens it was meant to serve. There are no longer any checks and balances to restrain the State from this unfettered and diseased growth. The United States has become far worse than the very nation we once fought a magnificent revolution against.

Liberals believe that flooding nations with hordes of migrants from the Third World constitutes progress. They view the fact that native British are becoming minorities in their own capital city of London as progress. But progress for whom? Certainty not for the native sons of Albion, who have inhabited that island for thousands of years. The same trend is happening all over Europe, and also in the US. In 1965, whites in the US made up nearly 90 percent of the population. In a little over fifty years, over fifty-nine million migrants have come to the US, bringing the white population down to 62 percent. In less than fifty years more, if present trends continue, white Americans will represent less than half of a population which will grow to nearly 450 million.[25] Liberals call this progress. And if their goal is to dispossess all the whites in America, the very people who built its civilization, then I guess this really *does* constitute "progress."

To be a Liberal progressive, particularly as regards mass migration, is to ignore the reality of crime against our people, the incredible financial costs involved, and the destruction of our culture. The Liberal progressives risk everything out of a blind and misguided trust in the idea that bringing Third World hordes into our lands will miraculously turn them into Westerners. This empty idealism, this thought that *other* peoples can carry on *our* culture, is possibly the greatest gamble they could make. They are risking the very future of civilization, all so they can feel good about themselves and consider themselves morally superior, all so that

25 "Modern Immigration Wave Brings 59 Million to U.S., Driving Population Growth and Change Through 2065" Pew Research Center's Hispanic Trends Project. September 28, 2015. http://www.pewhispanic.org/2015/09/28/modern-immigration-wave-brings-59-million-to-u-s-driving-population-growth-and-change-through-2065/. [http://archive.li/GN67z]

they can claim we are progressing towards something — even though they have no idea what that *something* actually entails.

Progressive Liberalism a disease which continues to spread farther and farther, destroying every good and just thing that stands in its path. Liberals the world over are determined to create a borderless and characterless society. I think I've seen enough of what they call "progress" to know exactly where this road leads.

Progress should mean movement toward the objective improvement of the human condition. If in the pursuit of an utterly illusory "progress" we find that we are moving further from real improvement of life for our people, then that man who most rapidly changes his course will in truth be the most progressive. The Left in its blind madness is charging toward an abyss that threatens the very fate of our civilization and our people: it is time for us to get off their wagon.

> "Not blind opposition to progress, but opposition to blind progress."
>
> — John Muir

4. Tolerance

Liberals endlessly espouse the false virtue of tolerance. They riot to shut down conservative speakers on campuses, they physically assault people for having the wrong viewpoint, even while demanding that we succumb to their every whim. Liberals are so *tolerant*, that they immediately conclude that anybody even slightly to the Right of Trotsky must be a Nazi. And against all "Nazis," they are swift to advocate violence. Liberals preach tolerance, even while promoting laws all over the Western world to fine and imprison people for "hate speech." And such speech is of course defined as any political opinion which differs from those of the Liberals in power.

A telltale sign of Liberalism is their requirement that others meet a standard which they do not set for themselves. The same Liberals with private armed security details are the ones who advocate for firearm bans. The same Liberals who teach the "value" of diversity live in gated communities and send their children to homogeneous private schools. The same Liberals who fight for "equality" want to ensure that certain groups still receive preferential treatment. The same Liberals who are so quick to affirm how progressive they are create laws and policies which cannot do other than turn the nations of the First World into nations of the Third World. The same Liberals who demand tolerance will denounce you as an ignorant bigot at the first sign of Wrong Think.

I like to think I'm a tolerant man. Perhaps I'm just tolerant of different things. But I am quite certain of one thing: I have run all out of tolerance for the Left.

The Left must never forget where it came from when it lectures us about "tolerance." The Liberals are the same people who gave us the Federal Reserve, the Income Tax Act, the very same people who have led us into nearly every unnecessary war we have suffered in the last hundred years. Even while lying to the American people about it all. Today, they are the party of oppressive taxation, mass migration, endless degeneracy, censorship, control, and thought policing. They are the people filling our society with spiritual poison and socially and politically corrosive policies. The global Left caused the rapes and murders in Rotherham, Nice, Berlin, and hundreds of other cities. The Left is the reason that abuse and sexual violence has become epidemic all over Europe, the reason that people are afraid to leave their houses in their own native lands.

It is the Left, and not the Right, which has made constant affronts to the freedom of expression, arms, and association. Liberals are the purveyors of lies, population replacement, and tyrannical taxation. They undermine our nation, our values, and our people, at every turn.

They are the party that supports late-term abortion, in which abortionists enter a woman's womb with scissors, cut the child's tiny limbs off, sever its brain stem, and crush its little skull.

The Liberal doctrine of mandatory tolerance frequently denounces those who are "judgmental." The Left advocates a total acceptance of everyone and everything. But I ask, where is the inherent moral wrong in judgment? Is it no longer reasonable to have an objective set of values and standards, to which one can refer in measuring and weighing morality and the actions of human beings? When one has no moral standards, it becomes impossible to measure the value of ideas or deeds. Which is exactly what Liberals want. Liberals vociferously abhor judgment because they do not believe in any sort of absolute moral or value standard. To the depraved mind of a Liberal, *everything* is subjective.

When we, as individuals or as a society, abandon all normative values, morals, and standards, we graciously invite the decay of our character and of our culture.

When we forego traditional, meaningful values, these are replaced with superficial, meaningless ones. How many times have we heard the terms "nice" and "funny" to describe personality traits? "He's so *funny*!" "She's so *nice*!" Yes, *everybody* is so nice, and so funny — and so fake. Who really cares how *nice* somebody is? Niceness is worthless. How many "nice and funny" people are also liars, thieves? How many are unreliable, untrustworthy? Ah! But at least they were friendly and made you laugh!

Honesty, dependability, discipline, perseverance, trustworthiness, honor, fearlessness — these are virtues worthy of our admiration. Yet society has become so decadent that people place a higher premium on how somebody makes them feel superficially, than on the profound qualities that actually matter. Society has reached a stage in which people are more concerned with their feelings than with truth and nobility. Yet it is truth and nobility which separates nice guys from good men.

Once objective virtues are replaced with subjective ones, everything becomes excusable and thus tolerable. Liberals are not even capable of reasonably evaluating character, let alone the outcomes of political actions and policy. They judge right and wrong based on how it makes them *feel*, as opposed to on the basis of actual real world consequences. We see this play out most clearly in Leftist immigration policy. Despite the fact it has been a total failure, costs billions annually, and leads to increased crime, it makes Liberals feel good — so they keep advocating for more. This is classic moral subjectivism, according to which feelings alone determine the consequential utility of actions.

Tolerance as a virtue was not taught by Jesus, the Romans, the Buddha; it is nowhere to be found in the Bushido, in the Nine Noble Virtues, nor in the code of Chivalry. Tolerance is not taught as a virtue anywhere by anybody, except by contemporary Liberals. Why is this? But the reason is simple. Tolerance is a virtue for those who have no honor, a "virtue" which permits one to forget one's own *lack* of honor.

Tolerance means putting up with or enduring something unpleasant. Which is precisely what the Left wants from us. They want us to capitulate to their destructive will. They want us to lie down and simply *tolerate* while they increase taxes to fund never ending "progress," to lie down and *tolerate* the destruction of our cultures, to peacefully *tolerate* as they inform us that we have no right to our own labor and efforts. Liberals preach tolerance as a virtue because they want society submissive — submissive to mass immigration and to mounting rates of rape and violence, submissive as they extort money from us to pay for the very same schemes that lead to these ends. Throughout Europe and America, tolerance is beaten into our heads through commercials, advertisements, films, by the news and by our politicians. Of course they want us tolerant as our culture is erased, our nations are ransacked, and our people are brutalized. Otherwise they may face a real existential threat to their entire empire.

> Tolerance and apathy are the last virtues of a dying society.
>
> —Unknown

If our *tolerance* were ever to run dry, the Left knows there would be hell to pay for their insolence.

Liberalism in Practice

Through history, the Left has everywhere gained power the same way: by demonizing and devaluing the worth of the individual in order to appease the collective. This strategy invariably devolves into mob rule, leading to tens of millions of deaths in the name of social justice and political correctness.

In its effort to create classless, egalitarian societies, in which everybody is the same, the Left has created more war, sickness, famine, and death than any other ideology in the history of man. The Left's thirst for blood and conquest is Biblical in proportion. It is indeed nothing short of cataclysmic. To protect its dogma, the Left has needed to exert total control over those it rules. The only way to control a population and force it into an unnatural order is through hyper-violence. Individuals and free thinkers cannot be tolerated in a Liberal "utopian" society; all dissent must be silenced lest the power of the Left be threatened. The Left needs a society of mindless golems, dependent on the State for their every need, in order for their "utopia" to work.

What the Left has created every time, without fail, is a dystopian hell on Earth, in which fear, starvation, disease, and murder reign supreme. And in this hell, everybody is indeed equal. After all, everyone is equal in death.

What becomes of those who don't believe in a society that advocates free love, a society in which everybody uses everybody else? Or those who see egalitarianism, the idea of taking from those who produce and giving to those who do not, as less of a utopia, and more of a misery?

What about all the rebels who don't quite fit into the socialist utopia? What about the ones who want to go forth, to struggle, and to overcome? The ones who want to push humanity a little further? The wild ones who still believe in becoming something greater than themselves? What happens to all the dreamers, revolutionaries, the rebels? What do socialist and communist societies do to *these* people?

They leave them dead in a snowy forest with a bullet in the back of their head.

People that do not docilely go along with the Liberal plan are a danger. They threaten to unfold the entire vision. People like me cannot be tolerated. People like you cannot be tolerated. We are seeing a manifestation of this currently in the constant calls of the American Left for coups, wars, and violence against those who dared vote against them.

How does the Left deal with dissidents? Free thinkers? Outliers? Those of us who threw a wrench in the Leftist machine. Those of us who denied the Liberal dream of open borders, increased taxation, and assault on civil liberties. What is the Left to do with such inconvenient persons?

- 45,000,000 dead under Chairman Mao's Great Leap Forward.
- 20,000,000 dead under Soviet rule.
- 9,000,000 dead after the October Revolution.
- 7,000,000 dead in the Holodomor.
- 2,000,000 dead in the Killing Fields.

An incredible number of these deaths were simply brought against those who had the wrong political opinion; hence the term "politically incorrect." High estimates are over fifty million deaths directly related to the Bolsheviks seizing Russia. Millions in Ukraine intentionally starved to death by the Jewish NKVD director, Genrikh Yagoda, a figure history has chosen to pass over in silence. Yagoda and the NKVD are responsible for far more civilian deaths than the Germans under Heinrich Himmler. Yet most of us only know *one* of their names.

700,000 deaths during Stalin's Great Purge. Most executed with a bullet to the back of the head. Millions more dead in Korea, Vietnam, Bulgaria, East Germany, Romania, and Cambodia under communist regimes. Most estimates are around 100,000,000 deaths as a direct result of communist ideology.[26]

Without a shadow of a doubt, communism and its purveyors have orchestrated the largest man-made disasters in all of human history.

There is a "Communist Club" on my University campus. It's not uncommon for me to see people wearing Che Guevara shirts, though the man was a famous communist, rapist, and murderer. Hammer and sickle pins on backpacks, fliers for their weekly meetings on bulletin boards. Every once in a while, the Communist Club writes in chalk on the campus sidewalks: "Capitalism = Work or Starve." I don't think these people have the intellectual capacity to perceive the dramatic, almost Shakespearean, irony of their message. Tens of millions literally starved to death because of people like them, yet they still have the audacity to scribble such utter filth. These people do not care if we are poor, starving, or dead, so long as they can call the results *equal*. This is the natural conclusion of egalitarianism: one hundred million bodies are the logical result of the communist equation.

Any relatively sane person will look not only at the communist idea, but at everything that comes of it, and conclude that it is absolutely devoid of any shred of morality or humanity. In *every attempt* at communism or socialism ever attempted, long before utopia is achieved, we all starve to death.

---

26 John J. Walters. "Communism Killed 94M in 20th Century, Feels Need to Kill Again" Reason.com. March 13, 2013. http://reason.com/blog/2013/03/13/communism-killed-94m-in-20th-century. [http://archive.li/7mJ1J]

Sure, capitalism could be construed to mean "work or starve." However, I would much rather that we all have the opportunity to work and buy food, than that we all starve to death together. Equally hungry.

I dream of a day when these devils dressed as humans, the advocates for socialism, communism, and the purveyors of any of its iterations, are heralded as the wretched, murderous scum they are. If somebody were to create a university "Nazi Club" calling for the dawn of the Fourth Reich, or wearing shirts with the Reichsadler on it, they would run immediately into hardship, and would likely even be expelled. But trumpet an ideology that has killed far more people than Hitler's, and it's considered perfectly acceptable. Why? Because the heralds of these ideas are on the *Left*, there is communism in the heart of every Liberal and Leftist, and the Left is in control. They care not if their political adversaries end up tortured to death, hanged, shot, or starved. In fact, that seems to be exactly what they are aiming for.

To hide their dark pasts, Leftist change their identity every so often. But their dogmatic principles of totalitarian collectivism remain constant through the ages. They have called themselves communists, Marxists, Trotskyites, Maoists, Bolsheviks, socialists, Democrats, Liberals, Progressives, Democratic Socialists, Progressive Democrats, neoconservatives, and many more names to boot. Yet the outcome is always the same: war, famine, pestilence, and death — the only things the Left has ever offered to any society.

The Left has been at war with us and our kind for quite some time. Sooner or later, we are going to need to wake up, to stop running, and to face them as the enemy they are. Those who fight the Left battle the devil.

Act II:

Fighting the Battles

I

Words Like Violence: The Left's Total War on Freedom of Speech

"HATE SPEECH IS NOT FREE SPEECH YOU FUCKING ASSHOLE!" the purple-haired, cigarette-smoking, degenerate, screamed at me from the top of her tiny, black lungs at a campus protest. Her hands clenched in fists of rage in front of her "Fuck Trump" tank top, she snarled at me with the rabid expression of hatred on her face, feverishly awaiting my reply.

"And that's where you're wrong, darling. Hate speech, is the noblest form of free speech," I calmly replied. As I sauntered down the brick walkway, on a cold autumn day, the wind blew my hair into a wild mane, my trench coat flowing eloquently behind me in some unintended, yet ornate display of regality.

Free speech is not, and has never been, a value of the oppressive Left.

And why would it be? In the face of really free speech, the false narratives of the Left, built upon half-truths and whole lies, would come crumbling down in a magnificent disaster, leaving them exposed as the charlatans they are.

Free speech in the United States is scarcely limited; the only restrictions are on speech which incites immediate violence. Nowhere else in the world is this liberty so protected.[1] In fact, as we will see, even many of our fellow American citizens do not share this value.

In Germany, hate speech and criticism of heads of state can result in five years in prison. German people have had their homes raided for comments they have left on social media criticizing the migrant population or the immigration policies that have caused a rape and crime epidemic in their nation.[2] I'm not talking about Germany during the Weimar Republic or Soviet-occupied East Germany; it happens frequently in the present day, under Angela Merkel — the German leader that Hillary Clinton said she most admired. This is worth reflecting on; this is how close we were to catastrophe in America. We were standing on the edge, looking into the abyss. There is no longer any time to mess around.

What is the justification for laws against certain kinds of speech? "Hate speech" might cause emotional turmoil for the "victim," or it might incite hatred against a certain group. Which means that currently, a person can be fined or imprisoned in so-called developed nations all over the world merely for *hurting somebody's feelings.*

The idea of fining or imprisoning somebody for speech is beyond barbaric. Considering how "progressive" the Left is, it is surprising that it has no issue instituting Draconian blasphemy laws of this kind. How ironic that the same group of people holding signs that read "No human being is illegal" seem to have no qualm making *you* illegal if you hold the wrong political views.

A man in Cambridge, UK, has been given four years in prison for making "hateful" comments online.[3] An 88 year-old woman in Germany, Ursula Haverbeck, has been sentenced to prison for two years for daring

---

1 Adam Liptak. "Hate speech or free speech? What much of West bans is protected in U.S" The New York Times. June 11, 2008. http://www.nytimes.com/2008/06/11/world/americas/11iht-hate.4.13645369.html. [http://archive.li/tdWl3]

2 Joshua Yasmeh. "Thought Crime: German Police Raid Homes Of People Who Made 'Hateful Postings' On The Internet" Daily Wire. June 21, 2017. http://www.dailywire.com/news/17801/thought-crime-german-police-raid-homes-people-who-joshua-yasmeh. [http://archive.li/u8j18]

3 Tom Pilgrim. "Cambridge extremist jailed for race hate" Cambridge news. March 11, 2017. http://www.cambridge-news.co.uk/news/cambridge-news/cambridge-extremist-jailed-four-years-12725791. [http://archive.li/zb96c]

question historical events dating back to seventy years ago; her crime is "Holocaust denial."[4] These two stories are by no means exceptional or extraordinary cases; they are the creeping norm in much of Europe today. In 2016 in the UK, over 3,300 people were arrested for offensive online comments. Let us repeat that. Per a communications act which makes it illegal to "cause annoyance, inconvenience or needless anxiety to another," over 3,300 people have been terrorized by their own government. Generally, these are only white citizens, as people making anti-*white* comments online are typically left alone.[5] European lawmakers now make a higher priority of jailing people for offensive comments, than stopping the massive sex trafficking rings and gang rapes that currently plague their nations.

Woe to whomever commits a Thought Crime; for that mistake, the Thought Police come knocking. Even tourists are now experiencing its tyrannical reach. Two Chinese men were arrested and fined for taking photos in front of the Reichstag building while making "illegal Hitler salutes."[6] Germany is no longer a serious country.

Here is a list to consider:

> Austria, Belgium, Denmark, Germany, Australia, Finland, France, Ireland, Norway, Poland, Iceland, Netherlands, Switzerland, Canada, United Kingdom.

None of the citizens of these nations are free folk.

They all have laws outlawing what politicians arbitrarily deem to be "hate speech" — or more accurately, Crime Think, as Orwell foretold.

---

4 Isabelle Gerretsen. "Nazi grandma Ursula Haverbeck sent to prison for holocaust denial." IBT. August 29, 2017. https://www.ibtimes.co.uk/nazi-grandma-ursula-haverbeck-sent-prison-holocaust-denial-1637098. [http://archive.is/dTgKs]

5 Jack Montgomery. "British Police Arrest At Least 3,395 People for 'Offensive' Online Comments in One Year." Breitbart . October, 14. 2017. www.breitbart.com/london/2017/10/14/british-police-arrest-at-least-3395-people-for-offensive-online-comments-one-year/. [http://archive.li/HEqoZ]

6 "Chinese tourists arrested for making Hitler salutes outside Reichstag" The Guardian. August 05, 2017. https://www.theguardian.com/world/2017/aug/05/chinese-tourists-arrested-for-making-hitler-salutes-outside-reichstag. [http://archive.li/pcKU3]

One in four countries across the globe outlaw blasphemy. Blasphemy laws are concentrated primarily in North Africa and the Middle East, places that have fallen under Islamic influence. However, blasphemy laws also exist in Europe and South America. Punishments range from fines and imprisonment to death.[7]

Thanks to the Left, many European countries claim that hate speech laws are an effort to stop fascism; in an effort to stop "authoritarianism," they became totalitarians themselves. Brilliant play lads. It is not that the Left has any real objection to authoritarianism, so long as *they* are in control.

But I'm starting to realize more and more that countries with theocratic totalitarian regimes are not all that different from "progressive" Liberal nations. And why would they be? Liberalism itself is more of a mentally deranged dogmatic cult than a political philosophy. Hate speech is blasphemy, and hate speech laws are blasphemy laws. Viewed in this light, everything starts to come together.

The United Nations has issued a "warning" to the United States, urging us to abandon our value of free speech, so that our inalienable rights are not "misused" to promote "hate speech."[8] The largest political organization on Earth is now agitating for the abolition of our most fundamental right. In a bygone time, better men would have seen this as an act of total war against our people by a hostile elite.

It is useful for us to look at what is happening in Europe today; it gives us a glimpse into our own future, — what might have been our present, had the 2016 election gone differently. This book is more than a political treatise; it does not seek only to illuminate and dissect the destructive nature of modern Liberal policies and ideals. This book is a warning of what lies ahead if we are not vigilant today. Our eternal vigilance has always been the high price we must pay for our freedom.

---

7 Angelina E. Theodorou. "Which countries still outlaw apostasy and blasphemy" Pew Research Center. July 29, 2016. http://www.pewresearch.org/fact-tank/2016/07/29/which-countries-still-outlaw-apostasy-and-blasphemy/. [http://archive.li/MV3Ad]

8 Margaret Menge. "United Nations Urges U.S. to Give Up Free Expression to Combat Racism." LifeZette. November 21, 2017. www.lifezette.com/polizette/united-nations-urges-u-s-give-free-speech-combat-racism/. [http://archive.li/6SZ8g]

University campuses all over the nation have already composed disturbing lists of banned words and phrases, side by side with acceptable phrases (Newspeak). College students with no moral convictions and weak characters have been calling for "safe spaces" and bans on hate speech for some time. Even US news organizations have urged a revision of our freedom of speech, modeled on the "progressive" European and Canadian speech laws. Their claim is similar to that of European nations and others that have enacted such laws: certain words or phrases create a "safety" issue for people. We should therefore silence this language in order to protect the exceedingly fragile and volatile Liberal mind from a state of danger. This is a classic example of the collective nature of the Left compared to the individualism of the Right. Even *if* preventing one person from speaking would spare the feelings of an entire group, that one person's freedom to speak should triumph over the hegemony.

Recent Pew research on the freedom of expression polled US citizens from the ages of eighteen to thirty-four, as to whether they thought the government should have the ability to prevent people from making offensive statements about "minorities." A whopping 40 percent of those surveyed answered in the affirmative: the government *should* have the ability to stop people from making "offensive statements." Democrats were twice as likely as Republicans to say the government should have the authority to regulate such statements. Of those surveyed in Europe, 49 percent were in favor of government intervention of offensive comments.[9]

There is some hope in the fact that 60 percent surveyed in America disagree with government censorship. On one hand, it is shocking that 40 percent of young Americans, people my own age, would be in favor of forfeiting their fundamental, inalienable, rights. On the other hand, it must be remembered that most people, long soaked in the propaganda of the Left, do not even realize that their thoughts are hardly their own anymore.

The startling aspect of the trend towards approval for hate speech laws is that each generation becomes more and more tolerant of censorship.

9 Jacob Poushter. "40 percent of Millennials OK with limiting speech offensive to minorities" Pew Research Center. November 20, 2015. http://www.pewresearch.org/fact-tank/2015/11/20/40-of-millennials-ok-with-limiting-speech-offensive-to-minorities/. [http://archive.li/4rY59]

Only 12 percent US adults aged seventy to eighty-seven were in favor of the government being able to regulate offensive comments. Each generation thereafter become more and more willing to submit to the State.

A 2017 study asked whether its subjects would support hate speech laws in the United States. 56 percent of black citizens supported hate speech laws. 58 percent of Hispanic citizens supported them. Only 33 percent of white Americans supported the banning of hate speech. 52 percent of Democrats were in favor of hate speech laws in America, while 27 percent of Republicans were in favor.[10]

It is clear to whom we must look for the defense of our freedoms.

Please Choose from the List of Approved Words and Phrases before Speaking

In Orwell's prophetic classic, *1984*, not only could a citizen be found guilty of a Thought Crime, but information that might threaten the official Party doctrine was also censored and destroyed. History books and articles were commonly rewritten to reflect the current agenda, and as always, thought criminals were routinely disappeared.

New York City passed a law that makes it illegal to address a person by the wrong title, pronouns, or gender. All businesses, professionals, and landlords, are required to address a person by their preferred title or pronoun. If a man wants to be referred to as "her," "ze," "xir," or any other randomly imagined name, employers, professionals, and landlords are required by law to abide, else they face a fine of $125,000 to $250,000. "Mis-gendering" a person is now illegal in New York City. The law also includes provisions to inhibit the enforcing a "gendered" dress code at work. Meaning, you cannot ask a male employee not to wear a dress and high heels to work. NYC has now made it illegal to observe a fundamental, biological reality.[11]

---

10 Emily Ekins. "The State of Free Speech and Tolerance in America" Cato Institute. October 31, 2017. https://www.cato.org/survey-reports/state-free-speech-tolerance-america. [http://archive.li/yWkD6]

11 Joe Tacopino. "Not using transgender pronouns could get you fined" New York Post. May 19, 2016. http://nypost.com/2016/05/19/

In California, State Senator, Scott Weiner, who is gay and Jewish, wrote a similar bill, one that would charge people criminally, and have them jailed for up to one year, for the crime of mis-gendering a person.[12] [13] Weiner also introduced a bill that would no longer make it a felony to knowingly infect another person with HIV. The bill applies to blood banks, meaning an HIV positive person would face only a misdemeanor, with a maximum penalty of six months in jail, for donating infected blood and not informing the blood bank of their HIV status.[14] In California, to call a person by the wrong gender now carries a heavier sentence, than does knowingly infecting a person with HIV. This is clown world.

I'm not against referring to people by their preferred name. In fact, if you want to paint your face green, wear a giant turtle shell, and carry around nunchaku, I'll gladly refer to you as Michelangelo from here to hereafter. Want to wear fangs, a cape, and only come out at night? You're Count Dracula for me. I'll be happy to entertain your delusion. I love a good character anyway.

The issue is that currently throughout the world, it is becoming a norm to criminalize and police language. I'm not appealing to some slippery slope, where I think this is going to spin out of control. It already has. Societies either need to decide that we can say whatever we want, or not. Somebody not calling you by your preferred name in no way inhibits you from being you. I would like it if from now on, everybody only referred to me as, King Richard the Wild Hearted, Last of his Kind, Hero to all Free Folk. Yes, the whole thing. I would like it quite a lot actually.

Imagine if everywhere I went, people affectionately greeted me that way. Walk into the coffee shop or the gym or class, "Good morrow, King

---

city-issues-new-guidelines-on-transgender-pronouns/. [http://archive.li/L38Hm]

12 Georgi Boorman. "CA Passes Bill To Punish Nurses Who Dont Use Trans Pronouns." The Federalist. September 15, 2017. thefederalist.com/2017/09/15/california-legislature-passes-bill-punish-elder-care-workers-dont-use-trans-pronouns/. [http://archive.li/Zjl5c]

13 C.W. Nevius. "In world of S.F. politics, Scott Wiener is a serious player." SFGate. January, 14, 2015. www.sfgate.com/bayarea/nevius/article/In-world-of-S-F-politics-Scott-Wiener-is-a-6015639.php. [http://archive.li/jy8am]

14 Alaa Elassar and Laura Diaz-Zuniga. "California lowers penalty for HIV exposure." CNN. October 10, 2017. www.cnn.com/2017/10/07/health/california-hiv-bill-signed/index.html. [http://archive.li/lxVj4]

Richard the Wild Hearted, Last of his Kind, Hero to all Free Folk, your standard espresso and muffin?" Life would be grand. But I do not think *forcing* anybody to call me by such a title under the threat of financial sanction or worse is reasonable in a fair and just society.

Hate speech laws are only the beginning. "Progressive" nations like Sweden quickly move on to censoring even the access of information, such as the recent denial by the Justice Minister at the request of updated crime statistics.[15] This is a classic tactic used by every communist regime we have ever seen. Controlling what people can say is a way to control what they think. Controlling what information people have access to is a way to control what they think. This is about keeping a population in the dark, stupid, weak, and dependent on the State. Liberals today have the same value system that communist dictators have always had. They are the very authoritarians that they claim to fight. The deceitful Left needs to censor speech and restrict access to information, for those are the only two necessary weapons in the battle for truth. Liberals can never win in a fair fight of facts and reason. So, they use the State to limit the arms of the opposition by denying us access to information, and denying us the ability to speak the truth. The Left by nature is anti-truth.

Incidents all over Europe have been intentionally covered up to keep people unaware of what is happening to their homelands. From the Rotherham sex-operation cover up, to the New Year's Eve sexual assault scandal in Germany, we are only scratching the surface. In Sweden, gangs of Afghan men raped and sexually assaulted girls as young as eleven at a music festival. When asked about the incident in an interview, a Swedish politician said that often times, they will leave out stories of this nature, as they worry the information may "play into the hands" of the Right-wing, nationalist party.[16] The Left understands what it is doing very well; it knows that if people knew the truth of their victimization they would naturally gravitate towards the Right and towards nationalism. It is

---

15 Virginia Hale. "Sweden Blocks Request for Data on Crime and Immigration" Breitbart. January 18, 2017. http://www.breitbart.com/london/2017/01/18/sweden-blocks-data-crime-immigration/. [http://archive.li/WbBqi]

16 Cynthia Kroet. "Sweden investigates sex assault cover-Up." POLITICO. January 11, 2016. www.politico.eu/article/sweden-sex-assault-migrants-cologne-muslims/. [http://archive.li/PBr7f]

intentionally keeping these stories, and thousands like them, under cover, at the grave expense of people's lives and safety — all so it may continue to rule with impunity.

Sadly, the same trend is beginning to emerge in the US as well. After a string of robberies committed by non-whites on the Bay Area Rapid Transit, San Francisco authorities chose to not release footage of the crimes. Despite the fact that releasing the footage would certainly help to apprehend the criminals, authorities felt releasing the video might perpetuate stereotyping. Further, one of the BART directors stated that the footage "would create a racial bias in the riders against minorities on the trains."[17] Once again we see that those in positions of authority are more concerned with protecting the people who victimize, than with stopping further victimization. There is a large-scale cover up the world over on the part of the Left of all the crimes non-whites commit against whites. This war against us is being deliberately waged under the guise of tolerance and political correctness.

Liberals in America have resorted to more indirect ways of silencing dissenters; due to our first two amendments, they cannot throw us in jail for speaking the truth. For now. The Left has therefore essentially privatized and outsourced the censorship. Instead of having the State censor us, as in so many other "advanced" nations, American censorship is done via private entities. Instead of using the State to directly police our voices — as happens in Europe — censorship has been out-sourced and renamed "terms of service." Liberals and tech giants now leverage their terms of service as little more than a virtual Article 58, a way to grant *carte blanche* to the cyber secret police.

Tech companies such as YouTube, Google, and Facebook have hired armies of people to find and remove upsetting or offensive content. *Not* content such as animal cruelty, violent pornography, and calls for rape and white genocide, but content that might be labeled as "hate speech,"

17 Amanda Prestigiacomo. "San Fran Transit: We Refuse To Release Crime Surveillance Videos Because It Will Make People Racist" Daily Wire. July 12, 2017. http://www.dailywire.com/news/18509/san-fran-transit-we-refuse-release-crime-amanda-prestigiacomo. [http://archive.li/UuMz9]

according to the Nuevo-Ministry of Truth.[18] [19] They are actively censoring and manipulating search results, in an effort to ensure we do not stumble upon any content they wouldn't want us to see. Thousands of accounts have been banned from social media such as Twitter and Facebook simply because they promote white interests and stand against mass migration. The Daily Stormer's website has become the most censored publication in history, being thrown off of dozens of domain-hosting companies.

Payment processing companies have followed suit as well, ensuring that those who sell Right-wing books and produce Right-wing radio shows or run Right-wing websites are hindered financially. None of these people are advocating violence, not one of them posts illegal content, as say videos of brutality against animals or violent pornography. *That* material can easily be found online. But political musing that cuts at the establishment is met with ferocious obstruction. There has been a virtual Hanging Order issued to suppress all forms of dissident thought.

Speaking of which, the Anti-Defamation League (ADL) is building a "command center," with the goal of combating hate speech, meaning anything Right-wing. It is easy to imagine what this will entail: a campaign to remove all instances of Wrong Think that might be found anywhere on the internet.[20] The ADL is working with Google, Twitter, Facebook, Microsoft, and YouTube to remove any content deemed to include "hate

---

18 Nikita Biryukov. "Google Turns to 'Quality Raters' to Combat Fake, Offensive Results" NBC News. March 17, 2017. http://www.nbcnews.com/tech/tech-news/google-turns-quality-raters-combat-fake-offensive-results-n735076. [http://archive.li/L6FoS]

19 Ingrid Lunden. "Facebook to add 3,000 to team reviewing posts with hate speech, crimes, and other harming posts" TechCrunch. May 03, 2017. https://techcrunch.com/2017/05/03/facebook-to-hire-3000-to-review-posts-with-hate-speech-crimes-and-other-harming-posts/.

20 Andrew Tobin. "ADL To Combat Online Hate From Heart Of Silicon Valley" The Forward. March 13, 2017. http://forward.com/news/breaking-news/365793/adl-to-combat-online-hate-from-heart-of-silicon-valley/. [http://archive.li/07mXt]

speech."[21] [22] The same group of people that declare cartoon frogs to be the enemy of mankind are now working with the largest video-hosting site, search engine, and social media networks on Earth to determine what people can and cannot access. Horrifying.

Large online book retailers have been pressured by Leftist organizations to ban "problematic" books. The most degenerate pornography is universally available—but books with the wrong political message are beyond the pale.

It is important to note that there is indeed a racial element to this. Those considered to be white nationalists are silenced with quick action. However, nationalists of other varieties are left alone, and generally even celebrated. Jewish nationalists, black nationalists, Latin nationalists, Muslim and Arab nationalists, are all welcomed. Nobody is censoring the many Zionist organizations, Black Lives Matter, La Raza, the Palestine Liberation Organization, or the Muslim Brotherhood. However, if you are pro-white the Left views that as an existential threat to their hegemony.

The Washington Post ran an article entitled, "How do you stop fake news? In Germany, with a law." The piece praises Germany for expanding their crackdown on Wrong Think by fining websites that do not remove "fake news" and "hate speech" quickly enough.[23] And who gets to decide what is and is not fake news and hate speech? The same people that claim there are more than two genders, that race is merely a social construct, that unborn humans are not living beings, and that public beheadings are the trappings of a peaceful religion.

---

21 Allum Bokhari. "YouTube Will Censor Non-Rulebreaking Content, Manipulate Search Results, And Work With ADL" Breitbart. August 01, 2017. http://www.breitbart.com/tech/2017/08/01/youtube-will-artificially-limit-reach-non-rulebreaking-videos/. [http://archive.li/UUzKf]

22 Allum Bokhari. "Google, Facebook, Twitter, Microsoft Join Forces With ADL to Create 'Cyberhate Problem-Solving Lab.'" Breitbart. October 10, 2017. www.breitbart.com/tech/2017/10/10/google-facebook-twitter-microsoft-join-forces-adl-end-cyberhate/. [http://archive.li/11eeR]

23 Anthony Faiola and Stephanie Kirchner. "How do you stop fake news? In Germany, with a law" The Washington Post. April 05, 2017. https://www.washingtonpost.com/world/europe/how-do-you-stop-fake-news-in-germany-with-a-law/2017/04/05/e6834ad6-1a08-11e7-bcc2-7d1a0973e7b2_story.html?utm_term=.9be78d7e114d.

German heads of state are so dedicated to the cause of censorship that they have hired a former Stasi agent to patrol social media for "xenophobic" content. How appropriate, granting a former member of the communist East German secret police the power once again to hunt down dissidents.[24]

German officials behind the new laws claim that the rise in violence in Germany and across Europe is the result of increased "hate speech," posted online. They actually have the gall to tell us that European citizens speaking out against the huge surge in rape and violent crimes, is the cause of the same. A United Nations Secretary General, a socialist, has expressed similar thoughts, by suggesting that the rise in global terror is caused by the rise of "Islamophobic hate speech."[25]

In a similar act of prodigious stupidity, New York City mayor Bill de Blasio blamed Donald Trump's "hate speech" on the rise of "hate crimes," thus attributing one totally imaginary thing to another.[26] This, despite the fact that hundreds of alleged "hate crimes" turned out to be hoaxes entirely fabricated by the "victims." In reality, the Left fabricates hundreds of "hate crimes" with one hand, and attacks the Right with the other, blaming those they attack for their own violent behavior, and then using it all as an excuse to silence opposing views.

Sweden passed a new law which makes it illegal to criticize migrants, the LGTBQ community, or government officials.[27] Even if such criticisms entail factual claims. Like the fact that the rate of rape in Sweden committed

---

24 Donna Rachel Edmunds. "Former Stasi Agent Hired By German Govt To Patrol Facebook For 'Xenophobic' Comments." Breitbart. September 17, 2015. www.breitbart.com/london/2015/09/17/german-govt-hires-ex-stasi-agent-patrol-facebook-xenophobic-comments/. [http://archive.li/AFLvS]

25 Leo Hohmann. "U.N. leader blames 'Islamophobia' for rising global terror." WND. February 17, 2017. www.wnd.com/2017/02/u-n-leader-blames-islamophobia-for-rising-global-terror/. [http://archive.li/kgW5K]

26 "NYC mayor blames Trump, hate speech for hate crime rise" Detroit News. December 06, 2016. http://www.detroitnews.com/story/news/nation/2016/12/06/trump-nyc-hate-crimes/95032236/.

27 Selwyn Duke. "New Swedish Law Criminalizes Anti-immigration Internet Speech" The New American. April 23, 2014. https://www.thenewamerican.com/world-news/europe/item/18116-new-swedish-law-criminalizes-anti-immigration-internet-speech. [http://archive.li/ZZ9Sv]

by Muslim migrants is over 20 times higher than that committed by native Swedes. Or the fact that the rise in rapes has been caused almost entirely by mass Muslim migration. Just for mentioning these demonstrable facts, you might face four years in prison.[28]

A police officer in Sweden is now being criminally investigated for speaking out against open-border policies and the crime they have caused. Officer Peter Springare did nothing but state publicly what everybody already knows. He affirmed that the investigations of violent crime he undertook per his detective job revealed that nearly all of the criminals are foreign, coming mostly from Muslim or African nations. For the offense of speaking the truth, Swedish government prosecutors are investigating officer Springare.[29]

London's first Muslim mayor, Sadiq Khan, recently launched a new police unit within Scotland Yard specifically devoted to policing "online hate crime."[30] It goes without saying that hate speech laws are never created to protect whites or Christians, despite the fact that whites and Christians are in fact the most persecuted group of people on planet Earth. Reports from the Center for Studies on New Religions reveal that in 2016 over 90,000 Christians were murdered for their faith.[31] Yet there are no special laws protecting them. We are seeing precisely what happens when a nation allows individuals with no connection to its own people or culture to make the laws and govern them. We hear constantly of the

---

28 Ingrid Carlqvist and Lars Hedegaard. "Sweden: Rape Capital of the West." February 14, 2015. https://www.gatestoneinstitute.org/5195/sweden-rape. [http://archive.li/cRcwf]

29 Virginia Hale. "Police Officer Who Spoke out on Migrant Crime Now Under Investigation for Racial Hatred" Breitbart. February 08, 2017. http://www.breitbart.com/london/2017/02/08/police-migrant-crime-investigated-hate/. [http://archive.li/QNZNU]

30 Justin Davenport. "New Scotland Yard unit to probe online hate crime launched" Evening Standard. April 24, 2017. http://www.standard.co.uk/news/crime/sadiq-khan-launches-new-scotland-yard-unit-to-probe-online-hate-crime-a3521941.html. [http://archive.li/TJx4E]

31 Perry Chiaramonte. "Christians the most persecuted group in world for second year: Study" Fox News. January 06, 2017. http://www.foxnews.com/world/2017/01/06/christians-most-persecuted-group-in-world-for-second-year-study.html. [http://archive.li/AxhTH]

rise in antisemitism, Islamophobia, and "hate crimes" targeting migrants, when in reality, nothing could be further from the truth.

Liberals hide behind the guise of not wanting to "incite hatred" or to "insult" anyone; they use this as an excuse to incessantly pass laws limiting public access to data about their own victimization. This has never been about protecting a targeted group of people. This is simply about forcibly protecting the Liberal multicultural doctrine.

The same lunacy is rearing its ugly head in the United States as well.

California recently introduced Senate Bill 1161, the California Climate Science Truth and Accountability Act of 2016. The new act would allow those who spoke out against the accepted "truth" of climate change to be sued for damages.[32] "Fraud" in regard to climate change would be grounds for prosecution. Liberals have even suggested jail time as an appropriate penalty for so much as challenging the climate narrative

Liberals would love to see us all in Room 101 or reeducation camps, so that we can learn what is politically correct—just as their Bolshevik forefathers once did.

Interestingly enough, when it came to light that the National Oceanic and Atmospheric Administration (NOAA) had manipulated data in their report for the United Nations 2015 climate conference in Paris, Liberals did not seem particularly interested in the news. NOAA was found to have been emphasizing and omitting data in order to exaggerate the effects of global warming, while downplaying the slowdown in warming patters.[33]

Where are the outraged Leftist organizations that claim to protect civil liberties during these blatant assaults on our freedom? They are naturally off supporting bills like the Anti-Semitism Awareness Act of 2016, which seeks to shut down criticism of Israeli foreign policy in higher education. This bill, which arose after pro-Palestinian activists dared protest the

32 Valerie Richardson. "California Senate sidelines bill to prosecute climate change skeptics" The Washington Times. June 02, 2016. http://www.washingtontimes.com/news/2016/jun/2/calif-bill-prosecutes-climate-change-skeptics/. [http://archive.li/4bVCK]

33 David Rose. "Exposed: How world leaders were duped into investing billions over manipulated global warming data" Daily Mail Online. February 04, 2017. http://www.dailymail.co.uk/sciencetech/article-4192182/World-leaders-duped-manipulated-global-warming-data.html. [http://archive.li/0VX07]

conflict between Israel and Palestine, makes "demonizing Israel" a legitimate cause for investigation of college students.[34]

Pro-Israeli lobbyist groups like The American Israel Public Affairs Committee (AIPAC) provide incredible financial incentives to sway our politicians to create laws prohibiting criticism of the foreign policy of foreign nations.[35] This is unacceptable: nobody, no idea, and nothing, is above criticism. Groups like the Anti-Defamation League (ADL) and The Southern Poverty Law Center (SPLC) are merely organizations furnishing weapons for the illegitimate war on Crime Think. The bills they urge Congress to pass are nothing but tools to police and humiliate dissenting opinions.

The same Liberal organizations that claim to support the protection of civil liberties are on the forefront of every movement to undermine them. No matter what they claim, it is clear from their actions that these virulent organizations do not support free speech whatsoever. They support *approved* speech, speech which does not threaten their narrative. And it is well worth asking why they find this so necessary. If Liberals were on the right side of the issues, if they had nothing to hide with regard to foreign conflicts, crime data, and migrant data, if they had the truth on their side, why would they go through such extreme lengths to ensure that nobody speaks about these topics?

It's incredibly telling that in America, you can freely criticize American foreign policy. Yet if you criticize the foreign policy of *Israel*, a country on the other side of the planet, groups with hundred-million-dollar budgets immediately lobby Congress to silence you. And our politicians, in an incredible show of cowardice and greed, capitulate. The US State Department even has an entire department called *The Special Envoy to Monitor and Combat Anti-Semitism*. Our tax dollars are going to provide

34 Colleen Flaherty. "Anti-Semitism Awareness Bill Passes Senate" Inside Higher Ed. December 02, 2016. https://www.insidehighered.com/quicktakes/2016/12/02/anti-semitism-awareness-bill-passes-senate. [http://archive.li/su7CP]

35 Richard Sandler. "We need to pass the Anti-Semitism Awareness Act to fight hate and bigotry" The Hill. April 07, 2017. http://thehill.com/blogs/pundits-blog/civil-rights/327801-we-need-to-pass-the-anti-semitism-awareness-act-to-fight-hate. [http://archive.li/yLl2m]

programs ensuring that certain foreign peoples are not having their feelings hurt. In America.

The absurdity of the situation is incredible. Imagine if there were a massive pro-Russia lobby that made it illegal to disagree with or criticize Russian foreign policy. Or what if there were a white anti-hate bill passed that could fine a private citizen up to a quarter of a million dollars for speaking negatively about white people? We are creating a society in which free-born Americans are going to be living in fear that what they say might be subjected to legislation like the Anti-Semitism Awareness Act. If this isn't stopped now, more will soon follow. One has only to glance at Europe if one wants the proof.

Censorship is so out of control we have essentially been reduced to dealing "hate facts" and truth on the black market through underground tunnels, ensuring we don't tip off the Stasi.

Do you think the Left would be very pleased if we reversed the roles for a change? Maybe it is time we lobby for anti-Anglo, anti-Celtic, anti-Russo, anti-Slavic, anti-Nordic, anti-Hellenic, anti-Native, anti-Saxon, anti-Orthodox, and anti-Christian laws — that is to say, laws against anything anti-white. Maybe once Liberals start facing investigation, fines, and jail, once their names are smeared merely because they have the wrong opinion about the wrong people, maybe then they will understand the totalitarian intolerance of their ways. In America, whites and Christians are fair game for criticism and mockery, yet everybody else is off limits. In fact, that is precisely how some "entertainers" have made their entire living. Everybody else is a part of some protected "minority" class, but the war on whites rages on.

I am beyond weary of their insolence. I am tired of foreigners coming to America, foreigners who have no connection to this land or people, foreigners who take advantage of the nation *our* ancestors built, using its own best qualities to destroy it in their attempt to rebuild a new nation in *their* image. If "anti-Semitism" is so bad, go home to Israel. If "Islamophobia" is so awful in America and Europe, go back to one of the fifty Muslim caliphates in the desert.

The idea of making it illegal for Americans to say whatever they want about anybody they want is an insurrection against the people native to this nation. Those who agitate for laws to protect any groups other than the ancestors of the people who built this nation should be immediately deported via helicopter. Jews are not the heirs to this land. Arabs and Muslims are not the heirs to this land. Africans are not the heirs to this land. Mexicans are not the heirs to this land. I am. We are. And I am sick of people trying to tell me what I can and cannot say in my own homeland.

An identical pattern repeats itself time and time again: a group of aliens migrate to a new nation; they play the victim; they complain that they are being discriminated against, that they are not well enough represented in government. The government in question acquiesces to their every demand. Then, once they possess a large enough percentage of the population or a strong enough influence, they vote their own group into power, and begin to pass laws granting themselves special immunities and privileges, heedless of the effects on the previous culture, or the erosion of the rights of the peoples who built these nations.

Advocating or passing "hate speech" laws or making it especially illegal to criticize one group, is fundamentally un-American, anti-Western, and inherently unequal. It flies in the face of true equality. Equality means we are all the same in the eyes of the law and of God. It does *not* mean that saying "All I want for Christmas is White Genocide" should be legal, while saying "All I want for Christmas is [Insert ethic or religions group here] Genocide" should be punishable. Either they are *both* accepted, or *neither* is: that is true equality.

The quantity of mainstream articles favoring censorship laws is illuminating. The outlets that produce them are not in the business of truth or honesty. They are interested in selling a very particular narrative. With the rise of the internet and independent media outlets, the Ministry of Truth is squirming to find a way to bury the truth.

Because Liberals cannot refute the facts or logic of our arguments, their only recourse becomes censorship. The Left sees too much danger in laying out the facts; it is threatened by the prospect of allowing people to make up their own minds.

Liberal narratives are eternally hollow and held up only by lies. The truth fears no investigation, and has no need of the crutch of censorship.

Silence or Violence

For quite some time now Liberals have resorted to simple name calling as a means to win arguments. Their ideas are weak and fragile. Factual reality weighs so heavily on their narrative that it would collapse at once in the added pressure of reasonable debate. To circumvent the onerous duty of actually proving their case, they label anybody who disagrees with them as sexist, racist, bigoted, homophobic, Islamophobic, antisemitic, transphobic, misogynistic — the list goes on and on. This tactic used to work well because of the social stigma attached to these terms. Liberals took full advantage of this, silencing dissident opinions with a label, thus forcing their interlocutors to defend themselves, rather than focusing on the argument and the facts at hand. This worked wonders for the Left. It did not need to defend its grotesque and harmful immigration policies, because its adversaries were too busy defending their character, explaining how they are *not* in fact racist, assuring everyone ad nauseam of how many black friends they had.

As the Right has caught onto this tired game, it has stopped being so effective; thus, the Liberals have moved on to the next level: when screaming "BIGOT!" and screeching horrifically at the top of their lungs fails to silence dissenters, violence is the natural next move in the Liberal strategy. The Left justifies violence against its political foes in a simple, two-step process.

First, it equates its opposition — that is, anyone who stands anywhere to the Right of Lenin — to generally despised historical figures or groups, like the KKK or the Nazis.

Second, it asserts that violence against groups like the KKK and the Nazis is in all cases inherently justified.

There's some sleight of hand going on here we must bring to light. The term "racist" and "Nazi" are now so loosely defined by the Left, the political spectrum has shifted so far its way, that anybody who is not willing to give up his nation to hordes of Third World invaders, pass hate speech laws on a whim, and limit gun rights, immediately becomes a racist and a Nazi. Liberals have moved so far into their collectivist group-thinking hive-mind, that merely wanting to enforce *current* immigration laws, makes you Himmler. That means *you too*, you who are presently reading this work of blasphemy against the Liberal god, have furnished enough evidence that the communist Left can label you a Nazi, and act accordingly.

There is a slogan I've seen online and on signs of protesters that read, "Make racists afraid again!" And how is the Left going to go about this? The same way it always has. The same way every Leftist regime has through history. With extreme violence.

During protests, the neo-KPD, based on the *Antifaschistische Aktion* group, known as Antifa can be frequently seen bearing a banner that reads, "The only good fascist is a dead one." The alarming part of this is that the Left has long openly declared Donald Trump a fascist, as well as all the nearly 63,000,000 people who voted for him. Logically meaning — they want us all dead. Not only has the ADL and SPLC covered for Antifa, but CNN has as well. CNN ran a piece about the group which claimed that Antifa "seeks peace through violence." NBC interviewed Dartmouth professor Bray, who explained the "ethics" of Antifa and their violent actions. Professor Bray defended and justified the virulent group, equating violence against the Right with "self-defense."[36]

The media, the press, and academia make these claims, thinking people will take them seriously, perhaps will even support political violence against us. But what are these Antifa even fighting for? Billion dollar corporations do not condemn them; in fact, they cover for them. Nor does the ADL, SPLC, or any Liberal politician disavow them. This Antifa claims to be the "resistance," yet every major organization, university, corporation, media outlet, and celebrity supports its messages and goals.

The truth is that the members of this "resistance" serve as the useful idiots for the international Left. It is painfully clear that they are fighting against us as a people. The Left fights for a debased democracy in which hordes of invaders on welfare have just as much a vote as those of us whose ancestors built these great nations. They fight for more mindless egalitarianism to achieve their debased pseudo-democracy; they fight for more ugliness, more disorder; they fight to destroy everything good and

---

36 Benjy Sarlin. "Antifa Violence Is Ethical? This Author Explains Why." NBC News. August 26, 2017. www.nbcnews.com/politics/white-house/antifa-violence-ethical-author-explains-why-n796106. [http://archive.li/14qHZ]

beautiful. They are fighting to censor us, disarm us, cheat us. Finally, they are fighting to orchestrate our eradication. They are fighting for a Final Solution to the White Problem.

The reason nobody on the Left will denounce Antifa is very simple. They share one and the same end goal. Antifa is simply the "street" division of the SPLC, the ADL, and the press. Every Leftists organization is moving in the same direction: *against* us and our people.

As the prevailing media, press, and politicians rush to defend the anarcho-communists, any whites that organize, hold rallies, and advocate for the interest of their people are violently shut down, de-platformed, and made into pariahs. They are called "terrorists" and "supremacists," in the total absence of supporting evidence, while Antifa and BLM burn entire cities, and nary a negative word uttered in reply. But when a white man advocates for his people, the world comes to a standstill. The real crime these whites seemed to have universally committed was being *white*, articulate, racially consciousness, and fighting for their people, when nobody else would. Simply wanting to opt-out of the massively failed experiment of multiculturalism is now grounds for accusations of terrorism.

As with the term "Nazi," the Left has now redefined "fascism" to cover anyone who opposes the open-border tyranny of globalism. It is used as a political smear. Simply a tool to demonize, dehumanize, and un-person political adversaries, so the truculent Left may justify its violence.

During the 2017 Presidential Inauguration, political author, advocate, and speaker Richard Spencer was attacked while giving an interview. Following the assault, social media as well as mainstream news outlets began debating the morality of whether or not it was acceptable to "punch a Nazi." Even the *New York Times* ran a piece asking, "Is it O.K. to punch a Nazi?"[37] *Mother Jones* published another entitled "The Long History of Nazi Punching."[38]

---

37 Liam Stack. "Attack on Alt-Right Leader Has Internet Asking: Is It O.K. to Punch a Nazi" The New York Times. January 21, 2017. https://www.nytimes.com/2017/01/21/us/politics/richard-spencer-punched-attack.html?_r=0. [http://archive.li/Oezm3]

38 Wes Enzinna. "The long history of "Nazi punching"-and the return of the "antifas" in the time of Trump" Mother Jones. June 26, 2017. http://www.motherjones.com/politics/2017/01/video-richard-spencer-punch-antifa-fascism. [http://archive.li/3PAg7]

The overwhelming reaction by the Left was *yes*, it *is* indeed not only reasonable, but morally righteous and even obligatory, to attack a random person for having different political views.

During the interview in which Spencer was attacked, he had just finished explaining to a protester that he was *not* a neo-Nazi, nor a Klan member. This, it was subsequently argued, was mere covering for his actual beliefs. But in truth, anybody that wishes to defend the sovereignty of Western nations, anyone who shows even a shred of nationalism, an iota of pride in his heritage, is now called a white-supremacist, a fascist, a Nazi, no matter what he really thinks about these positions.

Following Donald Trump's Inauguration, the *Forward*, published an article entitled, "Pulling No Punches In Fight Against 'Alt-Right' And Neo-Nazis." Discussed in the piece was the rise of the "Anti-Fascists," who are ready to use violence to suppress anybody they label a Nazi. A black-clad man was depicted stomping the face of another man supine on the ground. The man on the ground was wearing a shirt with a Celtic cross. A text around the image read, "Good Night White Pride."[39]

These groups advocating violence in the streets are of course never labeled as hate organizations by the ADL or SPLC. Richard Spencer, however, is listed by their organizations as a white supremacist. This despite the fact that he has never attacked anyone, nor advocated violence against anyone; to the Left, he is clearly the *real threat* to society. For while Richard Spencer does not pose an imminent threat, his ideas menace the Left's regime. His ideas, like so many of our ideas, are starting to make too much sense. They are becoming almost self-evidently true to too many people.

Let us be clear. People defending themselves from violent, hostile anti-white, Liberal aggression is not a manifestation of "white supremacy": it is simple self-preservation. Our enemies recognize that we are in a war: every other group can be Pro-black, Pro-Jewish, Pro-Muslim, Pro-Latino Pro-Gay, Pro-whatever, and be proud of their heritage and culture. But white Pride, and Christianity, clearly, need to be stomped out of existence.

39 Sam Kestenbaum. "Pulling No Punches In Fight Against 'Alt-Right' And Neo-Nazis" The Forward. March 08, 2017. http://forward.com/news/364726/pulling-no-punches-in-fight-against-alt-right-and-neo-nazis/?utm_source=rss&utm_medium=feed&utm_campaign=Main. [http://archive.li/XtXgK]

The Antifa is ready to do the stomping, the national and international press is ready to cover for them, and the organizations which proclaim themselves in favor of the First Amendment are ready to fund and defend the entire charade. Those of us who see clearly know what has happened: the essence of the First Amendment is dead; they have killed it.

> "If you want a picture of the future, imagine a boot stamping on a human face — forever."
>
> —*1984*, George Orwell

Riots

I watched as so-called Anti-Fascists rioted and burned the Berkeley campus in objection to the unacceptable prospect of journalist Milo Yiannopoulos giving a speech.[40] If you're unfamiliar with Milo, he is a gay, Jewish journalist from England, with a bit of character. He's anti-Islam, anti-abortion, and pro-Trump. The "tolerant and progressive" Liberal students were so outraged at his opinions that they physically attacked other students who were merely going to watch his speech. They held signs reading "This is war," "Kill Trump," and "Kill Fascists." The behavior we have seen all across the country by the violent Left, attacking conservatives, rioting, silencing dissident opinions, is actual, definitional authoritarianism. It is the very thing these "Antifa" are claiming to fight. We have really reached the point that a gay, Jewish, journalist from England is branded a Nazi and silenced accordingly.

During the riot coverage on the news I did not see police doing anything to halt the violence. It appeared they were ordered to stand down. Liberals are allowed to riot and attack their political opposition with total impunity while law enforcement, universities, and the media simply watch on. Nobody is holding them accountable. In fact, this kind of activity is actually being encouraged all over social media and in speeches

40 Madison Park and Kyung Lah. "Berkeley protests of Yiannopoulos caused $100,000 in damage" CNN. February 02, 2017. http://www.cnn.com/2017/02/01/us/milo-yiannopoulos-berkeley/index.html. [http://archive.li/244Tj]

given by other Leftists, reporters, celebrities (read: *court jesters*) at award ceremonies and protests.

This is nothing but the American Left showing its true colors now that power has been taken from it. I have said that they want us suffering, demeaned, and dead; that is no understatement. During an interview, Tim Kaine, once vice-president hopeful, urged his listeners to take the fight to the streets, saying that this is the time to "act."[41] While accepting an award at the Screen Actors Guild, actor David Harbour received a standing ovation after encouraging viewers to go out and punch people in the face — for their political views, of course.[42]

CNN referred to Milo as an "extremist" while reporting on the incident, but did not deign to comment in such terms on the violent rioters throwing bottles and attacking the students that wanted to see his speech. Ironically enough, Milo speaks quite a bit about the censorship of Right-wing thoughts, and had come to Berkeley to speak about this subject exactly. The only people who were injured in that riot were the students trying to see a damn speech. All the while, CNN has the audacity to refer to the "fake news" of independent journalists. The Left is nothing less than deranged.

Imagine if a group of Trump supporters violently rioted and forced the shutdown of a Left-wing speaker — which by the way, is a fair description of nearly every professor or speaker on college campuses. Imagine if a group of Trump supporters walked around cities in masks, starting fires, beating up Hillary supporters. Do you think CNN would have the same take on the event? Doubtful.

We have here yet another example of how the Left effectively silences heretics, those who dare attack the Liberal machine. This is neither the first nor the last time a Right-wing event is shut down by the Left. A Free Speech Rally in Martin Luther King Jr. Civic Center Park turned violent

---

41 Pam Key. "Kaine: Democrats Have to 'Fight in the Streets' Against Trump" Breitbart. January 31, 2017. http://www.breitbart.com/video/2017/01/31/kaine-democrats-fight-streets-trump/. [http://archive.li/W7WxH]

42 Scott Greer. "Hollywood Gives Standing Ovation For Punching Political Foes At Awards Show" The Daily Caller. January 30, 2017. http://dailycaller.com/2017/01/30/hollywood-gives-standing-ovation-to-punching-political-foes-at-awards-show/. [http://archive.li/tFIeZ]

as Antifa arrived to protest the *radical* Right-wing view that there should be free speech.[43] Evidently, free speech is not a value that the Left shares with us.

The Antifa, taking its inspiration from the Bolsheviks and German Communist Party (KPD), has staged protests and riots at numerous colleges in order to stop speeches from taking place. Free speech advocate Dave Rubin, was forced to cancel a talk at University of Southern California due to security concerns.[44] Ann Coulter had to cancel a speech for the same reason.[45] It would be tedious to recount all the examples that have occurred in the past year alone.

When violent mobs are not adequate for silencing those guilty of Thought Crimes, the Leftist faction at the Southern Poverty Law Center gladly steps in. The SPLC, which has declared itself the *de facto* Thought Police, labels any group or person it disagrees with politically a "hate group." Thus, the SPLC declared for instance that the non-profit research organization, Center for Immigration Studies, warrants a place on their "Hatewatch" list, alongside the likes of the KKK, the Skinheads, and the Black Panthers.[46] The SPLC answers to no one; it does not bother to explain why the violent Antifa group does not make the "hate list," while a data-collecting non-profit organization does. The SPLC claims to be a

---

43 Rob Shimshock. "Antifa And Trump Supporters Battle At Berkeley" The Daily Caller. April 15, 2017. http://dailycaller.com/2017/04/15/antifa-and-trump-supporters-battle-at-berkeley-again/. [http://archive.li/dqkVS]

44 Tom Ciccotta. "USC Shuts Down Scheduled Event with Free Speech Advocate Dave Rubin" Breitbart. March 02, 2017. http://www.breitbart.com/tech/2017/03/02/usc-shuts-scheduled-event-free-speech-advocate-dave-rubin/. [http://archive.li/sLw1V]

45 Susan Svrluga, William Wan, and Elizabeth Dwoskin. "There was no Ann Coulter speech. But protesters converged on Berkeley." The Washington Post. April 27, 2107. https://www.washingtonpost.com/news/grade-point/wp/2017/04/27/theres-no-speech-planned-but-protesters-are-converging-on-berkeley-today/. [http://archive.is/wc72R]

46 Mark Krikorian. "How labeling my organization a hate group shuts down public debate" The Washington Post. March 17, 2017. https://www.washingtonpost.com/opinions/how-labeling-my-organization-a-hate-group-shuts-down-public-debate/2017/03/17/656ab9c8-0812-11e7-93dc-00f9bdd74ed1_story.html?utm_term=.1fb0a3f43848.

neutral, non-partisan entity—yet it is quite clear it does not engage in any sort of objective neutrality, nor holds even a single objective standard.

Despite the fact that the Antifa group has physically assaulted Trump supporters at the 2017 Presidential Inauguration, the SPLC refuses to comment. Despite the fact that 230 Antifa members were arrested for felony rioting.[47] Despite the fact that they smash windows of businesses, set fires in the street, employ mob violence from Berkeley to D.C., the SPLC will not so much as mention their violence. Let alone grant them a coveted spot on its "Hatewatch" list.

The "hate list" is little more than a blacklist and defamation tactic, setting the innocent alongside the guilty and thus arbitrarily forcing guilt by association.

Limiting speech limits your thoughts. The ideas you cannot speak soon become the ideas you do not think. If you believe even for a second that censorship and hate speech laws are really about protecting somebody's feelings, understand—this is about protecting the *narrative*, this is nothing but a concerted effort to police thoughts. The Left fears that those who speak out against their lies might begin to awaken others to the false narrative of Liberalism. Free speech is deeply dangerous to the Left, which is precisely why we have seen an all out war on freedom of expression across the Western world.

Laws, policies, and actions that restrict speech are always instituted by the Left. Never the Right. For the Liberal narrative cannot compete in the marketplace of ideas or on the battlefield of facts in a fair fight. How could they? So far as *facts* go, they come unarmed. Silencing dissident views is for that reason a cornerstone of Leftist policy. Those who speak with honesty and integrity never fear what their opponent might say, for nothing is as powerful as the truth. The Left cannot defeat this. It will never be able to hide the truth, no matter how much it censors, bans, and lies. There will dawn a day when the truth the Left has fought so hard to bury will rise from the ash heap of history to triumph again.

---

47 Anna Hopkins. "Majority of 230 protesters arrested on Inauguration Day will face 10 years in prison and $25k fine as US attorney says they will be charged with felony rioting" Daily Mail Online. January 21, 2017. http://www.dailymail.co.uk/news/article-4144360/Anti-Trump-protesters-face-10-years-prison.html. [http://archive.li/r88jz]

Those of us who still have the courage of our beliefs will never tire and never despair. We will speak the truth when it costs us friends. We will speak the truth when it is unpopular. We will speak the truth when it becomes illegal. We will speak the truth when it is seen an as act of heresy. We will speak the truth even when our voices shake.

And sooner or later, our speaking of the truth will be the downfall of the international Left.

The Truth is No Longer Good Think

One fine autumn day, about a week before the 2016 election, a pro-life group set up a series of posters showing an unborn child's development. The posters depicted the size of the child in the womb compared to other objects for reference. There were photos of when the heart beats for the first time, photographs of facial development, of when babies start to yawn, of when they start to smile. As you walked through the display the tone changed. Suddenly there were photos of the abortion process. The suction method, the extraction method. In the latter, the child has its limbs severed, its tiny head decapitated, crushed, and forceps shoved into its spine to severe its little brain stem. And finally, posters that show actual photos of the aftermath of the murder.

Soon after the display was set up, a group of Liberal degenerates gathered round with signs to protest the right of the pro-life group to express their beliefs and show the truth of abortion procedures. They held signs reading "my body my choice," "get your religion out of my uterus," and "reproductive rights matter." These green-, blue-, and purple-haired mental patients stood at the ends of the walkway where the posters were set in order stop people from walking through the display and seeing the photos. They claimed they were there to keep people from feeling "unsafe" and to protest this act of "hate speech."

I had some time before my next class, so I was standing near one of the posters having a nice conversation with one of the people from the pro-life organization when I was accosted by a rabid Liberal woman (?) who was already screaming at me. Amidst her babble, I made out that I was creating an "unsafe environment" by being there and "normalizing" this act of "hate speech" and "aggression" against women. I was, she informed me, creating an unsafe environment for women on campus that have had abortions, and that I am inhibiting a woman's right to choose.

Being the sporting chap I am, I engaged her. I responded that women who have had abortions *did* have a choice — the choice to not get pregnant — and that they do not deserve a "safe space" to hide from their act of infanticide. That sent her into a wild tirade about my espousing of "hate speech." And suddenly I understood why Liberals are so hell-bent on censorship.

They know that if more people knew how soon this so-called "fetus" begins to look and act just like them, a tiny human, fewer and fewer voters would approve of the act of infanticide. They know that if people knew what "dilation" and "evacuation" procedures actually look like, fewer and fewer would vote for the wretched Democrats who support these barbarities.

The *New York Times* article, "When is Speech Violence?" sought to make the same claim as the rabid Liberal I encountered. They argued that because certain speech can cause *stress*, which can be seen as a form of harm, then stressful "hate speech" is consequently a form of violence:

> If words can cause stress, and if prolonged stress can cause physical harm, then it seems that speech — at least certain types of speech — can be a form of violence.
>
> By all means, we should have open conversations and vigorous debate about controversial or offensive topics. But we must also halt speech that bullies and torments. From the perspective of our brain cells, the latter is literally a form of violence.[48]

The argument of the Janus-masked Left goes like this;

1. People have the right not to feel unsafe or have their feelings hurt.
2. Some speech hurts feelings and makes people feel unsafe.
3. Therefore, you do not have the right to speech that make others feel unsafe or hurts their feelings.

But their first premise is deeply flawed. People do *not* have any intrinsic right to have their sentiments spared. This effete attempt to put the

48 Lisa Feldman Barrett. "When Is Speech Violence" The New York Times. July 14, 2017. https://www.nytimes.com/2017/07/14/opinion/sunday/when-is-speech-violence.html. [http://archive.li/LyBuh]

subjective value of feelings over that of the right to express one's ideas freely is a Pandora's box. Once we create laws based on the utterly subjective "feelings" of some Liberal goblin, everything becomes fair game, anything can be silenced, and the *real* right to freedom of speech, clearly identified by our Constitution, diminishes to the point of vanishing. Claiming your feelings are more important than another person's freedom of expression is the true violation of human rights.

Merely because I had looked at photos and engaged in conversation with one of the advocates for the human rights of unborn children, I was guilty of creating an "unsafe environment" for my fellow students. I did not speak to these students, I did not put up the photos, I did not provoke anyone in any way. I was simply an observer. Which was enough to make me an enemy of the Left—and thus, presumably, a Nazi, and fair target for Leftist violence.

> Violence can only be concealed by a lie, and the lie can only be maintained by violence.
>
> —Aleksandr Solzhenitsyn

In truth, the First Amendment is designed precisely to protect "hate speech." No one needs protection for run-of-the-mill, garden variety comments; it would be nonsense to make an amendment to the Constitution protecting a person's right to say something that everyone under the sun agrees with. It is only "hate speech" that needs protection from persecution.

Perhaps I feel this problem more sharply than others. I am, after all, a regular proponent of "hate speech." Some people golf. Some people play cards, or collect things. I like to make offensive and provocative statements. Most people, especially Liberals, are eternally worried about offending anybody, even by mistake. I, however, find great joy in the propagation of facts and thoughts which most find uncomfortable. I believe it to be one of the finer things in life. I don't even know how many forums, chat rooms, social media platforms, and comment sections I have been banned from for having the wrong views and opinions. For posting facts that discredit the narrative, for not appropriately participating in the Two Minutes of Hate, and for being the first to stop clapping.

So perhaps this is why, of all the perverse meanderings of Liberalism, I find the assault on free speech to be of the foulest. We owe it to our

First and Second Amendments if laws limiting our speech have not yet been passed in the US. Because the Left has already lost the argument. Our ideas, and the evidence we can adduce in their favor, are so much stronger that the only option the Left has now is censorship—turning dissenters into pariahs, against whom violence is not only acceptable but even encouraged.

We are the only ones being silenced because we are the only ones left with the courage to speak truth to power. The First Amendment exists to protect the likes of us, and the Left knows it. Every single time a Leftists regime has taken hold of country, one of the first things they do is silence those who speak against them. One way, or the other. From the Gulags to the Killing Fields, those who refuse to fall in line are dealt with severely. If the day ever comes to the United States when people are thrown in prison for "hate speech," as they are all over Europe, then people like myself will have only a few options left: do hard time in the Gulag, wind up dead in a snowy forest—or pick up a rifle.

Manifestations of the Liberal Illness: Freedom of Speech

During the 2017 White House Correspondence Dinner, member after member of the lying press stood up and accused Donald Trump of stifling freedom of press, of not understanding the First Amendment. Liberal after Liberal accused President Trump—with no supporting evidence—of doing precisely what the Left does on a constant basis.

This is a classic example of projection. The lying Liberal media, the same people who support "hate speech" laws and "fake news" censorship, are accusing the Right of their own attitude. The Left fails to see its own hypocrisy and the double standard in its actions and statements. You cannot say you support freedom of expression while advocating for hate speech laws.

Once again, the Left hides its contradictions by appealing to altered and redefined words. Claiming there is a difference between "free speech" and "hate speech" is the most egregious example. Feelings of victimization are again common here. The Left feels that if they hear things that upset them, they have moral grounds to shut that person down, one way or the other. Their feelings of victimization simultaneously enhance their feelings of moral superiority. We see this in the way they claim to be the arbiters of who can say what.

The desire to police speech is nothing but another form of the desire for control. Thus, the Liberal illness makes itself felt yet again. In the debate over free speech, we see symptoms 1, 2, 4, and 5 from Cluster I appearing, and symptoms 6, 7, 8, and 9 appearing from Cluster II.

Cluster I

1. Deceitfulness, indicated by repeated lying, grand exaggerations, or omission of contrary information, with the purpose to advance their chosen narrative and discrediting others.

2. Irritability or aggressiveness towards anybody that questions or opposes their views. Coupled with the inability to recognize they own hypocrisy, double standards, and doublethink.

3. Inability to adjust views when presented with information contrary to their own beliefs.

4. Frequent projections of their own traits onto others.

5. Difficulty in dealing with a loss of control or power, or a strong desire for control and power.

Cluster II

6. Appeals to altered and redefined definitions of words, or relies on fictitious terms for argumentation.

7. Consistent feelings of having been victimized or wronged, without any actual harm being done. Seen also as playing the victim after attacking others.

8. Intense sense of righteousness or moral superiority.

9. The inability to recognize the negative outcomes of their own actions. Often placing the blame on others.

10. Intense guilt or self-hatred, often manifests as hatred towards one's larger group identity.

II

Revolutionaries & Renegades: A Closer Look at the Second Amendment

> When loss of liberty is looming, as it is now, the siren sounds first in the hearts of freedom's vanguard ... because they know that sacred stuff resides in that wooden stock and blued steel. Something that gives the most common man the most uncommon of freedoms. When ordinary hands can possess such an extraordinary instrument, that symbolizes the full measure of human dignity and liberty.
>
> — Charlton Heston

There may be no other issue that attracts the ire and contempt of Liberals like the freedom to keep and bear arms. There is indeed something sacred hidden here, when the simplest of materials, in the hands of ordinary men, transforms both man and material into a single entity with the capacity of liberating himself from the wretched clutches of tyranny.

The history of gun laws in the United States makes for a fascinating and checkered tale. The Bill of Rights was ratified in 1791; following that, the federal government did not regulate firearms until the National Firearms Act of 1934, introduced by Democrat House Representative Robert Doughton, and signed into law by Franklin D. Roosevelt. The Firearms Act of 1934 was a reaction to the violence stemming from the Prohibition era and the organized crime which was its consequence. This Act created Title II weapons, often referred to as NFA weapons (short for National Firearms Act). These include short-barreled rifles, short-barreled shotguns, automatic and burst-fire weapons, explosives, and suppressors. The act created more stringent regulations on these weapons, and instituted a $200 tax on the transfer of the same.

The next major federal piece of gun control arrived in 1968. While the Roaring 20s, the Saint Valentine's Day Massacre, and an attempt on FDR's life paved the way for the NFA act of 1934, the assassinations of John F. Kennedy, Martin Luther King Junior, and Robert Kennedy all fueled efforts to pass the Gun Control Act of 1968. Democratic Senator Thomas Dodd and Jewish House member Emanuel Celler introduced legislation to ban mail-order weapons and to regulate the shipment and transfers of firearms. The 1968 act signed by Lyndon B. Johnson established the Federal Firearm Licensing (FFL) requirements for those in the firearm business.

In an effort to address allegations of abuse by the bureau of Alcohol, Tobacco, and Firearms, Republican Senator James A. McClure introduced the 1986 Firearms Owners' Protection Act, signed into law by Ronald Reagan. The act made several revisions to gun laws and prohibited a firearms registry for non-NFA weapons. The act also clarified and expanded the definitions of prohibited persons, specifying who may or may not purchase a firearm, and limited ATF inspections of Federal Firearms Licensed dealers to once annually, in an effort to curb allegations of ATF harassment. Additionally, Democratic Representative William Hughes of New Jersey proposed a ban on the sale of new automatic weapons to civilians once the Act was passed.

Herb Kohl, Jewish Democrat Senator from Wisconsin, introduced the Gun-Free School Zones Act of 1990, the bill that would ensure that school children are defenseless against all those who wish them harm. The Gun-Free School Zone act was one of a dozen or so bills incorporated into the Crime Control Act of 1990, which was introduced by Democrat Senator Joseph Biden and signed into law by George H. W. Bush. Our society routinely protects court houses, banks, sporting events, music venues, politicians, and office buildings with firearms, yet when it comes to our children, these elected officials have taken a different path.

Introduced by Jewish Representative, Chuck Schumer, and signed into law by Bill Clinton, the Brady Handgun Violence Prevention Act arrived in 1993. Named after James Brady, who was shot during the assassination attempt of Ronald Reagan in 1981, the Brady Act required background checks on anybody purchasing a firearm from a federally licensed dealer. The National Instant Criminal Background Check (NICS), maintained by the Federal Bureau of Investigation, was implemented along with the act to process the mandated background checks.[1]

A year later, the Federal Assault Weapons Ban, written by Jewish Senator Diane Feinstein, was added to the Violent Crime Control and Law Enforcement Act of 1994. The weapons ban was in part a reaction to the 1991 Luby's massacre that took place in Killeen, Texas. After that massacre, which left twenty-three dead and twenty-seven injured, Democrats sought to make certain weapons more difficult to obtain. The Right took a different approach.

Suzanna Hupp was with her parents at Luby's the day of the shooting. Both of her parents were killed in the massacre. Hupp had a gun in her car, but did not bring her weapon into the restaurant, as Texas law prohibited concealed carry at the time. After the massacre, Hupp became a leading advocate for concealed carry laws to be introduced and passed. In 1995, Texas passed its concealed carry law. Hupp then served five terms as a member of the Texas House of Representatives.

In response to gun violence, the Left seeks to further disarm us, while the Right fights for laws that enable us to protect ourselves. This is another prime example of the cultural differences between the Left and the Right. One favors individualism and self-determination, the other favors collectivism and a powerful state.

The Federal Assault Weapons Ban restricted numerous firearms and certain features for ten years. Numerous studies have been conducted, all of which found the Assault Weapon Ban to have been entirely useless for

1 "U.S. Gun Laws: A History" NPR. June 26, 2008. http://www.npr.org/templates/story/story.php?storyId=91942478. [http://archive.li/aHNiG]

stopping any crime or murder. Despite the evidence, many on the Left have demanded that the Act be renewed.[2] [3]

Over the last 100 years, the Federal government has already passed the majority of the "common sense" gun laws that Liberals like Hillary Clinton advocate. As we read on Clinton's website:

> Keep guns out of the hands of domestic abusers, other violent criminals, and the severely mentally ill by supporting laws that stop domestic abusers from buying and owning guns, making it a federal crime for someone to intentionally buy a gun for a person prohibited from owning one, and closing the loopholes that allow people suffering from severe mental illness to purchase and own guns. She will also support work to keep military-style weapons off our streets.

This all sounds reasonable enough. But there's a glaring problem to anybody who is paying attention. The Brady Act already covers the majority of what Liberals commonly refer to as "common sense gun control." There are two different criteria on background checks that specifically regard domestic violence. If you've ever been convicted of even a misdemeanor crime of domestic violence, or if you are the subject of a restraining order, you cannot purchase a firearm. If you have a felon status or have been found guilty of other crimes that could have landed you in prison for a year or more, even if the sentence was reduced or you received probation, you cannot purchase a firearm. Liberals call for violent criminals to be denied guns, yet the Brady Act goes even further by barring non-violent offenders access to firearms as well. The current background checks also consider mental health, ensuring that the buyer has never been committed to a mental institution or deemed in a court of law to be a danger to himself or others.

Clinton goes on to say we should make it a federal crime to purchase a gun on behalf of a prohibited person. Well, we already do. It is referred to as a Straw Purchase, and you can be sentenced to ten years in prison for

---

2 "Ban on assault weapons didn't reduce violence" The Washington Times. August 16, 2004. http://www.washingtontimes.com/news/2004/aug/16/20040816-114754-1427r/.

3 Tim Devaney. "Dems introduce bill to ban assault weapons" The Hill. December 16, 2015. http://thehill.com/regulation/263489-assault-weapons-ban-targets-semi-automatic-guns. [http://archive.li/IbkJC]

lying on a background check or for purchasing a firearm for somebody who is not eligible to do so themselves.

In any case, I'm not sure I even believe in the concept of a "prohibited person." If the person is such a danger to society that he cannot legally own a weapon, he should probably still be in prison. And if he is no longer a danger, his right to defend his home and family should be restored.

Further, I believe the idea of barring the "mentally ill" from owning firearms creates a dangerous precedent. Currently the laws are such that those people who have been legally committed to a mental institution are unable to purchase a firearm. However the push for further restrictions on the so-called mentally ill is beginning to sound eerily reminiscent of Article 58 of Soviet era Criminal Code, a catch-all served to criminalize and pathologize political dissidents. Those who were inconvenient to the regime and those who held beliefs not in-line with the state were "diagnosed" as mentally incompetent. The Left has long since declared that antisemitism, racism, and xenophobia are a sort of "mental illness." Soon, they will declare those with nationalist sentiments or a desire to retain their ancestral homelands unfit to purchase firearms. The effort will encroach slowly, first by including those who take any sort of medication for mental health issues, then expanding the definition of mental illness, until only those approved by the state will be allowed to exercise the basic right preserved in the Second Amendment. This disarming of dissidents will be accomplished entirely under the guise of "safety."

What Clinton and other Liberal politicians are doing is incredibly misleading at best. At worst — and more likely — it is intentional manipulation. By claiming they only want laws that keep guns out of the hands of violent criminals, the mentally ill, and domestic abusers, they are creating the myth that these people can now walk into any gun store they choose and purchase a firearm. This is simply not the case, and has not been the case for nearly a quarter-century. Yet the Liberal, who knows little about firearms, and even less about the laws, will believe the lying Democrats when they tell them that, as it stands, a domestic abuser or a violent felon can easily purchase a firearm. And so the rank and file Liberal supports more restrictive gun legislation.

The next point brought up on the Clinton website is commonly referred to the "gun show loophole."[4] Simply put, when two people who are not federally licensed dealers, such as two neighbors or friends or strangers at a gun show, decide to buy and sell to each other, no background check is required. Gun advocates oppose background checks for private sales because it would in essence make it illegal to sell a firearm to anybody, even your family members, without going through the State. Which in turn creates a *de facto* registry of who has firearms in their possession, and what firearms they possess.

Those in favor of background checks for private sales make the argument that a person who knows he cannot pass a background check will simply resort to buying a firearm from a private seller to avoid this obstacle. I can certainly understand both perspectives. Yet I often wonder why the Liberal default solution is always the addition of more laws? It is already illegal for the person in question to possess a firearm. He would already be actively breaking the law in purchasing the firearm. Yet somehow another law will succeed where previous laws have failed?

A more reasonable solution might be to only allow federally licensed dealers to sell at larger gun shows. That way gun shows would not be a "go-to" place for prohibited persons looking to buy a firearm. But this is almost too easy of a solution; I wonder if a *de facto* registry is not in itself the Liberal goal. When people advocate for "closing the gun show loophole," what they are really saying is that they wish to make the private sales of arms illegal.

The final point on Clinton's site is the most telling as far as the true Liberal agenda goes. Clinton would work to keep "military-style weapons off our streets," no doubt a reference to the panic-inducing "assault rifles." But the concrete claim that "civilians do not need assault rifles and should not have them" is made without any real justification, other than the sorry excuse that rifles apparently frighten Liberals quite a lot. Liberals often ask, "Why would anybody need an AR-15 or AK-47 to hunt deer?" and "Why do civilians need military-style weapons if they aren't fighting a war?" Sadly, I seldom see Republicans, conservatives, and those on the

4 "Hillary Clinton on gun violence prevention" Hillary for America. Accessed July 12, 2017. https://www.hillaryclinton.com/issues/gun-violence-prevention/. [http://archive.li/HDcuW]

Right offering the honest and genuine answers to these questions. So here it is.

Why do a civilians need military-style weapons? Because the government has military-style weapons, and you can't very well overthrow a tyrannical government with your granddad's old six-shooter. It's true, you do not need an M14, AR-15, FN-FAL, or AK-47, nor any other high-powered rifle of the kind, to hunt deer. These rifles are designed to hunt a far *more* dangerous game. The logic behind the Second Amendment was not to protect the people from the local deer population, nor to ensure their stock of venison. It was to protect the people from tyrannical government. Civilians need military-style weapons in order to wage another revolution, should such ever be needed. Too many have forgotten that this entire nation was born when a small group of men, who had committed high treason against the King, picked up their rifles to defend their rights. That heritage has been diluted and in many ways erased over the decades. But for some of us, the revolutionary spirit burns yet.

The purpose behind those "weapons of war" is simple — to keep the government afraid of the people, and not the other way around. Our Europeans cousins are being arrested and having their rights violated daily. They are routinely arrested, fined, tried, and harassed by their own governments for Thought Crimes. For political dissidents, there is a legitimate and substantial fear that once the right to keep and bear arms is limited, a domino effect will begin to erode all subsequent rights as well.

Although Americans have had many of their freedoms stripped, and much of their property and income taken, we still remain the freest people on Earth. Having those terrifying rifles, with thirty-round magazines, collapsible stocks, precision scopes, and even a suppressor if you'd like, is quite literally the last line that can be drawn in the sand to protect this freedom. Gun owners like myself, and others the country over, do not take our heritage or duty lightly by any means. These arms are far more than simple tools or hobbies or "weapons of war." What those rifles represent is quite literally the last hope, the final straw, the ultimate iron guard. They are the last vestiges of a dying breed. And maybe that is precisely the problem Liberals have with our rifles. Maybe they see us as an archaic and antiquated lot, nothing but a group of throwbacks that somehow missed a step in evolution while they were busy ushering in the new century. Perhaps they see us as the philistine Morlocks to their cosmopolitan Eloi.

And perhaps they are right. But there is one thing that keeps me up at night. It bothers me far more deeply than all the deaths caused by civilian gun violence.

It is estimated that in the last one hundred years alone, around 262,000,000 people, over a quarter of a billion, have been killed by their own governments. From Mao's Great Leap Forward to the Holodomor, from Stalin's Great Purge to the Armenian genocide, from the Killing Fields to the deaths in Bosnia and Rwanda. Genocides the world over, committed by governments against their own, *unarmed*, citizens. Men, women, and children. Nothing spared, and no defense that could be brought on behalf of the innocent against the juggernaut of these authorized massacres.[5]

If I had to take my chances with a bunch of mentally ill people right out of an insane asylum all armed with rifles on the one hand, or my own government on the other, I think I would try my luck with the lunatics. I am certain that not *all* of them would have genocidal intent — far more than I can say about the governments of the world.

Those people, whose corpses now rest in mass graves, trusted their governments, and many would have supported the very leaders that brought their demise. From a purely historical standpoint, I think it is more than reasonable to be incredibly skeptical of any person, especially any government figure, who has the intent to disarm his constituents.

Those 262,000,000 dead deserved at least a chance. At the very least, they deserved so little. And the very rifles Liberals loathe would have given them just that: a fighting chance.

I do not think it is irrational in the least to be concerned with a government turning tyrannical against its own people. It has happened over and over again throughout recent history, even in my own young lifetime, today even, in Venezuela. Based on the violence we have seen coming from the dark-hearted Left, I had no doubt that if they had their way, the Right-wing of the America and Europe would be the next Great Purge.

---

5 Rudolph J Rummel. Death by Government. New Brunswick, NJ : Transaction Publ., 1996.

Smallpox has killed over 300,000,000 people in the twentieth century. Governments have killed nearly as many humans as smallpox in the same time frame. This is absolutely staggering to consider. Governments have killed more of their own people the world over than all the people who have died in automobile accidents in the twentieth century. Yet nobody calls me paranoid when I wear a seat belt.

When I hear Liberals argue that the fear of a tyrannical government is baseless, irrational, and nothing more than a delusional, paranoid, conspiracy theory, I think of those mass graves and I wonder, what kind of monsters would mock these unarmed deaths as conspiracy theorists or fringe lunatics?

> I prefer dangerous freedom over peaceful slavery.
>
> —Thomas Jefferson[6]

The so called "assault rifles," whose ban Liberals constantly espouse, account for 300-500 murders per year. Those terrifying rifles that Democrats running for public office continually promise to protect us from, are used in fewer murders than knives (1,700 per year), clubs and hammers (600 per year), and bare hands and feet (800 per year). More people each year are beaten to death by unarmed persons, than are killed with rifles.[7] This horrifically absurd fact needs to be branded onto every Liberal politician's forehead until they — or we — understand.

The ten-year "assault weapon" ban that ended in 2003 had virtually zero effect on crime.[8] During 2003, the last year for the ban, rifles were used in 2.7 percent of murders. Over a decade after the ban was lifted, the number of people killed by rifles was 2 percent in 2014. Despite the

---

6 "Thomas Jefferson's Monticello" I prefer dangerous freedom over peaceful slavery (Quotation) | Thomas Jefferson's Monticello. https://www.monticello.org/site/jefferson/i-prefer-dangerous-freedom-over-peaceful-slavery-quotation. [http://archive.li/FGUy8]

7 "Murder Victims by Weapon, 2007–2011" FBI Expanded Homicide Data Table 8. September 21, 2012. https://ucr.fbi.gov/crime-in-the-u.s/2011/crime-in-the-u.s.-2011/tables/expanded-homicide-data-table-8. [http://archive.li/TGs2o]

8 "Ban on assault weapons didn't reduce violence" The Washington Times. August 16, 2004. http://www.washingtontimes.com/news/2004/aug/16/20040816-114754-1427r/.

low rates of crimes and murders involving these arms, Liberals are still obsessed with getting rifles out of our hands.

More people die from drowning at their own home each year, than are killed by rifles. More people die annually from overdosing on prescription Opioids than are murdered with firearms. More people die from prescription Opioids than any other drug.[9] Yet politicians make no campaign promises to rid society of these poisons. No politician runs ads promising to fight the evils of big pharmaceutical companies. Hillary Clinton wants to hold firearm manufacturers responsible for firearm deaths, but not pharmaceutical companies for the deaths causes by their drugs?[10] How telling.

If the Liberal goal were truly to save lives, they would have a long list of evils to face before a few hundred annual deaths from rifles found its way to the top. Yet the stated Liberal goal of "saving lives" and "making the streets safer," only ever applies to firearms. Thus the true Liberal agenda peeks out from behind the mask.

A Look at the Numbers

Liberal talking points and the data they choose to represent are incredibly dishonest. In the first place, Liberals nearly always include suicides in the data sets on gun violence and deaths, which I find abhorrent. The inclusion of suicides entirely minimizes and undermines the causes of suicide: clinical depression, schizophrenia, bipolar disorder, posttraumatic stress disorder, and a host of other anxiety and personality disorders. This is an issue that I take very seriously and I find it thoroughly repulsive that Liberals profit from the method which people use to kill themselves in order to politicize their gun agenda.

---

9 "Opioid Overdose" Centers for Disease Control and Prevention. February 09, 2017. https://www.cdc.gov/drugoverdose/data/analysis.html. [http://archive.li/lpm0S]

10 AWR Hawkins. "Hillary Clinton: 'Incomprehensible' that Gun Makers Aren't Liable for Misuse of Stolen Guns" Breitbart. October 16, 2016. http://www.breitbart.com/big-government/2016/10/16/hillary-clinton-incomprehensible-that-gun-makers-arent-liable-for-misuse-of-stolen-guns/. [http://archive.li/pz03E]

According to the World Health Organization, The United States ranks 50th in suicide rates compared to other nations.[11] In the nations in which firearms are uncommon, other methods become the number one method of taking one's own life, from hanging, to poisoning, to asphyxiation. Judging from data taken from the top fifty nations by suicide rate, banning guns does not prevent suicides at all; in many of these countries, people do not have easy access to firearms at all, yet they still kill themselves at an even higher rate than United States citizens. For Liberals and Democratic politicians to conflate the heartbreaking issue of suicide with firearm control is dishonest, grotesque, and embarrassing. They willingly stand on these graves in order to push a political agenda.

Every college textbook I have seen, and most news articles that depict graphs of intentional homicides by firearm in The United States as compared to other nations, always use the same trick. They place the US at the bottom of the list, and cherry pick twenty or so other countries with low homicide-by-firearm rates. The comparison countries are typically much smaller than the US, with mostly homogeneous populations, and have lower crimes rates in general. If you look up a global list of homicides by country, you'll see that the US is directly in the middle of all countries. The bogus graphs also only use the rate of *gun*-related homicides. Honduras for example, has an incredibly high murder rate, but when we only account for *gun*-related murders, the rate drops dramatically. They are still killing each other; they just find other methods.

The 2014 US murder rate per 100,000 people was 4.4. Broken down state by state, an interesting story begins to emerge. A dozen states have murder rates lower than 2.0. If those dozen states were their own countries, none would break the top 150 countries by homicide rate. On the other end of the spectrum, there are a dozen or so states with murder rates above 5.0, above and beyond the national average.[12] Looking at the murder rates of individual cities, we see an even more revealing picture.

11 "Suicide rates, age-standardized Data by country" World Health Organization. Accessed February 10, 2017. http://apps.who.int/gho/data/node.main.MHSUICIDEASDR?lang=en.

12 "Homicide Mortality by State" Centers for Disease Control and Prevention. January 11, 2018. https://www.cdc.gov/nchs/pressroom/sosmap/homicide_mortality/homicide.htm. [http://archive.li/6DRAr]

St. Louis, Baltimore, New Orleans, Newark, Detroit, Washington, D.C., all have murder rates above 24.0 per 100,000 people. St. Louis tops the chart at nearly 60.0 homicides per 100,000 people. Over 20 US cities have murder rates more than four times the national average, placing them among the most dangerous cities in the world.[13]

Murders in which a firearm is used are highly concentrated. 68 percent of all murders in which a firearm was used occur in just 5 percent of the nation's counties, per data from The Crime Prevention Research Center. More than 50 percent of all firearm related homicides are in just 2 percent of US counties. The majority of US counties, 98 percent, have a murder rate similar to that of Canada, less than 2.0 per 100,000 residents.[14] Perhaps most surprisingly, over half of all US counties have zero homicides.[15]

Liberals have long argued that more guns do not make a nation safer. Perhaps they are right, but it is curious to me that in Vermont, for example, the gun ownership rate is over 40 percent, while the murder rate is 1.3. Meanwhile in Maryland, the gun ownership rate is just over 20 percent, with a murder rate six times higher than in Vermont. Baltimore, Maryland, one of the most dangerous cities in the world, has a homicide rate of 55.0 per 100,000 people.[16]

In data taken from the Bureau of Justice Statistics, we can find an even more detailed view of murders in the United States. Men commit murder at a much higher rate than women. Rates of both being murdered and

---

13 Faraz Haider. "Most Dangerous Cities In The United States" World Atlas. February 18, 2018. http://www.worldatlas.com/articles/most-dangerous-cities-in-the-united-states.html. [http://archive.li/EeaMI]

14 Perry Chiaramonte. "US murders concentrated in 5 percent of counties" Fox News. April 26, 2017. http://www.foxnews.com/us/2017/04/26/us-murders-concentrated-in-5-percent-counties.html. [http://archive.li/b48mx]

15 "Murders in US very concentrated: 54 percent of US counties in 2014 had zero murders, 2 percent of counties have 51 percent of the murders" Crime Prevention Research Center. April 25, 2017. https://crimeresearch.org/2017/04/number-murders-county-54-us-counties-2014-zero-murders-69-1-murder/. [http://archive.li/kougT]

16 Deborah White. "How Many Gun Owners Live in Your Home State" ThoughtCo. April 28, 2017. https://www.thoughtco.com/gun-owners-percentage-of-state-populations-3325153. [http://archive.li/9DHIF]

committing murder are much higher for eighteen to thirty-four year-olds. When broken down by race, whites have murdered at an average rate of 4.5 over the years from 1980-2008, and blacks at a rate of 34.4, a difference of more than seven times. What this means is that black males, who make up around 6 percent of the population in the United States, account for half of all murders annually. If we were to remove murders committed by just 6 percent of the population, the murder rate of the United States would drop to levels similar to those in Nepal, Belgium, and Finland, placing the rate in the bottom 25 percent of the world's nations by homicide rate.[17] If black America were its own country, it would be one of the most deadly nations on Earth in terms of homicide rate.

Illegal invaders, making up only around 3.5 percent or so of the total population, commit a disproportionate rate of crime and murder, according to The General Accounting Office. In a 20 year span, at least 22,000 murders happened needlessly, inflating the murder rate in an artificial fashion. If we were to remove the black murder rate, the Hispanic murders, and the murders committed by illegals, which account for around 75 percent of all murders, the current, white only US murder rate would fall to just about 1.45 per 100,000. They would have among the lowest rates on Earth, while being among the most heavily armed groups of people on Earth. [18]

After sorting through piles of data, I have a hard time buying into the narrative that guns are somehow the root cause of murders in the United States — or anywhere else for that matter. Young men in America kill themselves and each other at incredible rates. 77 percent of whites that are killed with a gun are suicides. 82 percent of blacks that are killed with a gun are killed by other black men around their same age.[19]

---

17 Alexia Cooper and Erica L. Smith. "Homicide Trends in the United States, 1980-2008" U.S. Department of Justice. November 2011.

18 Ron Martinelli. "The truth about crime, illegal immigrants and sanctuary cities." The Hill. April 19, 2017. thehill.com/blogs/pundits-blog/crime/329589-the-truth-about-crime-illegal-immigrants-and-sanctuary-cities. [http://archive.li/Rpim8]

19 Richard V. Reeves and Sarah Holmes. "Guns and race: The different worlds of black and white Americans | Brookings Institution" Brookings. December 15, 2015. https://www.brookings.edu/blog/social-mobility-memos/2015/12/15/guns-and-race-the-different-worlds-of-black-and-white-americans/. [http://archive.li/VtiBT]

Not only do we find a very different pattern of gun deaths between races, but there is a pattern of percentage of firearm ownership that suggests the number of firearms in an area in no way predicts the relative amount of firearm violence.

If we were to seek actual, pragmatic ways of lowering the deaths related to firearms, we would look at demographic control, not gun control. Studies show that those who identify as Liberal are more prone to crime; the majority of convicted felons are registered Democrats, and black men make up over half of all murders.[20] [21] Further, most homicides are concentrated in a small percent of US counties. Perhaps the regulation we need does not concern firearms.

Data from the New York City Police Department reveals that in 2016, 73 percent of all firearm arrests were blacks, 22 percent Hispanic, and 3 percent whites. Time and time again crime data reveals that guns are *not* the issue. Yet the Left refuses to acknowledge any information that confirms the differences between groups in terms of behavior and criminality.[22]

Data from the National Crime Victimization Survey, conducted by Bureau of Justice Statistics, show that almost 68,000 times each year, a firearm is used for self-defense. That means at least 68,000 people who were not murdered, robbed, assaulted, or raped, and whose safety was guaranteed by owning a weapon. Over six times the amount of people used a firearm to protect themselves, than to kill.

This figure of 68,000 is the *lowest* figure I found reported. Florida State University criminology professor Gary Kleck has conducted research that shows firearms being used for self-defense at much higher rates than are

20 Paul Bedard. "Jail survey: 7 in 10 felons register as Democrats." Washington Examiner. January 1, 2014. www.washingtonexaminer.com/jail-survey-7-in-10-felons-register-as-democrats/article/2541412. [http://archive.li/Ut26x]

21 John Paul Wright, Kevin M. Beaver, Mark Alden Morgan, and Eric J. Connolly. "Political ideology predicts involvement in crime" Personality and Individual Differences 106 (October 2016): 236-41. doi:10.1016/j.paid.2016.10.062.

22 "Crime and Enforcement Activity Reports 2016" NYPD. Accessed January 10, 2017. http://www1.nyc.gov/site/nypd/stats/reports-analysis/crime-enf.page.

suggested in the Bureau of Justice Statistics report. Kleck estimates that firearms are used in self-defense at least 750,000 times per year.[23]

During his presidency, Obama signed an executive order that granted the Center for Disease Control (CDC) ten million dollars in order to research firearm violence. In 2013, the 110-page report titled *Priorities for Research to Reduce the Threat of Firearm-Related Violence* was released. Much to Liberal chagrin, the report found that firearm use for self-defense was not only prevalent, but represented an important tool for crime deterrent. When firearms were used defensively during attacks, the report states that those with guns had "consistently lower injury rates" as compared to those without guns. Further, criminals used guns in less than 6 percent of the total number of aggravated and simple assaults.[24]

Society-level, community-level, and individual-level factors were examined in relation to gun violence.

At the society-level, low income, low social capital (which is caused in part by increased diversity), and chronic environmental stressors were implicated in leading to higher levels of violence. The number of employment and educational opportunities also contribute to society-level factors.

On the community-level, residential turnover, unemployment, social isolation (again, a product of diversity), and neighborhood drug trafficking are all factors that contribute to more gun violence. Family disruption, low community participation, social disorganization, transiency, and poor economic opportunities also contribute to violence.

Finally, at the individual-level, substance abuse, unemployment, high levels of impulsivity, and low levels of education, all factored into the increase of gun violence.[25]

---

23 AWR Hawkins. "Researcher Reaffirms: At Least 760,000 Defensive Gun Uses a Year" Breitbart. February 19, 2015. http://www.breitbart.com/big-government/2015/02/19/researcher-reaffirms-at-least-760000-defensive-gun-uses-a-year/. [http://archive.li/eSbUk]

24 Kyle Wintersteen. "CDC Gun Research Backfires on Obama" Guns & Ammo. August 27, 2013. http://www.gunsandammo.com/politics/cdc-gun-research-backfires-on-obama/. [http://archive.li/b9UsT]

25 Bruce M. Altevogt, Margaret A. McCoy, Alan I. Leshner, Patrick W. Kelley, and Arlene F. Lee. Priorities for Research to Reduce the Threat of Firearm-Related Violence. National Academies Press, 2013.

Of all the factors mentioned, the report did not find any evidence to suggest that higher rates of gun ownership or gun carrying lead to higher rates of violence. Quite the opposite. The paper, *Crime, Deterrence, and Right-to-Carry Concealed Handguns*, by John Lott and David Mustard, found that after passing concealed carry laws, the rates of aggravated assault, rape, and murder, all *dropped* in the states that permit people to defend themselves.[26]

Gun Control Works! (Not Really)

Liberals frequently appeal to the gun restrictions of other nations such as England and Australia as examples of gun control that "works." They often cite misleading data which suggests that after England and Australia enacted strict gun control, including Australia's much praised mandatory buyback (confiscation) program, gun suicides and murders declined.

There are two crucial elements missing in this misleading data; first, they typically ignore the fact that gun-related suicide and murder rates were already declining *before* the strict gun laws were passed; and second, they neglect to mention the fact that violent crime overall *increased*. Further, although the rates of gun suicides of course dropped, other methods became more common. After the gun restrictions were enacted, both England and Australia saw a rise in robbery, home invasions, assault, and rape. The two "go-to" nations for supporting gun control, the two nations that Liberal politicians constantly laud as bastions of gun-free peace, are not so coincidentally both bearers of the highest rates of violent crime in the world. Since enacting strict firearm control, the rate of firearm use in crimes has doubled in the UK.[27] In both nations, home invasions, robbery, and rape have increased since their firearm bans.[28] The data show that United States citizens are victimized at *half* the rate of both England

26 John Lott, and David Mustard. "Crime, Deterrence, and Right-to-Carry Concealed Handguns" Journal of Legal Studies26, no. 1 (April 17, 1997).

27 AWR Hawkins. "How Gun Control Made England The 'Most Violent Country In Europe'" Breitbart. September 24, 2014. http://www.breitbart.com/national-security/2014/09/24/how-gun-control-made-england-the-most-violent-country-in-europe/. [http://archive.li/vxZZE]

28 Ibid.

and Australia. Despite the fact, or because of the fact, that there are not many guns in the UK or Australia, their citizens are far *less* safe than Americans.[29]

It is not hard to understand why. Imagine that you take away everyone's guns: criminals become more bold and less fearful, while law-abiding citizens are now defenseless. Perhaps if the Swedish people were allowed to carry guns they would not suffer the highest rates of rape on the planet. Perhaps if every woman were allowed to carry a gun, rapes and domestic abuse generally would plummet.

These are talking points the Left refuses to acknowledge, for they are far too damaging to the Liberal narrative that guns, and not people, are the problem. It's far too uncomfortable for a Liberal to face the fact that certain cultures and certain groups of people commit virtually zero crime, despite being heavily armed, while other groups commit an overwhelming amount of violent crime, armed or not.

But these facts fall beyond the pale. And by ignoring them, the Left is putting us all in danger. By trying to solve the crime problem by banning guns, they will do nothing but raise crime and cause more unnecessary violence against innocent people. The data from Europe and Australia prove this beyond any doubt. The suicide figures from the rest of the world again prove beyond any doubt that banning guns will not save more lives. All it will do is cause suicidal people to find other lethal methods, and embolden criminals to rape, plunder, and pillage more than they already do.

Switzerland drives the final nail into the proverbial coffin of the European gun-free utopia. Switzerland boasts one of the lowest rates of homicide in the world, a rate of 0.5 per 100,000 people—and the Swiss have the some of the *highest rates of gun ownership* in the world, with an estimated 50 percent of all Swiss citizens owning firearms. Switzerland has lower crime rates than England, Australia, and the United States, while having higher gun ownership rates.[30]

---

29 "Gun Control and Crime in non-US Countries" Gun Facts. Accessed March 02, 2017. http://www.gunfacts.info/gun-control-myths/guns-in-other-countries/. [http://archive.li/gooQd]

30 "Comparing murder rates and gun ownership across countries" Crime Prevention Research Center. March 31, 2014. https://crimeresearch.org/2014/03/comparing-murder-rates-across-countries/. [http://archive.li/ba3ct]

In an effort to reduce gun homicides and gun suicides, Liberals have not only overseen skyrocketing rates of violent crime and non-gun suicides, but also in vehicles used as weapons.

2016 — Nice, France. 86 deaths. 458 injuries.
2016 — Ohio State University, Columbus, Ohio. 13 injuries.
2016 — Berlin, Germany. 12 deaths. 56 injuries.
2017 — Westminster Bridge, United Kingdom. 6 deaths. 49 injuries.
2017 — Stockholm, Sweden. 6 deaths (5 human, 1 canine.) 15 injuries.
2017 — Paris, France. 6 injured.

All of these mass murders and attempted mass murders were accomplished without the use of a single firearm.

It's *almost* as if some groups of people are violently attacking other, more peaceful groups of people; its almost as if they have been doing so for better than a thousand years. Meanwhile the Liberal media and politicians incessantly blame — the guns. In Sweden, the most popular newspaper, *Aftonbladet*, suggested banning cars in cities as a solution to the recent wave of automobiles used to kill.[31] France, despite having incredibly strict gun laws, has nonetheless suffered the most violent incidents in Europe since the second World War, with nearly 500 casualties in November of 2015 alone. Liberals want to ban guns, ban cars, create gun-free and car-free zones, all the while refusing to address the actual issue, which the data makes painfully clear. The root cause of this violence does not fit their politically correct narrative. In the meantime, the rapes, murders, and vehicular homicides will continue apace.

Former President Barack Obama, has claimed on at least a dozen occasions that mass shootings are something exclusive to the United States:

> "We are the only advanced country on Earth that sees these kinds of mass shootings every few months."

---

31 Virginia Hale. "'Ban Cars to Stop Terror' Says Sweden's Best-Selling Newspaper After Stockholm Attack" Breitbart. April 11, 2017. http://www.breitbart.com/london/2017/04/11/ban-cars-newspaper-stockholm-attack/. [http://archive.li/14oVi]

> "At some point, we as a country will have to reckon with the fact that this type of mass violence does not happen in other advanced countries."
>
> "You don't see murder on this kind of scale, with this kind of frequency, in any other advanced nation on Earth."
>
> "I say this every time we've got one of these mass shootings: this just doesn't happen in other countries."[32]

Thankfully, the Crime Prevention Research Center has released reports that set the record straight. Because Obama specifically mentioned advanced nations, the Crime Prevention Research Center compared the United States mass shootings to twenty-eight countries in the European Union and Canada. They found that in frequency of shootings per one million people, the United States ranked twelfth in the list, behind the likes of France, Austria, and Norway. In terms of the death rate from mass shootings, the U.S. ranked eleventh.[33]

During the November 2015 Paris attacks, there were 498 casualties from shootings in one day. This means that there were nearly as many casualties in one day in France than there were in the United States during Obama's entire eight-year term presidency. Mass shootings not only happen in other advanced nations, but they tend to be even worse.[34]

---

32 Glenn Kessler. "Obama's odd series of exaggerated gun claims" The Washington Post. March 12, 2015. https://www.washingtonpost.com/news/fact-checker/wp/2015/03/12/obamas-odd-series-of-exaggerated-gun-claims/?utm_term=.55c3a874bf6a.

33 "Comparing Death Rates from Mass Public Shootings and Mass Public Violence in the US and Europe" Crime Prevention Research Center. June 23, 2015. http://crimeresearch.org/2015/06/comparing-death-rates-from-mass-public-shootings-in-the-us-and-europe/. [http://archive.li/j7aka]

34 "France had more casualties from mass public shootings in 2015 than the US suffered during Obama's entire presidency (532 to 527)" Crime Prevention Research Center. February 22, 2017. http://crimeresearch.org/2017/02/france-suffered-more-casualties-murders-and-injuries-from-mass-public-shootings-in-2015-than-the-us-has-suffered-during-obamas-entire-presidency-508-to-424-2/. [http://archive.li/GjMC5]

Irrational Fear

In an article published in *The Nation* and entitled, "We Fear Each Other, When Guns Themselves Are The Real Danger," Jewish professor Harold Pollack of the University of Chicago's Crime Lab argues that keeping a firearm for home defense is irrational and dangerous.[35] Pollack claims that because deaths from home invasions are rare, the greater threat is the gun itself and its presence in your home, so that the most logical course of action would be to remain unarmed.

Pollack further argues that keeping a firearm for home and self-defense is "obviously a primeval motive to have a gun by the bedside or whatever." Pollack reasons that because there are more suicides each year than there are deaths from home invasions, it is obviously much safer not to have a firearm in your home.[36] Again, Liberals are conflating the *method* of suicide with the *cause* of suicide. Guns simply do not cause suicide. Pollack is also appealing to the number of homicides during home invasions, while entirely ignoring the number of assaults and rapes that occur during home invasions each year.

Let us look into the data and see exactly how "primeval" and "irrational" the fear of home invasion truly is. According to the US Department of Justice Bureau of Justice Statistics, there are on average over one million home invasions per year. That means a situation in which a criminal unlawfully and forcibly enters into a residence while a person is home at the time. In over 266,000 of those home invasions, the person who was caught at home became a victim of violent crime at the hands of the invader. Among those 266,000 victims of home invasion, many were severely injured and raped.[37]

---

35 Harold Pollack. "We Fear Each Other, When Guns Themselves Are The Real Danger" The Nation. December 20, 2012. https://www.thenation.com/article/we-fear-each-other-when-guns-themselves-are-real-danger/. [http://archive.li/cc46B]

36 Ta-Nehisi Coates. "Gun Violence and the Irrational Fear of Home Invasion" The Atlantic. December 23, 2012. https://www.theatlantic.com/national/archive/2012/12/gun-violence-and-the-irrational-fear-of-home-invasion/266613/. [http://archive.li/LqhMx]

37 Shannon Catalano. "Victimization During Household Burglary" Bureau of Justice Statistics (BJS). September 2010. https://www.bjs.gov/content/pub/ascii/

For perspective, according to RAINN, the largest US anti-sexual assault organization, there are an average of 321,500 rapes and sexual assaults each year in the United States.[38] According to Pollack and many Liberals like him, the fear of a violent home invasion is "primeval," despite the fact that violent home invasions are nearly as common as rape and sexual assault. Would anybody tell young girls and women that taking precautions against possible rape is "irrational and primeval"? Not hardly. Yet Liberals constantly mock, berate, and denigrate those of us who look at the data and conclude that one million home invasions per year, over a quarter of which turn violent, is a more than reasonable rationale for arming oneself.

Appeals to the Second

A favorite Liberal tactic in the constant assault on the rights of gun owners is to appeal to the wording of the Second Amendment. Ironically, yet predictably, this appears to be the only time Liberals appeal to any of our founding documents or ideals. Their argument is that the line in the Second Amendment regarding "a well regulated Militia" implies that being able to keep and bear arms is entirely predicated upon participation in an official militia. Had Liberals bothered to read *The Federalist Papers*, or any of the individual States' Bill of Rights from the same era, they would have their answer, and see the absurdity in their argument. "Well regulated" at the time of writing meant little more than in working order. The Militia was described as the people. Not a formal government entity. The common man. The shopkeeper. The farmer. The tailor. The cook. They were the militia. *We* were the militia.[39]

---

vdhb.txt. [http://archive.li/sgX77]

38 "Victims of Sexual Violence: Statistics" RAINN. Accessed July 12, 2017. https://www.rainn.org/statistics/victims-sexual-violence. [http://archive.li/znYQI]

39 David W Brown. "How Alexander Hamilton solved America's gun problem — 228 years ago" The Week. June 15, 2016. http://theweek.com/articles/629815/how-alexander-hamilton-solved-americas-gun-problem--228-years-ago. [http://archive.li/rfx8i]

> Beyond the simple advantage of being armed, which the Americans possess to a greater extent than the people of almost every other nation, the existence of subordinate governments, to which the people are attached, and by which the militia officers are appointed, forms an almost insurmountable barrier against the enterprises of ambition. Notwithstanding the military establishments in the several kingdoms of Europe, which are carried as far as the public resources will bear, these governments are afraid to trust the people with arms. And it is not certain that with this aid alone they would not be able to shake off their yokes. But were the people to possess the additional advantages of local governments chosen by themselves, who could gather the national will and direct the national force, and of officers appointed by these governments out of the militia, it may be affirmed with the greatest assurance, that the throne of every tyranny in Europe would be speedily overturned in spite of the legions which surround it.
>
> — *Federalist* 46.[40]

Further, a simple question will illustrate the feebleness and thoughtlessness of the Liberal argument. If the writers of the Bill of Rights did not intend for the common people to have the ability to keep arms for their own defense, why did these men allow this situation to continue for their entire tenures as Statesmen? Surely if they meant that only the governmentally sanctioned armed forces were meant to have firearms, they would have done something about all the rifles that private citizens had in their possession, right?

Articles such as "The Second Amendment Doesn't Say What You Think It Does," published by *Mother Jones*, are commonplace on Liberal news outlets.[41] These articles all essentially argue the same thing: those who wrote the Second Amendment did not mean for individuals to be able to own firearms to protect themselves. While claiming that the wording of the amendment is vague and meant for a particular time in history,

---

40 Madison. "The Federalist Papers : No. 46." The Avalon Project : Federalist No 46. avalon.law.yale.edu/18th_century/fed46.asp. [http://archive.li/nCA1]

41 Hannah Levintova. "The Second Amendment doesn't say what you think it does" Mother Jones. June 19, 2014. http://www.motherjones.com/politics/2014/06/second-amendment-guns-michael-waldman/. [http://archive.li/Fi6IS]

the Left entirely ignores all other sources available to us in our investigation of the intended meaning of our most crucial freedom.

In the Constitutions of all but six states, the right to keep and bear arms is explicitly expressed.[42] Many of these were ratified after the US Bill of Rights, and are written in more explicit language.

Vermont's Constitution, Article 16:

> That the people have a right to bear arms for the defense of themselves and the State — and as standing armies in time of peace are dangerous to liberty, they ought not to be kept up; and that the military should be kept under strict subordination to and governed by the civil power.

Ohio's Constitution, Article 1.01, Inalienable Rights:

> All men are, by nature, free and independent, and have certain inalienable rights, among which are those of enjoying and defending life and liberty, acquiring, possessing, and protecting property, and seeking and obtaining happiness and safety.

Article 1.04, Bearing Arms:

> The people have the right to bear arms for their defense and security; but standing armies, in time of peace, are dangerous to liberty, and shall not be kept up; and the military shall be in strict subordination to the civil power.

Clear as day.

Furthermore, the Left claims that the Second Amendment is only applicable to the weapons available when the Bill of Rights was written. The Left frequently argues that the writers had no way of knowing what firearms might become over the course of 200 years. I disagree entirely. The line reads, "right to bear *arms*," not the "right to bear *muskets*." The

---

42 Dean Weingarten. "The Six States With No Constitutional Right to Keep and Bear Arms" The Truth About Guns. November 02, 2014. http://www.thetruthaboutguns.com/2014/11/dean-weingarten/six-states-without-constitutional-right-keep-bear-arms/. [http://archive.li/hf8Tl]

writers were not dense men. They knew the importance of citizens being able to possess weaponry on par with that available to the government.

I believe that requiring a permit to carry a firearm is an extreme infringement upon our rights. Currently around a dozen states have Constitutional carry laws; if you can legally buy a firearm, you can legally carry it on your person or vehicle without a permit. If we as law-abiding American citizens really have the inalienable right to defend our life, liberty, property, and safety, we should not be required to get a permission slip from the government expressly allowing the protection of that right. Our rights were not given to us for free; our ancestors spilled endless treasure and blood to bestow these rights upon us. There is nothing which can justify the notion that the State needs to know who carries and who does not. If you can legally own a firearm, there should be no further background check or permission required. The assumption that the State should be operating under is that we are a free and heavily armed society, and that those without a weapon are the exception rather than the rule.

Private ownership of arms serves as a bulwark against the State's exerting heightened control over its citizens. Any sort of registry or licensing requirement should be met with fierce skepticism. The state ought to be kept in the dark and should not know where, nor with whom, concentrations of arms lie within the nation, should they ever make the fatal error of crossing the line.

When we take a moment to read what the writers of the Bill of Rights expressed about arms, when we look at individual State Constitutions, and examine gun laws at the State and Federal level, it becomes quite clear the Second Amendment means exactly what gun rights advocates have always claimed. In no way does the Militia clause rescind the idea that individual citizens have the right to keep and bear arms: the contrary. Further, this very issue was argued in front of the Supreme Court as recently as 2008, in *District of Columbia v. Heller*. The case upheld the notion that private citizens do in fact, have the right to keep and bear arms for self-defense, even if they are *not* a part of any official militia.

The Heller decision, by the way, is one that Hillary Clinton felt the Supreme Court got wrong.[43] In an interview with Clinton, she stated, "If it [the right to keep and bear arms] is a constitutional right, then it, like every other constitutional right, is subject to reasonable regulation. And what people have done with that decision is to take it as far as they possibly can and reject what has been our history from the very beginning of the republic, where some of the earliest laws that were passed were about firearms."[44]

Actually, the first federal gun control law was not passed until 1934. In point of fact, some of the earliest laws regarded immigration. The Naturalization Act of 1790, for instance. The 1790 act allowed free white persons of good moral character, to apply for citizenship if they had been in the country for two years. Yet somehow I do not think that Clinton will be ready to accept a return to such legislation any time soon.

What part of "don't tread on" and "shall not be infringed" is so difficult to comprehend? I believe we are growing weary of the "repeated injuries and usurpations" that we constantly face from the Left. The last group of people that were dense enough not to understand how far they were pushing our kind ended up learning the hard way.

Christmas night, 1776. Patriot General Washington led a group of Revolutionaries across a frozen river, through the frigid darkness, to kill enemy soldiers. In their sleep. For freedom.

That revolutionary spirit lives on in all of us. We must never forget where we came from — all the more so, as it appears the Left already has.

---

43 Meghan Keneally. "Hillary Clinton Slammed for Her Characterization of Supreme Court Gun Ruling" ABC News. October 21, 2016. http://abcnews.go.com/Politics/hillary-clinton-slammed-characterization-supreme-court-gun-ruling/story?id=42965863. [http://archive.li/Cp6bz]

44 Jonathan H. Adler. "Opinion | Hillary Clinton on guns and the Second Amendment" The Washington Post. June 06, 2016. https://www.washingtonpost.com/news/volokh-conspiracy/wp/2016/06/06/hillary-clinton-on-guns-and-the-second-amendment/?utm_term=.8eb128e9bfc2.

Rational Fears

Liberals display an almost irrationally obsessive desire to control guns, limit their availability, and damage the industry as whole. There is no data supporting any of their stated agendas. It becomes clear that their position is one of fear and loathing toward what the hostile elite see as an "old America." The remnants of a WASPier and freer society. One they would prefer became extinct, substituted with more of their own elitist kin and their pet rootless hordes. They see us as the enemy, the last regiment of people fighting to keep this nation from being taken oven by an invasive, alien clique. And like any good war strategists would know, disarming us would greatly behoove them. Their interest is not in "saving lives" as much as it is in preserving their own kind, and disarming those they fear the most.

The Liberal desire to ban AR-15, AK-47, and M14 pattern rifles is not in the safety interest of the American people. It is simply about control. Leftist regimes for the last hundred years have needed an unarmed population so that they could continue to rule with impunity. The insatiable thirst to limit gun rights among citizens is not about the safety of the civilian population; it is about the safety of the ruling elite, an adversarial cabal that is terrified of a well armed population. They have manipulated their legions of useful idiots into believing that this is an issue of public health or public safety, when in reality it is the age-old issue of the ruling class holding down a citizen uprising.

You can do anything you want to a group of unarmed people. Liberals hate nothing more than a fair fight—as we've seen in their incessant desire for censorship of dissident thought. The desire to ban rifles is simply another expression of the desire to exert greater control over those whom they rule, and the only thing standing in their way, is the sacred force found within those rifles. For a rifle has the means to transform the most ordinary of men into the most exceptional of revolutionaries.

There is at least a remnant of the Wild West left in America. It's not all that uncommon to see somebody with a pistol at his side at the gas station, the market, on a hiking trail, or out on a bicycle trail. And every time I see it, I can't help but smile. There is an enduring sense that America is still an unbridled stallion, immune to taming by cosmopolitan dogmas.

Well armed citizens will only take so much. You can only push good men so far before their patience runs dry. And when that fateful day comes, and if those men are armed, Leftists everywhere know that nothing will save them.

Manifestations of the Liberal Illness: The Right to Bear Arms

Deceitfulness oozes out of every Liberal argument against the freedom to bear arms. They lie about the reasons behind the Second Amendment, they lie about the data regarding firearms in our day. Even former Presidents of the United States and people running for office lie. Obama lied about America's gun violence as compared to other nations; Hillary lied on her website about current gun laws and about the terms of background checks. Despite all the evidence that suggests that guns in the hands of private citizens act as deterrents to crime, Liberals refuse to modify their views on the matter. When confronted with the facts, Liberals often become agitated and angry, as their cognitive dissonance becomes too great.

The old Liberal maladies make their appearance here, too. The inability to recognize the negative outcomes of their actions, as demonstrated by Liberal claims that the UK and Australia are "doing gun control right," despite the rise of crime in the UK and Australia after their respective firearm bans The appeal to altered definitions in the language of the Second Amendment, despite mountains of evidence from the *Federalist Papers* and state Constitutions, even despite a landmark Supreme Court case. Feelings of being victimized, as when anti-gun groups like Moms Demand Action claim that guns make society unsafe, or politicians declare that "weapons of war" are threatening our collective safety. We also see the Liberal moral self-righteousness arising during gun debates. Liberals believe they are on the "right side of history" here, as everywhere else. Not near enough people remind Liberals that over one hundred million people are lying dead in mass graves due specifically to Leftist regimes, and that over 262 million were massacred because they had no way to defend themselves.

It is not idle to ask whether those 262 million would agree that the Left is on the "right side of history."

From Cluster I symptom 1, 2, 3, and 5, appear. Symptoms 6, 7, 8, and 9, are apparent from Cluster II.

Cluster I

1. Deceitfulness, indicated by repeated lying, grand exaggerations, or omission of contrary information, with the purpose to advance their chosen narrative and discrediting others.

2. Irritability or aggressiveness towards anybody that questions or opposes their views. Coupled with the inability to recognize they own hypocrisy, double standards, and doublethink.

3. Inability to adjust views when presented with information contrary to their own beliefs.

4. Frequent projections of their own traits onto others.

5. Difficulty in dealing with a loss of control or power, or a strong desire for control and power.

Cluster II

6. Appeals to altered and redefined definitions of words, or relies on fictitious terms for argumentation.

7. Consistent feelings of having been victimized or wronged, without any actual harm being done. Seen also as playing the victim after attacking others.

8. Intense sense of righteousness or moral superiority.

9. The inability to recognize the negative outcomes of their own actions. Often placing the blame on others.

10. Intense guilt or self-hatred, often manifests as hatred towards one's larger group identity.

III

Climate Change

The year was 1974, global cooling and disco were all the rage. Unfortunately, only one of those fads has continued into the next century. It's still the same old scheme, one that goes by an ever-changing name. But it is all too typical of the Left to change names and definitions to suit their current political agenda.

The global cooling scare of the 1970s, now dismissed as simple conjecture, was huge. It dominated news reports, papers, and magazine articles. The pollutants in the air were going to block out the sun's rays, causing massive cooling to the point we would not be able to grow food. Then, with no food, we all were going to die.

If you're wondering, that never happened.

Later, we saw feverish anxiety over global warming. The oceans would rise, coasts would flood, and all hell would break loose as millions of people were displaced.

Strangely, this, too, never came to pass. And in light of all these inaccurate predictions, we have now been introduced to the nicely noncommittal term, "climate change." Thus far, the only "inconvenient truth" has been the harsh reality for the Left that their incessant fear-mongering has never ceased to be mostly, if not entirely, built on conjecture.

Yes, the climate is changing. Just as it has since the dawn of time. But on the basis of this universal truth, the Left leaps to several invalid assertions and claims—everything from pretending to be the only party that cares about environmental issues, to wanting to levy the burden of this "crisis" solely on the Western world.

Legacy conservatives like Theodore Roosevelt were the men who truly fought to protect our national lands. When the petrified forests were being ransacked, and when the giant redwoods were being sold for cheap lumber, it was a Right-wing politician who stepped up and fought for conservation. Had it not been for men like Roosevelt and John Muir, it's quite possible the Grand Canyon would now be the world's largest privately owned trash dump, instead of being a revered destination the world over. The Liberal narrative that it is only coastal elites who care about our wild lands and naturalistic history is absurd, and based on no part of factual reality.

Nobody, regardless of political affiliation, wants poisoned rivers, toxic air, and a degraded Earth. The fundamental political disagreement hinges on two things. First, is there conclusive evidence of man-made climate change? And second, how do we solve the problem?

On the first question, the jury is still out. Since the beginning of industrialization, the global climate has warmed. It may be that the Earth was going to warm regardless of human activity, just as it had done for millions of years before we got here. If you look at graphs depicting climate change, you'll find that most start around 1860, and they all show an augment in temperatures after that year. But something funny happens if you go back many thousands or millions of years and look at temperatures based on ice and sediment cores: the upward slope for the last 150 years suddenly becomes unnoticeable. There are visible periods of warming, as well as ice ages, and even a fairly recent mini-ice age.[1]

The Left commonly makes an argument where they falsely claim that some 98 percent of the world's scientists believe that climate change is man-made. As for the specifics of this 98 percent figure that we have all heard, the statistic comes from an analysis done on climate-change articles published in scientific journals. And it just so happens that the majority of the scientists in question *do* believe in climate change. What about the

---

1 James Delingpole. "'Global Warming' Is a Myth, Say 58 Scientific Papers in 2017" Breitbart. June 06, 2017. http://www.breitbart.com/big-government/2017/06/06/delingpole-global-warming-is-myth-58-scientific-papers-2017/. [http://archive.li/jaI7Q]

climate scientists that *weren't* publishing articles about man-made climate change?

In 2016, George Madison University conducted a survey of 4,000 climate scientists.[2] They stumbled over — a few inconvenient truths. The most inconvenient being that there was no 98 percent consensus. Twelve percent of those surveyed reject the man-made climate change theory, believing the change to be either mostly or entirely natural. Fourteen percent of climate scientist believe the change in the temperatures are both man-made *and* natural. 38 percent believe that climate change is *mostly* (60 percent-80 percent) a function of human activity. And 29 percent believe humans are almost entirely responsible for the change in climate.

This study paints a radically different portrait of the community of climate scientists than the dogmatic 98 percent figure we so often hear. Over half of the scientists surveyed believe humans are at least partially responsible for climate change. Fully a quarter of those surveyed believed the change is only partially or not at all a result of human activity.

At this point, there are two conclusions we might draw. Either Liberals do not realize that the 98 percent figure they throw around with such utter abandon is a huge misrepresentation of the scientific community. Or else they do know, and are simply lying.

Liberals often like to attack those who question the current narrative of climate change and its possible solutions. They ask demeaning questions such as, "Do you not believe in gravity either since it's *just a theory*?" No, we believe in gravity; we're just waiting for the Left to get their theory straight before attempting to change the entire world because of it.

Even expert views are currently standing on shaky ground. Yet anybody who offers a dissident opinion is denounced as uneducated by our trustworthy Liberal proles. This type of rigid and unquestioning adherence to the narrative is something seen in cults — not in reasonable and logical discourse.

Now, for the sake of argument — and getting to the heart of this issue — let us assume that climate change is indeed man-made. Let's assume that the science is conclusive, and nobody on Earth disagrees with the

2 Edward Maibach, et al. "A 2016 Survey of American Meteorological Society Members about Climate Change" Center for Climate Change Communication (2016). DOI: 10.13140/RG.2.2.31946.98240

man-made climate change theory. Now what? This is the second very fundamental issue at hand, and the one that brings us back to politics. What do we *do* with this new information? If Liberals had it their way, there would be harsh regulations, increased taxation — and of course, only on Americans and Europeans.

The Climate Solution website suggests the following:

> It's simple. If we make carbon pollution expensive, we'll get less of it. Less carbon pollution means less climate change. Put another way, a price on carbon makes fossil fuels like coal and oil more expensive. And when that happens people switch to cheaper forms of energy like wind and solar.[3]

That's all very nice, but back here in the real world, I don't have an option to "switch" to wind or solar. If I could make myself entirely independent of fossil fuels, I would be one of the first to do so. Sadly, we aren't there yet. In the meantime, the Left wants to continue the assault on middle-class working families through taxation and increasing the cost of living essentials. The effect of such a measure would be a tremendous burden on the people who already struggle to get by. Those on welfare and the wealthy would notice no material difference in their lives, while the working families of middle America would be once again assailed by hostile elites. Proposals as offered by *The Climate Solution* effectively shift the burden of pollution onto those who have the *least* amount of influence on the issue.

New York Times article titles like "Earth's Hottest Year on Record" are rather misleading.[4] They convince the inattentive reader that we are living in the hottest period on Earth. I *know* this is what people think, because my classmates have told me time and time again that we are living in the hottest year in Earth's history. It is true that 2016 was the hottest year on *record* — but humans have only been keeping records since the mid 1800s. However, we can tell from ice and sediment samples that the Earth has

3 "The Solution to Climate Change" The Solution to Climate Change. Accessed July 10, 2017. https://theclimatesolution.com/.

4 Jugal K. Patel. "How 2016 Became Earth's Hottest Year on Record." January 18, 2017. The New York Times. https://www.nytimes.com/interactive/2017/01/18/science/earth/2016-hottest-year-on-record.html?. [http://archive.li/0XeD2]

been much hotter than it is now in different epochs of its history. Even as recently as the fifteenth century, temperatures were warmer than they are now.[5]

The issue of climate change, and environmentalism more broadly, displays the Liberal desire to take the moral high ground. It's entirely reasonable to think that excess carbon dioxide produced by humans is causing the global climate to rise in temperature. What is *not* reasonable is the fanatic politicizing of the issue which accompanies this belief.

Everybody should want to recycle more, to waste less, and to preserve our environment the best we can. However, that is not what we see from the Left. From the Left, we see a fanatical obsession and lust for control. Not long ago there was a video all over the news and internet of a woman being kicked off an airplane for berating a Trump supporter. What was her go-to topic of inquisition? Climate change, of course.[6]

Conservation is a great and worthy goal. I personally try to waste very little, and recycle nearly everything, so the smallest amount of my footprint ends up in a landfill. I traded in a fuel-inefficient truck for an older car with much better gas mileage. This after carefully researching electric cars, and realizing that the problem of fossil fuels remains, whether I'm using gasoline or using coal in the form electricity to charge the battery of an electric car. The Left wants to take this issue and weaponize it, as it does with everything. This shines a certain light on the character of the Left — how even in matters that most decent people should agree on, they can't help but deceive, falsely claim righteousness, and attack. Getting honesty out of a Liberal is like squeezing blood from a stone.

Clean air, clean water, successful species of flora and fauna, do not represent partisan issues. These questions affect humans and non-humans alike. Nobody wants trash being dumped into the lakes, sludge filling the rivers, and oil flooding the oceans. We are of course all in favor of ensuring

---

5 James Delingpole. "'Global Warming' Is a Myth, Say 58 Scientific Papers in 2017" Breitbart. June 06, 2017. http://www.breitbart.com/big-government/2017/06/06/delingpole-global-warming-is-myth-58-scientific-papers-2017/. [http://archive.li/jaI7Q]

6 "Woman kicked off plane for berating Trump supporter in viral video" Fox News. January 23, 2017. http://www.foxnews.com/travel/2017/01/23/woman-kicked-off-plane-for-berating-trump-supporter-in-viral-video.html. [http://archive.li/9TYSi]

a basic level of environmental protection. The issue is really simple: propose a solution that doesn't send us back into the Stone Age and I'm sure everybody will be on board.

This idea of increased taxation on America and Europe to solve a problem that may or may not exist is total lunacy and positively regressive in nature. The issue of climate change does not display the Left's passion for the environment nearly as clearly as it showcases its obsession to control and exert dominance over others. The proposed Carbon Tax is a thinly veiled means of wealth redistribution; it can do nothing other than weaken middle-class families, grant more power and control to the United Nations, and smooth the way for mass migration.

They want to fine or jail those they refer to as "climate deniers." The Left has made skepticism the new heresy, thus any skeptic of their narrative is labeled as a heretic and immediately dismissed as such. The question of human contribution to climate change is paramount for the Left and its agenda. It is so important, in fact, that the National Oceanic and Atmospheric Administration (NOAA) was found to be manipulating data in their climate reports for the 2015 United Nations climate conference in Paris, in order to exaggerate global warming.[7] I want a clean Earth, more than anybody. But I reject the Leftists ideal that taxation and mass migration are going to solve the issue.

If the government and the United Nation want to come together to work on alternatives to fossil energy, that would be great. They waste billions of dollars annually that could easily be put toward such a project. Maybe instead of burdening the everyday person with more taxation, we should throw the issue back on our "leaders" and make *them* find a reasonable alternative. Maybe the UN should offer a massive global reward, tens of millions of dollars, for any person or group that can find reliable, alternative energy solutions.

Naturally, they would never do such a thing. It would spoil such a nice *excuse*. We must be wary of any proposed solutions to any presumed problem that involves further governmental interference. Obama already

---

7 Valerie Richardson. "Climate change whistleblower alleges NOAA manipulated data to hide global warming 'pause'" The Washington Times. February 05, 2017. http://www.washingtontimes.com/news/2017/feb/5/climate-change-whistleblower-alleges-noaa-manipula/. [http://archive.li/vdM0X]

unveiled part of the plan in a final speech, when he asserted that there will be waves of climate refugees seeking asylum, and that "No challenge poses a greater threat to future generations than climate change." [8] [9] Challenge indeed. If we enforced closed borders and limited immigration, we wouldn't have to worry, now would we?

German Development Minister Müller has said that unless a massive Marshall-type plan is introduced, another 100 million migrants will move to Europe.[10] He claims that unless the European people are taxed in order to provide a better life for Africans and Arabs, they will encroach upon Europe *en masse*, increasing the population of Europe by 13 percent — a 13 percent which, as the majority of migrants now, will of course be on welfare. Considering these numbers from an economic point of view shows at once that such an exodus from the Third World into Europe would be entirely devastating. And the treasonous politicians do nothing to protect the people they are elected to serve.

The Liberal press drones on in endless preachments in the same wicked sermon:

> "Mass migration is no 'crisis': it's the new normal as the climate changes."
>
> — *The Guardian*[11]

---

8 Ian Johnston. "Barack Obama warns climate change could create refugee crisis 'unprecedented in human history'" The Independent. May 10, 2017.http://www.independent.co.uk/environment/barack-obama-climate-change-refugee-crisis-human-history-unprecedented-global-warming-paris-a7727881.html. [http://archive.li/4uE40]

9 Madison Park. "Obama: No greater threat to future than climate change" CNN. January 21, 2015. http://www.cnn.com/2015/01/21/us/climate-change-us-obama/. [http://archive.li/29gZX]

10 Jacob Bojesson. "Germany Says 100 Million African Refugees Could Head North" The Daily Caller. June 18, 2017. http://dailycaller.com/2017/06/18/germany-says-100-million-african-refugees-could-head-north/. [http://archive.li/PAwAv]

11 Ellie Mae O'Hagan. "Mass migration is no 'crisis': it's the new normal as the climate changes" The Guardian. August 18, 2015. https://www.theguardian.com/commentisfree/2015/aug/18/mass-migration-crisis-refugees-climate-change. [http://archive.li/XSYLI]

> "Climate Change Is Already Causing Mass Human Migration"
>
> — *Smithsonian*[12]

> "How Climate Change is Behind the Surge of Migrants to Europe"
>
> — *Time*[13]

Every article is the same: because the temperatures went up half a degree in the past forty years, we can expect millions of migrants to flood into our nations each year. And of course, we have only ourselves to blame for having the audacity to use cars and electricity.

Scientific American lists having only one child on their list of "10 Solutions for Climate Change."[14] Western nations already have among the lowest birth rates globally. But if children are the problem, why does the Left not advocate for contraception or sterilization programs in the Third World, whose populations produce litters of children in every family? The population in the Third World is exploding due to First World aid. If overpopulation is indeed an issue, cutting aid and sterilization would be the clear solution, not bringing them to the First World.

Or perhaps we could implement the Carbon Tax only on the Third World instead. They are among the heaviest polluters and having the most children, by far. Why hold only Americans and Europeans responsible? If the Left really cared about pollution and carbon dioxide, they would be chomping at the bits to demand that China and India stop dumping toxins into their rivers and poisoning the skies with their manufacturing. But strangely one never hears such calls from the Left.

---

12 Colin Schultz. "Climate Change Is Already Causing Mass Human Migration" Smithsonian.com. January 29, 2014. http://www.smithsonianmag.com/smart-news/climate-change-already-causing-mass-human-migration-180949530/. [http://archive.li/TTNHl]

13 Aryn Baker. "How climate change is driving migration to Europe" Time. September 07, 2017. http://time.com/4024210/climate-change-migrants/. [http://archive.li/9xIRK]

14 David Biello. "10 Solutions for Climate Change" Scientific American. November 26, 2007. https://www.scientificamerican.com/article/10-solutions-for-climate-change/. [http://archive.li/xFpVk]

The Guardian followed suit with their article, "Want to fight climate change? Have fewer children." Once more, the culprit is identified as the amount of carbon resulting from each additional human, and the solution is simply fewer children. It's worth noting that the photo prominently displayed in the article portrays three small *white* children.[15] This is most telling, given that present projections of global population through the year 2100 reveal that the American and European population will remain rather stable, showing no significant increase or decrease. The population of Asia, too, is predicted to remain more or less stable. However, in Africa, if trends continue, the population will rise from 1.2 billion to over 5.6 billion by year 2100. Half of the estimated eleven billion people on Earth in 2100 will be from Africa—a continent which already relies heavily on foreign aid, entirely from white nations.[16]

The *only* population issue we are facing is the monstrous growth of Africa, which will in turn lead to far more pollution than all Western nations combined. Yet the Left pushes for *whites* to stop having children, not Africans. This "migrant crisis" is never-ending only due to birth rates in the African and Arab world; yet not a peep from the Left about *that* particular conundrum.

Notice a trend yet? They tell us to stop having kids in the West, and simultaneously to open our doors to ever more abundant "climate refugees" from foreign lands. This isn't about clean water or air, and it never was; this is about control, about taxation, about forcing mass migration. This is about population and cultural *replacement.*

But we will have more to say on this riddle later on.

When President Trump pulled the US out of the Paris Climate Accords, that was a tremendously welcome sign for the American people. According to the US Chamber of Commerce, the Paris Accords would

---

15 Damian Carrington. "Want to fight climate change? Have fewer children" The Guardian. July 12, 2017. https://www.theguardian.com/environment/2017/jul/12/want-to-fight-climate-change-have-fewer-children. [http://archive.li/B5sV2]

16 Woollaston Victori. "World's population will soar to 11 billion by 2100 and HALF will live in Africa, claims report" Daily Mail Online. August 10, 2015. http://www.dailymail.co.uk/sciencetech/article-3192285/World-s-population-soar-11-billion-2100-HALF-live-Africa-claims-report.html. [http://archive.li/VM6YU]

cost over one million American jobs. Most large corporations in the US supported the Paris agreement, as it meant the closure of small businesses, automatically reducing market competition. The Heritage Foundation found that the agreement would increase the cost of electricity by 13 percent-20 percent per year, as well as significantly lower the average income for American households.[17] The Green Climate Fund would collect billions of dollars from the US, while the world's heaviest polluting nations would contribute almost nothing.[18] Nor would the proposed plan even mitigate climate change by any significant measure. It is merely a scam to extort more money from the US and Europe and to promote mass migration.

The Paris Climate Accord has been one the worst agreements to come out of France since 1919. We are well rid of it. But we won't soon hear the end of it from our Liberal comrades.

#Save the Ice-Age & The Pangaea One-Continent Summit: 175,000,000 B.C.

Sometimes I get bored and my mind wanders. I was stuck in traffic and starting thinking what Liberals would have been like during the end of the Little Ice Age. Chubby blue-haired Liberals desperately racing from village to village, screaming hysterically at everybody to put out their fires and torches, to stop global temperatures from rising. Panicking Liberals blubbering that if we end the Little Ice Age, we won't have eight months of winter anymore and we'll all burn to death once the average temperature rises too far above freezing.

Then my mind wandered even further back in geological history. What if Liberals had been around as Pangaea began to break apart? Could you imagine? Liberals lobbying to institute the Single-Continent Tax, to fund research efforts for ending tectonic plate shifting. They might even

17 John Carney. "Every Bad Thing We Will Avoid By Rejecting the Paris Climate Accords" Breitbart. May 31, 2017. http://www.breitbart.com/economics/2017/05/31/every-bad-thing-avoided-rejecting-paris-climate-accords/. [http://archive.li/qDKrJ]

18 "US Paid $1B to Green Climate Fund, Top Polluters Paid $0" Fox News. June 03, 2017. http://insider.foxnews.com/2017/06/03/paris-climate-accord-green-fund-america-paid-billion-united-nations. [http://archive.li/54D6T]

have staged marches with clever signs and catchy social media posts about the evils of a seven-continent-planet. "Keep the world united!" "No borders and no oceans!" "Save our one world government!" They would probably pass out pamphlets at university campuses, breathlessly regaling their startled recipients with the horrors of no longer being able to drive from the Northern Eurasia Provence to Southern Oceania, or the dire ramifications that continent breakup might have for cultural exchange or animal migrations. Maybe they would even find a way of blaming it all on their poorest constituents. "Excessive building development leads to tectonic fractures! Stop plate change now: live in a tent!"

What a thought.

Manifestations of the Liberal illness: Climate Change

Global cooling, global warming, climate change—they change the name so often that it's impossible to follow them. They lie and manipulate data, and would even like to throw deniers in prison. Liberals project their traits onto others by claiming that their opponents are ignorant, rigid, unscientific. But those of us on the Right are actually so open-minded and so in *favor* of science, that we want to make sure we have all the data before leaping to wild conclusions.

The Liberal fear and victim complex around climate change is intense. They believe they are slowly being killed by "climate deniers," while they make little effort to solve any of the issues at hand. Moral superiority is seen here, too. Liberals believe they are on the right side of history—and in a way, I agree. Their intentions here are noble. In good American tradition, I am a naturalist and a steadfast believer in conservationism. I would love a cleaner environment, and I believe in spending the time and money necessary to secure the existence of endangered animal species and a future for our planet. I am even against the factory farming of livestock and trapping. It is a devastating and barbaric practice both for the environment and for the wretched animals involved. In principle, I *agree* with the Left here.

However, the issue of climate change has evolved into a dogmatic ideology entirely detached from the concerns of wildlife conservation and environmentalism. The Left claims the moral high ground by conflating the two issues. They claim you simply cannot be concerned about the environment unless you fully accept *their* climate-change narrative. Further, their solution of mass migration and a Carbon Tax paid exclusively by those nations which pollute the *least* is frankly ridiculous. It doesn't take much scratching to see what lies beneath all of this: as with most Leftist crusades, the issue of climate change is but an excuse for garnering power.

I'm sure the average Liberal actually believes he is doing the right thing. Even so, his illness is seen in the way he dogmatically accepts the narrative, while remaining bitterly hostile to those who oppose him, to such a point that we cannot even work together on issues that affect us all.

All symptoms are seen from Cluster I. Symptoms 6, 7, and 8, are seen from Cluster II.

Cluster I

1. Deceitfulness, indicated by repeated lying, grand exaggerations, or omission of contrary information, with the purpose to advance their chosen narrative and discrediting others.

2. Irritability or aggressiveness towards anybody that questions or opposes their views. Coupled with the inability to recognize they own hypocrisy, double standards, and doublethink.

3. Inability to adjust views when presented with information contrary to their own beliefs.

4. Frequent projections of their own traits onto others.

5. Difficulty in dealing with a loss of control or power, or a strong desire for control and power.

Cluster II

6. Appeals to altered and redefined definitions of words, or relies on fictitious terms for argumentation.

7. Consistent feelings of having been victimized or wronged, without any actual harm being done. Seen also as playing the victim after attacking others.

8. Intense sense of righteousness or moral superiority.

9. The inability to recognize the negative outcomes of their own actions. Often placing the blame on others.

10. Intense guilt or self-hatred, often manifests as hatred towards one's larger group identity.

IV

Infanticide

There is no single issue that characterizes the immense depravity of the Liberal mind quite like infanticide. The nefarious and destructive nature of the Left is manifest in the annual average of over one million dead babies since 1970, when the CDC began keeping track of abortion rates.[1]

One million a year. That is one hell of a butcher's bill.

No other issue displays so total a disregard for the non-aggression principle, and of human life generally, as abortion. The Left is frantic to change the name of infanticide to anything else, to reframe the issue as anything but murder, and to appeal to any number of principles besides the one that matters most.

The non-aggression principle is likely as old as humankind and is arguably one of the simplest and noblest of all principles. In its simplest form, the non-aggression principle states that any sort of forced coercion or aggression against a person or his property is inherently wrong. This principle has appeared everywhere from the philosophy of old to the immortal writings of John Locke, which played an important role in our very own Declaration of Independence.

1 "Reproductive Health" Centers for Disease Control and Prevention. May 10, 2017. https://www.cdc.gov/reproductivehealth/data_stats/index.htm.

The principle is quite simple: to deprive another person of his property or right to life is inherently wrong and is at odds with natural law. To abandon this fundamental principle creates a moral and ethical dilemma in which people are not naturally entitled in their right to life and property. The basic right to life, freedom, and property is a cornerstone of Western society. Without it, there is nothing to stop a large mob of people from pillaging and raping small groups of other people for their own benefit. The non-aggression principle is the sole moral standard needed to debate and win against abortionist.

With the underlying principle out of the way, let us delve into the abysmal depths of the sickness known as Liberalism.

Re-Branding

The Liberals love to play the name-game. They rename their support of infanticide as "pro-choice"; they refer to a baby human as a "fetus" in order to obscure the truth. They reframe any abortion legislation as an issue of women's health or reproductive rights, and they refer to severing a child's neck with scissors as a simple "medical procedure."

When was the last time you heard the term "infanticide," by the way? No doubt it's been a while, and there's a reason for that. Liberals must re-brand every aspect of this question to gain mass appeal. Can you image Hillary Clinton standing on a podium and championing infanticide? Of course not. However, hearing a bleeding-heart Leftist drone on about "choice," "rights," and "freedom," leaves one with such a nice warm fuzzy feeling. Terms such as "women's health," "reproductive health," "women's rights," and "reproductive rights," are commonly used to circumvent the actual issue. The sound of the newly named issues are wonderful: who would *not* be in favor of women's health? Who would want to take away reproductive rights? Nobody of course!

Any truly dignified position, as for example the conservative's defense of unborn humans, has no need to rename or reframe the issue; a dignified position can call facts by their right names. The Left must play the name-game to divert the truth and conceal its devilish stance that some lives are worth taking, and that we have the right to take them. Killing a child, even an unborn child, is a clear and gross violation of the non-aggression principle, an abuse of our strength in the face of the most helpless.

The proper response to the deception of the Left is to insist on the real issue. The life of a child is the issue. Responsibility for one's actions is the issue. Being careless of human life is the issue. When debating a Liberal, do not allow them to use their term of "choice" in an attempt to reframe the conversation. They need us to argue on the basis of their terms, for they stand in clear violation of any decent moral principle underpinning a civilized society. Historically, infanticide is a classic hallmark of developing societies on the one hand and of crumbling societies on the other. Not of well functioning and civilized societies. What the Left calls "progress" is nothing but to recklessly race to the edge of total degeneracy. If we cannot defend the rights of the most defenseless in society, why bother to defend the rights of anybody at all?

In Bad Faith

Beyond playing games with the language, Liberals also try to use flawed reasoning and shaky arguments to make the case for abortion. There are several arguments I frequently see; we will discuss each separately. The first argument is that consenting to sex is not in any way consenting to conception. The second is that unborn humans have no rights; in the unborn stage, a human child is nothing but a clump of cells without sentience. Finally, there is even an appeal to the non-aggression principle itself: no human has the right to use another human's body or resources, and therefore the mother carrying the child can decide to kill the child in order to prevent it from using her resources and body for nine months.

Let us begin with the first of these arguments, the false distinction between consenting to sex, and consenting to pregnancy. The argument is that sexual consent implies neither consenting to becoming pregnant, nor consenting to carrying a baby to term. The main flaw in this argument is that you do not have the power to arbitrarily decide what realistic and logical consequences may come from a given act. For example, when I get into my car to drive to class or the market or the gym, I certainly do not *intend* to get into a car accident. I do everything I can to prevent being in one. However, if somebody broadsides me on a rainy Thursday afternoon,

I cannot undo the wreck by sustaining that I only consented to driving to the market, but not to the car wreck. That is not how reality works.

When you chose to partake in an activity, you assume, explicitly or implicitly, all logical and reasonable consequences of the activity in which you partake. Sex is as inextricably linked to pregnancy as driving is to the possibility of a car wreck. The only real way to avoid any potential car accident is to avoid cars all together.

Nobody would consider it remotely reasonable to say something along the lines of, "I'm going to consent to go skiing, but if I get hurt, I do *not* consent to any injuries." It's absolute nonsense. The same rule governs sexual intercourse, as is made clear from another of its possible side-effects: people often contract socially transmitted diseases, viruses, and infections from sex. I doubt most people explicitly "consented" to a case of Herpes or Chlamydia. Of course, people will attempt to treat these diseases with medicine. The Left would give a woman the "right" to do the same thing with her unborn child, essentially identifying human life with disease.

Which brings us to the discussion of whether unborn children have rights or not. Liberals, in their unquenchable lust for control, think they can be the arbiters life and death. But the argument that an unborn child has no rights is, once again, fraught with issues. The common claims are that at conception, and for sometime after, a child is merely a "blob" or "clump" of cells. These cells are nowhere near sentient, and are moreover not viable outside the womb; therefore the fetus cannot have human rights, since it is not yet a person. Well and good. But why do we not apply these principles universally to all humans?

There are many marginal cases of humanity. There are people with severe mental retardation and severe dementia; there are others in vegetative comas. A child even after it is born is utterly helpless and incapable of independent existence. All such cases lack sentience in the full human sense. What do we do with such cases? Do we have the right to violently end their lives with a pair of scissors to the base of the neck? Absolutely not. The case of marginal humans is a quick refutation of the sentience argument. We care for those who have lost or lack sentience, and rightly so.

So far as the question of "viability" goes, it is not any stronger. As humans we all have certain requirements if we are to continue living successfully. The healthiest of us only require around 2,000 calories of food, some water, and a few hours of sleep daily. Others require varying levels of resources to survive, such as a particular diet, medicine, or some sort of therapy. What if we took this idea of viability and expanded it to people that have been involved in traumatic accidents? Imagine paramedics arriving at the scene of a car wreck, and realizing that one of the people needs to be rushed to the hospital via helicopter due to blood loss and an inability to breath due to a partially blocked airway. Do they just shrug and say, "Oh well this person isn't viable any longer, they are no longer human, let them die"? Of course they don't. We recognize that these people are indeed still human beings, despite having particular needs at the moment. These special requirements may extend for sometime, in some cases months or even years; yet we still provide the care they need. Because they are human. And their lives matter.

Not that long ago there were cases of human beings ravaged by Polio who were not "viable" without an Iron Lung. Had we used the same principles and logic that Liberals use for an unborn child, we might have decided that children with Polio were no longer "viable" and left them to die.

The argument that a conceived child is merely a clump of cells (it is wretched to say, I know, but it's *their* argument, not mine), and not yet a human is really identical to claiming that the child is too young to have rights. The issue here is again quite simple. If we are speaking in strict biological terms, even the most complex and advanced living organisms (humans), are still nothing more than a blob of cells that have had sufficient time to go through more iterations of cell division. What about humans who are born without all their limbs due to some cellular mutation? Or those born prematurely? Do we decide it is justifiable to terminate their existences? Absolutely not. Because it's barbaric. But that is precisely what we are dealing with; Liberals are quite literally the barbarians at our gates.

The "blob of cells" argument is simply another age-based argument, much like the heartbeat argument that says there is no life until the first heartbeat. These are again arbitrary measures, unless we have some sort of conclusive evidence that the "spark of life" occurs precisely here, and not at conception. If you really force a Liberal to play out their arguments to the logical conclusion, you'll often find they have decided somewhere along the line what is and is not human.

No wonder, then, that the definition of life is a moving goalpost for Liberals. Many on the Left will claim that a human being becomes a human being after birth. Yet if a unicellular organism, or even the fossilized remains of one, were discovered on some distant planet by NASA, no one would deny that we had found alien life. It would be the story of our lifetimes. Every TV station and magazine would be covering the story of the new single-celled *life form*. Yet when it comes to humans, a "clump of cells" is evidently not to be considered a "life."

Possibly the strongest claim that these infanticidal maniacs like to make is that no other human, not even your own child, has a right to your body or resources. This argument relies of course on the non-aggression principle. The child is viewed as a trespasser, a parasite sucking the mother's vital resources. Thus the mother can terminate that life at any time during pregnancy, on the basis that the child is some sort of foreign invader in a land wherein it does not belong. And I *almost* agree. The argument is *almost* valid—except for the premise that the child is an uninvited guest. Even if the pregnancy was an accident, the mother and father still explicitly engaged in an activity that had the potential to create life. That life was therefore an invited guest. The baby is not a parasite, nor an invader, nor the property of the mother. The baby did not choose to be conceived; *the parents* made that choice, both deliberately and explicitly.

Moreover, if a child does not have any right to the resources of those who brought it into the world, why stop at nine months? What is the difference between this and, say, wanting to kill an eight year old child because it is using too many of its parents' resources? And while we're at it, perhaps tax payers should be allowed to execute welfare abusers, as they are unjustly wasting tax payer resources? When you apply the same logic to any other scenario, it becomes immediately clear how repulsive and absurd it is. (Except maybe the welfare abuser idea. That might work.)

Yet another irony lost on the humorless Left: the Left claims it is a moral imperative that our taxes provide resources for poor people and poor countries. An unborn child does not have a right to the mother's womb, but people, many not even Americans, have a right to our tax dollars? Imagine the rage of your run-of-the-mill Liberal, were anyone to suggest that such people might be "uninvited guests" or "parasites" abusing our resources!

The only place in this entire debate I would concede any ground to the Liberals would be in cases of rape. It is no wonder that the Left uses pregnancies resulting from rape or those that endanger life as a quick go-to argument. Because the rapist severely violated the non-aggression principle against the woman in question, it is at least reasonable to argue that any result of that violation cannot be legitimate. This does not of course account for the fact that the baby had no say in the matter. It does however pose a more complicated issue, as the responsibility for any consequences of this act no longer falls upon consenting adults.

But let us be clear. Rape, child deformity, and health complications for the mother or child, account for less than 10 percent of all abortions. The other 90 percent? Because the child was unwanted or inconvenient.[2]

Regressive Liberals talk an awful lot about choice in regards to abortion, but they somehow fail to mention the endless choices one can make *not* to get pregnant. You have the choice to not have sex, to use protection, and to sterilize yourself. Speaking of which — I personally think that sterilization is a fantastic idea. Anybody who is in support of infanticide should have himself or herself sterilized at once for a simple reason: it is unreasonable to assume that any person, man or woman, who supports the slaughter of the unborn would make a fit parent. People who kill three or more other humans are classified as serial killers, and if a woman has three or more abortions, I fully support labeling her as a serial killer too, and requiring sterilization to end the massacre. It's clear that such women are not responsible enough to stop from getting pregnant — not to speak of caring for another human. Instead of using tax dollars to support abortions, why don't we consider using tax dollars to pay for sterilization? It would solve the issue of abortion before it even begins.

I've often seen Liberals using the pro-life stance of conservatives against them through faulty logic. Liberals will claim that being pro-life

---

2 Lawrence B. Finer, Lori F. Frohwirth, Lindsay A. Dauphinee, Susheela Singh, and Ann M. Moore. "Reasons U.S. Women Have Abortions: Quantitative and Qualitative Perspectives" Perspectives on Sexual and Reproductive Health37, no. 03 (2005): 110-18. doi:10.1363/3711005.

must also mean favoring of mass migration of so-called refugees. But this is absurd. The principle is simple: conservatives do not believe in harming the innocent or initiating aggression upon people. Therefore it is immoral to harm unborn children. A man and a woman choose to bring their child into existence; thus the child becomes the responsibility of the parents. If they did not want that responsibility, they should not have created a child. Tax payers, on the other hand, made no equivalent choice as regards refugees. They are not responsible for them, nor are the refugees entitled to the resources of American or European citizens. No American tax payer ever made the *decision* to cause the never-ending chaos of the planet, nor did any one ever agree to spread his money all over the world to provide financial support for matters that do not concern him.

Liberals also love to claim that being simultaneously pro-life and pro-death-penalty is contradictory. Wrong again. The unborn child is being protected from violence and death. Any person facing capital punishment already initiated extreme violence against another person, thereby forfeiting his right to protection from the same.

The non-aggression principle allows for the defense of the innocent through force if necessary. Capital punishment merely takes the non-aggression principle to its extreme, by stopping further aggression against the innocent. I am in favor of capital punishment in such cases. Indeed, I would even extend capital offenses to include child abuse, animal abuse, rape, illegally entering the US, and the betrayal of citizens on the part of public officials who lead them to war and ruin. However, I favor capital punishment only in the most extreme circumstances, in which there is absolutely no doubt of guilt. For I believe it a far greater injustice to kill an innocent person, than to allow a guilty person to go free. Bringing about unjust violence is quite possibly the single most egregious moral act one can commit. And that is precisely why I believe that no one can reasonably defend abortion as a "choice," as well as why sterilization is the most reasonable solution in such cases.

Not that long ago there was a proposal in Texas to change the disposal practices for aborted children. I read the comments on the news articles, and watched the absolute outrage by the Left on social media. Liberals were almost as irate about this proposal as they were about Trump's election. They labeled the Texas proposal as "hate-filled," "misogynistic," and "sexist."

What was this new law that so powerfully called down the Liberal ire? It stipulated that instead of disposing of the children's bodies in a bin alongside other "medical waste," the remains were to be buried or cremated, as at a proper funeral.[3] The Left went off the deep end, claiming this law was being used to financially burden those seeking to commit infanticide.

I thought about the comments I was reading, the total lack of empathy they revealed for children that just had their heads separated from their bodies. I thought about all the animals I had rescued, cared for, and eventually had to bury when they passed away. I buried every single one, and I did so properly. I've even buried dead animals I found near my house that had been hit by cars. I thought about that gut-wrenching feeling as I read through the reactions to the new Texas law. No compassion to be found in these hearts of darkness. They saw this Texas law as nothing but a massive infringement upon "human rights." They were entirely outraged that they might be required to provide a burial for a human that once lived inside of them.

And it was at that moment I realized Liberals would never be like us. They are not of the same lineage. They are demented, they are sick, they are insidious in everything they believe. They are mentally ill beyond any doubt.

These truths are slowly becoming axiomatic to me.

Manifestations of the Liberal illness: Infanticide

When the issue of infanticide comes up, I often hear Liberals howling that abortion "is Constitutional." That is ironic. Liberals don't seem to care a whole lot for the Constitution when it comes to freedom of speech

3 Jon Herskovitz. "Texas passes a law requiring abortion providers to bury or cremate fetal tissue" Business Insider. June 07, 2017. http://www.businessinsider.com/texas-passes-a-law-requiring-abortion-providers-to-bury-or-cremate-fetal-tissue-2017-6. [http://archive.li/BOiu0]

or arms. They rarely appeal to the Constitution's provisions on limited government. They rarely appeal to the Constitution at all, for that matter. Which is very telling; the only sort of moral standards the Janus-faced Left believe in, are double standards.

When one brings the facts against them — reminding them, for instance, that abortions due to rape or health concerns account for less than 10 percent of the million children murdered annually — Liberals often become furious. Heaven forbid they might reconsider their view. Liberals pretend it is entirely normal to kill your own child; anybody who disagrees with this idea is misogynistic.

They manipulate our language, calling a baby a fetus, murder a medical procedure, and the decision to commit murder a choice. Liberals play the victim card *ad nauseam* here, claiming that their "rights" will be trampled on if abortion is even so much as curtailed. They mouth the idea that pro-life supporters are somehow bigoted, close-minded, Hell-bent on control, when in truth *they* desperately want the "right" to control the life and death of another human being. A sense of innate moral superiority abounds here as well; the Left really believes that it is moral to agitate for the freedom to murder innocent children. That speaks for itself.

All symptoms can be seen from Cluster I. In Cluster II symptom 6, 7, and 8, are apparent.

Cluster I

1. Deceitfulness, indicated by repeated lying, grand exaggerations, or omission of contrary information, with the purpose to advance their chosen narrative and discrediting others.

2. Irritability or aggressiveness towards anybody that questions or opposes their views. Coupled with the inability to recognize they own hypocrisy, double standards, and doublethink.

3. Inability to adjust views when presented with information contrary to their own beliefs.

4. Frequent projections of their own traits onto others.

5. Difficulty in dealing with a loss of control or power, or a strong desire for control and power.

Cluster II

6. Appeals to altered and redefined definitions of words, or relies on fictitious terms for argumentation.

7. Consistent feelings of having been victimized or wronged, without any actual harm being done. Seen also as playing the victim after attacking others.

8. Intense sense of righteousness or moral superiority.

9. The inability to recognize the negative outcomes of their own actions. Often placing the blame on others.

10. Intense guilt or self-hatred, often manifests as hatred towards one's larger group identity.

V

Highway Robbery

If I came to your house tonight with a group of my heavily armed friends and demanded that you give me a portion of your weekly paycheck, as well as an annual payment based on how much your house is worth, what might you call that? And supposing you did not capitulate, and I come back with my buddies, to present you with a few options (because, as mentioned previously, I'm a sporting chap): you can either pay up, you can come with me to prison (while I sell your house and belongings to raise the money you owe me), or you can try to resist (in which case we shoot you and take your stuff anyway) — well? Is there any other name for this than theft and extortion?

Now suppose me and my friends all get together and "vote" to take your money, and we claim that because we are the majority, you must obey. Does might suddenly make right here? Of course not. It would still be theft, and still be wrong. Or if I and my friends created some institution, some agency, which says you must give us your money — does this magically justify everything?

Yet that is almost exactly how United States taxation operates. Any involuntary taxation immediately violates the non-aggression principle. It is nothing more than extortion, and the IRS is nothing more than a group of State-sponsored thugs. The constant demands for more social programs, bigger government, and higher taxes, forms a perennial platform for the Left. Liberals are constantly in favor of exerting their will upon the rest of us by means of the State, and having violence brought upon us if we do not concede.

Taxes weren't always what they are today. Until 1913, we were burdened neither with the Revenue Act nor the Federal Reserve. Both were introduced by *Democrat* Congressmen, and signed into law by *Democrat* Woodrow Wilson.

Let us make clear what this means. For over 130 years after the birth of our nation, there was *no* permanent federal income tax. For over 130 years in our nation, most tax dollars collected came from excise taxes and tariffs. As they should be, and as our Constitution intended. Before the federal income tax was instituted in 1913, America still had roads, railroads, subways, ports, bridges, schools, colleges, and the armed forces. Despite the commonplace argument to the contrary, none of these things depends on income tax, and income tax was never meant to pay for them, as more than a century of our history demonstrates. Once the federal income tax was instituted, the government was able to spend our money with reckless abandon.[1]

The income tax and Federal Reserve were the first major attacks on US citizens' money. The next came with the abandonment of a gold-backed currency, and the switch to a worthless fiat currency — another affront brought against the American people by Franklin Roosevelt.

With the gold standard gone, the Federal Reserve operational, and the federal income tax in place, there was no longer any limit to the expansion of the federal government. It could print money as it pleased, and raise taxes to fund any effort, no matter how insane or unpopular. Not only could money be printed at will, but the money Americans earned and saved could also be devalued at will, as the only thing that ever makes it impossible to print money until it's totally worthless is some sort of security-backed standard — gold or silver.

The stories of post-World War I Germans in the Weimar Republic, who had to haul a wheelbarrow full of money to buy a cup of coffee, were a direct result of unchecked currency printing, the direct result of the exact system we employ today. And not only in the United States, but the world

1 Amy Fontinelle. "The History Of Taxes In The U.S" Investopedia. November 06, 2017. http://www.investopedia.com/articles/tax/10/history-taxes.asp. [http://archive.li/WYfNe]

over. No country uses a security-backed currency anymore. Furthermore, nearly every nation on Earth is overseen by a United Nations contrivance, the International Monetary Fund (IMF). The United Nations and the IMF are two massive entities paid for by the tax payers and filled with non-elected bureaucrats who are empowered to control our currency.[2]

An ounce of gold 200 years ago would buy about the same amount of goods as an ounce of gold does today. What you can get for around $1,300 today, you could have gotten for $20 then. Interestingly enough, the same trend can be seen the world over. Despite the massive amount of inflation that has occurred, the US Dollar stays relatively steady against most other currencies throughout the world. If the US and England, for example, were not connected through an international body that most people are not even aware of, would it make any sense that after all these years, our Dollar and their Pound have stayed so similar in value? If any single nation had kept a security-backed currency, it would today have easily the most valuable currency in the world. And if everybody had security-backed currency, the currency markets would not be so easily manipulated to benefit a few, while the rest of us see our money devalued at 3 percent a year, every year, forever.[3]

If you pick any year in United States history prior to the Revenue Act and the Federal Reserve Act, you'll find that government spending was less than 3 percent of total Gross Domestic Product (GDP). The only exception was a spike during the Civil War years, when spending rose to 13 percent GDP before dropping to 3 percent and below for the next forty years. Since the government was given the power to tax its citizens and to print money arbitrarily, spending has continually risen to the point that Federal spending alone makes up consistently over 20 percent of GDP. There is no longer any limiting factor to government growth.[4]

---

2 "About the IMF" International Monetary Fund. Accessed July 11, 2017. https://www.imf.org/external/about.htm. [http://archive.li/dzkcM]

3 "Why Did the U.S. Abandon the Gold Standard" Mental Floss. October 05, 2012. http://mentalfloss.com/article/12715/why-did-us-abandon-gold-standard. [http://archive.li/0QaLE]

4 "Government Spending Chart: United States 1800-2017—Federal State Local Data." US Government Spending. http://www.usgovernmentspending.com/spending_chart_1800_2017USp_18s2li011mcn_F0f. [http://archive.li/hPt06]

Not only is the income tax and lack of security backed currency a recipe for unchecked governmental growth, these innovations also fundamentally changed the relation of powers between the government and its people. The government, in America, was intended to serve the people, not the other way around.

Feudalist USA

The United States was created in part so that the King could not take our land or merely rent us our own land back to us through a feudalist system. Our great Revolution was also a rebellion against the burdens of unnecessary taxation and its stifling effect on freedom. We now live in a state of both unnecessary taxation and rampant feudalism.

If you live in a state that has property taxes, I have some bad news; you're living under feudalism. Thanks to property taxes, Americans never own their own homes. It does not matter if your house has been paid off for five generations. It does not matter if you saved the money for each and every piece of lumber and hammered each nail into it yourself. If you stop paying property taxes, the State can legally seize your land. If you refuse to leave, they will send men with guns to remove you. And if you resist them, you will be shot dead or thrown into prison, while the State sells your land and house to the highest bidder. In what diseased imagination does this system represent freedom or ownership? Under no circumstance, by no measure, no vote, no emergency, should it be even remotely comprehensible in America to force people to pay rent on their own land and homes. There is no single moral or logical claim that can be made in validation of property taxes. It means nothing other than charging indefinite rent on a people that is supposed to be free of feudalism.[5] In the "land of the free," we have been reduced to serfs in our own homeland.

For example, the US has an average property tax rate of 1.21 percent; on a home valued at $200,000, the property taxes are about $2,400 a year.

---

5 John Kiernan. "2017's Property Taxes by State" WalletHub. May 1, 2017. https://wallethub.com/edu/states-with-the-highest-and-lowest-property-taxes/11585/. [http://archive.li/1oG7x]

The average for all of America is $3,300 each year in property taxes.[6] Using the average rate on a $200,000 house, if you had a thirty-year mortgage, at the end of thirty years you will have paid $72,000 in taxes, more than enough money to pay off the house in around half the time on a thirty year loan, if you were applying the tax payments to principal. It is bad enough that we carry this burden to begin with, but it never ends. Long after the house is paid off, long after the house has been passed on to the kids, the taxes remain. The house could be in the family for generations: fail to pay the rent, and you're out on the street. No different than if you were renting a studio in Brooklyn and didn't pay up to the local slum lord.

I do not believe in property taxes whatsoever. Property taxes violate several tenants of our liberty, as well as the founding principles of this nation; they are forced upon us, and *en*forced through aggression. Our fellow citizens and the government at any level should have absolutely zero claim to another person's property. Anything less than full ownership is unacceptable. But the sad truth of the matter is that, as Americans, we are never allowed to own property. The idea of private property ownership is clearly nothing but a fiction in our nation.

Money is Time

Suppose somebody earns $100,000 per year. How would their actual taxes look? Using average rates, a person making $100,000 per year will pay $18,000 in Federal taxes, $7,600 in Social Security and Medicare, $3,000 in state taxes, and $500 to local city taxes. Add in the $3,300 average rate for property taxes, and we are sitting at $32,000 and change. 32 percent of income gone — before a single item is purchased.

The combined federal and state taxes on gasoline are about $.46 per gallon. Suppose somebody drives 2,000 miles a month, and that they average 23 miles to the gallon. That gives us eighty-seven gallons used a month, for a total of $40 in taxes per month, or about $480 annually. If

---

6 Constance Brinkley-Badgett. "Comparing average property taxes for all 50 states and D.C." USA Today. www.usatoday.com/story/money/personalfinance/2017/04/16/comparing-average-property-taxes-all-50-states-and-dc/100314754/.

another $2,000 is spent per month on taxable goods, taxed at a rate of 7 percent, that is another $1,680 annually.[7]

$34,360 each year paid in taxes on earnings of $100,000.

When we consider all of the hidden taxes that are included in the price of non-taxable items like food, the effective rate grows even more, as the same dollar is taxed many times, bringing the effective tax rate higher still. The average tax rate for all Americas is over 30 percent, and the average rate for most of Europe is even higher. The majority of the taxes being paid are not excise taxes, they are forced taxes. Which represents nearly one third of the hours we spend at work. From January to mid-April, we go to work, just to ensure the government can recklessly waste our money and time, with total abandon and zero accountability.

Ironically enough, tax day also happens to be in mid-April. That's a sick joke if I've ever heard one. We never get this time back. Ever.

> "One minute of time worth more than one ounce of gold."
>
> — Fortune Cookie

The majority of the taxes we pay as Americans are not voluntary. They were imposed on us. When people, especially Liberals, make the argument that taxation is constitutional, they are right, in the sense that the federal government always reserved the right to raise money through taxation. Which it did, prior to 1913, through voluntary excises taxes, tariffs, and bonds. In none of these cases were taxed extorted from people through the Internal Revenue Service.

Before the Revenue Act was passed, the Constitution had to be amended. When the Revenue Act was passed in 1913, it originally only applied to those making $20,000 or above, and ranged from 1 percent to 7 percent. Less than 100 years later, the lowest federal income tax is a rate of 10 percent, reaching up to 40 percent.[8] What was first paid by only a

---

7 "Free Income Tax Calculator — Estimate Your Taxes" Smart Asset. Accessed July 11, 2017. https://smartasset.com/taxes/income-taxes.

8 "2016 Federal Tax Rates, Personal Exemptions, and Standard Deductions" US Tax Center. Accessed July 11, 2017. https://www.irs.com/articles/2016-federal-tax-rates-personal-exemptions-and-standard-deductions.

small number of people, at a very low rate, has turned into an oppressive burden carried by us all.

We no longer own the rights to our own labor. Lockean natural law posits that a person's body is something he owns; therefore anything he produces as a result of his labor is his property. Involuntary taxation in turn means we do not own our own labor, nor our own persons. Meaning we are slaves. As soon as we begin to produce anything with our time, we must immediately sacrifice a portion to the government. And why? So that the government may give billions of dollars to foreign governments, billions to migrants, both legal and illegal, and billions to waste.

I would really love to know how the members of Congress think that giving over three billion dollars a year to Israel alone for Israeli defense is at all acceptable. That isn't *their* money. It's *ours*. How many hours of work does that $3 billion represent each year for Americans?[9] That's time we could have been with our families and friends, enjoying a day off, or a hobby. Why has it been decided for us that our time as Americans is not worth as much as the dozens of nations that receive our tax dollars? Why do we spend $1 billion dollars a year on Egypt? $320 million on Mexico?[10] That is *our* money. All to be given away to people that could not care any less about us. We are talking about theft on a scale the world has never known.

Property taxes have been passed through local elections for things like school board levies and police levies. The consequence? Police departments across the nation have become militarized, utilizing the latest cars, trucks, motorcycles, helicopters, weapons, and whatever else tax money can buy. I really doubt the safety of my neighborhood would be hurt if the local police helicopter program was scaled down a bit.

Police, fire, and schools no longer need to operate with a bottom line; they just continue to pass levies which permit them to expand indefinitely,

---

9 Nick Thompson. "U.S. foreign military aid: 75 percent goes to two countries" CNN. November 11, 2015. http://www.cnn.com/2015/11/11/politics/us-foreign-aid-report/. [http://archive.is/hTVSM]

10 Donovan Slack. "U.S. provides aid worth $320 million a year to Mexico; experts say yanking it could hurt" USA Today. January 26, 2017. https://www.usatoday.com/story/news/politics/2017/01/26/us-aid-320-million-mexico-wall-trump-specialists-backfire/97103024/. [http://archive.li/KW7u3]

all at the tax payers' expense. People have a right to vote and make decisions, but I reject the idea that our fellow citizens should be able to have their will forced upon others. Even supposing a majority vote I do not view this type of mob rule as legitimate. If they want to vote for higher taxes on *themselves alone*, well and good. Police, fire, schools, and road repair, could all be funded with excise taxes or selling bonds.

When local municipal institutions decide they need more money, they continually place their desired levy on local election ballots until eventually it passes. When one expires, another is right back on the ballot again. With no end in sight. Persistent mob rule is not the government style to which free folk should be subjected.

Can we not simply own our property, without anybody taking from us? Is that really such a wild idea?

The action of imposing or raising taxes is inherently identical to the threat of force. Suppose there is a local levy on the ballot, and Person A is in favor of the levy; suppose he votes in support of the increased or new tax. Person A has already decided he is willing to voluntarily pay the tax. Now suppose Person B does not want to pay the tax or knows the increase in property taxes will cause him financial hardship. He votes against the levy. If Person A is a member of the majority and Person B a member of the minority, then Group A is forcing its will on Group B. If the members of Group B do not want to pay or cannot pay the new tax, the government will force them, under the threat of incarceration or violence, to pay or to be put in prison. "Owing" money to the government is one of only two instances in America for which a man can be jailed for debt.

We have been indoctrinated into believing that democracy is the "will of the people," and further brainwashed to think that this "will of the people" is somehow just or legitimate or moral. There is no moral or logical principle that can justify forcing people to give up the money they have earned by trading their time and labor, merely so as to satisfy the majority. People can argue it is for the common good all they want: it is still illegitimate.

Initializing force for taxation is morally bankrupt and logically invalid. The only possible argument one can make is to appeal to the "common good" or the collective, as the Left has always done. It is exactly what the Bolsheviks did (Bolshevik derives from the Russian word meaning "of the majority"), and it is the same appeal Liberals give today for increasing the amount of taxes they collect. The Left always appeals one way or another to a collective totalitarianism, hiding the truth under pretty names. Not too long ago in human history, using mob rule and the authority of the State to impose one's will on others in order to gain access to their resources was seen as an act of war. Now we call it "democracy."

If people want to volunteer more money for a cause, I welcome them to do so. But they have no grounds to say what somebody else's "fair share" might be.

Every government agency is totally exempt from any sort of bottom line or budget. Enormous amounts of money are wasted, without anybody ever being held accountable for the costs, or even asked to justify their existence as an entity. We the people fund the defense of dozens of other nations, many of which belong to the First World and enjoy higher standards of living than the citizens of the United States. Our total amount of foreign and economic aid should be zero — no more and no less.

Enemies Foreign — but Mostly Domestic

The Marshall Plan, created in 1948 to help rebuild Europe after the second World War, was meant to end in 1953. Yet here we are in 2017, annually doling out more money than it took to help rebuilt Europe after the most devastating event in human history.

Foreign political lobbying is so prevalent that the Foreign Agents Registration Act requires foreign agents to register with the government and to disclose their intent. There are over 1,700 lobbyists, representing over 100 nations, who give US politicians money — and who knows what else.[11] [12] I find it hard to believe, impossible actually, that even one of those nations has the best interest of the American people at the forefront of their agenda. I sincerely doubt that foreign nations and entities are

11 "Revealing money's influence on politics" MapLight. Accessed July 11, 2017. http://maplight.org/us-congress/interest/J5100/view/all.

12 Alex Knott. "Foreign Lobbying Database Up and Running" The New York Times. May 30, 2007. http://www.nytimes.com/cq/2007/05/30/cq_2811.html. [http://archive.li/FuNJf]

interested in bribing our politicians to further benefit us, the American people. How this is legal in any way, how it is not considered a blatant act of treason, is far beyond me.

We have unsafe bridges, Third World airports, and crumbling roads; the programs for our veterans, disabled, mentally retarded, homeless, and elderly all lack funding; there are serious mental health and addiction issues which go unaddressed — all while we burn trillions in the Middle East and spread our tax dollars across the globe. Beyond atrocious.

Small business owners get possibly the worst abuse of all when it comes to taxation. States that have some type of gross receipt tax require businesses to pay taxes on their sales, whether or not there was any profit.[13] Not only is sales tax collected from the buyer, but the business must also pay taxes on those sales separately from sales tax — and again, regardless of profit. The owner of a business might be working for years until a profit is made, before he can pay himself, and all the while he must still pay the state. This practice is one of the most egregious in all of our sordid taxation schemes. The government is punishing people for trying their hand at starting a new business, for employing others, for trying to make their community a little nicer, for having the audacity to work for themselves. The government taxes employees on their earnings, the business owner pays an additional payroll tax, and on top of that, a gross sales tax, even when no profit is made, even during times of losses. Call it what you will: this is theft by any reasonable definition.

You should not have to constantly vote to keep your rights and property from being robbed. Such a thing should never even be up for a vote. But democracy is what happens when 51 percent of the people decide to eat the other 49 percent. With more and more people each year being imported into the country and destined, most of them, to go on the dole, it is no mystery that the politicians who promise more handouts are going to benefit. This is the slow path to communism. Instead of a violent revolution, you just keep importing those who will vote for the State, and keep giving more and more people welfare benefits, while the workers have to keep slaving away to provide for them. People arrive en masse to our nation, individuals with no connection to the people or heritage of

13 Jean Murray. "What is a State Gross Receipts Tax" The Balance. December 22, 2016. https://www.thebalance.com/what-is-a-state-gross-receipts-tax-398284.

those who built this nation. Over 50 percent of them are put immediately on welfare; they pay no taxes, contribute nothing to our society, raise the crime rate — and are given the same vote as the rest of us. This is a hostile invasion, a coup, wearing the mask of democracy. This is not the democracy of a serious nation; it is the debased democracy of a banana republic.

The American Left has always operated by the same principles. It values mob rule alone, and the collective. The most recent manifestation of the Left's philosophy is in wealth redistribution via income taxes and payroll taxes that favor the collective, once again, at the tremendous expense of individual freedoms. Business owners, even of small and medium-sized businesses, are being told by no less than the last president of the United States that they did not build their business themselves, so that taking more and more from them is justified.

This country was founded on the principle that the individual is the master of his own destiny, that the individual would not later be beholden to feudalism or to some king. Yet Americans pay more in taxes now than the Revolutionaries paid who fought King George. Once upon a time in America, we went to war over far less than what is happening to us today.

Many people still have this idea that we must continue down this dark path, or else the government and all worthy services will collapse. This is simply untrue, neither historically nor financially. Services like Medicare, providing assistance to the disabled, infrastructure, schools, military, roads, and certain other helpful welfare services can all be paid for by excise taxes, tariffs, and corporate taxes. The programs would all need to be redesigned, but it is entirely feasible. To begin with, if we cut all foreign aid, all foreign military aid, and any form of welfare to immigrants that have not been in the country at least thirty years, that would save enough money alone that we could reduce the federal income tax dramatically, effective immediately. About 90 percent of Middle Eastern migrants are on welfare — so let's stop bringing them here and forcing Americans to pay for their housing, schooling, healthcare, and food.[14]

---

14 Caroline May. "More Than 90 Percent of Middle Eastern Refugees on Food Stamps" Breitbart. September 10, 2015. http://www.breitbart.com/big-government/2015/09/10/more-than-90-percent-of-middle-eastern-refugees-on-food-stamps/. [http://archive.li/3csoi]

With the money we would save through just a few simple changes, we could probably fund that free universal healthcare that the Liberals so desperately want. I would even be in favor, so long as it was done through voluntary taxation. I would be happy knowing that the money I pay in sales taxes is going to somebody who is in need. I would be more than happy. In fact, I would gladly pay a higher sales tax, within reason, if that money went to help my fellow *Americans.* I am not willing however, to fund the entire planet through forced taxation. I am not willing to accept the fact that Americans should work the first three months of the year so that foreigners may extort their labor.

The lying press loves to espouse the idea that foreign aid or welfare to migrants only accounts for a small percent of the total budget. They use this tactic to minimize the burden we must carry as Americans for the rest of the world, to which we owe nothing. And they are right: if you look at each individual line item in the budget, it *does* only account for a small percentage. But something funny happens when you start adding up all the frivolous spending and waste that the Left doesn't bother to mention. It adds up. Tremendously.

With over 50 percent of immigrant households on welfare, and over a million new migrations coming to the US annually, we are quite literally operating a global soup kitchen.[15] [16] That amounts to tens of millions of people we are paying to come here, to do nothing but steal our money. Between the welfare of foreign nations, military aid and interventions, endless wars, domestic welfare to migrants, and burdensome government institutions that provide zero benefit to the American people, we could easily cut federal spending nearly in half. Anybody who says otherwise has not looked at the data, or is simply lying to advance an agenda that does not have the interest of the American people in mind.

---

15 Steven A. Camarota. "Welfare Use by Immigrant and Native Households" Center for Immigration Studies. September 10, 2015. http://cis.org/Welfare-Use-Immigrant-Native-Households. [http://archive.li/5uouk]

16 Jie Zong, Jeanne Batalova, and Jeffrey Hallock. "Frequently Requested Statistics on Immigrants and Immigration in the United States" Migrationpolicy.org. February 8, 2018. http://www.migrationpolicy.org/article/frequently-requested-statistics-immigrants-and-immigration-united-states. [http://archive.li/c6Hy7]

There are endless cuts that could be made tonight, and that would provide Americans, the people paying these outrageous bills, a better quality of life tomorrow.

In 2015, income taxes paid by individuals accounted for 47 percent of federal revenue or $1.48 trillion dollars.[17] The Cato Institute conducted a budget analysis and found that $100 billion a year is given to corporate welfare, mostly in subsidies and grants.[18] The endless War on Terror alone costs on average another $100 billion per year as of late.[19] This number is historically low; a study by Brown University states that since September 2001, the US has spent over $5 trillion on wars, over $23,000 for each American taxpayer.[20] A study done by the National Academies of Science, Engineering and Medicine, found that mass migration to the United States, both legal and illegal, costs over $300 billion per year.[21] Over $200 billion per year is paid on debt which we never should have had to begin with. Each year, we give away over $40 billion in direct aid to foreign nations.[22]

---

17 "Federal Revenue: Where Does the Money Come From" National Priorities Project. Accessed July 11, 2017. https://www.nationalpriorities.org/budget-basics/federal-budget-101/revenues/. [http://archive.li/7Oji3]

18 Scott Lincicome. "Calculating the Real Cost of Corporate Welfare" The Federalist. September 30, 2013. http://thefederalist.com/2013/09/30/calculating-the-real-cost-of-corporate-welfare/. [http://archive.li/tAIsf]

19 Kimberly Amadeo. "War on Terror Facts, Costs, and Timeline" The Balance. January 27, 2017. https://www.thebalance.com/war-on-terror-facts-costs-timeline-3306300.

20 Gillian Kiley. "U.S. spending on post-9/11 wars to reach $5.6 trillion by 2018." News from Brown. November 07, 2017. news.brown.edu/articles/2017/11/costssummary. [http://archive.is/BjyGP]

21 Stephen Dinan. "Mass immigration costs government $296 billion a year, depresses wages" The Washington Times. September 21, 2016. http://www.washingtontimes.com/news/2016/sep/21/mass-immigration-costs-govt-296-billion-year-natio/. [http://archive.li/C3Czs]

22 Max Bearak and Lazaro Gamio. "Everything you ever wanted to know about the U.S. foreign assistance budget" The Washington Post. October 18, 2016. https://www.washingtonpost.com/graphics/world/which-countries-get-the-most-foreign-aid/. [http://archive.li/jw41Q]

We contribute another $10 billion to that totally useless group of scoundrels known as the United Nations.[23]

If we ended corporate welfare, ended the endless War on Terror, ended immigration entirely, and stopped giving money to foreign nations, we would save $550 billion dollars a year. That is a little over one third of the taxes collected from individual workers per year. If there were no national debt to pay interest on, then over half of taxes paid by individual workers could be cut. At $116 billion per year, illegal immigration costs each American household an average of $1,000 per year.[24] Simply ending *all* migration, legal and illegal, would save each American household around $3,000 per year.

Could you and your family use another $3,000 each year?

We spend $600 billion a year on military spending. We have hundreds of military installations around the world, and there is no real way to know how much of that $600 billion benefits United States citizens who foot the bill.[25] I would guess that not a lot of it does. US taxpayers are forced to fund the security of other people's nations and borders, yet our government has utterly refused to secure our own. Our tax dollars went to help fund the construction of Israel's and Mexico's walls and security fences, yet everybody loses their mind when we want to build one ourselves!

NPR ran a propaganda piece about foreign aid titled, "Guess How Much Of Uncle Sam's Money Goes To Foreign Aid. Guess Again!"[26] In the article they not only called Americans ignorant for overestimating the

---

23 Brett D. Schaefer. "America, we pay way too much for the United Nations" Fox News. June 16, 2015. http://www.foxnews.com/opinion/2015/06/16/america-pay-way-too-much-for-united-nations.html. [http://archive.li/3USuX]

24 Matt O'Brien and Spencer Raley. "The Fiscal Burden of Illegal Immigration on United States Taxpayers " Federation For American Immigration Reform. September 27, 2017. http://www.fairus.org/publications/the-fiscal-burden-of-illegal-immigration-on-united-states-taxpayers. [http://archive.li/dzxy2]

25 "Federal Spending: Where Does the Money Go" National Priorities Project. Accessed July 11, 2017. https://www.nationalpriorities.org/budget-basics/federal-budget-101/spending/. [http://archive.li/BRtTl]

26 Poncie Rutsch. "Guess How Much Of Uncle Sam's Money Goes To Foreign Aid. Guess Again" NPR. February 10, 2015. http://www.npr.org/sections/goatsandsoda/2015/02/10/383875581/guess-how-much-of-uncle-sams-money-goes-to-foreign-aid-guess-again. [http://archive.li/ml2wz]

money we spend on foreign aid, but they then went on say that, considering how much money the United States has, we are not very generous at all. Considering that the people have not yet tarred and feathered every public official for subjecting us to such oppressive taxation, I would like to think we are an incredibly generous — and *forgiving* — lot.

If Liberals want to feed hungry people, that's noble enough, but I suggest they do it in the same way that Catholics and Christians do it all over the US and the world: namely, by collecting donations, opening soup kitchens and food pantries, and doing all of this without taking money they did not earn. Study after study shows religious conservatives are the most generous group of people when it comes to charitable giving. They help those in need, and they do it the proper way.[27]

Liberals themselves never help anybody. The create laws and vote for taxes that force one group to help another group. That is called *extortion*. The pathological altruism exhibited by Liberals is little more than a way flattering themselves and feigning moral superiority.

The current policy of taxing the hardest-working to subsidize the people who contribute the least to society is not sustainable. It is morally corrupt, and devoid of any reason. Taking money from responsible working families and giving it to corporations, foreign nations, migrants, and those who refuse to work, does nothing but create slaves out of honest, hard-working people. It creates a bizarre upside-down clown-democracy, in which those that contribute the least, can rule over those who contribute the most.

Welfare use in America has continued to increase since the War on Poverty started.[28] In my research for this book I came across a political idea originating with Liberal professors at Columbia, called the Cloward-Piven Strategy. The Cloward-Piven Strategy is simply socialism by other means. The idea is to end poverty by putting so many people on welfare that the welfare system becomes unsustainable and collapses. Then you take the income from the working class, and give it to those on welfare through a

---

27 "Who Gives Most to Charity" The Philanthropy Roundtable. Accessed August 02, 2017. http://www.philanthropyroundtable.org/almanac/who_gives_most_to_charity/. [http://archive.li/SfkZ5]

28 Rachel Sheffield and Robert Rector. "The War on Poverty After 50 Years" The Heritage Foundation. September 15, 2014. http://www.heritage.org/poverty-and-inequality/report/the-war-poverty-after-50-years. [http://archive.li/cqDif]

guaranteed basic income. Importing millions of migrants that are mostly on welfare, creating policies that send more jobs overseas, and promoting the destruction of the family unit, thus causing more mothers and children to be on welfare, all seem to be playing into this strategy. I wonder if Liberals who are in favor of a socialist "utopia," ever stop to consider what happens when those being taxed and those producing goods decide it's no longer worth it? I wonder if they ever stop to look at how every socialist wealth-redistribution program ever instated has worked out? Do they bother to see how the Venezuela bread lines are doing? Do they not care that the people of Venezuela have been eating their own pets and zoo animals to keep from starving, thanks to socialist ideals?[29] I wonder — have they stopped to consider what will happen when Atlas finally shrugs?

Socialism and its many offshoots have only ever appealed to the dredges of society. It is a scheme for losers and is absolutely anti-Western in nature. It is designed to pull the best members of a society down to the same trash heap as the ones who refuse to contribute.

If people still desire to help other nations, I think that's laudable and decent of them. I would suggest they start non-profits, raise money for their cause, and donate the money to those nations. But to create a tax and federal spending scheme that forces Americans to fund war efforts and infrastructure on the other side of the world, when we could desperately use that money back home, is unreasonable and unjust. Through buying our corrupt Congress members like the whores they are, the rest of the world has effectively enslaved the American people. I believe it's high time to break the chains.

Those who have enslaved us, stripped our rights to ownership, and taken control over our nation's money supply, could have never done so in one generation. It would have caused a revolution like no land has ever seen. Instead, they added a little bit each year, until today, we suddenly discover that we have no rights to our own property or even to our own labor. The first step was a low tax on the wealthiest, then the establishment of a central bank, then our removal from a gold standard. Then increased taxes on income, property, and goods. They carried all this out, even while assuring us that it has to be this way, that it is "our fair share."

---

29 "Thieves stealing Venezuela zoo animals to eat them, say police." The Guardian. August 16, 2017. www.theguardian.com/world/2017/aug/17/thieves-stealing-venezuela-zoo-animals-to-eat-them-say-police. [http://archive.li/D0Y70]

We have been seized by a small international clique that auctions off our labor to the highest bidder. Enough is enough.

10 Planks of Communism

We have fallen far from our original freedom. Compare Marx's vision of a Communist State in 1848 to modern day America.

In *The Communist Manifesto*, Marx outlines a list of principles that when enacted, will work together towards the creation of a socialist state by stripping away personal ownership of property, rights to ownership, and liberty. Going through the list written in 1848 and comparing Marxist policies to in the policies of contemporary America, it becomes rather clear that our once free nation has been seized by hostile and destructive forces. [30]

1. Abolition of property in land and application of all rents of land to public purposes.

We have no private ownership of land in the United States. Because of property taxes, which must be paid indefinitely, we are only a few months away from being forcibly removed from our homes, despite "owning" them. It does not matter if the home and land has been in the family for generations. If you do not pay property taxes, you're on the street.

What becomes of the property taxes we pay? They go to "public purposes," of course.

2. A heavy progressive or graduated income tax.

When the Federal Income Tax was imposed permanently in 1913, the taxes originally only applied to the highest earners, those with incomes equivalent of around $400,000 dollars today, adjusted for inflation. The tax rates were comparatively low, just 1 percent to 7 percent. Today, we have heavy graduated income taxes, where even small and moderate earners have their income confiscated before they so much as see it. The Marxists slogan, "From each according to his ability, to each according to his needs" is implicit throughout our subverted government.

30 Karl Marx and Friedrich Engels. The Communist manifesto. New York: Monthly Review Press, 1998.

3. Abolition of all rights of inheritance.

A further attack on private property. Every dollar in an inheritance has already been taxed by the government, yet when anything is left to the next generation, the money or property involved is heavily taxed a second time. So much so that in many cases that the taxes force the inheritor to liquidate any assets in order to pay the impost.

4. Confiscation of the property of all emigrants and rebels.

Consider tax liens, civil forfeiture, confiscation of property, RICO laws — all of which have been wrongfully applied to law-abiding citizens.

5. Centralization of credit in the hands of the state, by means of a national bank with State capital and an exclusive monopoly.

The Federal Reserve Act of 1913. There are many books on the subject, from Ron Paul's *End The Fed* to G. Edward Griffin's *The Creature from Jekyll Island: A Second Look at the Federal Reserve*. Creating a central bank is not a free-market tenet, by any means, but a method to imbue the state with power. Paul Moritz Warburg was an early advocate for creating the current Federal Reserve. Warburg wrote many papers lobbying for a central bank, and also played a major role in drafting the Federal Reserve legislation. Warburg was born into a wealthy Jewish banking family which migrated to the US; upon his arrival, before he was even a US citizen, he began to work towards creating the Federal Reserve, and later served on the Federal Reserve Board.[31]

6. Centralization of the means of communication and transportation in the hands of the state.

This one is a bit of a rabbit hole. There are a handful of companies, five or six, that own a tremendous share of the media, from TV, to movies, radio stations, magazines, newspapers, and news channels. It's estimated that 90 percent of all media is owned by the same handful of corporations — hundreds of television stations, thousands of newspapers and magazines, movie studios, thousands of radio stations, even video game

31 Roger Lowenstein. "The Jewish Story Behind the U.S. Federal Reserve Bank." The Forward. November 29, 2015. https://forward.com/culture/325447/the-man-behind-the-fed/. [http://archive.is/guOdc]

studios.[32] Nearly everything Americans and Europeans read or watch passes through the filter of a few companies that bend the narrative in any way they deem appropriate.

That itself is of course bad enough. What we learned this past election cycle causes this story to take a far grimmer turn. There was an unbelievable level of collusion between the Democratic Party and media outlets. Debate questions were exchanged before debates took place; emails between major news networks like CNN and the Democratic National Committee reveal debates on which questions were to be asked of DNC opponents.[33] Many of the owners and high ranking members of the media cartel have been exposed as huge donors to the DNC, which itself is not shocking.[34] Everyone has political affiliations and people make donations frequently. The issue arises when that bias then seeps into the sources from which Americans get their information. It is inconceivable that a news organization could provide an objective view of any issue, when it has become so clear the media is little more than the propaganda division of the international Left. When we see reporters asking permission from politicians to run certain stories, we have a bit of conflict of interest — assuming we are interested in the truth, not what they want us to believe.

In regards to travel and regulation — consider the Interstate Commerce Commission and the Federal Communications Commission.

7. Extension of factories and instruments of production owned by the State; the bringing into cultivation of waste-lands, and the improvement of the soil generally in accordance with a common plan.

32 Ashley Lutz. "These 6 Corporations Control 90 percent Of The Media In America" Business Insider. June 14, 2012. http://www.businessinsider.com/these-6-corporations-control-90-of-the-media-in-america-2012-6. [http://archive.li/nxbkT]

33 Michael Sainato. "New DNC Emails Expose More DNC-Media-Clinton Campaign Collusion" Observer. November 07, 2016. http://observer.com/2016/11/new-dnc-emails-expose-more-dnc-media-clinton-campaign-collusion/. [http://archive.li/HEtCq]

34 Alex Christoforou. "Here's a list of media companies who have donated to the Clinton Foundation slush fund" The Duran. August 24, 2016. http://theduran.com/list-media-companies-donated-clinton-foundation-slush-fund/. [http://archive.li/0I6Tg]

Wildlife Services, a little-known department within the United States Department of Agriculture, routinely kills between one million and five million wild animals each and every year. Each year thousands of animals are unintentionally killed, including pets, gray wolves, black bears, foxes, bobcats, turtles, owls, swans, and eagles. Coyote pups and fox pups are killed inside their own dens, along with hibernating bears. The Wildlife Services uses some of the most inhumane and grotesque methods to kill, including strangulation snares, leg hold traps (in which the animal can suffer for days before finally passing away), body grip traps, and cyanide poisoning, which makes it impossible for the animal to absorb oxygen and slowly suffocates it to death. Many of the pups were entangled in barbed wire, and then clubbed to death. Others were burned alive inside the den. Coyote and fox skins are often sold for revenue. The justification for using hundreds of millions of our tax money to slaughter wildlife and raze land? In order to make way for the corporate farms of big agriculture. With the massive influx of over a million migrants into the US each year, the demand for food continues to rise. The profits for corporate farming continue to increase, and wildlife and wild lands are yet other victims of the great replacement scheme our government is running. This is all entirely unsustainable. It is nothing shy of criminal madness.[35] [36] [37] [38] [39]

---

35 Daryyl Fears. "USDA's Wildlife Services killed 4 million animals in 2013; seen as an overstep by some." The Washington Post. June 07, 2014. https://www.washingtonpost.com/national/health-science/governments-kill-of-4-million-animals-seen-as-anoverstep/2014/06/06/1de0c550-ecc4-11e3-b98c-72cef4a00499_story.html?noredirect=on&utm_term=.c8cc61c1055f. [http://archive.li/5MvJk]

36 Center for Biological Diversity. "Wildlife Services Killed 1.3 Million Native Animals in 2017, Including Coyotes, Bears, Wolves." EcoWatch. April 24, 2018. https://www.ecowatch.com/wildlife-services-kills-native-animals-2562879506.html.

37 Richard Conniff. "America's Wildlife Body Count." The New York Times. September 17, 2016. https://www.nytimes.com/2016/09/18/opinion/sunday/americas-wildlife-body-count.html. [http://archive.li/vJY8h]

38 Christopher Ketcham. "The Rogue Agency: A USDA program that tortures dogs and kills engendered species." Harper's Magazine. March 2016. https://harpers.org/archive/2016/03/the-rogue-agency/. [http://archive.li/srKPt]

39 Heather Callaghan. "Wildlife Services killed 1.3 million native animals in 2017." Waking Times. April 30, 2018. http://www.wakingtimes.com/2018/04/30/wildlife-services-killed-1-3-million-native-animals-in-2017/. [http://archive.li/LERTW]

8. Equal liability of all to labor.

Through redistribution via heavy taxation, we become individually liable to serve the collective. We work to serve the government and those who do not work. Further, the women's "liberation" movement and modern feminism seek to ensure that all members of a family are in the workforce, and thus that all members of a family are paying taxes to the State.

9. Combination of agriculture with manufacturing industries; gradual abolition of all the distinction between town and country by a more equable distribution of the populace over the country.

Much like in case of the media, a handful of food production companies are involved in producing an incredible percentage of the food we consume. Factory farming has replaced family farming, and Monsanto, once a manufacturer of Agent Orange, has considerable control over the seed market. Further, mass migration patterns of "re-settling" foreign Arabs and Africans into the heartland is a creeping normality.

10. Free education for all children in public schools. Abolition of children's factory labor in its present form. Combination of education with industrial production.

Public schools and universities, were once places of freedom, creativity, and critical thinking. Now, they are indoctrination camps in which we are taught to never question authority, taught to think what they want us to think, taught how to conform socially and intellectually, by getting a job, consuming, paying debt, obeying the statue quo. And all along the way, they call this *freedom*.

Welcome to Bolshevik USA.

Marx, for all his faults, did make fair points about the abolition of child labor, and his theory of social alienation is rather keen. I personally struggle to find fault with Marx's view of late-stage capitalism. However, I do not agree that the solution to the failures of late-stage capitalism is to usher in an era of socialism and eventual communism. My primary divergence, in my short-lived Marxist agreement, is over his view of private property and class, and his theory of how society should progress out of late-stage capitalism.

There is this idea that because the US has a semblance of "private ownership" we must be living in a truly free society. It is true you can "own" a business, and when people think of Marxist or egalitarian economic models, they often think of state ownership — but is it really all that different? Why would the state decide to operate your factory when instead you can "own" your factory, pay the state sales tax, payroll tax, property tax, income tax, gross sales tax, inventory tax, permit and licensing fees, and have the privilege of working seventy-five hour weeks to ensure the business is a success? The state receives all the benefits of "owning" the factory, and in an open-border egalitarian state like the US, the wealth is transferred all the same.

The current economic system of global capitalism does nothing but emphatically foster an even more Left-wing structure. Capitalism, at least in its current incarnation, is globalist, not nationalist; it is anti-protectionist, anti-environment, and anti-isolationist. Massive corporations want open borders to allow for more consumers and cheap laborers, they want trade deals that allow them to seek the lowest possible human labor even if it means destroying local economies, they want to be able to use the cheapest materials and cheapest manufacturing processes despite harming animals and nature, and the capitalist approach to war manufacturing creates an environment in which there is a tremendous amount of money to be made in the armed conflict of nations. Instead of having a policy of ensuring that the best interest of our people comes before the market, we have the market dictating policy, which is inevitable when you have a consequentialist ethical theory that sees economic outcomes as a viable way of organizing a society. We have a system in which capital uses the nation for its own ends, instead of the nation using capital to best serve the people.

Julius Evola says it all:[40]

> This subversive character is found both in Marxism and in its apparent nemesis, modern capitalism. Thus, it is absurd and deplorable for those who

---

40 Evola, *Men Among the Ruins*, 2002 Inner Traditions, pp. 166-167.

pretend to represent the political 'Right' to fail to leave the dark and small circle that is determined by the demonic power of the economy — a circle including capitalism, Marxism, and all the intermediate economic degrees. This should be firmly upheld by those who today are taking a stand against the forces of the Left. Nothing is more evident than that modern capitalism is just as subversive as Marxism. The materialistic view of life on which both systems are based is identical; both of their ideals are qualitatively identical, including the premises connected to a world the center of which is constituted of technology, science, production, 'productivity,' and 'consumption.' And as long as we only talk about economic classes, profit, salaries, and production, and as long as we believe that real human progress is determined by a particular system of distribution of wealth and goods, and that, generally speaking, human progress is measured by the degree of wealth or indigence — then we are not even close to what is essential, even though new theories, beyond Marxism and capitalism, might be formulated.

The starting point should be, instead, a firm rejection of the principle formulated by Marxism, which summarizes the entire subversion at work today: *The economy is our destiny.* We must declare in an uncompromising way that in a normal civilization the economy and economic interests — understood as the satisfaction of material needs and their more or less artificial appendices — have always played, and always will play, a subordinated function. We must also uphold that beyond the economic sphere an order of higher political, spiritual, and heroic values has to emerge, an order that neither knows nor tolerates merely economic classes and does not know the division between 'capitalists' and 'proletarians'; an order solely in terms of which are to be defined the things worth living and dying for. We must also uphold the need for a true hierarchy and for different dignities, with a higher function of power installed at the top, namely the *imperium.*

— Julius Evola, *Men Among the Ruins*

Manifestations of the Liberal illness: Taxation

The entire foundation of any sort of socialism is theft. The idea of *forcing* people to give you money, for any reason, under direct threat of prison or death, is morally corrupt. Taxation is indeed worse than theft: it is servitude and slavery.

Liberals continually support and vote for larger governments, with larger spending, meaning more theft. The Left feels it has a moral duty to steal our money to fund its pet projects, and when taxes are cut to their programs, Liberals cry out as if we have personally stolen their money. Which is exactly what those programs have done to working Americans. Self-hatred is seen in the Liberal willingness to submit to foreigners, to give away lands and money to them. The problem is that not all of us want our money, land, and future to be given away. At some point, we are going to come to an impasse. These irreconcilable ideals can only coexist in one nation for so long.

The Left constantly lies and misdirects information about taxation and spending. Every program for which it advocates is justified by being *only* 0.5 percent to 2 percent of the budget. Apparently they believe nobody will catch on to how many 1 percent line items there are. They use the same tactic when proposing higher taxes, suggesting the new tax is *only* another $14 per month. When presented with the amount of spending on useless programs, like immigration, Liberals refuse to change or even adjust their views. To the Liberal, ideology reigns supreme, facts be damned.

When advocating for lower taxes or program cuts, Liberals project by accusing others of the very acts they are guilty of, by suggesting that those in opposition to the welfare state or high taxation "hate poor people," or the like. In reality, the Liberal policies from welfare to trade exacerbate poverty. The war on poverty started by Lyndon Johnson has cost taxpayers over twenty-two trillion dollars. This figure does not include Social Security or Medicare. Despite this stratospheric and ever-augmenting spending, poverty rates have remained nearly the same since 1970. However, the rate of single-parent families has increased tremendously.[41] Despite their good intentions, the Liberals' expansive welfare state has been a failure. And yet, in the teeth of the evidence, Liberals insist *more* government programs and spending is the solution.

---

41 Rachel Sheffield and Robert Rector. "The War on Poverty After 50 Years" The Heritage Foundation. September 15, 2014. http://www.heritage.org/poverty-and-inequality/report/the-war-poverty-after-50-years. [http://archive.li/cqDif]

The issue of taxation faithfully highlights the symptoms of Liberalism. The underling principles however reveal a more severe neurosis. The desire to take something from another, by force, shows a propensity toward aggression, power, and righteousness. Those in support of involuntary taxation suffer from a far worse illness than Liberalism alone. I believe antisocial personality disorder is the more accurate diagnosis. Antisocial personality disorder is marked by the total disregard and violation of the rights of others. A person suffering from this disorder takes from and victimizes others with no remorse. Supporting the theft of hard working Americans under threat of prison or violence is diametrically opposed to the principles our nation was founded upon.

Had income and property taxes been levied upon us overnight at their present rates, there would have been a violent and bloody revolution immediately following. The Liberal program was thus achieved incrementally, bit by bit over 100 years. Forced taxation has become a creeping normality. We are the metaphoric frogs sitting in hot water, who do not yet realize that we will eventually be boiled to death — and eaten.

All symptoms of Cluster I are apparent. Symptoms 7, 8, 9, and 10, are seen from Cluster II.

Cluster I

1. Deceitfulness, indicated by repeated lying, grand exaggerations, or omission of contrary information, with the purpose to advance their chosen narrative and discrediting others.

2. Irritability or aggressiveness towards anybody that questions or opposes their views. Coupled with the inability to recognize they own hypocrisy, double standards, and doublethink.

3. Inability to adjust views when presented with information contrary to their own beliefs.

4. Frequent projections of their own traits onto others.

5. Difficulty in dealing with a loss of control or power, or a strong desire for control and power.

Cluster II

6. Appeals to altered and redefined definitions of words, or relies on fictitious terms for argumentation.

7. Consistent feelings of having been victimized or wronged, without any actual harm being done. Seen also as playing the victim after attacking others.

8. Intense sense of righteousness or moral superiority.

9. The inability to recognize the negative outcomes of their own actions. Often placing the blame on others.

10. Intense guilt or self-hatred, often manifests as hatred towards one's larger group identity.

VI

White Privilege & Other Fables

The Fountain of Privilege

Racism has become a religion to the Left. "White privilege" has become the Original Sin, and the only way to absolve oneself and repent is through sufficient tithing of white guilt, and living a "virtuous" life of ethnomasochism.

Leftist "intellectuals" inhabit a world in which there are no objective individual or cultural differences. When a discrepancy in outcomes between two groups is discovered, Liberals clamor to find the cause. Reasonable objective thinkers might suggest that shared cultural values, upbringing, work ethic, and biology are responsible. Liberals, on the other hand, invent complex critical theories that accuse "whiteness" of being the root cause, not only of white success, but also of any other group's *lack* of success. A quick internet search of "white privilege" will return thousands of results ranging from articles in mainstream media publications to academic journal publications, from interviews with professors to entire books written exclusively on this subject. University textbooks such as Rothenberg's *White Privilege* are being used to teach entire courses dedicated to the subject.[1]

1 Paula S. Rothenberg. White privilege: essential readings on the other side of racism. New York: Worth Publishers, 2016.

The whole theory of whiteness and white privilege is predicated upon the idea that white people occupy all positions of power in government and business, and that they use this power to ensure that only whites can be successful, while keeping all other groups of people down a few rungs. Nearly every article from the sources that argue in favor of the existence of white privilege includes income information about white, black, and Hispanic households. They conveniently leave out Asians. This oversight is probably due to the fact that the data on Asians make so called white privilege look like the absurd joke that it is. 36 percent of whites hold a college degree, 23 percent of blacks, and 15 percent of Hispanics — while 53 percent of Asians have at least a bachelor's degree. Asians also have household incomes around 10 percent higher than whites, the highest incomes of those four ethnic groups.[2] Broken down even further by country of origin, we see the median income of many non-whites is much higher than that whites, with Indian citizens earning the most at over $100,000.[3]

Asian citizens make up such a small percentage of the US prison population that they are typically listed under the "other" race in the data I collected. Asian citizens are of course under-represented in prison populations with respect to their general population.

What we see looking at the data is that, by measures of income, education, and crime, Asian citizens fare far better than whites, blacks, and Hispanics. At this point we have a couple of options; we can conclude that there is something inherent to Asian culture that contributes to their success, or we can attribute it to "Asian privilege," the idea that Asians are given all sorts of favors and breaks in America to which other races are simply not privy. I would wager on the former.

The Chinese have a saying which they often say to each other: "No one who can rise before dawn 360 days a year fails to make his family

---

2 "Demographic trends and economic well-being" Pew Research Center's Social & Demographic Trends Project. June 27, 2016. http://www.pewsocialtrends.org/2016/06/27/1-demographic-trends-and-economic-well-being/. [http://archive.li/WC394]

3 "Indian-Americans Richest Community in US with Average Income $100,547" NDTV. April 30, 2015. http://www.ndtv.com/indians-abroad/indians-richest-in-us-with-average-income-100-547-759354. [http://archive.li/HqlRE]

rich."[4] The values that permeate one's culture have a profound effect on the individuals within the culture. When one group glorifies education, hard work, loyalty, and perseverance, is it any surprise that they succeed?

To the narrow-minded Liberal thinker, it is incomprehensible that Asian culture might lend itself well to success. It makes little sense to Liberals that there might be any connection between Asians making education a high priority and hard work an honorable virtue on the one hand, and their place as the top earners in America on the other. Asian citizens also have the lowest rates of single-parent families at 11 percent. Again, the Left sees this crucial piece of data as negligible, whereas in reality, it is quite possibly one of the single most influential factors of future success. The fact that more Asian children grow up with two parents is alone sufficient to explain the economic trends between races. White children have a single-parent rate of 26 percent, Hispanics of 43 percent, and blacks of 68 percent.[5]

Liberals utterly refuse to acknowledge these differences in race, culture, and their subsequent effects on life outcomes. Race denial is a necessary pillar of Liberal ideology. Recognizing aggregate biological differences between races in terms of intelligence, forward-thinking, self-control, abstract thought, and morality, would call into question the very foundation of equality, multiculturalism, mass migration, and affirmative action programs. If all groups are identical, then you can blame whites for the failures of other groups; however, if there are reasonable alternative explanations, such as biology, the entire concept of white privilege comes undone.

News articles and Liberal academics blaming racism as the root cause are all too common. *The Guardian* published a piece titled, "Black culture isn't the problem—systemic inequality is."[6] The article reduces

---

4 Malcolm Gladwell. Outliers: the story of success. New York: Back Bay Books, Little, Brown and Company, 2008.

5 Christina Huffington. "Single Motherhood Increases Dramatically For Certain Demographics, Census Bureau Reports" The Huffington Post. May 01, 2013. http://www.huffingtonpost.com/2013/05/01/single-motherhood-increases-census-report_n_3195455.html. [http://archive.li/GVDhN]

6 Boots Riley. "Black culture isn't the problem—systemic inequality is" The Guardian. April 09, 2016. https://www.theguardian.com/commentisfree/2016/apr/09/bill-clinton-black-culture-systemic-inequality-problems. [http://archive.li/sYTRl]

the inequality seen in income, crime, and prison rates within the black community to "systemic racism."

Children growing up with only one parent are twice as likely to be incarcerated as children with two parents. Even when controlling for income, the pattern holds true. Single-mother families live in poverty at a rate of 40 percent—five times that of two-parent families. Rates of high school graduation and college attendance are both lower for children from single parent homes as well. These rates all hold true across race: a white child from a single parent home is nearly as likely to drop out of high school as a black child from a single parent home.[7]

There seems to be few other factors that affects poverty rates, education outcomes, and incarceration rates, as much as growing up in a single parent home. It doesn't matter if the child is white, black, Hispanic, or Asian; they are *all* negatively affected by single parenthood.[8]

This correlation is not specific to the United States. Data in England from the Work and Pensions Secretary revealed that children from broken homes were nine times more likely to commit crime. Single-parent families were twice as likely to be living in poverty, and children from single parent homes have higher rates of drug addiction.[9]

Liberals often argue that the only reason single-parent rates are so high in the black community is mass incarceration, the war on drugs, and a prison system that targets blacks, all of these claims are made in Alexander's *The New Jim Crow*. It sounds reasonable enough, at least in the sense that incarceration could leave many black children without fathers. So I began looking at the data. Per the 2008 Bureau of Justice Statistics Special Report on prisoners with children, there are around 1.7 million children with parents in prison from all races.[10] According to the

7 Sara McLanahan. "The Consequences of Single Motherhood" The American Prospect. Summer 1994. http://prospect.org/article/consequences-single-motherhood. [http://archive.li/QHgFH]

8 Ibid.

9 Andy Bloxham. "Children from broken homes 'nine times more likely to commit crimes'" The Telegraph. November 04, 2010. http://www.telegraph.co.uk/news/politics/8109184/Children-from-broken-homes-nine-times-more-likely-to-commit-crimes.html. [http://archive.is/D77yQ]

10 Lauren E. Glaze and Laura M. Maruschak. "Parents in Prison and Their Minor Children" Bureau of Justice Statistics. August 08, 2008. https://www.bjs.gov/

census, about 17.2 million children in the US are being raised by single mothers.[11] Meaning that under 10 percent of children from single-parent homes owe their situation to incarceration.

Blaming the plight of the black community on the prison system is just another way to pass the issue onto some other group or entity without taking responsibility and addressing the problem. I want to see all communities of Americans doing better. I just don't believe that blaming whites for the shortcomings of others is the way to fix anything at all.

Regarding the war on drugs and its effect on the prison population — if every federal and state drug offender currently in prison were to be released in this moment, it would drop the prison population by only 14 percent.[12] That clearly still leaves the vast majority of prisoners. The notion that the war on drugs is the single greatest cause of mass incarceration is nonsense. However, entire books have been written on the premise that the war on drugs is the primary cause of incarceration rates.

When attempting to explain differences in education, crime, and income between races, Liberals default to the answers of white privilege and systemic racism. Neither of these theories can account for why Asians succeed at higher rates than whites, nor can they account for why, given alleged privileges and systemic advantages, so many whites end up in poverty and in prison. Yet when we look at correlations between single parent rates and outcomes in education, crime, and income, we see an entirely different story. A story that suggests there are factors beyond racism that contribute to the successes and failures of people. As an explanation, rates of single motherhood are far more powerful than "racism." Further, liberals also refuse to acknowledge the effects of genetic variations between races, which can lead to varying outcomes in terms of success and life trajectory.

Evidently we are to believe that this all-encompassing shield of white privilege is now selectively oppressing blacks and Hispanics, even while

---

index.cfm?ty=pbdetail&iid=823.

11 Dawn Lee. "Single Mother Statistics" Single Mother Guide. July 12, 2017. https://singlemotherguide.com/single-mother-statistics/. [http://archive.li/m8Efl]

12 Ollie Roeder. "Releasing Drug Offenders Won't End Mass Incarceration" FiveThirtyEight. July 17, 2015. https://fivethirtyeight.com/datalab/releasing-drug-offenders-wont-end-mass-incarceration/. [http://archive.li/WizCC]

ensuring that Asians and Indians are doing better than whites. I agree with the Liberals that there is clearly something endemic at play. We just disagree on what that something happens to be.

The very concept of white privilege is deeply harmful. It is yet another weapon in the war on whites. First, it tells the whites who believe in this degenerate trash that their success is not the product of hard work, talent, or intelligence, that anything they achieve was ill-begotten and inherently illegitimate. Further, it teaches non-whites that there is no use even attempting to work hard or develop talent and intellect, for all their work will be for naught so long as the system of oppression known as whiteness exists.

I once had a class that discussed contemporary race relations, including "white privilege." We discussed Scapegoat Theory, the idea that people often blame a despised and denigrated out-group for their own shortcomings or lack of success.[13] Shortly afterward we moved on to discussions of white privilege, by which society blames whites, especially white men, for all the problems that other groups face. I looked around the crowded lecture hall wondering if anybody else was struck by the irony. I caught one look; we made eye contact, and just starting laughing at the absurdity. Little moments like those made those days, filled as they were with Liberals and their trash theories, rather tolerable.

Universities and Left-wing blogs that masquerade as news organizations, publishing countless pieces of journalistic treasures, as for example *Salon*'s "White privilege: An insidious virus that's eating America from within," are not the only ones to blame for the perpetuation of the "systemic racism" myth.[14] Two-time presidential loser, Hillary Clinton, and Bernie Sanders both spoke about the issues of systemic and institutional racism caused by white privilege.

---

13 Neel Burton. "The Psychology of Scapegoating" Psychology Today. December 21, 2013. https://www.psychologytoday.com/blog/hide-and-seek/201312/the-psychology-scapegoating. [http://archive.is/vjQ8d]

14 Andrew O'Hehir. "White privilege: An insidious virus that's eating America from within" Salon. August 23, 2014. http://www.salon.com/2014/08/23/white_privilege_an_insidious_virus_thats_eating_america_from_within/. [http://archive.li/FNHSN]

> Clinton: "We need to recognize our privilege."[15]
>
> Sanders: "When you're white, you don't know what it's like to be living in a ghetto. You don't know what it's like to be poor. You don't know what it's like to be hassled when you walk down the street or you get dragged out of a car."[16]

Well if Mrs. Clinton or anybody else can prove that white people have some distinct, invisible, inherent, all-encompassing advantage, I'll listen. I've spent considerable time hunting high and low for the mythical Fountain of Privilege, and it eludes me still.

As for Mr. Sanders' comments, recent Census data reveals that about 10 percent, or 20,000,000, yes *million*, white Americans are living in poverty.[17] Further, a quick online search reveals a video from right after the November 2016 election, of a white man being dragged out of his car and beaten, while his attackers yell "Don't vote Trump!" I'm still awaiting retractions. I suppose all that socialism went to Bernie's brain and he forgot high profile incidents of profound racism, as for instance when Reginald Denny was beaten nearly to death for the crime of being in the wrong place in the wrong skin. Perhaps Sanders missed the brutal attack on a white man in Saint Louis, when a group of black and Hispanic teens pulled Zemir Begic, a Bosnian immigrant, out of his car during a protest, and beat him to death with hammers.[18] Maybe nobody briefed Bernie on

15 Steve Guest. "Hillary: White America Needs To 'Recognize Our Privilege' [VIDEO]" The Daily Caller. July 18, 2016. http://dailycaller.com/2016/07/18/hillary-white-america-needs-to-recognize-our-privilege-video/. [http://archive.li/gQ4L8]

16 Ben Kamisar. "Sanders's comment on white people and poverty creates social media stir" The Hill. March 06, 2016. http://thehill.com/blogs/ballot-box/presidential-races/271999-sanderss-comment-on-white-people-and-poverty-creates. [http://archive.li/xqAlW]

17 Carmen DeNavas-Walt and Bernadette D. Proctor. "Income and Poverty in the United States: 2014" United States Census Bureau. September 2015.

18 Snejana Farberov and Pete D'Amato. "St Louis authorities DENY that deadly hammer attack on Bosnian immigrant was racist ...as third suspect is charged with murder" Daily Mail Online. December 01, 2014. http://www.dailymail.co.uk/news/article-2855535/St-Louis-teens-beat-motorist-32-death-hammers-sparking-protests-Bosnian-community.html. [http://archive.li/kPXwY]

the fact that half of all the people killed by police are white. Or the fact that whites in America are the most frequent victims of violent interracial crime, being attacked at rates higher than any other group.

Every advantage Liberals claim that whites have, evidently due to some mystical force somewhere out in the ether, can be easily explained far more coherently by rates of growing up in single parent homes verses a two-parent home, and by easily verifiable aggregate differences between races, such as intelligence, forward-thinking, and impulsivity. The very reason there is a disparate rate of single-parent homes between races is itself likely a manifestation of racial differences playing out culturally.

The only valid contemporary examples of systemic racism are blatantly hostile towards whites: affirmative action, university admission criteria, "diversity" initiatives, and the crime epidemic targeting whites that has been largely covered up by the government and lying press. And just as the crime epidemic against whites is hushed, so is the massive wealth transfer forced on white families, whose taxation goes to provide for non-white families.

The claim that there is oppression of a systemic nature, inhibiting non-whites while simultaneously elevating whites, is little more than a ghost hunt. Every example of white privilege can be easily rendered invalid by mere seconds of research, and with minimal critical thinking.

Crime Rates are Racist

Liberals find racism is nearly every facet of life. We will go over a few of the more common ones I come across and discuss them through logic and data. There is no way to produce an exhaustive list, nor account for all the future ghost-hunting that Liberals will surely do in regard to racism. My hope is that these examples will help my readers to identify patterns in the Liberal narrative, see the flaws in their logic, and research further claims made by the Left, in order to see the full picture.

One of the most common arguments I've heard is that although surveys show that white and black Americans *use* drugs at roughly the same rates, blacks make up a higher rate of those *incarcerated* for drug crimes. This is simply comparing apples to oranges. A classic false equivalence fallacy.

The police are not arresting and incarcerating people merely for using drugs, which is what this argument assumes. Liberals look at two different sets of data — one showing drug use, the other showing incarceration rates — and suggest that they are one in the same. In reality, it's rare that people are even caught, let alone arrested, for getting high. The arrests and prison time come from the trafficking, distribution, manufacturing, selling, and possession of large quantities of drugs.

So this logically means one of two things. Either whites and blacks commit drug trafficking, distribution, manufacturing, selling, and possession crimes at the same rate, and the police are simply ignoring the whites that commit drug crimes. Or there is a difference in the number of violations between races. If there is no disparity in terms of drug crimes, that means that everything from the legislation of drug laws, to the DEA chiefs, to the beat cops, represents a massive race-based conspiracy which is predicated on ignoring all the white drug traffickers and manufactures, in order to systematically target blacks. The data simply does not support this wild Liberal theory. There are many whites in prison for drug violations. It just so happens that blacks are in prison at higher rates. Just as there is a different rate of single motherhood, education, income, and crime among the races as well. How naïve would we be to assume that every race on Earth is going to be represented perfectly in every aspect of life — including prison?

Data of drug use shows that women use drugs about half as much as men. 12 percent of men in America have used drugs in the past year, while 7 percent of women have used.[19] Yet men account for 93 percent of prison inmates, nearly fourteen times the rate of imprisonment over women.[20] Men use drugs at a rate of less than twice that of women, yet are fourteen times more likely to be in jail — but nobody is claiming the prison system is systemically sexist. Why? Because they correctly infer that when it comes to drug manufacturing, trafficking, and distributing, men make up

---

19 "Results from the 2013 National Survey on Drug Use and Health: Summary of National Findings" U.S. Department of Health and Human Services. September 2014.

20 "Inmate Gender." "Federal Bureau of Prisons. Accessed May 27, 2017. https://www.bop.gov/about/statistics/statistics_inmate_gender.jsp. [http://archive.li/pH0ig]

the majority of those involved in the drug trade. Nobody assumes that the usage rate of drugs between men and women should equate to the same rates of incarceration — so why do they assume the distribution should be identical between races? Does it not stand to reason that certain groups might be more likely to be involved in certain trades?

During Prohibition, nobody assumed that Italian men were being unfairly and systemically discriminated against due to the fact that they made up a large portion of those arrested for organized crime. The fact is, Italian men were involved in organized crime at a higher rate than any other group. If you had conducted surveys during Prohibition to see how many people were consuming illegal alcohol, I'm sure the distribution would have been more evenly spread across gender and ethnicity; yet when it came to the actual business of crime, there were certain groups more heavily involved. Not everybody who drank illegally was involved in running speakeasies, smuggling, and bootlegging. The same holds true today for the drug trade.

Liberals ignore this simple logic. Frequent articles with titles like *Huffington Post*'s "When It Comes To Illegal Drug Use, White America Does The Crime, Black America Gets The Time," continue to advance this invalid theory.[21] Their conclusion that rates of drug trafficking should be the same as usage rates simply does not follow. In the article in question, the author cites data from cocaine use alone. He argues that because 20 percent of whites have used cocaine, but only 10 percent of blacks have used cocaine, whites should be twice as likely to be in prison for drug crimes. Not only did he cherry pick data for cocaine and ignore the fact that for overall drug use the rate between races is nearly identical, but also, like most Liberals, he tries to glide over the difference between drug *use* and drug *trafficking*. According to data from the United States Sentencing Commission, 96 percent of offenders sentenced for drug crimes were for trafficking offenses.[22] Less than 2 percent of all drug crime sentences were

---

21 Saki Knafo. "When It Comes To Illegal Drug Use, White America Does The Crime, Black America Gets The Time" The Huffington Post. September 17, 2013. http://www.huffingtonpost.com/2013/09/17/racial-disparity-drug-use_n_3941346.html. [http://archive.li/2wTzL]

22 "Primary Drug Type of Offenders Sentenced Under Drug Guidlines" U.S. Sentencing Commission. Accessed July 13, 2017. https://www.ussc.gov/sites/

for simple possession. The majority of federal simple possession apprehensions take place at the US/Mexican border.[23]

Another very interesting bit of data regards the validity of the self-report surveys of drug use. In studies that compare self-reported drug use to hair samples, researchers find that blacks were six times more likely to lie about illicit drug use as compared to whites.[24] Blacks are also over three times as likely to go to the emergency room for use of illegal drugs.[25] These facts suggest that drug use is anything but equal between races. The very premise of the argument is faulty.

In regard to drug laws, Liberals often claim that racism can be seen in the difference between punishments for crack on the one hand and cocaine on the other. They allege that because cocaine is a rich, white person, party drug, it carries lower sentences than crack, which is thought to be used more widely by the black community. Again, not comparing apples to apples at all. First, the rise in the severity of punishment for crack came about as a direct reaction to the violence that police departments were seeing as a result of crack, as compared to other drugs, during the 1980s. Second, when we compare crack sentences to meth or PCP, both of which are seen as a more "white person" drug, the disparity in grams needed to land you five years in jail, nearly disappear.[26] The vast majority of people

---

default/files/pdf/research-and-publications/annual-reports-and-sourcebooks/2014/Table33.pdf.

23 "Weighing the Charges: Simple Possession of Drugs in the Federal Criminal Justice System." U.S. Sentencing Commission. September 2016. https://www.ussc.gov/sites/default/files/pdf/research-and-publications/research-publications/2016/201609_Simple-Possession.pdf.

24 David M. Ledgerwood, et al. "Comparison between self-Report and hair analysis of illicit drug use in a community sample of middle-Aged men." Addictive Behaviors, vol. 33, no. 9, 8 May 2008, pp. 1131–1139., doi:10.1016/j.addbeh.2008.04.009.

25 "Drug Abuse Warning Network, 2010: National Estimates of Drug-Related Emergency Department Visits." U.S. Department of Health and Human Services. November 2012. www.samhsa.gov/data/sites/default/files/DAWN2k10ED/DAWN2k10ED/DAWN2k10ED.htm [http://archive.li/lY5qj]

26 Eric E. Sterling. "Drug Laws And Snitching: A Primer" PBS. Accessed July 13, 2017. http://www.pbs.org/wgbh/pages/frontline/shows/snitch/primer/. [http://archive.li/LYedg]

in prison for meth are white.[27] Nobody claims that meth laws target poor whites.

Similar arguments were made about the controversial New York City Police Department practice of stop & frisk. Liberals claim that because blacks accounted for 55 percent of those stopped, there was clearly a racist motivation on the part of the police. In New York City, blacks account for 66 percent of the perpetrators of violent crimes, 70 percent of robberies, and 80 percent of murderers. Blacks are over-represented in every type of criminal behavior in New York from misdemeanors to rape, per the annual Crime and Enforcement Activity report released by New York City. With that in mind, blacks were actually stopped at a *lower* rate than what levels of black criminality would have warranted.[28] The same trend is true of Chicago: blacks account for more than 80 percent of all rape, robbery, and murder in the city.[29] In terms of the rate of crime in the black community, they are actually being under-policed.

The high crime rates of the American black population are in no way exclusive to the US. In London, England, blacks make up around 12 percent of the population, yet they account for 67 percent of gun crimes, 59 percent of robberies, and over 30 percent of sex crimes. Blacks in London also make up a disproportionate amount of street crimes: over 50 percent of muggings, assaults, purse snatchings, and pick pocket crimes, are committed by the black population.[30]

Another common Liberal argument for systemic racism in America today is that the chances of being pulled over by a police officer are higher for blacks and Hispanics, which they call the crime of "Driving While

27 "Crack Vs. Meth" Investor's Business Daily. July 28, 2011. http://www.investors.com/politics/editorials/crack-vs-meth/. [http://archive.is/5qY2Q]

28 Heather MacDonald. "Fighting Crime Where the Criminals Are" The New York Times. June 25, 2010. http://www.nytimes.com/2010/06/26/opinion/26macdonald.html?mcubz=0.

29 Edwin S. Rubenstein. "The Color of Crime, 2016 Revised Edition" American Renaissance. https://www.amren.com/archives/reports/the-color-of-crime-2016-revised-edition/.

30 Andrew Alderson. "Violent inner-City crime, the figures, and a question of race." The Telegraph. June 26, 2010. www.telegraph.co.uk/news/uknews/crime/7856787/Violent-inner-city-crime-the-figures-and-a-question-of-race.html. [http://archive.li/GTJEZ]

Black." The claim again is seductively simple: if blacks are stopped for speeding at a rate higher than whites, this must be due to systemic racist policies or racist cops.

A now infamous study conducted by the Public Services Research Institute in New Jersey was commissioned in light of numerous allegations of racial profiling and the unfair targeting of non-white drivers. The New Jersey Turnpike study set out to discover why around a quarter of traffic stops were of black drivers when blacks accounted for only 16 percent of the drivers on the Turnpike. Well, as fate would have it, after the study examined over 38,000 drivers, they found that black drivers were almost twice as likely to speed on the Turnpike. The study concluded that blacks were actually being stopped at a *lower rate* than whites, in terms of each group's propensity to speed.[31] There was indeed an unfair distribution of speeding tickets in regards to race and speeding; it just so happens that once again, the Liberal narrative inverted the truth.

Blinded by the theory of Cultural Relativism, Liberals refuse to acknowledge there might be differences between groups of people as a whole; they therefore conclude that all outcomes should be identical. But every time further research has been conducted into one of these issues, we find that different outcomes are the result of groups of people behaving differently.

The New York Times ran a piece titled, "Only Mass Deportation Can Save America." Its Jewish blogger, Bret Stephens, argues that Americans should be deported to make more room for migrants. Stephens claims Americans are now "Complacent, entitled and often shockingly ignorant on basic points of American law and history." He cites high rates of out-of-wedlock births and criminality as cause for deportation.[32] What Stephens fails to mention is that crime rates of migrants are only lower than those of black citizens. The same is true of out-of-wedlock births. Compared

---

31 David Kocieniewski. "Study Suggests Racial Gap In Speeding In New Jersey." The New York Times. March 21, 2002. www.nytimes.com/2002/03/21/nyregion/study-suggests-racial-gap-in-speeding-in-new-jersey.html. [http://archive.li/NNrv9]

32 Bret Stephens. "Only Mass Deportation Can Save America" The New York Times. June 16, 2017. https://www.nytimes.com/2017/06/16/opinion/only-mass-deportation-can-save-america.html?mcubz=1&_r=2. [http://archive.li/3bpKJ]

to whites and Asians, migrants commit more crime, have higher rates of single parent families, and produce more out-of-wedlock children.

The Liberal talking point on immigration and crime needs to be explained further. Liberals claim that the immigrant population in the United States actually commits lower rates of crimes than those born in America. They cite the figure from the American Community Survey, which finds that 1.8 percent of immigrant men between eighteen and thirty-nine are in prison, while 3.3 percent of native born citizens are in prison.[33] Yes, the average rate of incarceration is about 3.3 percent for US born males under the age of 40. However the incarceration rate varies widely between races. The Asian population in prison is negligible, the white American population is at 0.7 percent, Hispanic citizens 1.8 percent, and 4.7 percent of black American males are in prison.[34] Thus, though it is technically correct that immigrants commit less crime, they commit crime at about the same rates as Hispanics born in the US, double the rate of white Americans, and at a many times higher rate than Asian citizens. The reason the migrant crime rate is less than the average crime rate of native born Americans is solely because the rate of black crime is so high.

I've noticed something else in my discussions of racial issues with Liberals. They refuse to discuss any of these statistics. Any statistics that show racial discrepancies are racist in the Liberal mind. Liberals have gone so far as to define the merest suggestion of documented group differences as racism. They have effectively turned statistics and data into racists.

Taking a further look at some of those racist facts, one in particular stands out: the fact that blacks are twenty-seven more times likely to attack a white person in a violent crime than the other way around. Hispanics are eight times as likely to attack whites than the other way around. A large portion of crime takes place *within* races, meaning both the offender and the victims are of the same race. Yet when we look at data of crime *between* races, we see that whites are targeted at

33 Veronika Bondarenko and Skye Gould. "Despite Trump's speech, immigrants commit far fewer crimes than native-born Americans" Business Insider. March 01, 2017. http://www.businessinsider.com/immigrants-commit-less-crime-than-native-born-americans-trump-speech-2017-3/. [http://archive.li/Dfmg1]

34 "Prison Inmates at Midyear 2009 — Statistical Tables" Bureau of Justice Statistics. Accessed July 13, 2017.

an overwhelmingly disproportionate rate by both blacks and Hispanics. A tremendous amount of white victims of violent crime are attacked by non-whites.[35] This is striking when you consider the respective population rates, and the fact that whites are still a majority in the US; one can only imagine what happens when the white population falls below half. Because we are being forced to live with groups of people that have much higher crime rate, white victimization rate increases in an inordinate fashion as our relative numbers diminish. The media doesn't bother with these facts. These inconvenient truths are damaging to the Liberal narrative that the evil white man is abusing non-whites with total impunity.

In terms of interracial rape, almost 100 percent of rapes between blacks and whites are black men raping white women .[36] If the rates and roles were reversed, if whites were raping and murdering blacks at a rate of twenty-seven times more than the other way around, the media outrage would be non-stop. It's all we would hear about. But when whites are victimized, it is simply business as usual. The government and media are both actively engaged in covering up the over half a million violent crimes each year against whites by non-whites. While they constantly decry racism, it is whites who are by far the most victimized group in America.

There is an argument suggesting that the high victimization of whites is the result of a mere frequency effect. That is, because there are about five times as many whites in the US as blacks, we would expect whites to be victimized more often by mere chance encounter. And this theory *would* hold if rates of victimization were actually five to one between blacks and whites. But they are not five to one; they are twenty-seven to one.

When the Left does speak candidly about the incredible criminal variance between races, they often blame poverty and economic inequalities. As with most Liberal arguments, the idea that poverty causes crime is simply unsupported by all available data. This very theory was examined in an analysis by the New Century Foundation. New Century Foundation looked at rates of crime in all fifty states and Washington D.C. It found that violent

35 Jared Taylor. "New DOJ Statistics on Race and Violent Crime" American Renaissance. July 1, 2015. https://www.amren.com/news/2015/07/new-doj-statistics-on-race-and-violent-crime/. [http://archive.li/0dMuY]

36 "Criminal Victimization in the United States." National Crime Victimization Survey. Bureau of Justice Statistics Table 42. May 2011.

crime was correlated more strongly to the percent of the population that was black and Hispanic than it was to either poverty or unemployment, by a factor of more than double. Violent crime correlated to the percent of the population living in poverty at 0.36, the percent of the population that has not completed high school at 0.37, and to unemployment at 0.35. The violent crime rate and the percent of the population being black and Hispanic was a strong correlation, at 0.81.[37] Meaning a poor white neighborhood has less crime than more affluent "diverse" neighborhoods.

Researchers Richard Lynn and Tatu Vanhanen published an analysis of crime correlates which found that there is a relationship between low IQ and crime. The lower the IQ, the stronger a correlation to committing crime.[38] Also quite interesting is a recent study called "Political ideology predicts involvement in crime," by John Paul Wright et al. Wright found that people who self-report being conservative or very conservative have a lower correlation to criminal activity. While people who are Liberal or very Liberal are much more likely to be involved in criminal activity, with a high correlation.[39]

A journal article by Steven Levitt states that the lowest homicide rates found in the country were in the poorest white neighborhoods. The rate of crime and homicide is actually higher in black neighborhoods with higher median family incomes than in poor white neighborhoods.[40] In a study titled "Race, Wealth and Incarceration: Results from the National Longitudinal Survey of Youth," researchers found that at all income levels, even high income levels, blacks and Hispanics committed more crime than their white counterparts.[41] There is a tremendous body of literature

37 "The Color of Crime 2005" American Renaissance. Accessed July 13, 2017. https://www.amren.com/the-color-of-crime/.

38 Richard Lynn and Tatu Vanhanen. Intelligence: a unifying construct for the social sciences. London: Ulster Institute for Social Research, 2012.

39 John Paul Wright, Kevin M. Beaver, Mark Alden Morgan, and Eric J. Connolly. "Political ideology predicts involvement in crime" Personality and Individual Differences106 (October 2016): 236-41. doi:10.1016/j.paid.2016.10.062.

40 Steven D. Levitt. "The Changing Relationship between Income and Crime Victimization" Economic Policy Review5, no. 3 (September 1999).

41 Khaing Zaw, Darrick Hamilton, and William Darity. "Race, Wealth and Incarceration: Results from the National Longitudinal Survey of Youth" Race and Social Problems8, no. 1 (2016): 103-15. doi:10.1007/s12552-016-9164-y.

that entirely disproves the myth that poverty causes crime. Yet this work seldom makes its way into mainstream discourse.

Facts and statistics can *never* be racist, sexist, Islamophobic, anti-semitic, prejudiced, biased, or hateful. Facts are nothing but the mathematical and numerical representation of events in the real world. The untruthful Left shies away from facts to the point that France and several other European countries have outlawed the collection of demographic data of crimes, so that their citizens do not see how badly they are being victimized by foreigners. Liberals scream and cry when presented with facts like witches doused in Holy water. For their position is weak, and cannot stand up to even the most superficial scrutiny.

When a few numbers can make your entire narrative go up in flames, yet you stick to it adamantly nonetheless, what you have is no longer a political opinion. You no longer have a thoughtful argument. You are left with nothing but blind adherence to the narrative, no different than that of any member of a cult. You are left with a bankrupt ideology, one which you refuse to let die.

Redefinitions

Part of the Liberal strategy has been to redefine what it means to be racist; for without a redefinition, the already weak Liberal position would be entirely devoid of any substance. Racism once described the irrational treatment of others, for worse or better, simply on the basis of race. This was a simple and effective definition.

Today, Liberal academics have redefined racism to mean any acknowledgment of differences among racial groups. Further, they have defined racism to mean that one group holds higher levels of "institutional power," which can be used to oppress other groups.[42] This sleight of hand does two things; first it ensures that racism only applies to the actions of white people, as they are seen to hold the power in society; second, it makes any actions done against whites by non-whites, necessarily non-racist.

---

42 Rob Shimshock. "Only Whites Can Be Racist, Insists University" The Daily Caller. March 14, 2017. http://dailycaller.com/2017/03/14/only-whites-can-be-racist-insists-university/. [http://archive.li/XODJI]

So called racism, Islamophobia, and antisemitism do not exist in vacuums. More often than not, they are the normal reaction to the anti-white sentiments and behaviors coming from non-whites, Muslims, and Jews. The very basic assumption of Racism, Islamophobia, and antisemitism is that if you offer any criticism, no matter how legitimate, of a non-white person or group, then something is wrong with you. This entire paradigm should be outright rejected.

The Left goes so far as to refer to all white people as white supremacists, since their "unearned" privilege places them ahead of non-whites, whether they realize it or not. There is now no definitional differentiation between being white and being a racist or a white supremacist.

To provide some practical examples of what this means, a "racist" is essentially now anybody who has an understanding of crime rates and statistics, or the ability to recognize behavioral patterns within group dynamics. A recent study published in the *Journal of Experimental Psychology*, found that people who have a higher cognitive capability to recognize patterns, also tend to be more likely to form stereotypes.[43] This study, in a manner of speaking, found that those who the Left refer to as "racists," might simply be acute behavioral-pattern-recognition experts. What the Left calls "racism" is primarily little more than in-group preference coupled with pattern recognition — both traits being highly-evolved behaviors and markers of intelligence.

It is crucial to note that during the Presidency of Barack Obama, with Eric Holder and Loretta Lynch as Attorney Generals, the Left never once claimed that black citizens held institutional power. The narrative was still that only whites can be racist. But if we redefine racism to be applicable to whites alone, then the Left's *anti-racism* would have logically to be by nature *anti-white*.

The entire platform of race relations from the Left has been nothing but the demonization of whites. They use fictitious phrases for which they refuse to provide evidence, such as "white privilege," "systemic racism," or "power plus privilege equals racism," to provide answers as to why other

---

43 Olga Khazan. "How Intelligence Leads to Stereotyping" The Atlantic. July 29, 2017. https://www.theatlantic.com/science/archive/2017/07/intelligent-people-are-more-likely-to-stereotype/535158/. [http://archive.li/sN8Iy]

groups do not fare as well as whites — all the while conveniently ignoring the groups that prosper far better than whites.

Further, even the Liberal definition of racism never manages to logically elucidate how "institutional" power would benefit the average white person. The new definition essentially assumes that every white in society has the same degree of power and privilege that the elites of our society are afforded.

The Left has weaponized white guilt through constant propaganda in the media and the education system to ensure that feeble-minded whites kowtow to their agenda. Then, any white not guilt-ridden to the point of submission is automatically labeled a white supremacist. The Left uses white guilt to convince white folk to succumb to their demands, to roll over and die during their dispossession.

Liberal propaganda machines are constantly proliferating articles and films meant to destroy any remnants of heritage or pride in white culture. "Towards a Concept of White Wounding," by Jewish blogger, Jesse Benn, is the title of a recent article from *The Huffington Post*; it advances the idea that all white people, without exception, are indeed racists. By benefiting from the imaginary system of "white privilege," all white people are oppressing all other races.[44]

The anti-white propaganda is entrenched in society to such a degree that the phrase "white people don't have a culture" has become a commonplace. I've met countless people around my age that truly believe country music, fast food, and Walmart, is the full extent of white culture. And is that really any surprise? History classes in school restrain themselves to a four month section about American involvement in the Atlantic Slave Trade, followed by a four month section on the Holocaust — but nothing of *our* history. A *New York Times* article titled, "What Is Whiteness?" has this to say; "Whiteness is on a toggle switch between bland nothingness and racist hatred."[45]

---

44 Jesse Benn. "Towards a Concept of White Wounding" The Huffington Post. August 14, 2015. http://www.huffingtonpost.com/jesse-benn/towards-a-concept-of-whit_b_7985986.html. [http://archive.li/kuxbI]

45 Nell Irvin Painter. "What Is Whiteness" The New York Times. June 20, 2015. https://www.nytimes.com/2015/06/21/opinion/sunday/what-is-whiteness.html. [http://archive.li/G5MQw]

This is the work of the education system, the media, and the press. This is the work of cultural genocide.

We have become *personae non gratae. Damnatio memoriae*, exiles in our own lands. Complete with an iconoclasm brought against our past.

First they tell us we have no culture.
Then they erase the remnants of our culture and history.
Finally they rewrite our own history without us in it.

White culture is that of dreamers and inventors — the Wright Brothers, Tesla, Karl Benz, and Ferdinand Porsche. The brave culture of the Crusaders, the Centurions, the Spartans, and the Revolutionaries. It is the culture of the Enlightenment, the Renaissance, timeless architecture, the finest literature of the world, and the most romantic symphonic and operatic masterworks from Beethoven to Wagner.

White culture is little more than a record of every meaningful aspect of civilization as we know it today. Never let anybody tell you differently. Our culture is nothing less than the Promethean fire that first illuminated mankind.

White-European culture has surpassed all others in terms of invention, advancement, literature, music, art, engineering, architecture, aesthetics, and thought. Yet my view of the European peoples is not acceptable to the Left, their narrative of white guilt, their claims of the necessity for "cultural enrichment." For the view I hold, I am labeled a fringe, lunatic "supremacist." If a person is proud of his Muslim, Jewish, Hispanic, Asian, African, or homosexual identity, the Left sees that as acceptable and welcome. Yet having pride in your European heritage is cause for the Left to immediately label you as a hateful supremacist.

I have a respect and sympathy for the Japanese people and their rich culture. I even view their culture as objectively finer than most others in many ways. Yet nobody would ever consider me to be a "Japanese supremacist." Nor would they consider a Japanese person with those views to be a Japanese supremacist. The term is *only* applied to people of European heritage.

Wanting to live with people similar to yourself in a culture your ancestors built is not only entirely natural, it is human instinct, practiced by every group of people on Earth. Yet to the Left, that simple desire is entirely unacceptable in a white person, one that only the most ardent bigots and supremacists could ever forward.

During the spring of 1988, there was a student protest that shut down Gallaudet University, a school for the deaf and hard of hearing in Washington, D.C. The name of the protest was Deaf President Now, and the idea was simple: students felt the president of the university should be deaf, so that he could better understand and serve the community which he represented.[46] It makes perfect sense. It is normal and natural for people to want people who are similar to them, and who understand them, to represent them. I had a class in college in which the Deaf President Now protests were discussed, and the mostly Liberal class wholeheartedly supported their cause.

Japan would not likely elect a Swedish person to be Prime Minister. And I doubt Mexico would ever elect a person from Somalia to represent them. When over 90 percent of black citizens voted for Obama, nobody seriously considered racism to be their underlying motive. So why the double standard? Why is it seen as normal for deaf people, Japanese people, black people, to want to be represented by somebody like them, but whites are told they are racist and bigoted for wanting the very same thing? Isn't it ironic that charges of sexism were rampant when men did not want to vote for Hillary Clinton, yet when Right-wing women such as Marine Le Pen and Beata Szydło were running for office, sexism suddenly has nothing to do with the question? A stunning hypocrisy in both the Left more generally, and in modern feminism specifically. When Trump won the white vote by a little over half, it was seen as a "whitelash," and was obviously due to racism.[47] Yet the same standard is never applied to any other group, anywhere. For everybody else, it simply makes *sense*; but

46 "History behind Deaf President Now" Gallaudet University. Accessed July 15, 2017. https://www.gallaudet.edu/about/history-and-traditions/deaf-president-now/the issues/history-behind-dpn. [http://archive.is/F5bHb]

47 Josiah Ryan. "'This was a whitelash': Van Jones' take on the election results" CNN. November 09, 2016. http://www.cnn.com/2016/11/09/politics/van-jones-results-disappointment-cnntv/index.html. [http://archive.li/hkg1N]

whites are expected to choose national leaders who are totally foreign to them. Only whites are expected to hand over their civilization to hostile aliens, only whites are asked to allow themselves to be ruled by outsiders.

The Democratic Party makes the same play over and over again, and although it's easy to see through, the majority of our elected Republicans are apparently too dense to notice, or more likely, sufficiently Left-wing themselves. Democrats demonize whites, claim that every shortcoming of any other group is the result of systemic racism, oppression, white privilege, the glass ceiling, etc., and then the Democrats promise to protect them from the evils of "white supremacy," for which they still refuse to provide proof. By changing the definition of racism, Liberals have justified every horrific action committed against a white person.

In the United Kingdom, the Judicial College published a new Equal Treatment Bench Book for judges, which proclaims that in order to achieve true "equality," non-whites must be treated in an advantageous way.[48] Despite constant anti-white graffiti seen across the UK reading, "evil white failures", "bye bye whitey", and "every [white] death a good one"; despite the widespread and covered-up sex trafficking of white children; despite non-whites being given lighter criminal sentences than whites for the same crimes — despite all this, the official UK policy is still to enact anti-white pogroms against the native population. There are few clearer signs than this that the West is under hostile occupation.[49] [50]

When four blacks kidnapped a white, special-needs teen, and tortured him for two days, the black Chicago Police Commander, Kevin Duffin,

---

48 Steve Doughty. "Guilty of PC waffle! Top judge tells colleagues to not say 'postman', 'lady' or 'immigrant' in court because it might upset defendants and witnesses." Daily Mail Online. February 28, 2018. www.dailymail.co.uk/news/article-5447565/Judge-tells-colleagues-not-say-postman-immigrant.html. [http://archive.li/LzN1o]

49 Virginia Hale. "Official New Guidance Tells Judges That 'Real Equality' Means Favouring Minorities." Breitbart. March 02, 2018. www.breitbart.com/london/2018/03/02/judges-told-equality-favouring-minorities/. [http://archive.li/PTUlJ]

50 Steve Doughty. "Youths from ethnic minorities could get softer sentences after judges are told to consider 'discrimination' they may have suffered." Daily Mail Online. March 6, 2017. www.dailymail.co.uk/news/article-4288278/Youths-ethnic-minorities-softer-sentences.html. [http://archive.li/4baCH]

referred to the attack as "kids making stupid decisions."[51] CNN's Don Lemon refuted the idea that the torture was motivated by evil, instead offering the pearl of wisdom that it was merely a result of "bad home training."[52]

Liberals speak of the "dangerous rhetoric" coming from the Right, and they regale us with horrific accounts of alleged abuses resulting from Donald Trump's speeches. Yet they are eerily quiet when their constant barrage of anti-white propaganda and rhetoric ends up in violence against whites.

The complete refusal of the Left-wing to label any attack on whites as even potentially racist makes it quite clear they not only feel that racially motivated attacks on whites are a non-issue, but even that they are perhaps justifiable and acceptable. The way Liberals treat violence directed towards whites or conservatives is a classic example of their eternal double-standard.

Diversity has only ever meant one thing to Liberals: fewer white folk. Not diversity of thought. Not diversity of educational background. Fewer white people.

It's the same old word game the Left always plays, and will never cease to play. If we do not stop the Left, even the term "terrorist" will soon be redefined to mean anybody the Left deems to be racist, antisemitic, or xenophobic — meaning, naturally, *white.*

Liberals maintain that only whites can be racist, explaining that only those with more "social power" can commit acts of racism. Is that why blacks victimize whites in violent crimes at a rate of twenty-seven times higher than whites victimizing blacks? Or why Hispanics victimize whites in violent crimes at a rate of eight times higher than whites victimize Hispanics? Or why, in European countries, the Muslim male population

---

51 Natalie Musumeci. "Cops slammed for downplaying black teens' attack on white special-needs man" New York Post. January 05, 2017. http://nypost.com/2017/01/05/cops-slammed-for-downplaying-black-teens-attack-on-white-special-needs-man/. [http://archive.li/KmcwD]

52 Douglas Ernst. "Don Lemon: Chicago torture video suspects are victims of 'bad home training'" The Washington Times. January 05, 2017. http://www.washingtontimes.com/news/2017/jan/5/don-lemon-chicago-torture-video-suspects-are-victi/. [http://archive.li/02MHJ]

accounts for over 75 percent of rapes?[53] If I didn't know better, I would even suspect that the data shows whites to be the *victims* of racism in America, and that white victimization is being entirely ignored in favor of perpetuating the *myth* of white privilege. Fortunately, the Liberals are here to keep me from drawing such unsociable and unsound conclusions.

Perhaps in the warped world of the Liberal mind, being forced to subsidize the world's indigent, even while they brutalize your race, is indeed a privilege. Or maybe Liberalism is a pathological criminal madness.

Everything is Racist — Including Maps

During a Criminology class one Summer day, the class was discussing examples of systemic racism and white supremacy. The topic of world maps came up, and much of the class quickly began claiming that the typical map we are used to seeing in classrooms and in online direction websites is racist. It turns out that others have written about the same subject in articles such as "Your Map is Racist, Here's How."[54] The map they call "racist" is known as the Mercator Projection. Its "racism" lies in the fact that on the Mercator world map there are size distortions among landmasses. South America and Africa are presented as being smaller than they are in reality, while Europe, the United States, and Greenland are presented as being larger. Liberals claim that this distortion is meant to minimize the importance of non-white nations.

When early cartographers were trying to map the world, they struggled with the complex problem of accurately representing a three-dimensional object, the planet, on a two-dimensional plane, a paper map. Removing a dimension causes unavoidable distortions, either in the size of landmasses, in directionality, in parallel lines, or in distance. When Mercator was creating his now famous map, he decided that in the year 1569, the most important aspect of a map was that it can be used accurately

---

53 Tom Tancredo. "Political Correctness Protects Muslim Rape Culture" Breitbart. January 02, 2016. http://www.breitbart.com/big-government/2016/01/02/political-correctness-protects-muslim-rape-culture/. [http://archive.li/pfl91]

54 Nathan Palmer. ""Your Map is Racist" Here's How" Sociology In Focus. March 26, 2014. http://sociologyinfocus.com/2014/03/your-map-is-racist-and-heres-how/. [http://archive.li/0Sxq0]

for navigation; thus, he decided to adjust the size of land-mass sizes in order to preserve the reliable calculation of true distances and direction. If you use a map projection that is accurate with respect to land-mass size, it becomes difficult to properly chart a path for maritime navigation. The reason map websites show a Mercator Projection is not due to white supremacy: it's because the purpose of a map is to get you from point A to point B.

There is another map projection called the Gall-Peters Projection, which depicts land sizes in more accurate terms. It is *not* used for navigation.[55] If Liberals want to use the Gall-Peters projection to accurately portray the size of everyone's homeland, great! I'm all for it! But perhaps they could check their data before declaring *everything* a racist conspiracy theory.

No, Really — Everything

I read a lot of studies. It's a bit of a hobby of mine. It is rather rare for me to read an article or study, and to be legitimately dumbfounded by the result or conclusion. However, coming across a study about premature birth rates among black American women truly left me without words. The study found that the infant mortality rate is three times higher for black women than for white women in America. These mortality rates are still higher than those of whites, even when accounting for age, education, and income. So what was the conclusion reached by the researchers as to the disparity? *The stress of chronic racism.*[56] That's right: the stress associated with being exposed to racism or to the perception of racism, allegedly causes premature births, which lead to higher infant mortality rates.

They didn't stop to wonder if there might be any connection between the high infant mortality rates of blacks living in Africa and those in

55 Christina Sterbenz. "The Most Popular Map Of The World Is Highly Misleading" Business Insider. December 12, 2013. http://www.businessinsider.com/mercator-projection-v-gall-peters-projection-2013-12. [http://archive.li/PpZfv]

56 Janet Taylor. "Stress of racism can cause premature births for black moms" The Grio. November 23, 2009. http://thegrio.com/2009/11/23/stress-of-racism-can-cause-premature-births-for-black-women/. [http://archive.is/GigOo]

America, on account of genetic similarities. They never looked at the fact that white women are nearly 50 percent less likely to be the victims of domestic violence than black women.[57] They never stopped to examine the difference in coping styles, support structure, or spousal support. Black citizens have the highest rates of single motherhood in America. Is it not possible that the stress of being a single parent might be the culprit? Nope, let's just blame racism and the evil white man. Japan and South Korea have some of the lowest rates of infant mortality in the world; I suppose a Liberal researcher would attribute this to a *lack* of racism, not any potential cultural, racial, or biological difference. More disturbing of a potential explanation are the rates of infant homicide among races. Blacks kill their own infants at a rate of over twice that of the national average.[58]

Professor of Equality and Diversity, Kevin Hylton, wrote an article titled "The unbearable whiteness of cycling."[59] He posits the theory that blacks do not ride bicycles as much as they should because of white privilege and racism. Hylton believes that whites create barriers that do not allow non-whites to participate in cycling. An idea conceived in good Liberal tradition. Maybe Hylton should survey black communities and white communities. He might just find that certain demographics prefer certain sports over others.

Imagine the uproar, had a white or Asian professor written a piece titled "The unbearable blackness of basketball." Imagine a white or Asian person claiming that more whites and Asians would enjoy basketball if it were just *less* black.

The Center for Disease Control conducted a sleep study, which *New York Magazine* covered in an article titled, "Nobody Sleeps Better Than White People, Says Study." The article is filed under the "privilege"

---

57 "Demographics and Domestic Violence" DomesticShelters.org. January 7, 2015. https://www.domesticshelters.org/domestic-violence-statistics/demographics-and-domestic-violence. [http://archive.li/XS2cy]

58 "Infant Homicide" Child Trends. Accessed April 14, 2018. https://www.childtrends.org/indicators/infant-homicide/.

59 Kevin Hylton. "The unbearable whiteness of cycling" The Conversation. April 27, 2017. http://theconversation.com/the-unbearable-whiteness-of-cycling-76256. [http://archive.li/PQtbm]

category of the site.[60] The CDC study found that 66.8 percent of whites get at least seven hours of sleep per night, which is more sleep than any other racial group. Black people and multiracial people were getting the least sleep, with around 53 percent of those surveyed getting seven hours of sleep per night.

So what was the conclusion drawn from the different patterns of sleep behavior? That non-white groups are kept awake at night by racism and concern at racism. Meanwhile, whites, not burdened by racism, can sleep much more soundly through the night. While the Left is determined to find racism under every stone, I decided to look at some alternative factors. After not much research, I found a report from a research organization, Nielsen, that reported black citizens watching 37 percent more TV than other demographics.[61] Perhaps, some groups stay up later watching TV, while other groups turn in earlier. But such a hypothesis is of course blasphemous to the Liberal religion of ubiquitous rabid racism.

When crimes happened on our around my university campus, students would receive emails notifying us of the crime, with a description of the suspect. After noticing a certain trend, many of my Liberal peers complained about the racist "profiling" that was taking place in the emails, noting the description of the suspect was nearly always black. They claimed that this creates a negative stereotype — namely, that blacks commit most of the robberies targeting students.

I then started to notice that the race of the suspect was no longer being included in the email descriptions. His height, weight, clothing, facial hair, hair style, were all included — but not race. Apparently, accurately describing a criminal, and thus protecting potential victims, is racist.

---

60 Susan Rinkunas. "Nobody Sleeps Better Than White People, Says Study" The Cut. February 28, 2016. https://www.thecut.com/2016/02/white-people-get-the-most-sleep-per-CDC.html. [http://archive.li/SvtSm]

61 Courtney Garcia. "Nielsen report confirms blacks watch more TV than any other group" The Grio. September 27, 2013. http://thegrio.com/2013/09/27/nielsen-report-confirms-blacks-watch-more-tv-than-any-other-group/. [http://archive.li/iOG0P]

Babies—Yes, Even Babies—Are Racists

Even Babies Discriminate —*Newsweek*[62]

Your Baby Is a Racist—and Why You Can Live With That —*Time*[63]

Your baby is a little bit racist, science says —*New York Post*[64]

Do babies show bias? Researchers seek the roots of racism —*CBC News*[65]

According to recent studies, your little one is likely to be a bundle of joy, and also a hateful, bigoted, sexist, racist, xenophobic, little fascist. Just like his parents. I am, of course, joking. But the Liberals are not.

Newsweek, Time, CBC, and *The New York Post* all have run stories about university "research" that found, shockingly, that babies seem to prefer looking at and paying attention to people of their own race. Babies also were found to associate positive music with their own race. *The New York Post* wrote, "It's not clear why the infants made these associations." While *Newsweek* states that "It's horrifying to imagine kids being proud to be white."

Since Liberals are clearly at a loss to explain how in their first year of life, innocent, bright-eyed children can turn into Klan-robe wearing, Hitler-hailing monsters, I'll have a go at it.

In-group favoritism is a well known psychological concept, and it is an adaptive trait for survival. When humans lived in small tribes, they

62 Po Bronson and Ashley Merryman. "Even Babies Discriminate: A NurtureShock Excerpt" Newsweek. September 04, 2009. http://www.newsweek.com/even-babies-discriminate-nurtureshock-excerpt-79233. [http://archive.li/scV5E]

63 Jeffry Kluger. "Your Baby Is a Racist—and Why You Can Live With That" Time. April 17, 2014. http://time.com/67092/baby-racists-survival-strategy/. [http://archive.li/Rlm2y]

64 Molly Shea. "Your baby is a little bit racist, science says" New York Post. April 13, 2017. http://nypost.com/2017/04/13/your-baby-is-a-little-bit-racist-science-says/. [http://archive.li/7Afgd]

65 Nicole Mortillaro. "Do babies show bias? Researchers seek the roots of racism" CBC News. May 19, 2017. http://www.cbc.ca/news/technology/science-racism-racial-bias-1.4074603. [http://archive.li/rmv7e]

needed to be able to quickly discriminate members of their own tribe from others, since out-group members could pose a threat to their very existence. Babies, being entirely defenseless, are wired to prefer their own in-group, as it is more likely that the people who looked most like them, would be the same people to care for them and keep them safe; people who look differently, meanwhile, those in the out-group, had uncertain intentions. It's a good thing public money is going to pay professors' salaries so that they can unearth these groundbreaking discoveries, and it's even better we have such fearless journalists, who are willing to present these chilling scientific conclusions to us plebeians.

And what do professors and journalists recommend as the remedy for the problem of racist babies? Expose them to more diverse groups of people and to more diversity in the media, of course. We wouldn't want our newborns missing out on mandatory tolerance and diversity indoctrination, would we?

Anti-Defamation League & The Southern Poverty Law Center

The ADL and SPLC are two of the most influential and well-funded Leftist organizations for promoting the Liberal narrative and denigrating political opposition. In true Leftist fashion, the main tactic used by the Anti-Defamation League to attack those with thoughts outside of the official narrative is to defame their work and character. Both the ADL and SPLC are nothing but glorified Judeo-supremacist think tanks that seek to advance Leftist, Jewish, and anti-white political agendas. They behave in a more hateful manner than those they claim to oppose; these groups, which claim to be the *de facto* experts on extremism and hate, are in fact exponents of the same. Both organizations essentially exist essentially to defame whites.

Any group that publicly defends vehement anti-white partisans such as Tim Wise, who openly admits to hating whites and fails to condemn professors for calling for the complete destruction and annihilation of the white race, has zero moral ground to stand on.[66] If these were truly unbiased groups that honestly wanted to combat hate and extremism, they could declare George Ciccariello-Maher an anti-white extremist in no way fit to be a university professor. If you're unfamiliar with him, Dr. Ciccariello-Maher is the university professor who publicly stated that the racially motivated rape and murder of whites in Haiti "was a good thing," shortly after publicly expressing his "Christmas wish" for "white genocide."[67] The ADL and SPLC see no problem with him, or others like him. Which really comes as no surprise given their history. The ADL was founded to stop "antisemitism," after a Jewish factory boss, Leo Frank, had beaten, raped, and strangled a thirteen-year-old factor worker, named Mary Phagan. Frank was found guilty of the crime, but due to appeals, his execution was postponed several times and finally commuted. Growing weary of legal proceedings that were preventing justice from being served, a group of armed men stormed the penitentiary where Frank was being held, kidnapped him, and hung him from a nearby tree.[68] To this day, the ADL claims the lynching, which it considers the impetus for its organization, was due to "antisemitism," and not Frank's vicious crimes.

I searched the ADL and SPLC websites for Tim Wise, George Ciccariello-Maher, and Noel Ignatiev, to name a few. Not much is listed on any of them, and certainly nothing negative. These people are calling for the genocide of an entire race, yet the groups that take in millions of dollars annually to "combat racism and hate" are both strangely quiet when it comes to the advocacy of the rape and death of whites.

In true stereotypically neurotic ADL fashion, before the 2016 election, this organization declared a cartoon frog named Pepe a hate symbol.

---

66 "White Supremacists Target Two Anti-Racist Intellectuals" Anti-Defamation League. March 18, 2015. https://www.adl.org/blog/white-supremacists-target-two-anti-racist-intellectuals. [http://archive.li/OBNqQ]

67 Warner Todd Huston. "Drexel University Professor's Christmas Wish: 'All I Want for Christmas is White Genocide'" Breitbart. December 25, 2016. http://www.breitbart.com/big-government/2016/12/25/drexel-univ-professors-christmas-wish-want-christmas-white-genocide/. [http://archive.li/djLht]

68 Alexander Baron. "The murder of Mary Phagan — 99 years ago today" Digital Journal. April 26, 2012. http://www.digitaljournal.com/article/323026. [http://archive.li/vDLCY]

That's right; a green, cartoon, talking, frog, is now an icon of hate.[69] They were serious about this, by the way.

The ADL uses its enormous budget to ensure that the world is safe from a wide-eyed, fictitious frog, while they remain totally silent regarding calls for white genocide. There is a lot of money to be made protecting people from imaginary hate crimes. In fact, it appears to be one of the best-selling works of fiction, one of the largest industries to date.

Further illustrating the actual agenda of the ADL and SPLC is the case of Black Lives Matter. When I first heard about BLM, it was sometime around the death of Eric Garner. I recall seeing signs and shirts that read, "I can't breathe," shortly after Garner's death. At first I was deeply sympathetic to the group and their cause. There are indeed many instances of police brutality, corruption, and tremendous lapses in judgment. And there have been indeed many cases of people killed by police who should be alive today. Reforms are needed. Those responsible for wrongful convictions and deaths should be held fully accountable. There is nothing worse in the justice system than putting an innocent man behind bars or killing a man needlessly. I disagree however that Black Lives Matter is helping anything, or even moving in the right direction; at this point it is really nothing more than a glorified anti-white hate group.

It wasn't long after Eric Garner's death that Ferguson went up in flames as a result of Mike Brown being shot and killed during a confrontation with police.

"Hands up don't shoot," became the BLM slogan. Except there was a glaring problem. Mike Brown never *had* his hands up. Brown was attacking officer Wilson. Yet the line "hands up don't shoot," persisted on the mainstream media, all over social media, and on the signs of protesters who quickly mutated into rioters. Instead of working towards actual resolutions, these mobs decided to parrot a lie, and burn a city.

Neither the ADL nor the SPLC recognizes Black Lives Matter as a hate organization. Yet they do list the group White Lives Matter as a hate

---

69 "ADL Adds "Pepe the Frog" Meme, Used by Anti-Semites and Racists, to Online Hate Symbols Database" Anti-Defamation League. September 27, 2016. https://www.adl.org/news/press-releases/adl-adds-pepe-the-frog-meme-used-by-anti-semites-and-racists-to-online-hate. [http://archive.li/bXNsP]

group.[70] As far as I know, White Lives Matter has yet to advocate for anybody's death, nor have any of their supporters killed anybody. More than can be said for BLM.

During a July 2016 protest, a shooting in Dallas left five police officers dead. The killer, Micah Johnson, stated that he was upset about white officers killing blacks, and that he "wanted to kill white people." Less than two weeks later in Baton Rouge, another police shooting took place during protest over the death of Alton Sterling, in which six officers were shot by Gavin Long, a member of a black separatist group.

FBI reports implicated BLM in the shootings in Dallas and Baton Rouge, stating that the shooters were influenced by the BLM narrative. The FBI report also cited the news and media as contributing to hostility towards police.[71] It's not hard to see why, when the mainstream media, the national organization of Black Lives Matter, and politicians, continue to disseminate false information, while never bothering to correct the record.

The fact that both the ADL and SPLC claim to be non-partisan is ironic to say the least. Contradiction after contradiction, complete hypocrisy, and reckless double-standards define these organizations at their root. They have an astonishingly clear agenda, one that falls nicely along party lines, and one that is tremendously anti-white.

The SPLC maintains a list of Right-wing terror attacks. They listed both Micah Johnson and Gavin Long as Right-wing terrorists.[72] So if you're keeping track, all whites that speak out against violence against whites and advocate for their own people are Right-wing extremists — as are blacks that want to kill white people, and blacks who do murder whites.

---

70 Katie Mettler. "Why SPLC says White Lives Matter is a hate group but Black Lives Matter is not" The Washington Post. August 31, 2016.https://www.washingtonpost.com/news/morning-mix/wp/2016/08/31/splc-the-much-cited-designator-of-hate-groups-explains-why-white-lives-matter-is-one/. [http://archive.li/whJQX]

71 Valerie Richardson. "EXCLUSIVE: FBI report finds officers 'de-policing' as anti-cop hostility becomes 'new norm'" The Washington Times. May 04, 2017. http://www.washingtontimes.com/news/2017/may/4/fbi-report-officers-de-policing-anti-cop-hostility/. [http://archive.li/lssvL]

72 "Terror from the Right" Southern Poverty Law Center. November 04, 2015. https://www.splcenter.org/20100126/terror-right.

When you see the lying press reporting on the "rise of Right-wing extremism," or claiming that "Right-wing terrorism is more prevalent than Islamic extremism," now you know just how they classify these rampant acts of terror.[73] Further, many "lone wolf" attacks by Muslims are often not counted as terrorism by reports because the individuals in question are not "officially" a member of an Islamic terror organization. Yet they classify Right-wing terrorism as the actions of anybody holding a Right-wing political ideology. Indeed, as we've seen, a criminal can even be far to the *Left*, and these organizations will still blame the Right for his deeds. The SPLC uses no objective standards to classify hate groups or terrorism. They exist exclusively to smear and defame the Right — and the white race along with it.

Professor Andrew Holt released a paper looking at Islamic terror versus Right-wing terror in the United States. What he found was that, excluding September 11th, there have been nearly twice as many deaths due to Islamic terror than to Right-wing terror.[74] However the media still downplays fear of Muslim terror as "Islamophobia," and insists that Right-wing terror is the *actual* threat to society. Really, the argument about white terrorist versus Muslim terrorists should be a non-issue. The only terrorists in the US or Europe *should* be white. There is no reason to even allow Muslims into our nations; they should never have the opportunity to terrorize us in the first place.

What is most startling is the fact that the majority of Islamic terrorists in the US and Europe have been born in the West. "Extreme vetting" will not work, since the second generation of Muslims in the US and Europe are far more likely to become terrorists than their migrant parents. And the second largest group of Islamic terrorists are *naturalized*

---

73 Mirren Gidda. "Here's why the U.S. needs to focus on right-wing, not Islamist, extremism" Newsweek. June 22, 2017. http://www.newsweek.com/right-wing-extremism-islamist-terrorism-donald-trump-steve-bannon-628381. [http://archive.is/RdSuz]

74 Andrew Holt. "Right Wing Extremism vs. Islamic Extremism in the United States: A Look at the Numbers" Accessed July 10, 2017. https://apholt.com/2016/01/11/right-wing-extremism-vs-islamic-extremism-in-the-united-states-a-look-at-the-numbers/. [http://archive.li/HF9w3]

citizens—meaning, they have already made it through our vetting processes.[75]

Perhaps, if we were supplied with the truth, we could find productive strategies to solve these issues. Instead we are fed lie after lie, all while the media and Leftist organizations hope and pray that nobody is paying enough attention, or bothering to read any real reports

The central Black Lives Matter argument stems from the fact that, while making up 13 percent of the population, blacks make up a much larger share of police shootings than their representative demographic. This crude analysis of course does not take in account rates of crime and police interactions within each community. While making up only 13 percent of the population, blacks account for nearly half of all assaults, a third of all rapes, over half of all robberies, and half of all murders, which in turn causes blacks to have a much higher rate of encounter with police. In 2016, the number of blacks killed by police was 233, 24 percent of all police killings.[76] [77]

Further, FBI reports from 2004 to 2013 show that 511 police officers were killed. Of the offenders, 52 percent were white and 43 percent were black. Meaning that blacks are more than three times as likely to kill a police officer than is a white person.[78] The entire BLM narrative is predicated on a lie, namely that the police are hunting down black men for sport. This lie is perpetuated by the media, the press, and politicians daily. The reality is that, when we account for levels of criminality, whites are the group being disproportionately fined and killed by police.

---

75 Peter Bergen, Albert Ford, Alyssa Sims, and David Sterman. "Terrorism in America After 9/11" New America. Accessed July 10, 2017. https://www.newamerica.org/in-depth/terrorism-in-america/what-threat-united-states-today/.

76 "Crime in the United States, Arrests by Race, 2011—Table 43" FBI. Accessed July 13, 2017. https://ucr.fbi.gov/crime-in-the-u.s/2011/crime-in-the-u.s.-2011/tables/table-43. [http://archive.li/GDR0p]

77 "Police shootings 2016 database" The Washington Post. Accessed July 13, 2017. https://www.washingtonpost.com/graphics/national/police-shootings-2016/. [http://archive.li/QCQUM]

78 Michelle Ye Hee Lee. "Are black or white offenders more likely to kill police" The Washington Post. January 09, 2015. https://www.washingtonpost.com/news/fact-checker/wp/2015/01/09/are-black-or-white-offenders-more-likely-to-kill-police/. [http://archive.li/zgn76]

In truth, blacks are 20 percent less likely even to be shot at by police than whites are. These findings come from Harvard economist Roland Fryer, who conducted a controversial study which found that, in terms of rates of police interactions, whites are more likely to be killed by police than blacks.[79] [80] Also of interest, a study using data from the New York City Police Department found that black officers were three times as likely to shoot a suspect compared to white officers.[81]

In 2016, according to *The Washington Post* database, 963 people were killed by police. Half of them were white. Yet you likely never heard of any of them. When Daniel Harris, a white, deaf, mute, unarmed man was killed by a black State Highway Patrol officer in his neighborhood for speeding, it was indeed just as tragic.[82] Yet there were no protests. There was no fanfare. No cities burned. The national press never made a show of their stories or sought to investigate further. It doesn't fit their narrative.

The Washington Post wrote, "when adjusted by population, black males were three times as likely to die as their white counterparts."[83] Which is true, but they don't bother to tell you that when crime rates were factored in, white men are more likely to be shot and killed by police. Using the

---

79 James Barrett. "6 Facts From New Study Finding NO RACIAL BIAS Against Blacks In Police Shootings" Daily Wire. July 11, 2016. http://www.dailywire.com/news/7343/new-study-no-racial-bias-police-involved-shootings-james-barrett. [http://archive.li/ds4SU]

80 Roland Fryer. "An Empirical Analysis of Racial Differences in Police Use of Force" The National Bureau of Economic Research, 2016. doi:10.3386/w22399.

81 Greg Ridgeway. "Officer Risk Factors Associated with Police Shootings: A Matched Case–Control Study" Statistics and Public Policy3, no. 1 (2015): 1-6. doi:10.1080/2330443x.2015.1129918.

82 Michael Gordon. "Autopsy released in state trooper fatal shooting of Charlotte deaf man" Charlotte Observer. October 6, 2016. http://www.charlotteobserver.com/news/local/crime/article106360877.html. [http://archive.li/hMcJj]

83 Kelly Kimbriell, Wesley Lowery, Steven Rich, Julie Tate, and Jennifer Jenkins. "Fatal shootings by police remain relatively unchanged after two years" The Washington Post. December 30, 2016. https://www.washingtonpost.com/investigations/fatal-shootings-by-police-remain-relatively-unchanged-after-two-years/2016/12/30/fc807596-c3ca-11e6-9578-0054287507db_story.html. [http://archive.li/eluCS]

population rate factor is only logically relevant assuming that the crime rates between the races are identical. In reality, they are anything but.

The media and politicians continue to give credence to the BLM narrative, to the point that Obama invited BLM organizers to the White House.[84] President Obama furthermore sent three White House aides to Mike Brown's funeral, further legitimizing the group and its narrative.[85] One of the BLM leaders invited to the White House was responsible for organizing the shutdown of the I-35 freeway in Minneapolis.[86] Founder of Black Lives Matter Toronto publicly declared whites to be sub-human, genetic defeats, and inferior in every way to blacks. She even suggested that blacks should wipe out the white race.[87]

Ironically enough, yet all too predictably, the ADL and SPLC do not condemn Black Lives Matter when their organizers call white people "sub-human." Despite the fact that the justification for placing the group White Lives Matter on their hate list is precisely the racist remarks made by one of its leaders.

I would assume that if a group of white people shut down a freeway, or declared Muslims or Jews or Asians or Hispanics or blacks to be sub-human and worthy of eradication, the ADL and SPLC just *might* refer to that group as "extremist" or "supremacist." I would further assume that if that group of white people found many of their high profile marches and demonstrations ending in the violent deaths of police, the ADL and

---

84 Jordan Fabian. "Prominent Black Lives Matter activist to attend Obama meeting" The Hill. July 13, 2016. http://thehill.com/blogs/blog-briefing-room/news/287593-prominent-black-lives-matter-activist-to-attend-obama-meeting. [http://archive.li/aAhYZ]

85 "Obama Sending White House Aides To Attend Michael Brown's Funeral" CBS St. Louis. August 25, 2014. http://stlouis.cbslocal.com/2014/08/25/obama-sending-white-house-aides-to-attend-michael-browns-funeral/. [http://archive.li/Eogq7]

86 Laura Yuen. "Meet the young activists behind the I-35W shutdown" Minnesota Public Radio News. December 05, 2014. https://www.mprnews.org/story/2014/12/05/activists-35w-shutdown. [http://archive.li/pbx8H]

87 Joseph Curl. "BLM Leader Says Whites 'Sub-Human,' Should Be 'Wiped Out'" Daily Wire. February 13, 2017. http://www.dailywire.com/news/13418/blm-leader-says-whites-sub-human-should-be-wiped-joseph-curl. [http://archive.li/nMho6]

SPLC might just put them on one of their "Hatewatch" lists. I would even further assume that if Donald Trump invited the leaders of such a group to the White House, the ADL, SPLC, the media, and every Liberal on Earth, might lose whatever is left of their minds. Yet because the group Black Lives Matter fits the narrative, and is appropriately Left-wing and anti-white in nature, all of their hateful and violent transgressions are forgiven. No doubt so that the ADL and SPLC can focus on other hoaxed hate crimes, and track down the whereabouts of a suspicious cartoon frog.

The SPLC's Hatewatch lists serves as more of a hit list than anything. The SPLC assassinates the character of political foes by placing them along side actual terrorist organizations. The Center for Immigration Studies, the Federation for American Immigration Reform, and even Ben Carson, have all made appearances on the Hatewatch list.[88] [89] These additions to the SPLC Hatewatch list, particularly of organizations that publish nothing but factual data, reveals the true intent of the likes of the ADL and SPLC. The Hatewatch list seeks to silence and de-platform anybody that these people, whose names are not even generally known to the public, deem politically dangerous to their insidious objectives.

The total hypocrisy of the ADL and SPLC is seen in the curious case of two former Klan leaders and politicians, David Duke and Robert Byrd. I searched the ADL and SPLC websites for Byrd, Democrat politician, friend and mentor to Hillary Clinton, and the longest-serving United States Senator in history.[90] There was nothing to be found but an old archived article. When I searched for David Duke, a former Republican

---

88 Mark Krikorian. "Opinion | How labeling my organization a hate group shuts down public debate" The Washington Post. March 17, 2017. https://www.washingtonpost.com/opinions/how-labeling-my-organization-a-hate-group-shuts-down-public-debate/2017/03/17/656ab9c8-0812-11e7-93dc-00f9bdd74ed1_story.html?utm_term=.a0e9bd58eaeb. [http://archive.li/LPnjB]

89 Jessica Chasmar. "Ben Carson placed on Southern Poverty Law Center's 'Extremist Watch List'" The Washington Times. February 08, 2015. http://www.washingtontimes.com/news/2015/feb/8/ben-carson-placed-on-southern-poverty-law-centers-/. [http://archive.li/oE2Rq]

90 Dulis, Ezra. "Flashback: Hillary Clinton Praises 'Friend and Mentor' Robert Byrd (a KKK Recruiter)" Breitbart. August 25, 2016. Accessed July 16, 2017. http://www.breitbart.com/2016-presidential-race/2016/08/25/hillary-clinton-friend-mentor-robert-byrd-kkk/.

State Representative, I found expansive biographies and pages of articles. Byrd filibustered the Civil Rights Act of 1964, was in favor of the Vietnam War, and voted against confirming both Thurgood Marshall and Clarence Thomas.[91] I am not suggesting these facts alone make Byrd a racist, nor do I care; perhaps he had his legitimate reasons. Giving Byrd the benefit of the doubt, perhaps he saw the Civil Rights Act, for instance, as a grave infringement upon freedom of association. Perhaps he had philosophical differences with Marshall and Thomas. However, I can say with certainty that the same open-mindedness, the same granting a man the benefit of the doubt, would never be afforded to a person on the Right. Despite his history in the Klan, and Byrd's Congressional voting record, the Democratic party considers him a hero. David Duke, meanwhile, is still identified almost entirely with his involvement in the Klan over forty years ago. The SPLC and ADL actively update their files on Duke. During the 2016 Presidential election race, Donald Trump was asked numerous times to disavow Duke, after Duke expressed support for Trump. Although the two had never met, the Left made a point of associating their names, and asking Trump time and time again to disavow. Politicians on the Left were never asked to do the same with Byrd.

As far as public opinion, the media, politics, and Left-wing organizations are concerned, if you're on the Left side of the political spectrum, any former affiliations can easily be forgotten and forgiven. However if you're Right-wing and pro-white, your past will forever stain you. The ADL and SPLC will see to that.

This is a perfect example of how the Left forces the Right to play by one set of rules, while they play by another. The Left is never asked to denounce Antifa or BLM, they are never asked to denounce groups further to the Left and more extreme than themselves. Yet politicians on the Right are incessantly asked to denounce any and all Right-wing groups — and in displays of righteous cowardice, they capitulate every time.

The ADL and SPLC do not fight hate. They propagate hate. The justify hate. They weaponize hate. They incite and inspire hate. They are entirely silent when Leftists call for the total destruction of an entire race of people — white people. They not only refuse to condemn their own

91 "Robert C. Byrd" Biography.com. March 18, 2016. Accessed July 15, 2017. https://www.biography.com/people/robert-c-byrd-579660.

tribe, they rush to its defense. They call everybody Right-of-center an "extremist," yet the title is never used for the far more radical Left. Anybody that dares oppose the ADL and SPLC is labeled and defamed as a white supremacist or a white nationalist. Both organizations are ferociously quick when it comes to denouncing alleged hate crimes and indicting "antisemitism." Yet when it turns out the crimes in question were really hoaxes committed by their own, as so many have been, they are sluggish to retract the story—supposing they do at all. When those on the Right of the spectrum are attacked at rallies or on the streets for their beliefs, they ADL and SPLC never put out an article or social media post condemning the action, yet they demand that everybody, up to and including the president, condemns "hate crimes" and acts of "Islamophobia" and "antisemitism," which in so many cases have turned out to be entirely fabricated and contrived.

Though they do not hesitate to throw around terms like "supremacist" and "extremist," neither organization, neither the ADL nor the SPLC ever bothers to attack the data and arguments presented by people like Tomislav Sunic, Greg Johnson, Jared Taylor, Richard Spencer, Daniel Friberg, Lana Lokteff, Kevin MacDonald, or Ann Coulter. Because they cannot. The Left attacks the person, calling him a racist, a bigot, but it never addresses his data or the conclusions he draws from his data. Why is that? Simple. *The data sets are correct*—and the Left knows it. Right-wing writers are constantly referred to as "pseudo academics" by the ADL and SPLC, yet they never demonstrate this through arguments.

The SPLC has dedicated articles to attacking and defaming the sources that Ann Coulter cites in her books, yet they never once show any of these sources to be inaccurate.[92] Calling data that doesn't fit the Liberal narrative "white supremacist" or "racist" only works on people who mindlessly accept everything an organization or authority figures tell them. For the rest of us, who seek the truth, it doesn't fly. I could have written an entire book which did nothing but cite selected texts from Liberals, calling them names, mocking them, pointing out their hypocrisy, and so forth. But

92 "Ann Coulter Cites White Nationalists, Anti-Muslim Activists and Other Racists in New Book" Southern Poverty Law Center. June 29, 2015. https://www.splcenter.org/hatewatch/2015/06/30/ann-coulter-cites-white-nationalists-anti-muslim-activists-and-other-racists-new-book. [http://archive.is/6rxhP]

that's a base way to win in the war of ideas. It is intellectually lazy to take the easy road, plucking at the low hanging fruit along the way. For one, it's insulting to readers that are looking for more of a substantive debate; secondly, it is far better to refute core Liberal ideology with facts, data, real world outcomes, and logic. Even if the Left refuses to engage.

Quite apart from that, the people which these organizations so love to defame are in truth *good people.* I urge you not to take my word for it, or anybody else's. Take a look at the books, articles, and speeches of these individuals. Make up your own mind. When you see that many of the figures the Left has demonized so viciously are honestly motivated by nothing but a love for their people, you begin to realize who the enemy truly is.

Louis Farrakhan is another controversial figure labeled an extremist by the ADL and SPLC. Since I didn't want to take their word for it, I watched some of his speeches and read some of his work. He, like most of the people the organization labels as a "extremists," seems to be motivated not at all out of hate, but out of a love for his own people. If you look at the works of David Duke, you'll find similar sentiments. These men, who hold to values that not long ago were perfectly common, are now cast out as pariahs. We live in a society in which people promoting communism are lauded; they even run for president, and sometimes win. However, those trying to protect their own people are vilified and defamed.

Why is being a nationalist inherently wrong anyway? It was white nationalists who built America, as well as nearly every First World nation. What is so wrong about loving your own people and wanting them to have a homeland and a future? Every other group on the planet is afforded this simple luxury. Our ancestors didn't fight and die to protect our nations so that they could become North Algeria and North Mexico a few generations later.

Ethnic nationalism, despite what the media would like you to believe, has nothing to do with supremacy, subjugation, or domination of other groups. It is simply the advocacy for your own people and the preservation of your own homelands, desire for self-determination. At this point, nationalism is the rescue mission of our people and our culture.

Speaking of which, the ADL has even declared the phrases, "Love your race," "We have a right to exist," and "It's okay to be white," as white supremacist hate speech.[93] Think of the absurdity in this claim. Leftist organizations are trying to convince white people that it is somehow morally abhorrent for them to love their own people.

Each year there are over 500,000 incidents of violent black-on-white crimes, never so much as mentioned by the ADL and SPLC in all their incessant cries about "the rise in hate crimes." The clear message is that they simply do not care about the victimization of whites. In fact, I would go as far as to say they *condone* it, through their silence if nothing else.

When graffiti reading, "Die whites die," "Kill white people," "Death to white power," was seen all over large cities leading up to and after the 2016 election, neither the ADL nor the SPLC released statements about the rise in "anti-white hate incidents."[94] The mainstream media was also silent on the topic. During the August 2016 Black Lives Matter Milwaukee riots, video footage shows black rioters seeking out and beating white people, for their race. Chants of "Black power!," and screams of "He white, get him!" were commonplace.[95] The same scene played out in the September 2016 Charlotte riots. A white man was chased into a car park, surrounded, and beaten by a mob of black rioters. Because he was white. The same weekend a white journalists covering the riots was knocked unconscious and thrown into a street fire. Thankfully, he was pulled to safety by police officers.[96]

---

93 "Love Your Race" Anti-Defamation League. Accessed July 13, 2017. https://www.adl.org/education/references/hate-symbols/love-your-race. [http://archive.li/ZKcQX]

94 John Binder. "'Die Whites Die': Anti-Trump Rioters Vandalize NOLA Monuments" Breitbart. November 10, 2016. http://www.breitbart.com/texas/2016/11/10/die-whites-die-anti-trump-rioters-vandalize-nola-monuments/. [http://archive.li/rHJud]

95 Chase Stephens. "Video: Milwaukee Rioters Target White People For Beatings" Daily Wire. August 14, 2016. http://www.dailywire.com/news/8354/video-milwaukee-rioters-target-white-people-chase-stephens. [http://archive.li/qXNxS]

96 Maryse Farag, and Jon Lockett. "Shocking footage shows white man begging rioters for mercy while being beaten" The Sun. September 23, 2016. https://www.thesun.co.uk/news/1836515/shocking-footage-shows-white-man-begging-rioters-for-mercy-while-being-beaten-as-a-reporter-is-nearly-dragged-into-a-fire/. [http://archive.li/u3NGJ]

The most troubling aspect of the ADL and SPLC is their relationship with law enforcement. The SPLC puts out "training" videos and propaganda to law-enforcement agencies all over the US, and the ADL trains over 14,000 officers annually.[97] [98] These programs serve to indoctrinate the people we pay to "protect and serve" us into believing that white men are the enemy — that white men and white "extremist" organizations are their biggest threat. I have no doubt that these programs are at *least* partially responsible for the clear anti-white bias revealed by the fact that whites are over-policed per their levels of criminality, and fined and killed by police at higher rates than are warranted. The ADL training program was developed in partnership with the United States Holocaust Memorial Museum, in order to ensure that the police and law enforcement agencies are used first and foremost to protect Jewish interests, while entirely ignoring, even covering up, the abuse whites face at the hands of non-whites. The people we pay to protect us are corrupted and turned against us by hostile cliques. This is what an occupation government looks like.

When whites are the victims of horrific hate crimes, their stories seldom make national headlines. They get a little local coverage — if they are lucky. As an example, an Ohio man named Pat Mahaney was walking home when a group of six black teenagers attacked him from behind, beating him with such brutality that he spent nearly a month in the hospital. Pat was forty-six years old, and took care of his elderly mother in their Cincinnati home. He never fully recovered from his injuries and died eleven months after the beating. The six teenagers were arrested; they claimed the attack was motivated by boredom. For their crimes, they were given probation and counseling.[99] There was no national media coverage. No national outcry. No riots. Just another black-on-white hate crime, nearly entirely ignored.

97 "Law Enforcement Partnerships." Anti-Defamation League. www.adl.org/what-we-do/combat-hate/law-enforcement-partnerships. [http://archive.li/HQosN]

98 "Law Enforcement Resources." Southern Poverty Law Center. www.splcenter.org/what-we-do/fighting-hate/law-enforcement-resources.

99 David Boroff. "Ohio man beaten by six teens last year dies" NY Daily News. July 16, 2013. http://www.nydailynews.com/news/national/ohio-man-beaten-teens-year-dies-article-1.1399794. [http://archive.li/0I0ZO]

When Pat Mahaney had his life cut short by feral thugs, the incident was not the topic of month-long discussions. It was not seen on talk shows or heard on radio shows, no books were written about it, President Obama did not comment, and certainly did not send anybody to Pat's funeral. There were no funds set up to help Pat's family.

When a black daycare worker tortured and killed eight-month old Reese Bowman, the racially charged story did not dominate headlines.[100]

Yet when Trayvon Martin was shot by George Zimmerman in self-defense, every Liberal, up to and including Barack Obama, decided it was the most crucial issue of the day. Obama lamented that Trayvon could have been his son. But for Pat Mahaney, little Reese Bowman, and millions of other victims, it was business as usual. Just another day. Just another dead white person. There were no riots. No protests. Nothing.

But perhaps—perhaps there should have been. Maybe we need to start sending a message that probation and sweeping these deaths under the rug will no longer be acceptable. Maybe a little more *intolerance* is exactly what we need. The current malaise of the West is perhaps best exemplified by scenes of white men rioting and taking to the streets after a sporting event, but doing nothing in the wake of the rape, brutalization, and murder of our own people. Perhaps it is time for us to wake up to what really matters.

These organizations like to proclaim that "white supremacy" is everywhere. My message to them is this: they have never in their lives experienced White Imperium. But if they continue down this path, they will most certainly one day find themselves standing face-to-face with everything they fear most.

Shots Fired

The concept of "white privilege" is merely a battle tactic in the war against whites in America and in Europe. It is a tool used to delegitimize a people

100 Rick Ritter. "New Charging Documents Reveal Gruesome Details In Murder Of Infant" CBS Baltimore. May 26, 2017. http://baltimore.cbslocal.com/2017/05/26/new-charging-documents-reveal-gruesome-details-in-murder-of-infant/. [http://archive.li/zxYLa]

in their own homelands. What "white privilege" and its proponents really represent are parts of a larger cause: Leftists view "whiteness" as an intrinsic problem that must be solved. The ceaseless promotion of more diversity is at root an attempt to make whites the minority in their own lands. Globalization and the open-border policies that cause hordes of Third World migrants to flood into Europe and America is part of the Liberal Final Solution for the White Question. Evidence supporting my claim, can be drawn from just about every possible source — the media, advertisements, university campuses, academic articles, and the lying press.

In an "Open Letter to the White Right," Jewish blogger and so called anti-racism activist, Tim Wise, goes on an unhinged rant about how he will revel in the demise of the white race:

> Because [white people] you're on the endangered list. And unlike, say, the bald eagle or some exotic species of muskrat, you are not worth saving. In forty years or so, maybe fewer, there won't be any more white people around...
>
> Do you hear it? The sound of your empire dying? Your nation, as you knew it, ending, permanently? Because I do, and the sound of its demise is beautiful.[101]

In March of 2016, leading up to the presidential election, Wise had this to say:

> White people: this is the moment of truth. Will we choose multiracial democracy or white nationalism? Know this: if you support Donald Trump or would even consider voting for him for president, you have chosen the latter. You are my enemy. I will not seek to co-exist with you. I will not make nice. I will not pretend we believe in the same things but merely have different opinions about how to get there. You are the enemy, plain and

101 Tim Wise. "An Open Letter to the White Right, On the Occasion of Your Recent, Successful Temper Tantrum" November 03, 2010. http://www.timwise.org/2010/11/an-open-letter-to-the-white-right-on-the-occasion-of-your-recent-successful-temper-tantrum/. [http://archive.li/SwCAO]

simple. And you must be stopped. You must lose and not just by a little. By a lot. A crushing defeat that leaves no doubt in your mind that the country you prefer is gone and is never coming back.

Georgetown University law professor, Preston Mitchum:

"Yes, ALL white people are racist. Yes, ALL men are sexist."

"If you're apart of any dominant group when it comes to race, gender, sexuality, etc., you contribute to the oppression of groups period."[102]

Texas A&M professor, Thomas Curry:

"In order to be equal, in order to be liberated, some white people may have to die."[103]

Several quotes from Jewish professor Noel Ignatiev:

"The goal of abolishing the white race is on its face so desirable that some may find it hard to believe that it could incur any opposition other than from committed white supremacists."

"There can be no white race without the phenomenon of white supremacy."

"Treason to whiteness is loyalty to humanity."

"The task is to bring this minority together in such a way that it makes it impossible for the legacy of whiteness to continue to reproduce itself."

---

102 Anthony Gockowski. "Prof: 'ALL white people are racist,' 'ALL men are sexist'" Campus Reform. July 24, 2017. https://www.campusreform.org/?ID=9480. [http://archive.li/yP7il]

103 Anthony Gockowski. "Prof: 'some white people may have to die'" Campus Reform. May 11, 2017. https://www.campusreform.org/?ID=9166. [http://archive.li/E55mv]

> "Make no mistake about it: we intend to keep bashing the dead white males, and the live ones, and the females too, until the social construct known as 'the white race' is destroyed, not 'deconstructed' but destroyed." [104] [105]

Quotes from Mexican professor and founder of La Raza Unida Party, Jose Angel Guiterrez:

> "We have got to eliminate the gringo, and what I mean by that is if the worst comes to the worst, we have got to kill him."
>
> "Our devil has pale skin and blue eyes."
>
> "This is not a white country. It is not going to be a white country. And we will paint this White House brown."[106]

None of these people or those like them, nor even their legions of useful idiots, are interested in seeking equality. They want to dominate us.

After reading these quotes by university professors, it becomes clear why during so many revolutions throughout history, "journalists," academics, and professors were the first people to be rounded up and physically removed from society. Eventually, people come to an end of their tolerance; their patience for the incessant insolence, and provocations against them, runs dry.

---

104 Noel Ignatiev. "Abolish the White Race" Harvard Magazine. September-October 2002. http://harvardmagazine.com/2002/09/abolish-the-white-race.html. [http://archive.li/Qa2ct]

105 "Harvard professor argues for 'abolishing' white race" The Washington Times. September 04, 2002. http://www.washingtontimes.com/news/2002/sep/4/20020904-084657-6385r/. [http://archive.li/SnD8s]

106 David Horowitz. The Professors: The 101 Most Dangerous Academics in America. (Regenery, 2007).

A few headlines:

> White men must be stopped: The very future of mankind depends on it—*Salon*[107]
>
> Straight, White Men Are The Root of Our Problems —*Affinity Magazine*[108]
>
> I Don't Know What to Do With Good White People —*Jezebel*[109]
>
> Ten Things White People Need To Quit Saying —*The Huffington Post*[110]
>
> Yes, Diversity Is About Getting Rid Of White People —*Thought Catalog*[111]
>
> Escaping Whiteness —*The Huffington Post*[112]
>
> A Sermon on the Unbearable Whiteness of America —*The Washington Post*[113]

---

107 Frank Joyce. "White men must be stopped: The very future of mankind depends on it" Salon. December 22, 2015. http://www.salon.com/2015/12/22/white_men_must_be_stopped_the_very_future_of_the_planet_depends_on_it_partner/. [http://archive.li/m6i2D]

108 Alex Brown. "Actually... Straight, White Men Are the Root of Our Problems." Affinity Magazine. December 27, 2016. affinitymagazine.us/2016/12/27/actually-straight-white-men-are-the-root-of-our-problems/. [http://archive.li/6a6ng]

109 Brit Bennett. "I Don't Know What to Do With Good White People" Jezebel. December 17, 2014. https://jezebel.com/i-dont-know-what-to-do-with-good-white-people-1671201391. [http://archive.li/QFV4E]

110 Melody Moezzi. "Ten Things White People Need To Quit Saying" The Huffington Post. April 27, 2016. http://www.huffingtonpost.com/melody-moezzi/ten-things-white-people-n_b_9765436.html. [http://archive.li/IwAh7]

111 Emily Goldstein. "Yes, Diversity Is About Getting Rid Of White People (And That's A Good Thing)" Thought Catalog. May 26, 2015. http://thoughtcatalog.com/emily-goldstein/2015/05/get-rid-of-white-people/. [http://archive.li/DwyH1]

112 Jennifer Delton. "Escaping Whiteness" The Huffington Post. July 12, 2015. http://www.huffingtonpost.com/jennifer-delton/escaping-whiteness_b_7781914.html. [http://archive.li/nof5X]

113 Carlos Lozada. "A sermon on the unbearable whiteness of America" The Washington Post. January 06, 2017. https://www.washingtonpost.com/news/book-party/wp/2017/01/06/a-sermon-on-the-unbearable-whiteness-of-america/?utm_term=.92a6318ae691. [http://archive.li/43yLs]

Do White Men Really Deserve to Vote? —*Affinity Magazine*[114]

The Sugarcoated Language Of White Fragility —*The Huffington Post*[115]

17 Deplorable Examples Of White Privilege —*Buzzfeed*[116]

White Families Are Engines Of Inequality —*The Huffington Post*[117]

What Is Whiteness? —*New York Times*[118]

The Case for Banning White Male Americans From America —*Slate*[119]

White Identity Offers Bland Nothingness or Racism —*The Huffington Post*[120]

---

114 Malia Rolt. "Do White Men Really Deserve To Vote" Affinity Magazine. August 01, 2017. http://affinitymagazine.us/2017/08/01/do-white-men-really-deserve-to-vote/. [http://archive.li/thEJn]

115 Anna Kegler. "The Sugarcoated Language Of White Fragility" The Huffington Post. July 22, 2016. http://www.huffingtonpost.com/anna-kegler/the-sugarcoated-language-of-white-fragility_b_10909350.html. [http://archive.li/egRG5]

116 Michael Blackmon. "17 Deplorable Examples Of White Privilege" BuzzFeed. October 27, 2013. https://www.buzzfeed.com/michaelblackmon/17-harrowing-examples-of-white-privilege-9hu9. [http://archive.li/77wPC]

117 Jessie Daniels. "Opinion | White Families Are Engines Of Inequality." The Huffington Post. Februray 27, 2018. www.huffingtonpost.com/entry/opinion-daniels-white-black-wealth-gap_us_5a947f91e4b02cb368c4bf48. [http://archive.li/7yMqE]

118 Nell Irvin Painter. "Opinion | What Is Whiteness" The New York Times. June 20, 2015. https://www.nytimes.com/2015/06/21/opinion/sunday/what-is-whiteness.html. [http://archive.li/G5MQw]

119 Ben Mathis-Lilley. "The Case for Banning White Male Americans From America" Slate Magazine. March 06, 2017. http://www.slate.com/blogs/the_slatest/2017/03/06/white_u_s_men_should_be_banned_by_trump_administration_logic.html. [http://archive.li/3Nemw]

120 Ian Reifowitz. "White Identity Offers Bland Nothingness or Racism -- An Inclusive American Identity Is the Answer" The Huffington Post. June 30, 2015. http://www.huffingtonpost.com/ian-reifowitz/white-identity-offers-bla_b_7695138.html. [http://archive.li/7CsPD]

Defending 'White interest' can never be right —*The Times*[121]

And if these publications are not enough to re-educate you, thankfully there are classes white folk can take to help them! *Everyday Feminism* offers a ten-week online class titled "Healing from Toxic whiteness."[122] There are even white privilege conferences around the country, where you can pay to be properly indoctrinated.

For the college-bound, the University of Wisconsin Madison offers a class titled, "The Problem of Whiteness."[123] Hunter College offers another titled, "Abolition of Whiteness," in which eager young minds can be warped by Cultural Marxism and learn all about "white supremacy and violence."[124] And Stanford offers a course in Anthropology focused on "abolishing whiteness."

I'm sure other universities will follow suit. As if the social sciences were not already filled enough with the degenerative virus that is Critical Theory, they are going to ensure this is now part of the required curriculum (read: propaganda program), as well.

The people who pass as today's "intellectuals," professors, journalists, those authoring books and articles on white privilege, are without a doubt, some of most hate-filled, self-righteous, lowliest vermin on the planet right now

White guilt has been transformed into an industry, in which non-whites not only are able to teach whites to hate themselves further, but

121 David Aaronovitch. "Defending 'white interests' can never be right" The Times. March 15, 2017. https://www.thetimes.co.uk/article/defending-white-interests-can-never-be-right-83hlb2xpm. [http://archive.li/pJvzz]

122 Kashmira Gander. "Healing from Toxic Whiteness: The woman behind a course helping white people tackling internalised racism" The Independent. February 23, 2017. http://www.independent.co.uk/life-style/toxic-whiteness-healing-white-people-internalised-racism-woman-sandra-kim-new-york-a7595216.html. [http://archive.li/UzpIk]

123 Thomas Columbus. "University offers class on 'The Problem of Whiteness'" The College Fix. December 19, 2016. https://www.thecollegefix.com/post/30434/. [http://archive.li/vadkT]

124 Anthony Gockowski. "'Abolition of Whiteness' course offered at Hunter College" Campus Reform. May 25, 2017. http://www.campusreform.org/?ID=9231. [http://archive.li/SbmCA]

can even profit greatly from it as well. From books to classes to seminars, the market for ethnomasochism grows by the day.

Based on my own experience and research, it seems to me that many modern university programs now serve as indoctrination centers for communist radicalization, places to stomp out critical thinking. Perhaps even more troubling is how this mind-plague of Liberalism will begin to affect the young. Conferences are now being held in which school teachers, from kindergarten to high school, will be taught how to deal with, and talk to, their students about white privilege, the problems of "whiteness," and how to address "microaggressions" in the classroom.[125] Children as young as six years old are now going to be exposed to the same Cultural Marxism and Frankfurt School Critical Theory as college students. Young whites will learn to hate themselves, hate their race, and bear a sense of collective guilt; they will be taught they are inherently evil for being white. Nobody is born hating their own people; ethnomasochism is not innate — it is a learned behavior. It must be taught to the young. These are all very clear signs we are being subjected to the control of a hostile elite.

"White devil," "white trash," "toxic whiteness," "the white race is the cancer of humanity," "dead white male," "white genocide," "abolish the white race." The media, the news, professors, Liberals, all snivel about the "dangerous rhetoric" coming from the Right, while they freely and openly discuss ways to rid the world of the White Problem. No one is coming to check these people's hate. It's up to us to end these affronts against our people.

If we truly lived in a country of white supremacy, as the Left claims, would these be the kind of headlines we would see? Would the press, academia, and the media be permitted such vehement and openly anti-white comments? In a nation of true white supremacy, would slurs of "white trash" and calls for "white genocide" be made with impunity? If we lived in a nation of white supremacy, would any of these people have jobs the next day? Of course not. If Liberals truly believe that their ability to openly mock us and promote our dispossession is the consequence of

---

125 Nathan Rubbelke. "Conference teaches K-12 educators how to combat 'whiteness in schools'" The College Fix. July 28, 2017. https://www.thecollegefix.com/post/34912/. [http://archive.li/pfxz1]

"white supremacy," they are in for one hell of a shock. They are creating the very monsters they fear most.

If these statements were made about any other group of human beings, people would call for the heads of those who had made them. Why do we allow this to go unchallenged in our own nation, built by our own ancestors? Do you think *they* would be proud of us? These men who fought and died for our nations—would they be proud of what we have become? Allowing an invasive species to come into our homeland, attacking us with such uppity displays and insolence, and with such total impunity?

No other group on Earth would tolerate this. Nor would our own ancestors of a mere century ago.

"Whiteness," despite the rhetorical pseudo-intellectual excuses its users make for it, is simply a code word for white people or Europeans. Our enemies don't have the mettle to declare total war outright. So they hide behind their Liberal dog whistles. Whiteness means white people, "racist" now too means white people, and, of course, diversity simply means fewer white people. As if it weren't enough that these people support policies across the globe that persecute and destroy our race, they laugh about it, they cheer it on.[126] They gloat over the fact that whites are becoming a minority in our own homelands.

Fake-news extraordinaire, *The Washington Post*, published a piece titled, "The 'war on whites' is a myth—and an ugly one." In the article the authors describe white economic achievement relative to blacks and Hispanics as "proof" that there is no war on whites. Of course, they leave out Asian economic achievement, which is higher than that of whites'.[127] Their article is only proof of the widespread cover-up of what is happening. They conveniently leave out the fact that 85 percent of violent, interracial crimes, amounting to over half a million each year, comprise blacks

126 Matt Stoller. "On Mocking Dying Working Class White People" Medium. March 24, 2017. https://medium.com/@matthewstoller/on-mocking-dying-working-class-white-people-d0ea653a91a9 [http://archive.li/eFBfv]

127 Christopher Ingraham and Heather Long. "The 'war on whites' is a myth—and an ugly one" The Washington Post. August 14, 2017. https://www.washingtonpost.com/news/wonk/wp/2017/08/14/the-war-on-whites-is-a-myth-and-an-ugly-one/?utm_term=.db1f14355231. [http://archive.li/wpXbE]

attacking whites. They chose to ignore the fact that nearly 100 percent of interracial rapes are white women raped by non-whites.[128] They failed to mention the somewhere near one-million white women and children that have been raped by Arab and African Muslims in England alone in the past forty years. They ignored the fact that, due to those economic achievements, whites are forced to fund the lifestyle and families of blacks and Hispanics, who are perennial net negatives to the fiscal budget. Our monuments are being destroyed and vandalized, we are being written out of our own history books, our identity devalued, deconstructed, until we are unpersoned. We are murdered, raped, beaten, and extorted by non-whites at totally disproportionate rates, while the media covers up the crimes and excuses them — because whites have a higher average income than blacks and Hispanics.

An article titled "The Last Days of a White World," discusses population data and projections. The conclusion: before long, there will not be a country, state, or city, on Earth, in which whites are a majority.[129] The Asians will always have Asia. The Africans will always have Africa. The Jews will have Israel. Arabs will have the Near East. The Hispanics will have Central and South America. And for us Europeans? We will not even have a single city to call our own. Even in our own homelands, we are being displaced. If this were happening to any other group on the planet, it would be called a genocide; yet for us, it is welcomed. An internet search of "white genocide," will assure you that it is nothing but a "racist conspiracy theory." They cheer on our demise, and then use the media to tell us nothing is happening.

Then let us set the record straight. Immigration *is* genocide. Through our tax dollars, we are forced to fund the war on our own people. The war is waged with our own money, on our own soil. The ethnic cleansing of whites is happening in our own homelands. Be it mass murder or mass migration, the end results are the same. There is no term *other* than ethnic

---

128 Jared Taylor. "New DOJ Statistics on Race and Violent Crime" American Renaissance. July 01, 2015. https://www.amren.com/news/2015/07/new-doj-statistics-on-race-and-violent-crime/. [http://archive.li/0dMuY]

129 Anthony Browne. "The last days of a white world Non-whites will be majority in US and Europe by 2050" The Guardian. September 03, 2000. https://www.theguardian.com/uk/2000/sep/03/race.world. [http://archive.li/e41uQ]

cleansing to describe the reality that were will not be a single nation, state, or city left where whites are the majority. Our homelands are being ripped away more and more each day.

In many cases, these efforts to eradicate the whites are purely cultural. Take the Eiffel Tower, perhaps one of the best known symbols of the modern Occident. The famous Parisian monument was recently desecrated by the first ever mural to be painted at its base. An "artist" named Cleon Peterson, who has a portfolio of work that depicts white women being beaten, beheaded, and raped by black men, was chosen to paint the mural. Titled "Endless Sleep," the scene is of black figures on top of white figures, arranged in a six-pointed star, with a black man and a white woman "embracing" in the center.[130] The Eiffel Tower is an explicit expression of European culture and of the European peoples. The "art" that was chosen as the first to adorn this space in the Tower's more than century old history, is an open depiction of whites being replaced, by an "artist" who built his career around violent scenes of white people being tortured, raped, and murdered, by non-white people.

Pay attention: it's all around us. The war is raging, silently but surely. They call for white genocide, then shirk when pressed, calling the whole thing a conspiracy theory. If anybody on the Left wants white genocide, that's fine. But own it. Don't be a coward when confronted. Professor George Ciccariello-Maher was on the Tucker Carlson show; he claimed his comments about whites being raped and killed were simply jokes and that his "white genocide Christmas wish" was merely satire on an "imaginary concept."[131] Don't call us racists when we want sovereign borders, when we seek to save our nations and our people from your diabolical politics and genocidal intentions. Declare your war, let everybody know your intentions, so we may respond accordingly.

---

130 Priscilla Frank. "This Massive Painting Is Best Viewed From The Eiffel Tower." The Huffington Post. September 30, 2016. www.huffingtonpost.com/entry/cleon-peterson-eiffel-tower-mural_us_57ee7444e4b082aad9bacd2a. [http://archive.li/YMPzz]

131 "Fiery Tucker Battles Prof Offended by Airplane Passenger Giving 1st-Class Seat to Soldier" Fox News. March 30, 2017. http://insider.foxnews.com/2017/03/30/tucker-carlson-tonight-debate-drexel-university-professor-george-ciccariello-maher. [http://archive.li/GY1Gp]

Fin

The hordes are coming for you, my friend. If you think you're safe because you voted for the open-border candidate or because you posted an "I support Black Lives Matter" photo on social media, you're gravely mistaken.

Take a look at how whites are treated in South Africa. If you think for a second that Europe and America will not follow the same route when Europeans are no longer a majority in our own homelands, think again.

If you think having a "Coexist" bumper sticker might save you, consider this. In South Africa, whites makes up less than 10 percent of the population, yet they are raped and assaulted at a rate of over four times that of anybody else. They are quite literally being hunted to extinction, while the world sits idly by. The murder rate of whites in South Africa is 313 per 100,000 people. Higher than any other group of people on planet Earth. Not only are they murdered, they are tortured daily in the most vile and horrific ways imaginable. South African whites are facing genocide, while the world remains silent.[132]

We stand at a crossroads such as we have never before seen at any point in the history of the West. It is high time to think long and hard about which way you are going, Western man.

Manifestations of the Liberal Illness: Racism

Constant lies abound in discussions of race with Liberals. They parrot the lie that blacks are being gunned down by police, and the lie that white privilege is the cause of the plight of certain non-white groups. The lying press never makes mention of the data that proves whites are victimized at higher rates than any other racial group, nor do they care to cover those stories in the media. They only care about preserving their narrative.

---

132 Ilana Mercer. "Damned Lies and Statistics About Black-on-White Farm Murders in South Africa" American Renaissance. May 01, 2017. https://www.amren.com/commentary/2017/05/black-white-farm-murders-south-africa-statistics-ilana-mercer/. [http://archive.li/MH1IT]

When confronted with facts, when told white privilege is a myth, and the problem with certain communities is their own choices and actions, Liberals lose their minds.

Yet these terms, like "systemic racism" and "white privilege," are empirically bankrupt. Liberals provide no evidence to support their theory of white privilege. Nothing but words made up by sociologist to belittle the hard work of Westerners and undermine all of our accomplishments. Just words made up by sociologist to try to explain why some people can succeed and others are stuck in the Stone Age and struggle to meet even the most minimal of Western standards.

What the Left and non-whites refer to as "white privilege," is nothing more than white competency. White industriousness. White struggle. White perseverance. And ultimately, white culture. Through our own efforts we became great, not due to some unearned "privilege" that exists in an insubstantial metaphysical realm. Never let anybody tell you otherwise.

Despite those facts that entirely blow the Liberal narrative apart, Liberals still vehemently stick to their story. Liberals claim that whites are the racists, while they consistently denigrate whites and white interests.

We see the Liberal mind projecting its own bias, hatred, and bigotry, upon the Right. Liberals claim that the Right is guilty of that which the Left does non-stop. When Liberals seek to come up with conspiracy theories about white privilege, they are trying to blame another group for their own failures. They have no ability to recognize their own responsibility.

Redefined words run amok in this connection. The idea that only whites can be racists is a perfect example. Feelings of persecution are also seen throughout this discussion of race. It's always the evil white man who is keeping everybody else down — except, of course, for the Asians, and the Indians, and really anybody who stays in school, doesn't commit crime, and goes to work.

Liberals are always vying for power for their own group, even while trying to denounce their out-groups. They garner support by telling people they are victims of racism, by assuring people that they will save everyone from those horrors.

An exaggerated sense of moral superiority is seen in the way Liberals and extremist groups like the ADL and SPLC unilaterally declare themselves to be *the* moral authority on all things race-related.

Self-guilt and hatred are manifested in many Liberals, who are consumed by white guilt. All over Europe and even in America we see the symptoms of ethnomasochism. The claim that whites or Europeans have no culture of their own is only a single prime example.

The desire to control and silence their out-group, whites, is rampant.

Every symptom, in both Clusters, can be found in the discussion of race.

Cluster I

1. Deceitfulness, indicated by repeated lying, grand exaggerations, or omission of contrary information, with the purpose to advance their chosen narrative and discrediting others.

2. Irritability or aggressiveness towards anybody that questions or opposes their views. Coupled with the inability to recognize they own hypocrisy, double standards, and doublethink.

3. Inability to adjust views when presented with information contrary to their own beliefs.

4. Frequent projections of their own traits onto others.

5. Difficulty in dealing with a loss of control or power, or a strong desire for control and power.

Cluster II

6. Appeals to altered and redefined definitions of words, or relies on fictitious terms for argumentation.

7. Consistent feelings of having been victimized or wronged, without any actual harm being done. Seen also as playing the victim after attacking others.

8. Intense sense of righteousness or moral superiority.

9. The inability to recognize the negative outcomes of their own actions. Often placing the blame on others.

10. Intense guilt or self-hatred, often manifests as hatred towards one's larger group identity.

VII

Feminism and the Downfall of Western Women

Modern, third-wave feminism, as it exists today, seeks to destroy the family unit, cause more dependency on the State, and make women miserable. Feminist theory seeks to pit women against men, undermine traditional values, and alienate women. *None* of what feminists are advocating helps women in any fashion. In reality, it does precisely the opposite.

Modern feminism claims to seek gender equality, but nothing could be further from the truth. Feminists are not interested in equality in the slightest. They are not concerned with the fact that men pay the majority of taxes, while women use the majority of government benefits.[1] They are not concerned with the fact that health insurance companies are no longer able to charge women higher rates than men, despite the fact that women use health insurance more often than men and frequently have

1 Derek Thompson. "7 Facts About Government Benefits and Who Gets Them" The Atlantic. December 18, 2012. https://www.theatlantic.com/business/archive/2012/12/7-facts-about-government-benefits-and-who-gets-them/266428/. [http://archive.li/2827b]

more expensive health care.[2] While in automobile insurance, companies are still allowed to charge men higher rates than women, because men are riskier to insure due to their higher rates of drunk driving and speeding tickets.[3] Feminists claim there is a "glass ceiling" that prevents more women from becoming CEOs of companies, yet they are oddly silent on the fact that over 90 percent of workplace fatalities are men.[4]

Where are the marches demanding that men and women pay the same rate for auto insurance? Where is the outrage that women are not required to register for the Selective Service Act in order to receive college financial aid? Where is the organization that volunteers young women for the most dangerous and the dirtiest jobs? 99 percent of garbage collectors are men — but feminists do not want any part of *that* equal share.[5]

Over 70 percent of all homeless people and suicides are men.[6] [7] Yet I rarely see anybody expressing grave gender-based concern for the young men on the streets, or those who take their own lives. Feminists will march in the streets and demand free birth control from the government, paid for by tax dollars which mostly come from men, yet they are oddly silent about the grave issues in our society. The Women's March on Washington was outstanding in its level of entitlement. Demanding that the tax payers

---

2 "ObamaCare No Discrimination" Obamacare Facts. Accessed July 10, 2017. http://obamacarefacts.com/no-discrimination/. [http://archive.li/DwzwG]

3 "Why women pay less for car insurance" Esurance. Accessed July 10, 2017. https://www.esurance.com/info/car/why-women-pay-less-for-car-insurance.

4 Andrew Knestaut. Fewer Women Than Men Die of Work-Related Injuries, Data Show. U.S. Bureau of Labor Statistics. Census of Fatal Occupational Injuries. June 1996.

5 Elland Road Partners. "14 Behind-the-Scenes Secrets of Garbage Collectors" Mental Floss. March 05, 2015. http://mentalfloss.com/article/62038/14-behind-scenes-secrets-garbage-collectors. [http://archive.li/RO6B2]

6 Daniel Freeman and Jason Freeman. "Why are men more likely than women to take their own lives" The Guardian. January 21, 2015. https://www.theguardian.com/science/2015/jan/21/suicide-gender-men-women-mental-health-nick-clegg. [http://archive.li/FkRIl]

7 Glen Poole. "Homelessness is a gendered issue, and it mostly impacts men" The Telegraph. August 06, 2015. http://www.telegraph.co.uk/men/thinking-man/11787304/Homelessness-is-a-gendered-issue-and-it-mostly-impacts-men.html. [http://archive.li/0qr67]

fund the hobby of recreational sex. Demanding free birth control, free STD screening, and free abortions. The fact that modern feminists see these things as fundamental rights does not do much to bolster their posturing as fighters for equality. I have many hobbies, but I could not imagine demanding that the government pay for my new camera lens, or bicycle tires, or target ammunition. Imagine being so self-righteous that you truly believe it is somebody else's responsibility to fund what you do in your spare time!

I find the broader issue of women's reproductive rights to be incredibly one-sided and unequal. Considering that these agitators are claiming to seek equality, it is odd to me that they offer men almost no rights at all regarding children, from the moment of conception all the way to child support. If a man and woman are in a relationship and the woman becomes pregnant, the man has no legal voice at all as to what becomes of the pregnancy. If the man desperately wants the child, yet the woman wants an abortion, she can unilaterally decide to have an abortion, with no input from the man. If the woman decides to have her child, on the other hand, she can take the man to court for child support, which he must pay, though he is granted only limited custody rights. There is nothing equal at all about this arrangement. The woman has the authority to make every decision in the life of that child, while the man has little to none.

Feminists want equality in only the most Orwellian sense of the word: everybody is equal, but some are a little *more equal.*

The Myth of the Wage Gap

The single largest myth that feminists perpetuate is the "gender pay gap." Feminists from purple-haired Gender Studies majors, up to Hillary Clinton and Bernie Sanders, all drone on endlessly about the wage gap. The claim is that women are only paid around 75-80 cents for every dollar a man makes. Let's see how well this holds water.

The data showing that men earn more money than women was determined by looking at the total amount of money earned by men, and dividing that by the number of men in the workforce; the same was done for women, and the result was that men, on average, earn more money than women. Liberal feminists like to conflate this simple fact with the notion that men are earning more for the exact same job, which is not at all the case. The alleged wage gap does not take into account education level, occupation, or hours worked.[8] What we find when we look at the data more closely is that men work more hours than women, they work more overtime, they choose college programs and careers that are higher paying, and they take less time off from work. The claim that men make more than women does not account for the fact that the majority of jobs like software development and network engineering are occupied by men, while most human resource managers and administrative assistants are women.[9]

Further, studies that factor in all those aforementioned variables find that the "pay gap," falls to within 2 percent.[10] That is, when men and women have the same education level, the same amount of work experience, and the same career, they are paid an almost identical amount, with women earning even more on average in many fields.[11] The framing of the "pay gap" problem by Liberal feminists is incredibly misleading and dishonest.

A quick thought experiment shows the total absurdity of the idea that women are paid less than men for precisely the same job. Imagine you are the owner of a company that has ten employees, five men and five women. And imagine that everybody in the company does the exact same job and has the same amount of productivity, but the women are all paid $35,000 per year, while the men make $50,000 per year. Annually this means a total of $250,000 to the men and $175,000 to the women, for a total of $425,000 being paid out in salaries. If the company were to fire all 5 men,

8 "Fallacy of the Gender Wage Gap" PayScale. April 10, 2013. http://www.payscale.com/career-news/2013/04/fallacy-of-the-gender-wage-gap. [http://archive.li/Kmegs]

9 Steve Tobak. "8 Reasons Why The "Gender Pay Gap" Is A Total Sham" Business Insider. March 11, 2011. http://www.businessinsider.com/actually-the-gender-pay-gap-is-just-a-myth-2011-3. [http://archive.li/HiBAr]

10 Aimee Groth. "The Gender Gap Is Much, Much Smaller Than Anyone Realized" Business Insider. May 30, 2013. http://www.businessinsider.com/the-gender-pay-gap-is-overblown-2013-5. [http://archive.li/ot2Ww]

11 Patricia Garcia. "These 10 Careers Pay Women More Than Men" Vogue. April 20, 2017. http://www.vogue.com/article/careers-pay-women-more-than-men. [http://archive.li/mvuN8]

and to hire 5 more women at the lower rate of $35,000, it would immediately save $75,000 per year, a labor savings of close to 20 percent. If men were truly making a significantly higher amount of money for the exact same jobs, as many feminists claim, there isn't a single man in the country that would be able to find work. If companies with tens of thousands of employees that pay tens of millions of dollars in payroll yearly could cut their payroll costs by 20 percent overnight by only hiring women, don't you think they would have done so by now?

So we've come to an impasse: either every company in the nation is so sexist that it is willing to pay men a substantially higher amount of money for no other reason than their gender; or else the idea that women make less than men the for same job is a lie. The studies that have been made into this question, and logic itself, will both suggest which of these possibilities is more likely.

Perpetuating the wage gap myth is another way Liberals try to sell their narrative that women and non-whites are oppressed by the evil white man, so that they can be the noble crusaders for "social justice." It's the same old trick with a slightly new veneer — and purple hair.

Rape Culture

Feminists define rape culture as an environment in which the prevailing norms enable rape to happen more frequently, to be covered up, trivialized, and ignored.

There is indeed a rape culture, and one that is increasingly prevalent; Liberal feminists and myself agree up to this point. However, that is where our agreement diverges: For the very people who perpetuate and cause rape culture, are feminists, Liberals, and open-border globalists.

There is a current denial of widespread rape in the Western world, and the denial is encouraged by none other than the Liberal feminists themselves. They deny the fact that there have been hundreds of cases of Muslim rape gangs; they deny the sex trafficking of women and young children which is happening all over Europe and the United States.[12] The

12 "Rotherham child abuse: Cases in other towns" BBC News. August 27, 2014. http://www.bbc.com/news/uk-28953549. [http://archive.li/lDTyI]

cases have largely managed to stay out of the media and press, despite the fact that many of the incidents involve hundreds of victims and have lasted for a decade or more. Feminists refuse to acknowledge the fact that Arab and African men in Europe and America commit a disproportional amount of sex crimes as compared to European men. Feminists ignore the fact that since enacting open-border policies, places like Sweden have seen incidents of rape increase from 400 per year, to over 6,000 per year.[13] They ignore the fact that nearly half of Swedish women are afraid to leave their home now, in their own country, and they ignore the fact that the same trend is following for women all over Europe.[14]

The Swedish government describes itself as the "first feminist government in the world."[15] Where have these feminists leaders led the women of Sweden? To some of the highest rates of rape in the world and to a constant state of fear and anxiety which is so strong that many women do not even feel comfortable leaving their homes alone. Nor is it any wonder: the National Crime Prevention Council released a report showing that one out of every four Swedish women will be raped at least once in their lifetime if the upward trend continues.[16]

Feminists are quiet on the prevalence of acid attacks all over the world, and they are equally quiet about their rise in the West. Over 1,500 acid attacks have been reported in London alone in the last few years — a

---

13 Ingrid Carlqvist and Lars Hedegaard. "Sweden: Rape Capital of the West." February 14, 2015. https://www.gatestoneinstitute.org/5195/sweden-rape. [http://archive.li/cRcwf].

14 Oliver JJ. Lane. "Scared Sweden: Almost Half Of Women 'Afraid' To Be Out After Dark In Europe's Rape Capital" Breitbart. March 04, 2016. http://www.breitbart.com/london/2016/03/04/scared-sweden-almost-half-of-women-afraid-to-be-out-after-dark-in-europes-rape-capital/. [http://archive.li/LqrsJ]

15 "A Feminist Government" Government Offices of Sweden. Accessed July 10, 2017. http://www.government.se/government-policy/a-feminist-government/. [http://archive.li/LBvpD]

16 Daniel Greenfield. "1 in 4 Swedish Women Will Be Raped as Sexual Assaults Increase 500 percent" Frontpage Mag. January 29, 2013. http://www.frontpagemag.com/point/175434/1-4-swedish-women-will-be-raped-sexual-assaults-daniel-greenfield. [http://archive.li/xhVbd]

lovely custom which the Muslims brought with them to the West.[17] It is estimated that over one million British women and girls have been raped by migrant men in the past forty years.[18] Mass sexual assaults are plaguing nearly every city in Europe, while the lying press rushes to cover up the atrocities. There is no telling how many more millions of girls and women have been raped across Europe by invading Saracen hordes of non-European men. These are millions of girls and women that would have never been subjected to such horror and torture had the borders of their nations remained secure and closed.

There is a rape culture being imported into the West at alarming rates, yet feminists take the low-hanging fruit every time. They are endlessly outraged at the Brock Turner case, while they refuse to discuss the case of Edgar Mendoza, an illegal invader that raped a six-year old girl in her own home.[19]

Why? Because the Turner case fits the feminists narrative of a "privileged white athlete" being able to get away with anything. Cases of non-whites and migrants raping women and children at a disproportionately high rate, meanwhile, do *not* fit their Liberal narrative of poor young refugees just trying to make a better life for themselves in the West.

I've seen almost no media coverage of a couple that was on vacation in Germany, when an African migrant raped the woman at knife point, nor the case in Sweden of two African migrants who raped a girl and beat

---

17 Saagar Enjeti. "1,500 Acid Attacks Hit London Since 2011" The Daily Caller. March 16, 2017. http://dailycaller.com/2017/03/16/1500-acid-attacks -hit-london-since-2011/. [http://archive.li/Zcdkj]

18 Dale Hurd. "'Easy Meat.' Britain's Muslim Rape Gang Cover-Up" CBN News. October 29, 2016. http://www1.cbn.com/cbnnews/world/2016/august/easy-meat-britains-muslim-rape-gang-cover-up. [http://archive.li/iUxqY]

19 "Illegal immigrant breaks into NJ home, rapes 6-Year-Old girl, police say." Fox News. October 07, 2017. www.foxnews.com/us/2017/10/07/illegal-immigrant-breaks-into-nj-home-rapes-6-year-old-girl-police-say.html. [http://archive.li/YUV8o]

her friend to the point of permanent brain damage.[20] [21] These criminals received just three years for their crimes. No outrage attended their acts.

In Italy a Polish couple was vacationing in the Adriatic coast, when four African men beat the man unconscious with bottles, then proceeded to gang-rape his girlfriend. After the horrific attack, a Muslim who works at an Italian reception center for migrants commented, "Rape can be enjoyed like normal sex by women once they calm down."[22] This is our real rape culture — the one feminists will not acknowledge.

Feminists often cite "toxic masculinity" as the underlying issue that predisposes young men to rape women. Yet they forget to mention that per FBI data, a third of rapes in the United States are committed by black men, who make up less than 6 percent of the population.[23] In every single aspect of violent crime against women, from domestic abuse to rape, we see severe ethnic and racial discrepancies. In European countries, reports show that foreign migrants are responsible for nearly 100 percent of all gang rapes, and for over 75 percent of all sexual assaults.[24] [25] It appears

---

20 Alan Hall. "Boyfriend forced to watch as refugee rapes his girlfriend at knifepoint during camping trip in Germany" Daily Mail Online. April 09, 2017. http://www.dailymail.co.uk/news/article-4395310/Boyfriend-forced-watch-refugee-rapes-girlfriend.html. [http://archive.li/HhMGZ]

21 Jack Montgomery. "African Migrants Brutally Rape Swedish Teen; Leave Male Friend With Brain Damage" Breitbart. April 14, 2017. http://www.breitbart.com/london/2017/04/14/african-migrants-brutally-rape-swedish-teen-leave-male-friend-brain-damage/. [http://archive.li/3B9FS]

22 Jack Montgomery. "Muslim 'Mediator' Defends Gang Rape After Attack: 'Enjoyed Like Normal Intercourse When Woman Calms.'" Breitbart. August 30, 2017. www.breitbart.com/london/2017/08/30/rimini-attack-muslim-cultural-mediator-says-rape-can-enjoyed-like-normal-intercourse-woman-becomes-calm/. [http://archive.li/j5Gfi]

23 "Crime in the United States, Arrests by Race, 2011 — Table 43" FBI. Accessed July 13, 2017. https://ucr.fbi.gov/crime-in-the-u.s/2011/crime-in-the-u.s.-2011/tables/table-43. [http://archive.li/GDR0p]

24 Chris Tomlinson. "9 in 10 Gang Rapists In Sweden Have Foreign Origins" Breitbart. March 23, 2017. http://www.breitbart.com/london/2017/03/23/report-9-in-10-gang-rapists-in-sweden-have-foreign-origins/. [http://archive.li/bob9g]

25 Tom Tancredo. "Political Correctness Protects Muslim Rape Culture" Breitbart. January 02, 2016. http://www.breitbart.com/big-government/2016/01/02/

that "toxic masculinity" is a bit more prevalent in some cultures than others. Yet Liberal feminists will not address a single one of these glaringly obvious trends. "Toxic masculinity" is an incredibly obtuse theory and thoroughly lacking when measured against reality. The statistics in terms of violence against women would lend much themselves much better to theories of Toxic blackness and Toxic Islamism.

After Ohio State student, Reagan Tokes, was abducted, raped, and murdered just months before her graduation, Liberals wasted no time blaming "toxic masculinity." In a letter to the editor, the university paper *The Lantern*, a graduate student suggested that male privilege was to blame for the girl's rape and murder. He writes that men must be "fearless" in speaking up about this "culture" and bringing about the change needed in the unfair dichotomy between men and women.[26] [27] The letter never made mention of the fact the attacker was a black man who had recently been released from prison.

Although I agree there is a disproportionate level of violence between men and women, there is an even larger disproportion in the level of violence between races. There is an especially profound dissonance in terms of rape between races, which nobody has been "fearless" enough to address. Why is it that in 85 percent of interracial crimes between whites and blacks, whites are victimized? Why is it that nearly 100 percent of interracial rapes involve white women being raped by non-whites?[28] The theory of toxic masculinity fails short here. Toxic blackness, meanwhile, would account for these differences. Surely East Asian and white men, who commit far lower amounts of crime, are not behaving in toxic ways — so why indict them as well?

---

political-correctness-protects-muslim-rape-culture/. [http://archive.li/pfl91]

26 Joachim Bean. "Letter to the Editor: Constant violence directed at women highlight male privilege" The Lantern. February 14, 2017. http://thelantern.com/2017/02/letter-to-the-editor-constant-violence-directed-at-women-highlight-male-privilege/. [http://archive.li/RT3tt]

27 Amanda Tidwell. "Student blames brutal rape, murder of Ohio State co-ed on 'toxic masculinity'" The College Fix. March 02, 2017. http://www.thecollegefix.com/post/31447/. [http://archive.li/Mn1lE]

28 Jared Taylor. "New DOJ Statistics on Race and Violent Crime" American Renaissance. July 1, 2015. https://www.amren.com/news/2015/07/new-doj-statistics-on-race-and-violent-crime/. [http://archive.li/0dMuY]

Vice "news" published an article titled, "Immigrants Aren't Responsible for Rape Culture in Germany," in which *Vice* blamed the laws in Germany, not the rapists, for the crime epidemic.[29] Isn't that the very essence of rape culture, per the Liberals' own definition? A culture in which you blame the victim, the environment, and not the actual rapists? Liberals advocate mandatory sexual consent classes on college campuses in which they "teach" young men not to rape women — only to turn around and make excuses for migrants who do the same.[30]

Over half of all German women are afraid to be alone in their own neighborhoods at night, citing the recent rise of crime as the cause for their fear.[31] Police all over Europe have issued warnings to women, telling them not to go out alone.[32] In the United Kingdom, police let over 1,500 men charged with sexual assault walk away with only a "warning." Forty-five of the men were admitted rapists, who had also received warnings before being released back onto the streets.[33] In Denmark, a seventeen year-old girl used pepper spray to fight off a would-be rapist, and was later

---

29 Stefanie Lohaus and Anne Wizorek. "Immigrants Aren't Responsible for Rape Culture in Germany" Vice. January 08, 2016. https://www.vice.com/en_us/article/rape-culture-germany-cologne-new-years-2016-876. [http://archive.li/NF4xB]

30 Laura Burnip. "Students forced to attend consent classes telling them how not to rape" Mirror. October 02, 2016. http://www.mirror.co.uk/news/uk-news/oxbridge-students-forced-attend-consent-8960756. [http://archive.is/XKDCo]

31 Donna Rachel Edmunds. "Half Of German Women Feel Unsafe In Their Own Neighbourhoods" Breitbart. January 09, 2017. http://www.breitbart.com/london/2017/01/09/half-german-women-feel-unsafe-neighbourhoods/. [http://archive.li/gijRx]

32 Tom Wyke. "Migrant rape fears spread across Europe: Women told not to go out at night alone after assaults carried out in Sweden, Finland, Germany, Austria and Switzerland amid warnings gangs are co-ordinating attacks" Daily Mail Online. January 31, 2016. http://www.dailymail.co.uk/news/article-3390168/Migrant-rape-fears-spread-Europe-Women-told-not-night-assaults-carried-Sweden-Finland-Germany-Austria-Switzerland-amid-warnings-gangs-ordinating-attacks.html. [http://archive.li/wLU7Z]

33 Samuel Osborne. "Police let 45 men who admitted rape walk away with a caution" The Independent. May 07, 2017. http://www.independent.co.uk/news/uk/crime/police-45-men-admitted-rape-walk-away-with-caution-jail-a7722376.html. [http://archive.li/rfS0a]

charged by the police for defending herself.[34] Since carrying pepper spray is now illegal in much of Europe, she will be prosecuted for her "crime." These are sure signs of a sick society, one that has been subverted and led far off course. The institutions that created this sort of perversion must be burned down, with the purveyors inside.

If feminists actually cared about the well being of women, they would adamantly seek to stop the violent crime that their own Liberal politicians and policies are inflicting upon them. If they actually cared about the safety of women and ending the "rape culture," they would close their borders, stop making excuses for non-whites and migrants, and stop covering up the crimes of these men. If feminists and Liberals actually cared about women, they wouldn't import rapists, make it illegal to criticize the rapists, make it illegal for women to defend themselves, and then keep the stories out of the news. UK citizens have been arrested for "inciting racial hatred," merely because they brought these stories to light. I myself have been banned from social media accounts for discussing this rape epidemic. The establishment is so complicit in these crimes that we are no longer even able to publicly discuss what is happening to our people.

Once upon a time, in a bygone era, when men from another nation came to a given land, raped the women, attacked the men, and refused to assimilate, we called that invasion. Today, it's called "cultural enrichment."

Feeling enriched, my friends? I hope so — because we are all about to become a whole lot richer.

Feminism Makes Women Miserable

Feminist culture, which is advanced in universities, online, in the press, and in the media, tells women that their careers are paramount, that being a housewife is degrading, and that "liberation" amounts to being a

34 Jennifer Newton. "Danish 17-year-old girl who used a pepper spray to fight off a rapist near migrant asylum centre is told SHE will be prosecuted for carrying the weapon" Daily Mail Online. January 27, 2016. http://www.dailymail.co.uk/news/article-3418751/Danish-17-year-old-girl-used-pepper-spray-fight-rapist-near-migrant-asylum-centre-told-prosecuted-carrying-weapon.html. [http://archive.li/g65fq]

whore. This lesson is embodied in every film, sitcom, song, reality show, and female "role model."

The cover story on a recent *Time* magazine, "The Childfree Life: When having it all means not having children," is a perfect example of placing the value of self-indulgent materialism over that of making a family.[35] At heart, feminism is nothing more than conspicuous consumerism for women, which tells them that nothing will make them happier than their next promotion or new car, or that hideous handbag they've been yearning for. Books on the subject, like *All the Single Ladies: Unmarried Women and the Rise of an Independent Nation*, seek to promote a similar aim: to glorify the single career women, with her "hobbies," wine habit, and never ending supply of Zoloft.[36] In theory, if these tenets of feminism made women objectively better off, I wouldn't bother to argue against them. However, they do not, and it is demonstrable.

In a study called "The Paradox of Declining Female Happiness", researchers found that in the past thirty five years, women's well being, life satisfaction, and happiness, have all dropped.[37] Today, one in four women use anti-depressants — the highest levels in history.[38] Feminism has made women atomized and depressed, and has replaced meaningful values with a worthless job and mountains of trinkets.

Further, feminism has contributed to the destruction of traditional family units and marriages. A study from The National Marriage Project found that as the number of sexual partners increased prior to marriage,

---

35 Vaughn Wallace. "The Childfree Life" Time. August 01, 2013. http://time.com/75964/behind-the-cover-randal-fords-america/.

36 Rebecca Traister. All the single ladies: unmarried women and the rise of an independent nation. New York: Simon & Schuster, 2016.

37 Stevenson, Betsey and Justin Wolfers. "The Paradox of Declining Female Happiness" American Economic Journal: Economic Policy, American Economic Association, 2009. doi:10.3386/w14969.

38 Katherine Bindley. "Women And Prescription Drugs: One In Four Takes Mental Health Meds" The Huffington Post. November 16, 2011. http://www.huffingtonpost.com/2011/11/16/women-and-prescription-drug-use_n_1098023.html. [http://archive.li/VZizq]

levels of marriage happiness dropped.[39] [40] As the number of sexual partners increases, so do rates of single motherhood and rates of sexually transmitted diseases. And rates of happiness decrease as the rates of sexual partners increase.[41] [42] Moreover, the most commonly abused children are those living with a single parent and the single parent's partner.[43]

A study of over 3,000 women and their life satisfaction found that the happiest women, with a life satisfaction score of 87 percent, were stay-at-home moms. They scored higher than women with careers in charity, creative design, leisure, and tourism. The least happy women were ones with careers in marketing, public relations, and advertising, with scores in the low 50 percent range.[44]

---

39 Taryn Hillin. "New Study Claims People Who've Had More Sexual Partners Report Unhappier Marriages" The Huffington Post. August 21, 2014. http://www.huffingtonpost.com/2014/08/21/more-sexual-partners-unhappy-marriage_n_5698440.html. [http://archive.li/JoxNc]

40 Khaleda Rahman. "So how many is TOO many? Experts reveal the number of sexual partners you've had could determine how likely you are to get a DIVORCE" Daily Mail Online. January 03, 2017. http://www.dailymail.co.uk/femail/article-4085758/Experts-reveal-sexual-partners-ve-determine-likely-DIVORCE.html. [http://archive.li/HhIGV]

41 Tyree Oredein. "The Relationship between Multiple Sexual Partners and Mental Health in Adolescent Females" Journal of Community Medicine & Health Education (2013).

42 Lawrence B. Finer, Jacqueline E. Darroch, and Susheela Singh. "Sexual Partnership Patterns as a Behavioral Risk Factor For Sexually Transmitted Diseases" Guttmacher Institute. September 02, 1999. https://www.guttmacher.org/journals/psrh/1999/09/sexual-partnership-patterns-behavioral-risk-factor-sexually-transmitted. [http://archive.li/GJyTQ]

43 Andrea J. Sedlak, Jane Mettenburg, Monica Basena, Ian Petta, Karla Mcpherson, Angela Greene, and Spencer Li. "Fourth National Incidence Study of Child Abuse and Neglect (NIS-4): Report to Congress: Executive Summary" U.S. Department of Health and Human Services. doi:10.1037/e565022012-001.

44 Steve Doughty. "The job that makes us happiest? Housewife! Survey finds stay-at-home mothers are more satisfied than any other profession " Daily Mail Online. June 10, 2016. http://www.dailymail.co.uk/news/article-3634473/The-job-makes-happiest-Housewife-Survey-finds-stay-home-mothers-satisfied-profession.html. [http://archive.li/RDIv7]

The results of a similar yet much larger study of 165,000 people were identical. The Office for National Statistics study conducted in the UK found stay-at-home moms, and those who did not return to work after having a child, were happier, reported fewer feelings of boredom, and a greater sense of worth.[45]

Following the October Revolution, the Bolsheviks legalized abortion until birth and made it easy to obtain. No-fault divorces were enacted, enabling couples to be married and divorced in a matter of minutes. This was seen as "women's liberation."[46] The communists sought to destroy the family unit and to "liberate" women — meaning they were now free to work uninterrupted. Destroying the family unit served to facilitate more women's depending on the State for support; the State now became a parent to the child, and was free to instill the "proper" values into the next generation. Liberals today, one hundred years later, are carrying on the Bolshevik tradition of family destruction. They undermine marriage, promote behavior that erodes the family, and argue that a career is the most important endeavor any person could embark upon.

Feminism has always existed to help facilitate a socialist state. Communists parties from the Bolsheviks to Mao's Communist Party of China to the Democratic National Committee in the US, have all utilized feminism as a way to transfer more power to the State.

Feminism sells the idea that working at a public relations firm for $42,018 a year, sending trivial emails from a laptop at the coffee shop during the thirty-minute lunch break, is a worthy goal for women to pursue. Why? So they can feel "empowered and liberated"? Slaving for an impersonal entity that uses them like cattle?

The neo-Western tradition of sending children off to be raised by strangers so the parents can work is horrid. Many negative effects have been shown to come from children spending more time away from their

---

45 Steve Doughty. "Stay-at-home mothers are the happiest: Women who don't return to work suffer less from feelings of boredom and worthlessness" Daily Mail Online. July 30, 2013. http://www.dailymail.co.uk/news/article-2381647/Stay-home-mothers-happiest-Women-dont-return-work-suffer-feelings-boredom-worthlessness.html. [http://archive.li/Goj70]

46 Becky Yeh. "The abortion ripple effect: Russia's tragic abortion tale" Live Action News. June 27, 2014. https://www.liveaction.org/news/the-abortion-ripple-effect-russias-tragic-abortion-tale/. [http://archive.li/V4KZT]

primary caregiver in daycare scenarios. Lower levels of social-emotional functioning, higher levels of stress, more behavioral problems, and conflicts with parents and teachers, all arise with just ten hours a week of daycare.[47] If you're sending your children to an institution on a regular basis, even a "high-quality" one, so you can afford a bigger house, newer car, or nicer electronics, you're making a tremendous mistake. Favoring your gadgets and a slightly larger McMansion does a great disservice not only to your child, but to you yourself, your family, and your society. You're choosing consumerism over ensuring your child has a strong and secure foundation for life.

The effects of all of this are most strikingly visible in what is perhaps the saddest and most frightening fact: while life expectancy in the US has remained stable in recent years, even increasing for blacks and Hispanics, for white women, life expectancy has dramatically declined. Increasing rates of suicide, drug and alcohol use are among the causes of the shortened lives of white women.[48] Collapsing job prospects for the middle class, reduced marriage rates, increased divorce rates, and poor mental health are all thought to contribute to the malaise that women, particularly white women, are so viscerally experiencing, in what are being called "deaths of despair".[49] All of these factors arise from a breakdown of social capital and breakdown of communities, in which increased diversity plays no small role.[50]

---

47 Hara Estroff Marano. "Daycare: Raising Baby" Psychology Today. April 29, 2007. https://www.psychologytoday.com/articles/200704/daycare-raising-baby. [http://archive.li/c34fl]

48 Joel Achenbach. "Life Expectancy for White Females in U.S. Suffers Rare Decline." The Washington Post. April 20, 2016, www.washingtonpost.com/news/to-your-health/wp/2016/04/20/cdc-life-expectancy-for-non-hispanic-white-women-dips-for-first-time-in-decades/. [http://archive.li/YT0XC]

49 Jessica Boddy. "The Forces Driving Middle-Aged White People's 'Deaths Of Despair.'" NPR. March 23, 2017. www.npr.org/sections/health-shots/2017/03/23/521083335/the-forces-driving-middle-aged-white-peoples-deaths-of-despair. [http://archive.li/SXJLK]

50 Robert D. Putnam. "E Pluribus Unum: Diversity and Community in the Twenty-first Century The 2006 Johan Skytte Prize Lecture" Scandinavian Political Studies 30, no. 2 (2007): 137-74. doi:10.1111/j.1467-9477.2007.00176.x.

Between 1999 and 2014, the period of time covered by a recent CDC report on suicide, suicide rates of women increased drastically.[51] The rate of suicide among young girls has tripled, leading overall rates to a thirty-year high.[52] Between 1999 and 2015, the alcohol-related death rate increased for white women by 130 percent, far higher than Asian, Hispanic, and black women. Compared to Asian, Hispanic, and black women, white women drink more; they drink more days per week, more times per week, and binge drink at a far higher rate.[53] Diversity and feminism are creating horrific environments for white women in particular. These movements ensure they are surrounded by hostile invaders; the rates of crime and rape steadily increase, while economic and family opportunities are increasingly rare. Feminism, far from being interested in helping women, is vastly more concerned with, and more effective at, destroying Western society. White women are its primary victim.

If feminists and Liberals actually cared about women, instead of promoting promiscuity and going through life atomized, deracinated, and alone, they would promote the values of modesty, elegance, and family. Our Liberal culture is telling women that a career and new possessions will make them happy and fulfilled, while the data, traditional wisdom, and common sense all suggest otherwise. Women are more miserable than ever — not *despite* feminism, but *because* of feminism.

I know it's difficult to believe. Who would have thought that abortions, promiscuity, boxed wine, Zoloft, and worthless consumerism were *not* the keys to happiness?

---

51 Carina Storrs. "U.S. Suicide Rates up, Especially for Women." CNN. April 22, 2016. www.cnn.com/2016/04/22/health/suicide-rates-rise/index.html. [http://archive.li/6DQUs]

52 Sabrina Tavernise. "U.S. Suicide Rate Surges to a 30-Year High." The New York Times. April 22, 2016. www.nytimes.com/2016/04/22/health/us-suicide-rate-surges-to-a-30-year-high.html. [http://archive.li/6Mk8M]

53 Dan Keating. "Nine Charts That Show How White Women Are Drinking Themselves to Death." The Washington Post. December 23, 2016. www.washingtonpost.com/news/national/wp/2016/12/23/nine-charts-that-show-how-white-women-are-drinking-themselves-to-death/. [http://archive.li/yqFSt]

Manifestations of the Liberal Illness: Feminism

Feminism lies to women from beginning to end. Not only does the feminist narrative espouse lies like the pay gap myth, it promotes a lifestyle that is empirically proven to make women less happy. Despite the overwhelming evidence standing against their claims, feminists dismiss anybody who disagrees with them or with their dogma as a misogynist.

Rampant hypocrisy is found in the very foundation of feminism. The feminists are clearly not interested in equality, but only in *more equality* for themselves. Feminists hold marches for their "rights," and cry out continually that their rights are being eroded, without ever providing a scrap of evidence to support these claims.

In typical Liberal manner, feminists feel they are the victim of fictitious entities such as the "glass ceiling," the "patriarchy," and "male privilege." They display a sense of moral superiority in their claims that *they* are the true champions of women's and children's rights, while all those who oppose them must be haters of women and children. And in blatantly disregarding the facts and the evidence suggested by any number of studies, they willfully bring harm and unhappiness to precisely the group of people they claim to be defending.

All symptoms of Cluster I are readily apparent. Symptoms 6, 7, 8, and 9 from Cluster II are shown.

Cluster I

1. Deceitfulness, indicated by repeated lying, grand exaggerations, or omission of contrary information, with the purpose to advance their chosen narrative and discrediting others.

2. Irritability or aggressiveness towards anybody that questions or opposes their views. Coupled with the inability to recognize they own hypocrisy, double standards, and doublethink.

3. Inability to adjust views when presented with information contrary to their own beliefs.

4. Frequent projections of their own traits onto others.

5. Difficulty in dealing with a loss of control or power, or a strong desire for control and power.

Cluster II

6. Appeals to altered and redefined definitions of words, or relies on fictitious terms for argumentation.

7. Consistent feelings of having been victimized or wronged, without any actual harm being done. Seen also as playing the victim after attacking others.

8. Intense sense of righteousness or moral superiority.

9. The inability to recognize the negative outcomes of their own actions. Often placing the blame on others.

10. Intense guilt or self-hatred, often manifests as hatred towards one's larger group identity.

VIII

Ministry of Truth

The freedom of press was intended to protect those speaking the truth, and to ensure that the truth will come to public attention. The mainstream media has bastardized this freedom, transforming it into the freedom to lie to the general public, to only report that which confirms their bias and aims, while withholding any information contrary to what Big Brother would like us to believe.

The leaked DNC emails revealed not only clear collusion between the DNC and CNN in regard to interview questions, debate questions, and which stories to run; they also revealed DNC correspondence with at least a dozen other news organizations.[54] [55]

None of these revelations was startling. Why would they be? It is obvious to anybody paying attention that the American mainstream media is little more than the propaganda division of the global Leftist cabal.

---

54 Daniel Chaitin. "WikiLeaks: DNC and CNN colluded on questions for Trump, Cruz" Washington Examiner. November 06, 2016. http://www.washingtonexaminer.com/wikileaks-dnc-and-cnn-colluded-on-questions-for-trump-cruz/article/2606651. [http://archive.li/GpMCA]

55 Lee Stranahan. "Wikileaks Reveals Long List of Media Canoodling with Hillary Clinton" Breitbart. October 14, 2016. http://www.breitbart.com/wikileaks/2016/10/14/wikileaks-reveals-long-list-clinton-media-canoodling/. [http://archive.li/7PYZl]

Sadly, it appears that the basic function of the lying press has always been to advance the appropriate narrative to its eagerly anticipating herd of soft-brained golems.

The press coverage of the 2016 election, and the interviews with Hillary Clinton, were disgusting. Alleged journalists acted much more like star-struck groupies with backstage passes to meet their favorite rock star, than like professional journalists seeking objective truth. The vast majority of writers, journalists, and anchors within the mainstream media are little more than drooling fans, opinion bloggers, and propagandists with clear agenda-driven narratives. It was stomach-turning to watch grown adults fawn over a woman who has caused so much horror in the world. It was chilling to watch her cackle like a deranged fiend at the death of Muammar Gaddafi.[56] Yet the lying press continued to worship her, as the cowardly bootlickers they are.

The lying press serves as a clear looking glass into the mental illness known as Liberalism.

Clear and Present Bias

Truth, honesty, accuracy, objectivity, impartiality, and accountability.[57] When you read these values, does the mainstream media come to mind? I would wager the contrary. If anything, the lying press would only come to mind because these tenets, which journalists claim to uphold, are diametrically opposed to what we actually see from the media today. Being honest, truthful, accurate, objective, and impartial, requires a degree of neutrality on the part of the journalists in question. Nothing could be further from reality in the case of those journalists, reporters, commentators, and anchors that cover the "news" today—or rather, who present what they want us to believe.

56 "'We came, we saw, he died': How Gaddafi was hunted and brutally killed" RT International. October 20, 2016. https://www.rt.com/news/363454-timeline-gaddafi-death-anniversary/. [http://archive.li/4Ea9g]

57 "Five Principles of Journalism " Ethical Journalism Network. Accessed July 10, 2017. http://ethicaljournalismnetwork.org/who-we-are/5-principles-of-journalism. [http://archive.li/6INLT]

Professors of journalism, Lars Willnat and David Weave, have been conducting research tracking journalism since 1971. Their recent survey entitled *The American Journalist in the Digital Age*, found that 50 percent of all journalists consider themselves politically Independent. If this were the case, one might assume that 50 percent of media coverage would be somewhat impartial. As we will see, it is anything but. Journalists that identify as Democrat account for 28 percent of those surveyed, while Republicans make up only 7 percent of journalists in the study. Even if 100 percent of those who claim Independent status are being truthful — and there is reason to doubt this — Democrats outnumber Republicans in the field by four to one.[58]

Now that we know what political affiliation journalists *claim* to have, let's take a look at how this plays out in terms of press coverage. The Media Research Center (MRC) has been examining and tracking press coverage since the 1980s. They recently released data on the media coverage for Donald Trump's first three months in office. Evaluating the three big news networks, ABC, NBC, and CBS, the Media Research Center found that over half of all news coverage for the period was directly related to President Trump. Of that coverage, MRC found that 88 percent of the coverage was negative and hostile towards President Trump.[59] Conversely, after President Obama's first hundred days in office, the same media organizations not only devoted much less time to covering the new President, but they were largely supportive, with over 50 percent of all coverage being favorable towards President Obama.[60]

A similar study was conducted by Harvard professor Thomas E. Patterson. Patterson's media study also included *The New York Times*,

58 Chris Cillizza. "Just 7 percent of journalists are Republicans. That's far fewer than even a decade ago" The Washington Post. May 06, 2014. https://www.washingtonpost.com/news/the-fix/wp/2014/05/06/just-7-percent-of-journalists-are-republicans-thats-far-less-than-even-a-decade-ago/. [http://archive.is/0xBcX]

59 Jennifer Harper. "Press coverage of Trump in first month of office: 88 percent 'hostile,' says new study" The Washington Times. March 02, 2017. http://www.washingtontimes.com/news/2017/mar/2/press-coverage-of-trump-in-first-month-of-office-8/. [http://archive.li/ZhwZQ]

60 Mike Ciandella. "FLASHBACK: Media Gushed Over Obama's First 100 Days" NewsBusters. April 19, 2017. http://www.newsbusters.org/blogs/nb/mike-ciandella/2017/04/19/flashback-media-gushed-over-obamas-first-100-days.

Washington Post, *Wall Street Journal*, and Fox. During Trump's first 100 days, Patterson found that 80 percent of all coverage, including that by Fox, was negative. The study found that fully 93 percent of CNN reports were negative, while *only* 52 percent of Fox reports were negative. Fox was the only news organization that displayed an even split between negative and positive coverage. Fox, the organization which Liberals so clearly despise, the organization which Liberals so often label as "fake news," "faux news," "not really news," and the like, was the only organization to show any level of impartiality. Of all the topics covered, immigration received the most negative press, with 96 percent of statements being negative; economics, meanwhile, was merely 54 percent negative.[61]

In terms of print newspapers, the bias was no better. Of the top hundred major papers in the US, only two endorsed Donald Trump in the 2016 election. The majority endorsed Clinton, while a few supported Gary Johnson. A handful of low-circulation, independent papers, also endorsed Trump in his 2016 run.[62]

An analysis by the Center for Public Integrity found that during the election cycle leading to November 2016, 96 percent of all campaign donation dollars from the media industry went to Clinton. Of the 480 media donors, 430 donated to Clinton.[63]

Two elements are worthy of note here. The first is the number of journalists that are Left of center as compared to those on the Right. The second is the fact that a mere six corporations control 90 percent of the media outlets in America. In the 1980s, there were over fifty companies that controlled the press, radio, TV, and film studios. Due to deregulation, abetted by the Telecommunications Act of 1996, which eased regulations

---

61 Thomas Patterson. "News Coverage of Donald Trump's First 100 Days" Shorenstein Center. May 18, 2017. https://shorensteincenter.org/news-coverage-donald-trumps-first-100-days/. [http://archive.li/WjcL2]

62 Reid Wilson. "Final newspaper endorsement count: Clinton 57, Trump 2" TheHill. November 06, 2016. http://thehill.com/blogs/ballot-box/presidential-races/304606-final-newspaper-endorsement-count-clinton-57-trump-2. [http://archive.li/k8bHp]

63 Katie McHugh. "Study: 96 Percent of Media's Campaign Donations Go to Hillary Clinton" Breitbart. October 18, 2016. http://www.breitbart.com/2016-presidential-race/2016/10/18/revealed-96-percent-of-medias-campaign-donations-went-to-clinton/. [http://archive.li/HdXaa]

and removed the limit placed on radio station ownership, companies were able to buy up smaller entities until only a handful now control nearly everything that we see and hear. Clear Channel Communications, now iHeart Media, went from owning around forty radio stations in 1995, to over 850 stations since the Telecommunications Act of 1996 was passed.[64]

Previous laws would not allow conglomerate media companies to create an oligopoly; media regulations existed for a reason. Our freedom of press, and the media regulations which helped defend it, existed because statesmen of long ago recognized the danger that consolidated media could pose. The threat of having all information filtered through a small clique was understood as being detrimental to freedom. This danger has been demonstrated in our day. The mainstream media empire now exists not to inform us, but to tell us what to believe. Everything is now screened through a handful of companies that dictate what we are supposed to care about. Between the media oligopoly and the government's role in deciding what is taught in schools, everything, literally everything, is transformed into some deviated and diluted version of the truth.

Pew Research published an article entitled "Political Polarization & Media Habits," which examined the differences between Liberals' and conservatives' media habits. The article thoroughly praised Liberals for using more news sources as compared to conservatives. While 47 percent of conservatives named Fox News as their primary news source, Liberals sought an "array" of sources — that is, CNN, MSNBC, NPR, and *The New York Times*. What the Pew Research article did *not* mention while they were busy painting conservatives as shallow, uniformed, ignorant plebeians living in an echo chamber, was that the "array" of sources Liberals use all parrot one and the same ideology right back to them. According to the studies just discussed, Fox is by far the most impartial and balanced source of news. Yet Pew Research went to great lengths to use the fact that most conservatives prefer Fox News as a way to denigrate them as simple-minded, insular, and biased.

---

64 Ashley Lutz. "These 6 Corporations Control 90 percent Of The Media In America" Business Insider. June 14, 2012. http://www.businessinsider.com/these-6-corporations-control-90-of-the-media-in-america-2012-6. [http://archive.li/nxbkT]

The article paints a negative portrait of conservatives, while entirely ignoring the clear media bias of most news organizations. Pew Research also found that Liberals are so incredibly *tolerant and progressive*, that they are more likely to block and un-friend people on social media who do not share their political views. They rush past this bit. The profound irony of a research article on the bias of media preferences which itself shows clear biases had me wondering if I was reading satire.[65]

The extreme media bias documented in regard to coverage of Presidents does not only apply to heads of state. This clear and present bias is found in nearly every article, on nearly every talking point. The press is majority pro-Islam, anti-white, sympathetic to Black Lives Matter and Antifa, while they denounce any pro-white organizations and accuse them of being composed of "supremacists." When whites are the victims of violent crimes, which they usually are, the story hardly makes the papers; when the victim is black and the perpetrator white, the coverage is non-stop. Anything that can be used to forward the Liberal narrative is exploited to the utmost. Meanwhile, the frequent events that fly in the face of the Liberal narrative are relegated to local press, and seldom make national headlines.

War is Hell

For over 100 years, the press and government have been conspiring in the dark to lead the US into unnecessary wars. The RMS *Lusitania* was used as a US battle cry to enter the First World War. The *Lusitania*, besides carrying Americans, was also carrying munitions for the British, unprotected, through a war zone, while the Germans were fighting a British blockade. The Allied media reports omitted those crucial details in order to stir up

65 Amy Mitchell, Jeffrey Gottfried, Jocelyn Kiley, and Katerina Eva Matsa. "Political Polarization & Media Habits" Pew Research Center's Journalism Project. October 21, 2014. http://www.journalism.org/2014/10/21/political-polarization-media-habits/. [http://archive.li/EjFf6]

more resentment towards the Germans and to muster American support for war.[66] [67]

The Second World War is overbrimming with lies. The Japanese attack on Pearl Harbor was, and still is, sold as a "surprise attack," when in reality, FDR had been waging an increasingly aggressive economic war on Japan with increasingly hostile provocations for months prior. President Franklin Roosevelt had seized all Japanese assets within the US, and placed a devastating oil embargo on the Japanese, months before Pearl Harbor.[68]

The Katyn Forest massacre was one of the most notorious and brutal mass murders of the Second World War. 15,000 unarmed Polish prisoners were executed and buried in mass, shallow graves in the snowy Katyn Forest. The massacre was used in Allied propaganda to foment anti-German sentiment, and showcase the German lack of humanity. But Polish investigations from 1943 revealed that it was in fact the Russian secret police, the NKVD, who had massacred the Poles, not the Germans. The German army had not even been in the region when the massacre took place. Yet the true story was covered up for years, and the NKVD was never held responsible for their war crimes. In fact, Germans were tried for the Katyn Massacre after the war ended — tried by a Soviet court in Leningrad.[69]

The Gulf of Tonkin incident is strikingly similar: lying government intelligence agencies, followed slavishly by the lying press who ran with

---

66 Doug Bandow. "Sinking the Lusitania: Lying America into War, Again" Cato Institute. May 07, 2015. https://www.cato.org/blog/sinking-lusitania-lying-america-war-again. [http://archive.li/OdRaF]

67 Bandow Dou. "Sailing And Sinking The RMS Lusitania: A Century Of Lying America Into War" Forbes. May 06, 2015. https://www.forbes.com/sites/dougbandow/2015/05/06/sailing-and-sinking-the-rms-lusitania-a-century-of-lying-america-into-war/. [http://archive.li/8k9sc]

68 "United States freezes Japanese assets" History.com. Accessed July 31, 2017. http://www.history.com/this-day-in-history/united-states-freezes-japanese-assets. [http://archive.li/h5tZK]

69 "Soviets Admit Blame in Massacre Of Polish Officers in World War II" The New York Times. April 13, 1990. http://www.nytimes.com/1990/04/13/world/upheaval-east-soviets-admit-blame-massacre-polish-officers-world-war-ii.html. [http://archive.li/HbJHp]

the story in order to manipulate the citizens that trusted them. The official narrative of North Vietnam launching two unprovoked attacks against US ships was almost entirely fabricated. The story has it that on August 2nd 1964, the US ship, USS *Maddox*, was on patrol when an unprovoked attack came from the North Vietnamese. What the government and media failed to mention was that the day before, North Vietnam had been attacked by the South Vietnamese Navy in the same Gulf of Tonkin.

Two days after the first "attack" on the USS Maddox took place, the Pentagon and media claimed that another US ship was attacked. The second incident never took place, yet it was all the justification Lyndon Johnson needed to enter into the war. Forty years later, it would be revealed that the NSA had falsified information to "create" the second attack. There are over 58,000 Americans, and hundreds of thousands of Vietnamese dead, as a result of that lie. And nobody was ever held accountable.[70] [71]

The entirely fabricated Nayirah testimony was used as justification for entering the Gulf War. The fifteen year-old daughter of a Kuwaiti ambassador lied before the Congressional Human Rights Caucus. Nayirah told a harrowing tale of having personally witnessed Iraqi soldiers going into a hospital in Kuwait, throwing Kuwaiti children out of incubators, and leaving them on the floor to die. The story was entirely fabricated. The press of course ran with it, and government officials used the work of fiction to paint the Iraqis as monsters, so as to justify yet another war.[72]

Government "intelligence" agencies around the globe and the media sold the Weapons of Mass Destruction lie. Saddam Hussein was built up to be the largest existential threat to the West of his time. Our very survival was predicated on a war with Iraq, according to both intelligence agencies

---

70 Gene Healy. "Happy Gulf of Tonkin Anniversary (and Thanks, NSA, for Lying about It for 40 Years)" Cato Institute. August 08, 2013. https://www.cato.org/blog/happy-gulf-tonkin-anniversary-thanks-nsa-lying-about-it-40-years. [http://archive.li/eior0]

71 Jeff Cohen and Norman Solomon. "30-year Anniversary: Tonkin Gulf Lie Launched Vietnam War" FAIR. July 27, 1994. http://fair.org/media-beat-column/30-year-anniversary-tonkin-gulf-lie-launched-vietnam-war/. [http://archive.li/y8ECu]

72 Tom Regan. "When contemplating war, beware of babies in incubators" The Christian Science Monitor. September 06, 2002. http://www.csmonitor.com/2002/0906/p25s02-cogn.html. [http://archive.li/N0bg]

and the press. Years later we are left with thousands of dead Americans, hundreds of thousands of dead Iraqis, and absolutely nothing to show for this carnage.

United States and NATO involvement in the Libyan Civil War, which ultimately lead to the brutal slaying of Muammar Gaddafi, was entirely justified through Colonel Gaddafi's alleged massacre of his own citizens. Intervention by the US and NATO came under the guise of humanitarianism; they created a monster out of Gaddafi, armed his opponents, then murdered him.[73] As happens time and time again, we are sold the same tired boogeyman story. We are expected to believe that war is a reasonable "humanitarian" solution. The Ministry of Truth is so brazen that they openly espouse blatant contradictions, and so insulting, that they expect us to actually pretend that these manipulations are normal.

If the Ministry of Truth would so shamelessly lie to us about these watershed events, they will lie about anything.

The media and government is now trying to do the same thing to Assad and Putin. Liberal-controlled media and "intelligence agencies" have been forwarding a Russian conspiracy theory since the 2016 election. They have presented no evidence, per their usual, but they insist on the narrative regardless.

How suitably ironic that the same people who favor mass migration and the abolition of borders, now pretend to be deeply concerned with national sovereignty. The same people who go about chanting "Build bridges not walls!" and "No human is illegal!" are suddenly terribly worried about Russian influence, to the point of advocating war with one of the world's largest superpowers.[74]

The United States has toppled governments and assassinated leaders; Obama threatened the UK with penalizing trade policies before

---

73 Micah Zenko. "The Big Lie About the Libyan War" Foreign Policy. March 22, 2016. http://foreignpolicy.com/2016/03/22/libya-and-the-myth-of-humanitarian-intervention/. [http://archive.li/V9Gf2]

74 Glenn Greenwald. "A Consensus Emerges: Russia Committed an 'Act of War' on Par With Pearl Harbor and 9/11. Should the U.S. Response Be Similar?" The Intercept. February 19, 2018. theintercept.com/2018/02/19/a-consensus-emerges-russia-committed-an-act-of-war-on-par-with-pearl-harbor-and-911-should-the-u-s-response-be-similar/. [http://archive.li/XZ1Xd]

the Brexit referendum.[75] Liberals had no issue with Obama and Hillary hunting Colonel Gaddafi down like an animal, which in turn exacerbated the European migrant crisis. But alleged Russian interference is just too much to take. It's remarkable when you think about it. *That's* what finally did it for the Left? Seeing the truth about their corrupt and depraved Democratic National Committee from some leaked emails? And how ironic that Liberals were more upset about the *method* in which the truth was revealed, than they were about the *contents* of the emails themselves.

In true Orwellian manner, the Ministry of Truth wants us to believe that "war is peace." That we needed be involved in every war throughout history. That we needed to invade Iraq. That Gaddafi needed to be overthrown. And that Putin and Assad are presently our greatest threats. But I ask, are *those* men the ones responsible for the opening of our borders? Is our tax money being sent to *their* nations? Are *they* the ones robbing us, lying to us, stealing our hard-earned money and time? Are any of these foreign leaders responsible for creating our oppressive tax system, our welfare state, our absurd immigration policies, and the ceaseless attacks on our liberties?

Not at all. The enemy is within. If you want to know who the real enemies are, follow the money, and ask yourself what groups you are not allowed to freely criticize.

Looking back at the history of armed conflicts, ask yourself a simple question — how could this have possibly benefited Americans? You'll be hard-pressed to find a single answer. Nonetheless, we have spilled endless treasure and rivers of blood. For what? What do we have to show for our involvement in any of history's wars? Nothing, save a long list of good men that never made it home.

If this past election and these stories have not caused you to question every single narrative upheld by the mainstream media over the last century, I'm afraid you have not learned to ask the right questions.

Fearing that too many people had begun to ask too many of the right questions, Congress leaped into action. A bipartisan bill called the

---

75 Anushka Asthana and Rowena Mason. "Barack Obama: Brexit would put UK 'back of the queue' for trade talks" The Guardian. April 22, 2016. https://www.theguardian.com/politics/2016/apr/22/barack-obama-brexit-uk-back-of-queue-for-trade-talks. [http://archive.li/FKRln]

Countering Foreign Propaganda and Disinformation Act would be added to the National Defense Authorization Act (NDAA), in an effort to fight "fake news."[76] This is a new low, even for invertebrate swamp creatures. Who gets to arbitrarily decide what is and is not "fake news"? How will "fake news" be countered? With a visit from the Thought Police and a three night stay in Room 101? Does Congress think we are too pedestrian to discern "fake news" from "real news"? Or do they have so much to hide, that an addition to the already overreaching NDAA needed to be made?

The same group of people that brought us such insights as "Iraq has weapons of mass destruction," "The NSA is not spying on US citizens," and "Hillary has a 99 percent chance of winning the election," want to be the gatekeepers of "fake news." Thoroughly horrifying.

The truth will never need laws to protect it. The truth will always stand with two feet on solid ground, while lies stand on but one. The truth is out there. Patiently waiting for the lies to collapse under their own weight, so that it may triumph once again.

The Lie Factory presents: Hate Crime Hoax Hysteria

The latest perverse and degenerate Liberal fetish is the fake hate crime. The rise of fake hate crimes since November 2016 has been meteoric. The Southern Poverty Law Center kicked this circus off with their propaganda literature entitled "Ten Days After: Harassment and Intimidation in the Aftermath of the Election."[77] The SPLC's scare piece begins with the tragic story of the burning of a Mississippi church, and a message painted on the side of the building that read, "Vote Trump." Well, the truth rose from the

---

76 Craig Timberg. "Effort to combat foreign propaganda advances in Congress" The Washington Post. November 30, 2016. https://www.washingtonpost.com/business/economy/effort-to-combat-foreign-propaganda-advances-in-congress/2016/11/30/9147e1ac-e221-47be-ab92-9f2f7e69d452_story.html?utm_term=.1723bef50a81.

77 "Ten Days After: Harassment and Intimidation in the Aftermath of the Election" Southern Poverty Law Center. November 29, 2016. https://www.splcenter.org/20161129/ten-days-after-harassment-and-intimidation-aftermath-election. [http://archive.li/g6nhi]

church's ashes like a triumphant phoenix: a member of the church itself had written the message and started the fire.[78]

According to the SPLC over 1,000 "bias related incidents" occurred in the month after the 2016 presidential election. Of those "incidents," the SPLC counted a group of middle-school children chanting "Build the wall!" during lunchtime as a "bias related incident."[79] Apparently the SPLC does not take kindly to twelve year-olds who support sovereign borders. Who knew?

Interestingly, the SPLC has maintained silence on the hundreds of instances of violence against the Right. The attacks on Trump supporters make it onto their list only to discredit and downplay them. Violent Left-wing groups are ignored, and the SPLC makes no comment on incidents such as a man being shot at on the freeway simply for having a Make America Great Again flag flying on his truck.[80]

For over a year, the Liberal media was infatuated with the rise of hate crimes. This has been its favorite method to defame those of us on the Right as violent lunatics.

> Here Are 28 Reported Racist And Violent Incidents After Donald Trump's Victory —*Buzzfeed*[81]

---

78 Samira Said and Darran Simon. "Parishioner charged in Mississippi church fire" CNN. December 22, 2016. http://www.cnn.com/2016/12/21/us/mississippi-black-church-arson-arrest/. [http://archive.li/OIPaz]

79 "Update: 1,094 Bias-Related Incidents in the Month Following the Election" Southern Poverty Law Center. December 16, 2016. https://www.splcenter.org/hatewatch/2016/12/16/update-1094-bias-related-incidents-month-following-election. [http://archive.li/4uukX]

80 Debra Heine. "Shots Fired at Truck Flying 'Make America Great Again' Flag in Indiana" PJ Media. June 15, 2017. https://pjmedia.com/trending/2017/06/15/shots-fired-at-truck-flying-make-america-great-again-flag-in-indiana/. [http://archive.li/kDjnB]

81 Tasneem Nashrulla. "Here Are 28 Reported Racist And Violent Incidents After Donald Trump's Victory" BuzzFeed. November 10, 2016. https://www.buzzfeed.com/tasneemnashrulla/racist-incidents-after-trumps-victory. [http://archive.is/9vvtJ]

> Hate crimes spike, most sharply against Muslims —CNN[82]
>
> Anti-Muslim Hate Crimes Surged Last year, Fueled By Hateful Campaign —SPLC[83]
>
> 2016 was a horrible year for anti-Semitic hate crimes. 2017 is much worse. —ThinkProgress[84]
>
> Anti-Muslim Hate Crimes Are Spiking In The U.S. Donald Trump Won't Speak Up. —*The Huffington Post*[85]

The lying press constantly ran the story of increasing antisemitism, citing a string of bomb threats to Jewish centers and Jewish cemetery vandalism as the most egregious incidents. As fate would have it, the "neo-Nazis" behind over one hundred bomb threats turned out to be a single Jewish man living in Israel, along with a black, Liberal journalist.[86] [87] It doesn't get much better than that.

---

82 Azadeh Ansari. "FBI: Hate crimes spike, most sharply against Muslims" CNN. November 15, 2016. http://www.cnn.com/2016/11/14/us/fbi-hate-crime-report-muslims/. [http://archive.li/tIxpu]

83 Mark Potok. "Anti-Muslim Hate Crimes Surged Last Year, Fueled by Hateful Campaign" Southern Poverty Law Center. November 14, 2016. https://www.splcenter.org/hatewatch/2016/11/14/anti-muslim-hate-crimes-surged-last-year-fueled-hateful-campaign.

84 Jack Jenkins. "2016 was a horrible year for anti-Semitic hate crimes. 2017 is much worse" Think Progress. April 24, 2017. https://thinkprogress.org/report-anti-semitic-spike-this-year-bdf97cbe762. [http://archive.li/Wa7Mz]

85 Carol Kuruvilla. "Anti-Muslim Hate Crimes Are Spiking In The U.S. Donald Trump Won't Speak Up" The Huffington Post. February 25, 2017. https://www.huffingtonpost.com/entry/trump-islamophobia-anti-semitism_us_58b08debe4b0780bac2938b4. [http://archive.li/SKpF8]

86 "Bipartisan bill would boost penalties for anti-Semitic bomb threats" Jewish Telegraphic Agency. March 27, 2017. http://www.jta.org/2017/03/27/default/bipartisan-bill-would-boost-penalties-for-anti-semitic-bomb-threats.

87 Peter Beaumont. "Israeli teenager arrested over bomb threats to US Jewish targets" The Guardian. March 23, 2017. https://www.theguardian.com/us-news/2017/mar/23/israeli-police-arrest-man-over-bomb-threats-to-us-jewish-targets. [http://archive.li/VpmuF]

Or does it?

Do you remember all those tombstones in Jewish cemeteries that were vandalized? The tombstones, for whose repair over $100,000 were raised through donations?[88] The cemeteries that were plastered all over the news as a sure sign of the rise in Right-wing "neo-Nazi" terror? Well, the New York City Police Department hate-crime task force investigated the "vandalism," and found that the "desecrated tombstones" had actually been damaged by "environmental" factors. Meaning — a strong storm blew the headstones over. The cemeteries were in such disrepair and had been maintained so poorly, that high winds were able to topple the headstones. The tombstones became dilapidated as a result of utter neglect, and antisemitism was declared the cause.[89] To be clear, according to the Left, nature is now antisemitic. And, of course, it's our fault. As a result of the fake bomb threats and fake hate crimes, the bipartisan Combating Anti-Semitism Act of 2017 has been introduced to Congress. The Act seeks to create harsher penalties for those who target religious institutions. Just as acts of violence are so often used to restrict individual liberty, now even imaginary violence is being used as a justification to pass Draconian laws and usher in a far more authoritarian State.[90]

To be entirely objective, I looked at the FBI database of hate crimes, to see if perhaps the Liberal narrative had any trace of credibility. In 2015, the FBI reports 5,818 hate crime offenses. Out of those, eighteen were murders and thirteen were rapes.[91] To put the 5,818 hate crimes in perspective, over

---

88 Mary Emily O'Hara. "Muslim Fundraiser to Repair Jewish Cemetery Raises $100k" NBCNews.com. February 23, 2017. http://www.nbcnews.com/news/us-news/muslim-fundraiser-repair-jewish-cemetery-raises-100k-n724221. [http://archive.li/Q6iwJ]

89 Azadeh Ansari and Joe Sutton. "Tombstones damaged at New York cemetery not vandalism, say police" CNN. March 06, 2017. http://www.cnn.com/2017/03/05/us/brooklyn-jewish-cemetery-tombstones-overturned/. [http://archive.li/uBdle]

90 "Bipartisan bill would boost penalties for anti-Semitic bomb threats" Jewish Telegraphic Agency. March 27, 2017. Accessed July 10, 2017. http://www.jta.org/2017/03/27/default/bipartisan-bill-would-boost-penalties-for-anti-semitic-bomb-threats.

91 "Incidents and Offenses 2015 Hate Crime Statistics" FBI. Accessed July 10, 2017. https://ucr.fbi.gov/hate-crime/2015/topic-pages/incidentsandoffenses_final. [http://archive.li/lltQQ]

half were either classified as "intimidation" or property damage and vandalism. Also in 2015, the FBI estimates there were 1,197,704 violent crimes. Over 15,000 murders, and over 90,000 rapes and sexual assaults. Despite the narrative that hate crimes are committed by whites against others, the data shows that whites are under-represented as hate crime perpetrators, and blacks are over-represented by a factor of double their population percentage.[92]

According to the Department of Justice's National Crime Victimization Survey, the vast majority (85 percent) of interracial crimes are whites victimized by blacks. In 2013 there were around 660,000 interracial crimes that involved blacks and whites. Less than 100,000 of those crimes were whites attacking blacks. The remaining 560,000 were blacks attacking whites. The rate of blacks attacking whites is twenty-seven times higher than that of whites attacking blacks. More than 20,000 rapes per year are black men raping white women, yet these are never counted as hate crimes, nor does the media so much as bother to cover these stories.[93] The Liberal press is too busy ghost hunting racism, Islamophobia, and antisemitism to be bothered with real crime epidemics that show clear signs of racism.

Out of the multitude of "bias related incidents" and "hate crimes" with which the media has been infatuated, many, if not the majority, have turned out to be entirely fabricated by the "victim." While many of the higher profile "crimes" have remained in the news for weeks or months, the revelation of hoax is seldom covered. Here are a few of such "crimes" which were later revealed as a ruse:

> Jewish man arrested after spray painting swastikas on his own home in Upstate NY — *Syracuse*[94]

---

92 "2015 Hate Crime Statistics Released." FBI. November 14, 2016. www.fbi.gov/news/stories/2015-hate-crime-statistics-released. [http://archive.li/lcnHm]

93 Jared Taylor. "New DOJ Statistics on Race and Violent Crime" American Renaissance. July 1, 2015. https://www.amren.com/news/2015/07/new-doj-statistics-on-race-and-violent-crime/. [http://archive.li/0dMuY]

94 Ben Axelson. "Jewish man arrested after spray painting swastikas on his own home in Upstate NY" Syracuse.com. March 21, 2017. http://www.syracuse.com/state/index.ssf/2017/03/jewish_man_arrested_after_spray _painting_swastikas_on_his_own_home_in_upstate_ny.html. [http://archive.li/aYIRY]

Muslim Woman Made Up Hate Crime on Subway — *The New York Times*[95]

Muslim girl who claimed she was pushed in front of a train because of her headscarf faces prosecution in Austria after CCTV shows she invented the story — *Daily Mail*[96]

Man Faked 'KKK' Crimes —*Breitbart*[97]

Indiana State Professor Fabricated Anti-Muslim Hate Crimes —*Daily Caller*[98]

University of Michigan student pleads guilty to reporting fake hate crime after President Trump's election — *NY Daily News*[99]

Jewish suspects arrested over swastika graffiti on synagogues — *The Times of Israel*[100]

---

95 Christopher Mele. "Muslim Woman Made Up Hate Crime on Subway, Police Say" The New York Times. December 14, 2016. https://www.nytimes.com/2016/12/14/nyregion/manhattan-yasmin-seweid-false-hate-crime.html. [http://archive.li/9ARJz]

96 Chris Summers. "Muslim girl who claimed she was pushed in front of a train because of her headscarf faces prosecution in Austria after CCTV shows she invented the story " Daily Mail Online. January 19, 2017. http://www.dailymail.co.uk/news/article-4136730/Muslim-girl-claimed-pushed-cried-wolf.html. [http://archive.li/5V0HQ]

97 John Binder. "Hate Hoax: Man Faked 'KKK' Crimes, Abduction" Breitbart. December 14, 2016. http://www.breitbart.com/texas/2016/12/14/hate-hoax-man-faked-kkk-crimes-abduction/. [http://archive.li/RFZcl]

98 Chuck Ross. "Police: Indiana State Professor Fabricated Anti-Muslim Hate Crimes" The Daily Caller. April 24, 2017. http://dailycaller.com/2017/04/22/police-indiana-state-professor-fabricated-anti-muslim-hate-crimes/. [http://archive.li/w1WY8]

99 Jessica Schladebeck. "Michigan student pleads guilty to reporting fake hate crime" NY Daily News. March 08, 2017. http://www.nydailynews.com/news/national/michigan-student-pleads-guilty-reporting-fake-hate-crime-article-1.2992019. [http://archive.li/yiCQ9]

100 Stuart Winer and Judah Gross. "Jewish suspects arrested over swastika graffiti on synagogues" The Times of Israel. June 11, 2017. http://www.timesofisrael.com/jewish-suspects-arrested-over-swastika-graffiti-on-synagogues/. [http://archive.li/nekQC]

It is hard to tell what percent of alleged hate crimes were real and what percent were fake. Many of the stories that revealed the crimes to have been hoaxes were only covered in local papers, while the original "crimes" frequently made national headlines. I can tell you that I have personally come across hundreds of articles and police reports which found that previously reported hate crimes had been entirely manufactured by the warped Liberal mindset of the "victims." After researching these "crimes," it appears that the hoaxes outnumber the actual crimes.

Several "victims" claimed that, although the incident they alleged was fake, they were still helping to "raise awareness" about the rise of hate in America. Perhaps even more grievous than the people who hoaxed crimes is the fact that so many news organizations and "anti-Hate" groups seldom bother to retract the original stories. It's one thing when a deranged individual fakes a crime; it's another issue entirely when massive organizations actively participate in gaslighting the ordeal.

By claiming to be daily victimized by the Right, the Left has created an atmosphere in which violence against political opposition is justified as simple act of "retaliation," *lex talionis*. As a result, over 200 *actual* crimes have been perpetrated against Trump supporters merely on account of their political views. The violence from the Left, directed to the Right, has all but been ignored.[101] And these 200 crimes do not even count the Trump supporters that have been pepper-sprayed, beaten, hit with rocks, and had urine thrown on them by protesters all over the country, without a single arrest being made in consequence. In several cases, it appears the police were told not to intervene, nor to arrest the Liberal rioters at many California protests.[102]

An analytics company named Dataminr found that since the Inauguration, over 12,000 people have called for the assassination or

---

101 Westley Parker. "Anti-Trump Hate Map" American Renaissance. Accessed July 10, 2017. https://www.amren.com/archives/reports/anti-trump-hate-map/. [http://archive.li/JQ0h4]

102 Jim Hoft. "Breaking: Berkeley Mayor Told Local Police to Stand Down So conservatives Could Get Pummeled During Riots" The Gateway Pundit. May 02, 2017. http://www.thegatewaypundit.com/2017/05/breaking-berkeley-mayor-told-local-police-stand-conservatives-get-pummeled-riots/. [http://archive.li/Kf8TT]

threatened assassination of Donald Trump on Twitter.[103] Celebrities and Liberal politicians have of course also joined in on Hate Week, some calling for violence in the streets, others proclaiming their fantasy of blowing up the White House, others yet carrying out mock executions of President Trump.[104] Yet the Left still accuses the Right of violence, even while its useful idiots attack speakers, politicians, and everyday citizens for holding the wrong political views.

If the media were interested in really troublesome trends, they would focus on the rise of Left-wing violence since the 2016 election. As the collective Left and the press bemoans the rise of "neo-Nazis," they entirely ignore the global rise of neo-Bolsheviks. From Antifa to Black Lives Matter, the Left is totally out of control. Communists have killed around 100 million people in the twentieth century—a staggering figure that seldom receives mention, but which we cannot repeat too many times. The violence we are seeing now is merely an extension of a long tradition on the Left—the Left which is the rightful heir to the October Revolution, the Katyn massacre, the Gulags, and the NKVD.

The Liberal media reminds me an awful lot of Iago, the puppet master and villain from Shakespeare's *Othello*. From garnering support for endless wars to inciting political violence, they can masterfully manipulate and twist nearly anything so that it favors them politically.

Shifting Blame

Just as Liberals blame crime and poverty on "systemic racism" and "white privilege," so terrorism is also framed as being brought about by abstractions such as "lack of tolerance." A few recent headlines to this effect:

---

103 "More than 12,000 tweets have called for Trump's assassination since the inauguration" Daily Mail Online. February 03, 2017. http://www.dailymail.co.uk/news/article-4189124/More-12-000-tweets-call-Trump-s-assassination.html. [http://archive.li/tLBzl]

104 Daniel Nussbaum & Jerome Hudson. "15 Times Celebrities Envisioned Violence Against Trump and the GOP" Breitbart. June 14, 2017. http://www.breitbart.com/big-hollywood/2017/06/14/15-times-celebrities-envisioned-violence-against-trump-and-the-gop/. [http://archive.li/rRUZ6]

> Donald Trump's 'Muslim ban' will only make terrorist attacks, more, not less likely — *Independent*[105]

> Donald Trump's Muslim Bashing Aids Cause of Terror Networks, Say Experts — NBC News[106]

> How Trump has inspired violence across the country, in one map — ThinkProgress[107]

These examples point to Donald Trump specifically, and by implication to Trump supporters. However, the press has been playing this same game for years. The Benghazi attack was blamed on an anti-Muslim video, and the *Charlie Hebdo* attack was blamed on a cartoon. No matter what happens, it is always *our* fault when we are attacked.

According to the Left, if we do not let Muslims into our countries, they will attack us out of rage. If we criticize Muslims, this will incite violence against us. If we do not give them enough welfare, they will attack us in retaliation. Liberals blame the victims, claiming that they have not been welcoming enough, not tolerant enough, not accepting enough. In what warped mind could this make any sense?

After every terrorist attack, the Liberal media, Liberal politicians, and their flocks of underlings, all rush to "remind" us that Islam is not the problem. Articles such as, "After the Paris attacks, the fear of Islam runs

---

105 Patrick Cockburn. "Donald Trump's 'Muslim ban' will only make terrorist attacks, more, not less likely" The Independent. January 30, 2017. http://www.independent.co.uk/voices/trump-muslim-ban-terrorism-isis-only-make-it-worse-a7552776.html. [http://archive.li/reYyc]

106 Corky Siemaszko and F. Brinley Bruton. "Donald Trump's Muslim Bashing Aids Cause of Terror Networks, Say Experts" NBCNews.com. December 08, 2015. http://www.nbcnews.com/storyline/isis-terror/donald-trumps-muslim-bashing-aids-cause-terror-networks-say-experts-n476221. [http://archive.li/vjMTL]

107 Kira Lerner. "How Trump has inspired violence across the country, in one map" ThinkProgress. March 17, 2016. https://thinkprogress.org/how-trump-has-inspired-violence-across-the-country-in-one-map-6ab5e096a627. [http://archive.li/G47OG]

rampant in the United States,"[108] "Muslim hate crime rises in London,"[109] and "Hate crime in Manchester has doubled since terror attack,"[110] are all too common. After Muslims rampaged through Paris, murdering 130 people, torturing dozens, injuring hundreds, wouldn't it be at least slightly normal for fear to increase? Are fear and horror not the normal reactions to these nefarious actions? Many of these alleged "hate crimes" are nothing more than people voicing their thoughts about the rise of Muslim terror online. Is this really abnormal?

We are being victimized at incredible rates, but the Left is only worried about racism, Islamophobia and antisemitism. The Liberal cries out in pain as he attacks you. It is an integral part of his character — to play the victim while on the attack.

This is the result of political correctness run amok. It's literally getting us killed at this point; the government and media are engaging in massive cover-ups and soft-peddling, in order to avoid offending anybody. Instead of warning us of the crime and violence we face, they pretend that everything is normal, so as not to offend the fragile feelings of non-whites. The same is true in America in terms of black on white crime, which largely stays out of the news despite accounting for over 500,000 violent crimes per year. The silence on this topic can do nothing but lead to an increase in white victimization.

NPR ran an article about the fears in the Muslim community the day after a Muslim student at Ohio State ran his car into a group of people, jumped out of his car with a butcher knife, and started stabbing people. The article discussed how fearful the Muslim community is about a potential "backlash" — which virtually never happens, by the way. NPR went on to discuss the plight of the Muslim community in an article entitled,

---

108 Susan Milligan. "No Welcome Mat" U.S. News & World Report. November 20, 2015. https://www.usnews.com/news/the-report/articles/2015/11/20/after-paris-islamophobia-is-on-the-rise. [http://archive.li/PqpUe]

109 Vikram Dodd and Sarah Marsh. "Anti-Muslim hate crimes increase fivefold since London Bridge attacks" The Guardian. June 07, 2017. https://www.theguardian.com/uk-news/2017/jun/07/anti-muslim-hate-crimes-increase-fivefold-since-london-bridge-attacks. [http://archive.li/K6mou]

110 "Manchester attack: Hate crime 'doubles' after incident" BBC. May 27, 2017. http://www.bbc.com/news/uk-england-manchester-40064424. [http://archive.li/jVQY7]

"Muslim Community Fears Backlash After Ohio State Attack," which painted Muslim students as the *real* victims of the campus terrorist attack.[111] The reader learns that the *real* tragedy of these events is found in the fact that Muslims are a little uneasy the day after one of their own tried to kill as many Westerners as he could. I guess they never considered how *we* feel, being surrounded by invaders in our land, who every so often try to kill as many of us as they can by any means available.

Three months after the campus attack, the Ohio State Middle East Studies Center even hosted a discussion on Islamophobia, so that students could be properly educated out of their fear of Islam and Muslims.[112] Maybe I'm just paranoid, but it seems to me that having a healthy level of apprehension towards a group of people that hunt us for sport is a natural reaction. To my mind, calling the fear of Islam a "phobia" is a misnomer in itself. A phobia is an *irrational* fear of something. It is perfectly rational to fear an alien culture, in which more than one in four of their members justifies our massacre for having insulted their cult.[113]

The Washington Post published the article, "Attacks like Portland's will keep happening unless we all fight white supremacy,"[114] in which the author incorrectly claims that "The greatest threat facing our country comes from homegrown white supremacists, not Muslims or refugees." From *Newsweek*: "Homegrown Terrorism and Why the Threat of Right-Wing

111 Esther Honig. "Muslim Community Fears Backlash After Ohio State Attack" NPR. November 29, 2016. http://www.npr.org/2016/11/29/503693426/police-search-for-motive-in-ohio-state-attack. [http://archive.li/8vw7S]

112 Amanda Tidwell. "After Ohio State students attacked by radical Muslim, campus hosts 'Islamophobia' talk" The College Fix. February 18, 2017. https://www.thecollegefix.com/post/31262/. [http://archive.li/xPEv4]

113 David Morgan. "Poll: 26 percent Of Young U.S. Muslims OK Bombs" CBS News. May 22, 2007. http://www.cbsnews.com/news/poll-26-of-young-us-muslims-ok-bombs/. [http://archive.li/7TA2m]

114 Arjun Singh Sethi. "Attacks like Portland's will keep happening unless we all fight white supremacy" The Washington Post. May 29, 2017. https://www.washingtonpost.com/posteverything/wp/2017/05/29/attacks-like-portlands-will-keep-happening-unless-we-all-fight-white-supremacy/. [http://archive.li/eT0gS]

Extremism is Rising in America."[115] The media is selling a false narrative. Not only has it been proven that Muslims have killed over twice as many people as white supremacists and Right-wing terrorists combined, but the media frequently ignores and downplays Muslim terror. They have to, else their sob stories about Muslim victimhood would immediately fall apart. In all of the West over the past two decades, a dozen or so Muslims have been killed due to "Islamophobia"; meanwhile, Muslims kill us daily.

In slander pieces such as *The Nation*'s "Why Does the Far Right Hold a Near-Monopoly on Political Violence?"[116], *The Huffington Post*'s "Most Of America's Terrorists Are White, And Not Muslim,"[117] and *The New York Times*' "What About Terrorism of the Far Right?"[118], they all blatantly espouse lies. That is, that white men, not Muslims, are the *real* terrorists. Per a study by New America, after September 11th, 2001, there have been fifty-three deaths due to Right-wing terrorists, and ninety-five by Muslims Jihadists in America.[119] Incredible, considering that Muslims are about 1 percent of the US population and whites are over 60 percent of the US population. The most superficial of research into terrorist ideology reveals that despite their small numbers, Muslims are far more prone to terrorism

115 Arie Perliger. "Why far-right extremism in America is rising" Newsweek. June 04, 2017. http://www.newsweek.com/homegrown-terrorism-rising-threat-right-wing-extremism-619724. [http://archive.li/u6GOt]

116 Joshua Holland. "Why Does the Far Right Hold a Near-Monopoly on Political Violence" The Nation. June 23, 2017. https://www.thenation.com/article/why-does-the-far-right-hold-a-near-monopoly-on-political-violence/. [http://archive.li/KlrnX]

117 Sarah Ruiz-Grossman. "Most Of America's Terrorists Are White, And Not Muslim" The Huffington Post. June 22, 2017. https://www.huffingtonpost.com/entry/domestic-terrorism-white-supremacists-islamist-extremists_us_594c46e4e4b0da2c731a84df. [http://archive.li/Kpl6n]

118 Amarnath Amarasingam and Jacob Davey. "What About the Terrorism of the Far Right" The New York Times. June 21, 2017. https://www.nytimes.com/2017/06/21/opinion/finsbury-park-terrorist-attack-far-right.html. [http://archive.li/RMklR]

119 Peter Bergen, Albert Ford, Alyssa Sims, and David Sterman. "Terrorism in America After 9/11" New America. Accessed July 10, 2017. https://www.newamerica.org/in-depth/terrorism-in-america/what-threat-united-states-today/.

than whites; but the lying press continues to churn out garbage article after garbage article, with the intent to defame whites and mislead.

In the last decade, the number of Muslims killed in Western nations due to "Islamophobia" is in the single digits. The citizens of France, England, United States, Sweden, and all other nations terrorized regularly by Muslims, have seldom retaliated against their resident Muslim communities. Muslims kill more Americans and Europeans in single attacks, than Muslims have been killed collectively across Europe and the US over the last twenty years by Westerners. Keep that in mind the next time you see an article, anchor, or social media post that argues the irrationality of Islamophobia, and how we must learn to be more tolerant. Despite what the Liberal media would have you believe, Muslims living in Western nations are the *least* likely group to be victimized. Yet the Liberal media only cares about them and their "feelings." Tolerance is not an effective strategy towards barbarians. It never has been, not at any point in history, and it will not work now. There is only one thing that has ever brought an end to hordes of violent invaders. Maybe a little more intolerance is exactly what we need.

These people are entirely alien to us. They come to our nations speaking other languages, dressing like they are still in the desert, bringing drastically different cultures. And by all measures, it appears that most of them are not too fond of us. I'm tired of constantly hearing about how racist, Islamophobic, antisemitic, bigoted, and xenophobic Americans are. None of it is true. The only reason some Americans appear to be racists, is because we point out facts about crime rates that some people do not want to hear. The only reason we are called antisemitic and Islamophobic is that Muslims and Jews seem to have made a hobby of fabricating hate crimes. Claiming that the evil white man spray painted a Swastika on your house or ripped off your hijab is nothing short of a revelation of a depraved pathology. These people should have all been deported for their insurrection.

Election Meddling

The press has been struggling to make an issue of "foreign influences" in the election. In a sense, I agree that there is some foreign meddling.

Let's start by asking ourselves why the American Israel Public Affairs Committee (AIPAC) exists, which uses its vast lobbying network to connect current Congressmen and those running for office, with pro-Israeli donors who then donate millions of dollars to our politicians each year. It *might* have something do to with the fact that Israel is the beneficiary of the largest aid agreement in the history of planet Earth. I'm still waiting for somebody to explain to me what the American tax payer gets out of this aid package to a single country, which costs us over three billion dollars a year. There are of course hundreds of lobbyist groups funded by various foreign nations. It just so happens that AIPAC is one of the largest and most influential, and the recent aid deal was the largest of its kind.[120]

Here's a wild idea. How about, if Mexico, Israel, Egypt, Morocco, or any other nation on Earth needs more money, it can raise taxes on its own people, instead of giving our politicians millions of dollars in exchange for billions of our tax dollars? We are literally being sold like cattle. For these transgressions, no fate would be too severe for those who have been masquerading as our representatives.

The *elected* get their thirty pieces of silver, and we get a knife in the back.

The billions we provide the rest of the world each year in economic and military aid does not represent just a balance-sheet figure. At bottom, those dollars represent hours worked by every American tax payer. Hours of our lives we will never have back, hours that we must spend away from our homes and families, so that other countries can enjoy the benefits of our labor.

When Russophobia was running rampant under headlines of "election hacking," I found it odd that Liberals were not much concerned about money from Saudi Arabia making its way into the hands of US politicians. One of the biggest human-rights violators on Earth was paying our politicians for *something*—yet *this* was not worthy of an investigation. I also find it interesting that our politicians turn a blind eye to the Saudi and

120 L. Michael Hager. "The Best Congress AIPAC Can Buy." Foreign Policy Journal. March 22, 2106. www.foreignpolicyjournal.com/2016/03/22/the-best-congress-aipac-can-buy/.[http://archive.li/5D1Kf]

Yemen conflict, or the Israel and Palestine conflict, while being curiously interested in intervention in Libya, Iraq, Iran, Russia, and Syria.

There has been an deafening cry of outrage over the mere possibility of "Russian election influence." To be sure, the idea that a hostile international clique might be subverting the American will is indeed alarming. Yet I cannot help but wonder if this concern over foreign meddling is misplaced. The Jewish Telegraph Agency reports that the top five campaign donors to Clinton's presidential run were Jewish.[121] *The Jerusalem Post* reports that 50 percent of the donations to the Democratic Party and 25 percent of donations to the Republican Party were contributed by Jewish donors. The article reports that 70 percent of Jewish voters supported Clinton, and further notes that "The degree to which liberalism and liberal ideas has been good for the Jews in America helps explain why so many American Jews think liberalism and Judaism are the same."[122] A similar trend was present during the Obama years: according to *The Times of Israel*, top Obama donors were also Jewish.[123] *The New York Times* recently discussed a shift in funding of pro-Israeli donors towards the Republican Party. The influx of millions of dollars in donations to support Israeli and Jewish causes has led the Republican Party to accept "little dissent on the topic of Israel." [124]

In a discussion of alleged Russian interference in the US election, Brexit leader Nigel Farage had this to say: "There are other very powerful lobbies in the United States of America, and the Jewish lobby, with its

---

121 "Clinton campaign tally shows 5 top donors are Jewish." Jewish Telegraphic Agency. October 26, 2016. www.jta.org/2016/10/26/top-headlines/5-top-donors-to-clinton-election-bid-reportedly-are-jewish.

122 Jeremy Sharon. "US Jews contribute half of all donations to the Democratic party." The Jerusalem Post. September 27, 2016. www.jpost.com/US-Elections/US-Jews-contribute-half-of-all-donations-to-the-Democratic-party-468774#/. [http://archive.li/fosAa]

123 Ilan Ben Zio. "Jewish donors prominent in presidential campaign contributions." The Times of Israel. October 20, 2012. www.timesofisrael.com/jewish-donors-prominent-in-presidential-campaign-contributions/. [http://archive.li/c74tk]

124 Eric Lipton. "G.O.P.'s Israel Support Deepens as Political Contributions Shift." The New York Times. April 04, 2015. www.nytimes.com/2015/04/05/us/politics/gops-israel-support-deepens-as-political-contributions-shift.html. [http://archive.li/ouF30]

links with the Israeli government, is one of those strong voices."[125] When Russian President Vladimir Putin was asked about potential Russian interference he replied, "Maybe they're not even Russians. Maybe they're Ukrainians, Tatars, Jews, just with Russian citizenship."[126] Putin's comments are particularly fascinating in light of a Jewish Telegraph Agency report from several years ago, in which Putin is reported as remarking, while speaking at Moscow's Jewish Museum, that the majority of the first Soviet governments, the governments that slaughtered millions of Orthodox Russians, were in fact ethnically Jewish.[127] This is perhaps best corroborated by the fact that not long after the Bolshevik Revolution, antisemitism was declared a crime, one punishable by death.[128]

On one hand we have the more Liberal J Street Jewish political action committee, on the other we have the hawkish neoconservative Emergency Committee for Israel, and AIPAC in the middle, all helping to fund *both* parties, so long as the "elected" officials adequately support Jewish interests. While stories of Russian election interference are constant, any discussion of Jewish influence in the West is immediately decried as antisemitism. Does it not stand to reason that when there are very well-funded organizations spending considerable resources in both American political parties, there may be some conflict of interest? If Russia was allegedly able to influence a US election and US politicians by publishing a handful of articles, surely another group would be able to influence public policy by infusing tremendous sums of money into American politics, no?

There may very well *be* a hostile international clique of interlopers that are subverting our nation. However, I do find it odd that we are not

---

125 Nicole Goodkind. "Jews should concern Americans more than Russian influence, Nigel Farage says." Newsweek. November 01, 2017. http://www.newsweek.com/trump-russia-jewish-farage-brexit-698486. [http://archive.li/curpj]

126 Madison Park. "Putin: Maybe Jews or minorities behind US election interference." CNN. March 12, 2018. www.cnn.com/2018/03/12/politics/putin-comment-jews-russian-minorities/index.html. [http://archive.li/HYEbl]

127 "Putin: First Soviet government was mostly Jewish." The Times of Israel. June 19, 2013. www.timesofisrael.com/putin-first-soviet-government-was-mostly-jewish/. [http://archive.li/qM0dx]

128 "Reply to an Inquiry of the Jewish News Agency in the United States." Marxists Internet Archive. January 12, 1931. www.marxists.org/reference/archive/stalin/works/1931/01/12.htm. [http://archive.li/m8qjO]

sending billions of dollars to Russia each year, or fighting endless wars at the behest of Russian dual-citizens, while Russian dual-citizens lobby to enact gun-control, undermine free speech, and free association. I do not see many ethnically *Russian* members of Congress introducing constant legislation to undermine our right to bear arms (Schumer, Kohl, Feinstein), nor do I see Russian organizations working with Facebook, Twitter, Google, and Microsoft to censor the lawful speech of Americans online (The Anti-Defamation League). I do not recall it being Russians or Russian organizations who fought to open our nation up to mass migration (Celler, Javits, Hebrew Immigration Aid Society, American Jewish Congress). And it is certainly not ethnic Russians who own and operate the majority of American news, media, and advertising organizations.

No, it's not *Russia* that is the problem.

Manifestations of the Liberal Illness: The Press

Bias, lies, exaggeration, and the omission of facts, are pillars of the Liberal media establishment. The lying press will only cover stories that fit neatly into their narrative. The press in America never reports on the economic disaster and civil unrest in Venezuela. They never cover the massive slaughter of whites in South Africa by the hands of blacks. Those stories do not fit well into their multicultural utopia or into their white-privilege conspiracy theories. The very same people who bemoaned the "horrors" of Apartheid, non-stop, for years, are silent on the current genocide currently facing white South Africans. The same people who booed white South Africans in the US, the same people that boycotted South African goods, the same people who herald Mandela as a hero, do not even mention how whites are being tortured and hunted down by blacks in South Africa — or anywhere for that matter.

The members of the lying press serve as propagandists to atomize those with thoughts contrary to the Liberal establishment. The propaganda is designed to make you feel alone, ostracized, incorrect, and psychotic for daring to swim against the stream. By only presenting a very particular story, and only reporting on events which reinforce its narrative, the press spins a vast web of deceit, one that is based on the principles of crowd manipulation. In providing fake and rigged studies, the press manipulates the masses by providing false social proof for their views through an argument by consensus or by reliance on the authority of the many. Humans naturally seek conformity and communal reinforcement, and the press plays on these social psychological concepts in order to mold the consensus into anything they wish.

When they are called out for their behavior, they violently attack and lash out while playing the helpless victim. Despite all evidence against their narrative, the press sticks with its story to the point that it will plainly deny reality on live TV. In true Liberal form, the mainstream media loves to name other media outlets the purveyors of "fake news," when it has better than a century-long record of being just that.

Perhaps most damaging is the Liberal inability to recognize the negative outcomes of their actions. The government intelligence community in concert with the mainstream media has literally gone to war on the basis of lies. Hundreds of thousands, if not millions, have been slain due to this negligence. All with total impunity to any consequence. If we truly seek a fair and just society, marching the war mongers and lying press to the gallows would be the place to start.

The Liberal press claims that the "violent rhetoric" from Trump and Trumpian "racists" has caused an increase in crime, when in reality it has been the Left to incite and engage in most of the violence. The media has screamed since the election that Trump is illegitimate, that his supporters are all Nazis, that American children and lives are endangered by his administration, that the government has been taken over by the Russians, and the resulting violence from the useful idiots is a response to injustice. When people take the Liberal press' lies seriously, the result cannot help but be riots, beatings, shootings, and killings.

Neither the election of Donald Trump, nor the Right itself, created this hatred. It only revealed it.

Fictitious terms and redefined words are disseminated proudly through the mainstream media. From white privilege to the wage gap myth and the false Black Lives Matter narrative, the media snap it all up with a patent sense of moral superiority. The brazen approach the media takes to telling us what to believe while assuming nobody will ever catch on to its manipulations is another manifestation of the Liberal's total loss of touch with reality.

If you watched the 2016 election coverage, you are surely familiar with the crisis brought on the Liberal media by the loss of their power. Votes against their candidate were seen as indefensible acts of ignorance. The fact that Americans had the sheer audacity to go against what the media had been telling them to do enraged these people to the core. It brought them to tears on live TV; they were "literally shaking" out of despair.

Despite the Liberal pretentiousness and feigned sophistication, Liberals are clueless and emotional sheep. They are manipulated by each and every emotionally evocative news segment, played with concerto skill. The ease with which the media can twist the Liberal mind is yet more proof that Liberals are a herd of unquestioning, brainwashed sycophants.

Symptoms 1, 2, 4, and 5 from Cluster I are readily apparent. From Cluster II, symptoms 6, 7, 8, and 9, are seen.

Cluster I

1. Deceitfulness, indicated by repeated lying, grand exaggerations, or omission of contrary information, with the purpose to advance their chosen narrative and discrediting others.

2. Irritability or aggressiveness towards anybody that questions or opposes their views. Coupled with the inability to recognize they own hypocrisy, double standards, and doublethink.

3. Inability to adjust views when presented with information contrary to their own beliefs.

4. Frequent projections of their own traits onto others.

5. Difficulty in dealing with a loss of control or power, or a strong desire for control and power.

Cluster II

6. Appeals to altered and redefined definitions of words, or relies on fictitious terms for argumentation.

7. Consistent feelings of having been victimized or wronged, without any actual harm being done. Seen also as playing the victim after attacking others.

8. Intense sense of righteousness or moral superiority.

9. The inability to recognize the negative outcomes of their own actions. Often placing the blame on others.

10. Intense guilt or self-hatred, often manifests as hatred towards one's larger group identity.

IX

Which Way Western Man? Salvos Against Mass Migration

There is a startling trend in worldwide migration: certain nations are allowed to remain sovereign homelands for their native peoples, while Western nations, particularly Western Europe and the United States, are required to keep their doors, money, and borders wide open for everybody the world over. At face value, the ideas of inclusion and openness sound very nice, yet they have an incredibly high cost. However, I am not making an appeal against immigration solely as regards the financial cost. I am appealing against the destruction of cultures, homelands being ripped away from their rightful owners, and future generations risking the loss of a cultural identity, heritage, or a future.

Japan for Japanese.
Algeria for Algerians.
Germany for everybody.

Korea for Koreans.
India for Indians.
France for everybody.

China for Chinese.
Mexico for Mexicans.
The United States for everybody.

If Liberals are not troubled by the idea that Japan is for the Japanese, Israel is for the Jewish, Mexico is for the Mexicans, but they are troubled by the idea that France is for the French and Italy is for Italians, then Liberals are in fact displaying tremendous double standards. They are effectively saying that some races and ethnicities have an intrinsic right to exist, to be left alone, to preserve their homelands, and secure the future for their children — but not Europeans. They are effectively advocating the invasion and eventual genocide of the white race and the white race alone. When diversity, multiculturalism, and open borders are all forced upon a group, and it becomes illegal for the members of that group even to speak out against the invasion, that is genocide. Intentionally creating a hostile environment for a group of people based on race or ethnicity is quite literally genocide, as defined by the United Nations in Article 2 of the Convention on the Prevention and Punishment of the Crime of Genocide from 1948:

The United Nations legally defines genocide as;

> Any of the following acts committed with intent to destroy, in whole or in part, a national, ethnical, racial or religious group, as such: killing members of the group; causing serious bodily or mental harm to members of the group; *deliberately inflicting on the group conditions of life calculated to bring about its physical destruction in whole or in part ; imposing measures intended to prevent births within the group; [and] forcibly transferring children of the group to another group.*

By the standards accepted by the United Nations itself, the current pogroms being enacted at the very highest levels of world governments, from the oligarchs down to the beat cops, are not simply anti-white, they are genocidal.

Only in white European nations, is the millennial custom of preferring native majorities to foreign minorities referred to as supremacist and seen as unnatural. Only in white European nations is multiculturalism praised and pushed. Only in white European nations are borders called racist. Only in white European nations, are people forced to assimilate to invaders in their own homelands, rather than the other way around. Only in white European nations are the native populations expected to invite the rest of the world into their lands. Only in white European nations is it unacceptable to be proud of your heritage. Liberalism has moved so far to the Left that Liberals are now outraged at the radical notion that white people, too, might have a right to exist in *our* own homelands, which *our* ancestors created.

If you think any of this is a bit far-fetched, I ask, can you name a single non-white nation which is embracing diversity and multiculturalism? I've looked. There isn't one. If this realization does not make you question why this might be so, I'm not sure there is anything else to be said: you may not be very interested in globalism and population replacement, but I can promise, that globalism and population replacement are very interested in you.

Only in white European nations is white guilt and white hate promoted. No other region on Earth has a school system that tells their children that they are evil oppressors. Slavery, war, and colonialism are not unique to white European nations. Every group on Earth is guilty of having been involved at one point or other in the slave trade, in war, and in colonialism. In fact, those "evil white European" nations were the first places where slavery was ended, and indeed to this day they are among the minority of regions which have ended slavery. There are more slaves in the world today than there were in the entire history of the Atlantic Slave Trade.[1]

It is interesting, by the way, that there is virtually zero mention today of the Barbary slave trade, which enslaved over one million white Europeans over a course of several hundred years at the hands of Muslim and Jewish slave traders.[2]

---

1 Annie Kelly. "Modern-day slavery: an explainer" The Guardian. April 03, 2013. https://www.theguardian.com/global-development/2013/apr/03/modern-day-slavery-explainer. [http://archive.li/HkbbN]

2 Mikhail Kizilov. "Slaves, Money Lenders, and Prisoner Guards: The Jews and the Trade in Slaves and Captives in the Crimean Khanate." Journal of Jewish Studies, vol. 58, no. 2, Jan. 2007, pp. 189–210., doi:10.18647/2730/jjs-2007.

Prior to 1965, the US' immigration laws were designed to maintain the relative demographics of the nation. This was based on a simple idea that the people who built this nation and made it great had a right to see themselves and their posterity reflected in the nation they had created. This was an extension of the belief that a nation has a right to maintain its culture, heritage, cohesiveness, and sovereignty: for without a sovereign homeland and self-determination, people are never truly free.

Then the Immigration Act of 1965 was enacted. This act firmly established an anti-American, anti-white, and globalist immigration policy. The Immigration Act sought to change, and indeed has effectively changed, the makeup of our nation in a totally inorganic fashion, by enabling people with no connection to our history, values, or beliefs to come to America, sponsored financially by US tax payers. Also known as the Hart-Celler Act, this legislation was nothing but another effort to destroy our culture by importing millions of people that would become dependent on our generous welfare system, the majority of whom would vote Democrat to keep the welfare checks rolling in. Critics of previous immigration laws, such as Emanuel Celler, referred to the prior laws as racist, exclusionary, and discriminatory, which is nothing but a typical Judeo-Leftist tactic to get his way by claiming some sort of tendentious morality. Billions of our tax dollars have been spent to help defend other nations' borders, but we cannot defend our own without being called "racists"? There is absolute nothing racist about wanting to maintain your culture.

Our trouble didn't stop with the Immigration Act: Jimmy Carter soon after signed the Refugee Act of 1980, which would increase the annual number of refugees from 17,400, as specified in the act of 1965, to 50,000 a year, the majority of which would vote Democrat and go immediately on welfare. The Refugee Act, like the Immigration Act of 1965, was introduced by Ted Kennedy, and was heavily lobbied for and influenced by Jewish organizations.[3]

We cannot have both a welfare state *and* open borders allowing over a million migrants to arrive legally every year. It is suicidal. As historian Arnold Toynbee wrote, great civilizations seldom die of natural causes or

3 Fred A. Lazin. "Refugee Resettlement and 'Freedom of Choice': The Case of Soviet Jewry" CIS.org. July 01, 2005. https://cis.org/Report/Refugee-Resettlement-and-Freedom-Choice-Case-Soviet-Jewry. [http://archive.is/Ys84b]

by murder, they die from suicide.[4] Our act of suicide was allowing interlopers into this nation, people that we knew were snakes from the beginning. Our suicide is in our sitting idly by and naively taking for granted all that our ancestors had sacrificed, even as we passively let others work toward its destruction.

These policies of open borders and mass migration are obviously not for the benefit of Americans — not when we must fund over 50 percent of the invaders with our tax dollars.[5] These policies were created by the Left in order to secure votes and power for the future, while destroying our homeland and people — perhaps the ultimate goal. If you look at immigration patterns pre-1965, you see a high amount migrants from Western and Northern European nations. When you allow migration to come from the Third World under the guise of diversity and inclusion, you end up with more welfare-users, more crime, more social dysfunction, and more societal decay. The same story is playing out everywhere it has been tried.

Another odd trend — many of the migrants to the United States are being resettled in the American Midwest, so that the Midwest is in consequence seeing the highest rate of demographic change. This is not organic. This is not a family of Somalis deciding one day to up and move to the middle of Ohio. This is part of the plan to turn key swing states into Democrat voting states; and those who are pushing this agenda are accomplishing it via forced migration and welfare programs. There is no cultural enrichment happening for the residents of these resettlement towns. They only thing they get from all this are groups of people who refuse to assimilate into our so called "melting pot," people who cost us far more in tax dollars than they will ever contribute. There are cities all over Europe that already look like they belong somewhere in the Middle East or Africa. You'll see far more people wearing the exact same "diverse" uniform of a black hijab and burka than you will see wearing European fashion. Nobody asked the residents of those European towns, or of these American ones, if they wanted these boatloads of invaders. They didn't

4 Arnold J. Toynbee. A study of history: abridgement of volumes 1-6. New York: Oxford Univ. Pr., 1948.

5 Steven A. Camarota. "Welfare Use by Immigrant and Native Households" Center for Immigration Studies. September 10, 2015. http://cis.org/Welfare-Use-Immigrant-Native-Households. [http://archive.li/5uouk]

get to vote on whether their tax dollars should go to fund a relocation program to ensure their demographic evisceration. Nobody invited us to that meeting. We were never asked. If I wanted to walk around downtown and see the majority of people covered head to toe in black trash-bags, we would long ago have moved from my homeland to some Third World slum. Strangely, immigration seems to always go in the other direction.

This forcible imposition of "diversity" is a form of terrorism. It is weaponized migration. We are no longer free to associate with whom we wish. That right is being ripped away by open border policies, mass migration, foreign invaders, and state-enforced integrated housing. Nobody ever asked us if we were alright with the idea of our neighborhoods being turned into little Mogadishus, North Mexico Cities, and East Karachis.

In fact, when people *do* bother to ask the native people of Europe and America how they feel about immigration, most respond negatively. Over half of those surveyed in the US say they would cut immigration by half, or reduce it to zero.[6] Of those surveyed in Europe, over half say migration makes their nations less safe, and makes their countries worse places to live.[7] Alas, mass migration is forced upon us all the same. A recent Harvard-Harris poll revealed that 81 percent of Americans want reduced migration numbers, with 35 percent wanting under 250,000 migrants per year.[8] The US currently allows in well over one million migrants per year, to contribute to the immigrants already there, who make up over 13 percent of the current US population.[9] A massive poll of all twenty-eight European Union nations found that almost 80 percent of

---

6 Katie McHugh. "Poll: 54 Percent Want Immigration Halved—or Reduced to Zero." Breitbart. November 7, 2016. www.breitbart.com/big-government/2016/11/08/poll-54-percent-want-immigration-halved-reduced-zero/. [http://archive.li/UiSSo]

7 Jacob Poushter. "European opinions of the refugee crisis in 5 charts." Pew Research Center. September 16, 2016. www.pewresearch.org/fact-tank/2016/09/16/european-opinions-of-the-refugee-crisis-in-5-charts/. [http://archive.li/apo2m]

8 Charles Lehman. "Here's How Americans Feel About People Immigrating to the US." Washington Free Beacon. January 23, 2018. freebeacon.com/issues/4-5-americans-want-less-immigration/. [http://archive.li/ACNsQ]

9 Steven A. Camarota and Karen Zeigler . "Immigrants in the United States." CIS.org. October 03, 2016. cis.org/Report/Immigrants-United-States. [http://archive.li/GSLw0]

citizens want strict border controls, that Europeans feel mass migration is harmful to their nations, and they fear the rising tide of non-European migration.[10]

The vast majority of us do not want mass migration and state-enforced diversity. We never voted for this. Yet they call this occupation government a "democracy," they tell us, "This is what democracy looks like." Is it really? If so, perhaps this is why I and so many others view modern "democracy" as nothing but an illusion. At the present time, and for many years now, we have had no real democracy. Time and time again our voices have been silenced, our will thwarted, and our votes debased. Without asking, they opened the floodgates to alien races of interlopers who would vote against us, while they tell us this is how democracy must function. But democracy is *only* present when the will of the people is carried out.

I've been called many things for my views — most typically, "intolerant." I won't argue. I do *not* tolerate forced assimilation. I do *not* tolerate forced taxation to fund a hostile invasion. I do *not* tolerate perverse and savage ideals being imported into this great land. This land is not for the Liberals to give away. They have no right to do so. They never fought for it: they were the "persons inimical to the liberties of America," as the Patriots called the Tories.

Do you think that if all the immigrants from Europe had voted Democrat, the Democrats would have cared to change the law in 1965? Do you think Liberals would be protesting and carrying signs that say "Muslims belong here" and "Make America Mexican Again" if Muslims and Mexicans voted monolithically Republican?

If the vast majority of immigrants voted Republican, did not need welfare, and supported an armed society, Democrats would have already built a southern wall that could be seen from outer space decades ago. Or imagine if Republicans began to flood New York and California with Right-wing Russians and Eastern Europeans that all voted Republican, respected traditional values, and loved the freedom to own rifles. I have

10 Thomas D. Williams. "Survey: 78 Percent of Europeans Want Tighter Control of Borders" Breitbart. March 29, 2018. http://www.breitbart.com/london/2018/03/29/survey-78-percent-europeans-want-tighter-control-borders/. [http://archive.is/w1ozB].

the feeling that the Left, in such a scenario would suddenly take a keen interest in border control.

In fact, that's not such a bad idea.

The Myth of the Melting Pot

"We are a nation of immigrants. We are a melting pot. Immigration is a basic human right." Have you heard all of this before? These arguments supporting mass immigration are wrong, wrong again, and dead wrong, in no particular order. Nations exist for the protection of one thing, their most precious possession; their peoples. Japan is rightfully interested in the protection and preservation of its own history, values, culture, and above all else, its people. Nations do not exist for the betterment of individuals on the other side of the world, who do not share their history, traditions, or culture. But somewhere along the way, the Western world decided the contrary. That is a mistake that might destroy everything we have ever held dear.

We are not a melting pot of primordial ooze. Until the borders were flung wide open with the Immigration Act of 1965, the US was nearly 90 percent culturally and ethnically European.

"We are and always will be a nation of immigrants," proclaimed Barack Obama, as justification for amnesty to illegal migrants.[11] But there is an important distinction to be made regarding this ubiquitous claim that "we are a nation of immigrants," and the distinction lies between the people that came to the US *before* the New Deal, and those who came *after*. The Legacy American immigrants (those who came prior to the New Deal) were quite an exceptional group of people. They did not come here expecting anything to be given to them. They had no welfare safety net, there was no inherent monetary incentive, and still they came to the United States. Prior to the New Deal, anyone who came to America knew it was up to them and their family if they were to succeed. And as a result

---

11 Paul Lewis. "Barack Obama: 'We are and always will be a nation of immigrants'" The Guardian. November 21, 2014. https://www.theguardian.com/us-news/2014/nov/20/obama-plan-shield-five-million-undocumented-migrants-deportation-speech. [http://archive.li/fYI5X]

America in those days attracted the most tenacious, the hardest-working, the most brilliant, and the most hopeful. American exceptionalism is no mistake. We opened our doors to those who had little prospect or hope in their home countries; all we offered them was a chance. And I'm glad those brave souls decided to get on those boats for the long journey to a foreign land. Though they did not know the language, had no family or friends here, and were penniless, they still were willing to take a wild shot in the dark. And their gamble helped make America great.

Each group of those immigrants brought something crucial to America: farming, culinary arts, the skills to build beautiful cathedrals; but most of all, the dream of making a better life *through their own struggle*. Which might just be the very essence of American exceptionalism. There was essentially a self-selection process prior to the welfare state, one in which only the hungriest had the desire to come to a new land. Far removed from the welfare tourists of today's migrants.

Those who advocate for open borders today, use the success of early, primarily white European immigrants to argue for increasing the rate of African, Arab, and Latin migrants. But the two groups cannot be compared. Coming from Europe, the early immigrants had an average IQ of around 100; with that came the ability to learn the language and contribute within a short period of time to their new homeland. Migrants today coming from the Third World often have substantially lower levels of intelligence, and can do nothing but become a perennial drain on society.[12]

The concept of an American melting pot only came about in the last century of our history. The term was popularized in 1908 by a play by Israel Zangwill called *The Melting Pot*. The play depicted an America where there was no longer any national or ethnic identity, simply a muddled concoction devoid of any sort of heritage.

Zangwill was born to Jewish migrants living in England, and he himself never lived anywhere else. He had no connection to America at any point, nor any understanding of our nation. Most of his writings were concerned with the history of the Jewish peoples, promoting Jewish culture and interests, as well as the establishment of a Jewish state. The idea that this man, who had no first-hand knowledge of America or our

---

12 Richard Lynn and Tatu Vanhanen. IQ and the Wealth of Nations. Praeger, 2002.

values, could somehow be the best arbiter of our immigration policy, is something only a deranged Liberal might accept.[13]

Liberals also love to cite the Statue of Liberty as evident justification for mass migration. But the Statue of Liberty was given to the US as a gift from the people of France to celebrate our independence: it has *nothing* to do with immigration. The table held by Lady Liberty reads, *JULY IV MDCCLXXVI*—July 4th, 1776. The woman depicted is the Roman goddess *Libertas*, who of course represents freedom, liberty, and independence.

The Statue of Liberty predates the construction of Ellis Island. The famous plaque with the poem by Emma Lazarus that reads, "Give me your tired, your poor, Your huddled masses yearning to breathe free, The wretched refuse of your teeming shore …" was not added until seventeen years after the dedication of the statue. The poem by Lazarus was added by a friend of Lazarus', who almost unilaterally saw to it that this poem was mounted under the statue. Like Zangwill, Lazarus was of Jewish decent, and also very preoccupied with the establishment of a Jewish homeland.[14] It appears they both were quite interested in diverting the national interest of America, to bring it in more line with the interests of their own people, rather than those of the American people. In 1882 Lazarus wrote, "I am all Israel's now. I have no thought, no passion, no desire save for my own people."[15]

The Melting Pot play, and "The New Colossus" poem, do not represent the ideas that we built our nation upon. They are nothing but propaganda pieces. They have both become immortalized as rallying cries by the Left in their incessant agitating for mass migration and the erosion of our true history, heritage, and culture. Both Zangwill and Lazarus were advocates for a Jewish homeland, and the relatively young America seemed to be a perfect fit at the time. Perhaps not coincidentally, Emanuel Celler, the Congressman who spent his entire career fighting for unlimited mass

13 "Israel Zangwill" Poetry Foundation. Accessed July 15, 2017. https://www.poetryfoundation.org/poems-and-poets/poets/detail/israel-zangwill. [http://archive.li/LuCrL]

14 "Emma Lazarus" Jewish Women's Archive. Accessed July 15, 2017. https://jwa.org/womenofvalor/lazarus. [http://archive.li/M4tOh]

15 Emily Taitz, Sondra Henry, and Cheryl Tallan. The JPS Guide to Jewish Women: 600 B.C.E.to 1900 C.E.Philadelphia: Jewish Publication Society, 2003. p. 253

migration to the United States, was also Jewish. Celler just happened to be a vehement critic of American isolationism and of a national origin quota for immigration.[16] He spent his entire career fighting to open US borders; he was joined by Jewish Senator Jacob Javits and many influential Jewish organizations dating back to the 1920s, such as the American Jewish Committee, the Anti-Defamation League of B'nai B'rith, and the American Federation of Jews from Eastern Europe.

Ironically enough, now that the Jewish people have their own ethnostate, they take in virtually zero refugees or non-Jewish migrants, and regularly deport non-Jews.[17]

The Founders of this nation explicitly stated in the Preamble that America was a nation for "ourselves and our posterity." The Founding Fathers had no intention of creating a homeland for all the world. Which is why until 1965, European immigration was favored, and why there was an origin-based quota system. This notion of a "nation of immigrants" was invented by people who deliberately sought to change America from its original European ideals into a nation without any sort of ethnic, religious, or cultural identity.

The poem on the base of the Statue of Liberty needs erasing. It subverts the true meaning of the Statue, and is used as a false rallying cry. As if our highest achievement as a nation is to become the dumping ground for foreign refuse. It is a subversive poem, arguing essentially for hostile invasion and insurrection, for the displacement of the rightful heirs to this nation, in our own homeland.

Liberals are attempting to equate pre-New Deal immigrants with those of today. And you simply cannot compare the two groups. People once immigrated here because they had fallen in love with the American dream. Not simply to get handouts.

---

16 James Krammar. "The Hart-Celler Immigration Act of 1965" CIS.org. September 30, 2015. https://cis.org/HartCeller-Immigration-Act-1965. [http://archive.li/NSFxv]

17 Daniel Estrin. "Israel Gives African Asylum-Seekers A Choice: Deportation Or Jail." NPR. February 22, 2018. www.npr.org/sections/parallels/2018/02/22/587858424/israel-gives-some-asylum-seekers-a-choice-deportation-or-jail. [http://archive.li/47SqA]

Until 1965, the majority of those who came to the US were from Western and Northern Europe. There was relatively little assimilation needed for these people. There were of course cultural differences between them, but these were mostly minor. As many of the European peoples were once united by the Roman Empire or Byzantine Empire, they shared similar values already. Many of the early European tribes had fought alongside each other to fend off foreign invaders. We were a nation of primarily European and Christian culture. Not a nation of Africans, Arabs, Asians, Hispanics, Muslims, and Jews. Those arguing that we are a "nation of immigrants" always intentionally leave out the fact that we were in truth a nation of *nearly homogeneous white European* immigrants; they are trying to conflate one group of people with another, to disastrous consequences.

The Left would like you to believe that the migrant hordes of today built the United States of America. They would like you to believe that the men and women who carved this great nation out of the wilderness are somehow cut of the same cloth as the Third Worlders pouring into it today. Nothing could be further from the truth. The fact that there was an Ellis Island and a New York City already built for immigrants to come to, already proves that the idea that "immigrants built the USA" is logically invalid. It simply does not follow chronologically.

Aside from attempting to conflate two entirely different groups under the single umbrella-term "immigrants," the argument "we are a nation of immigrants" attempts to posit the idea that because immigrants once came to America, they should continue to come here forever. But this is ridiculous. The amount of foreign born "Americans" (read: paper citizens) is at an all time high, more than ever before are on welfare, and we are still accepting people that have no connection whatsoever to our culture or history.

In 2013, nearly 300,000 babies were born in the US to illegal immigrant parents, making up 8 percent of the total US births that year. This figure is a drop from the 370,000 anchor babies born in the US in 2007.[18] Birthright

---

18 Jeffrey S. Passel and D'Vera Cohn. "Number of babies born in U.S. to unauthorized immigrants declines" Pew Research Center. September 11, 2015. http://www.pewresearch.org/fact-tank/2015/09/11/number-of-babies-born-in-u-s-to-unauthorized-immigrants-declines/. [http://archive.li/qZfQZ]

citizenship has become an all out disaster, and brings absolutely no benefit to the US. It needs to end immediately. The United States Department of Agriculture reports that 1.5 million illegal immigrants and 4 million anchor babies receive food stamps each year.[19] Averaging $254 dollars a month per household, this costs Americans billions of dollars — and it is just one of the many government welfare programs non-citizens enjoy. Considering that half of all legal immigrants also use welfare, we get into Mesospheric costs quite quickly. American taxpayers have essentially become slaves to welfare-using migrants. We go to work and allow the government to confiscate about a third of our money, so that it can invite in and pay for foreigners. It is bad enough that we have many *Americans* choosing to live off the tax payers; add to this mass migration, and the result is a totally corrupt and unsustainable predicament.

Mass migration does nothing but increase our tax burden and increase the levels of crime in our neighborhoods. And even *if* mass migration did somehow benefit us, we still have a right to our own homeland, and the right to be left alone, to live peacefully with our own people, in the civilizations our ancestors built. Just because the Left wants to give our nations and our money away, in accord with some ill-defined moral authority, their "want" does not justify any of these affronts. Even *if* migrants were not such drains on society and did not create so much dysfunction and the loss of so much social capital, we still have the right to keep our culture without foreign interlopers rebuilding *our* nation in *their* image. It is unconscionable that taxpayers are forced to fund the total living expenses of foreigners. Over 90 percent of migrants from the Middle East are on welfare.[20] These are people who will not contribute, people that do not believe in our values, and people that have no reason to care about our traditions or our ways. People that will ultimately alter our nation forever.

---

19 Katherine Rodriguez. "Immigrants Canceling Their Food Stamps over Fears of Being Deported" Breitbart. March 16, 2017. http://www.breitbart.com/big-government/2017/03/16/immigrants-canceling-food-stamps-fears-being-deported/. [http://archive.li/aiOJU]

20 Caroline May. "More Than 90 Percent of Middle Eastern Refugees on Food Stamps" Breitbart. September 10, 2015. http://www.breitbart.com/big-government/2015/09/10/more-than-90-percent-of-middle-eastern-refugees-on-food-stamps/. [http://archive.li/3csoi]

There should be zero welfare of any sort available to people have not been in the country for at least several decades.

Pilgrims, explorers, pioneers, and early settlers, came into a tough, harsh, and unforgiving environment. They needed a special type of grit and indomitable determination to go forth and succeed in order to form a nation out of the wild lands. Today, migrants have every luxury possible. They are given air-conditioned apartments, food, cash, everything they need, while doing nothing to earn it. To somehow say the people who came to America under harsh and often desperate conditions with little more than a dollar and a dream are the same as the hordes clamoring for welfare today, is not only insulting, it's sickening. To suggest that those pilgrims, pioneers, explorers, settlers, and revolutionaries were "immigrants" is an absurd sophistry, one only a deranged Leftist could possibly dream up.

The Left has pushed this immigration on us in the name of "cultural enrichment." What a brazen insult. The Occidental tradition has created the vastest and richest cultures the world has ever known. The greatest literature, music, art, architecture, philosophy, and inventions, all come from the sons of Europe. And Liberals want to tell us we need to become more diverse and enriched? By a group of people that still practice honor killings and have not figured out running water? We are going to somehow become more enriched and worldly by being forced to be neighbors with groups of people that dress nearly homogeneously in burkas and hijabs?

We already *have* a tremendous amount of our own "diversity." The suggestion that we might need more is offensive. If you've ever traveled the US or Europe you are surely familiar with the variety of unique cultures we already enjoy. Europe has over two dozen nations, each with its special food, architecture, traditions, and heritage. If you dropped me off in Prague, I would know I was in Prague by the look of the city alone. The same is true all over Europe. Each country is unmistakable. These are not the qualities of people who lack culture or identity.

In America, there are at least as many localized sub-cultures as there are in Europe. The Pacific Northwest has an entirely different look and feel as compared to Northern California or to Southern California. I would know quite quickly if I was randomly dropped off in the French Quarter, as opposed to somewhere in New England. The assumption that we need hordes of people form the Third World to "enrich" us, as if *we* are the cultureless hordes, is tremendously denigrating.

The end result of forced assimilation is seen all over Europe: people from radically different cultures do not come to the West with the intention to become citizens of their new nation, they come to dominate and bring their backwards and depraved traditions along with them.

Lines in the Sand

When foreigners flood your streets, burn buildings and cars, wave foreign flags, take your resources, kill and rape the native population, this once meant your homeland was being invaded. It still does.

Leftists the world over claim that the very concept of borders, sovereign nations, and immigration laws or quotas, are all fundamentally racist, bigoted, xenophobic, and unnecessary. But nowhere is it written that people have the right to freely enter other countries. For the entirety of human history, people who did just that were referred to as invaders, and they were usually put to sword and fire.

America was not created to be the dumping ground for the rest of the planet. If you do not share our fundamental heritage, you do not have any right to come to America, or to European countries, no more than I have any fundamental right to live in Japan or Argentina or Somalia. I have zero right to go and take resources from African nations, I have zero right to go pillaging for diamonds or gold. I have no right to the rainforests of South and Central America. I have no right to migrate to South Korea, to then impose my beliefs and culture upon the South Koreans.

A recent *Salon* article was titled "Everyone's wrong on immigration: Open borders are the only way to defeat Trump and build a better world."[21] The *de facto* function of the Left is to facilitate globalization and to create a world where there is not a single white majority country anywhere on Earth. I think at this point the real agenda is clear to anybody paying

21 Anis Shivani. "Everyone's wrong on immigration: Open borders are the only way to defeat Trump and build a better world" Salon. March 15, 2017. http://www.salon.com/2017/03/15/everyones-wrong-on-immigration-open-borders-are-the-only-way-to-defeat-trump-and-build-a-better-world/. [http://archive.li/7Z5pq]

attention. The title of the article says it all, "build a better world" through "open borders." The author further argues that the distinctions between legal and illegal are meaningless, and that immigration is a human right. He then claims that the red-tape of immigration is far too complicated. And of course, he claims that immigration laws are racist and exclusionary. Those, like this author, who advocate for a "path to citizenship" for illegals seem to forget there is already a very clear path: over a million people annually manage to navigate it just fine.

This article was written by a man named Anis Shivani — not a particularly Western name. A few questions for the Liberals, who evidently see Europe and America as evil white empires that must to be dismantled: If white people are so awful and racist, and oppressive, why does the entire planet want to live with them? If white people are such a problem, that the only way to build a better world is to eliminate them from power in the very lands that they built, why are people flocking here and trying to get all their relatives in as well?

Imagine if a bunch of French people, say a million per year, moved to Japan. Then imagine if they started complaining that there were too many Asians there, and that the Japanese have too much power, and they should not get to be the majority in their own nation. Imagine if the French started telling the Japanese that celebrating their holidays, which they have celebrated for generations upon generations, was exclusionary and racist. At some point, the Japanese would probably round up all the French, and either deport them or bury them, once their patience and tolerance inevitably ran dry. And I somehow doubt that the Liberals would utter a single objection.

Do you think the Japanese people would be okay if every neighborhood in Kyoto was filled with nothing but white Texans, flying Texas flags, and opening Texan BBQ stands on every corner? Is it "racist" of them to want to remain Japanese, rather than see Kyoto turned into a Texan colony? The cultural disparity need not be as wide as that between the Japanese and the Texans: if the Chinese or the Koreans suddenly flocked to Japan, the culture would inevitably shift away from Japanese, and towards Chinese and Korean.

Japan has very strict immigration because they understand that neither Europeans nor Africans nor anybody else can carry on their heritage and culture for them. Only the Japanese are able to do so. By manipulating our populace, instilling in us all a sense of collective racial guilt, and brainwashing us into believing that there is something wrong with the preservation of our nations, Liberals have used immigration to expand the state, import voters by the millions, and cement their power. Imagine the amount of inculcation it would take to get a nation such as Japan or South Korea to forfeit their culture, land, history, and values. It's nearly incomprehensible to imagine a non-white nation being forced to sacrifice the very body of their history in order to appease the false god of diversity.

Liberals are pushing the limits of madness when they claim that "illegal" is a racist word. We went from *illegal alien*, to *illegal immigrant*, to *undocumented immigrant*, to *mis-documented worker*, to *mis-documented American*, to the ever so illustrious moniker, "*dreamer*." Let's stick with *invader*; it is far more accurate.

As regards migration, something else I find both ironic and telling: Before the 2016 election, all the many Liberals proclaiming they would move to a different country if Trump won, announced they would move—to Canada! *Not* Mexico. *Not* Pakistan. *Not* Somalia. Not any of the nations they want to force us to welcome en masse. But Canada. A country even whiter than America. How telling.

Nothing More Sinister

There is nothing new in all of this. The entire mass migration scheme has been planned for quite some time by a hostile international clique of global Leftists. What we are seeing happen in Europe and America today is the direct result of nearly 100 years of planning to undermine European civilization through the mass migration of non-Europeans. In 1923 a book was published called *Pan-Europa*, by Richard von Coudenhove-Kalergi. *Pan-Europa* laid the groundwork for what would become the European Union.[22] Its agenda, often referred to as the Kalergi Plan, called for the destruction of sovereign nations in Europe. Kalergi envisioned a united

22 "Pan-Europa—The parent idea of a united Europe" Internationale Paneuropa Union. Accessed July 15, 2017. http://www.paneuropa.org/gb_int/geschichte.html. [http://archive.li/z62Fc]

Europe with no borders, subject to the mass migration of non-European peoples. The stated goal of the Pan-Europa movement was to create a single European population with no sense of history, identity, culture, or tradition, so that the ruling elite would be able more easily to control the population. Kalergi had written the early manifesto of what we now refer to as demographic genocide.

There is an award given every other year to those politicians who most work to further the globalization agenda, ironically called the Charlemagne Prize. The first prize was given to Coudenhove-Kalergi for his plan. Notable winners have included George Marshall, Henry Kissinger, Tony Blair, Bill Clinton, and Angela Merkel. Notice a trend? These people all are working toward the sinister plan to create a one world government with no nations, no borders, no identity. When politicians utter the phrase "diversity is our greatest strength," they aren't lying. They mean it is *their* greatest strength to undermine the values of individual cultures and nations, create chaos, and make for a weak society that is easily controlled and manipulated.

The Kalergi Plan has had its echoes throughout recent history. In 1941, Jewish businessman, Theodore Kaufman, wrote a book titled *Germany Must Perish!*, in which he advocated a sterilization plan for all German men as well as the dissection of Germany. Although his book was published during World War II, Kaufman had pushed for the sterilization and destruction of both Germans and Americans through the 1930s in a series of pamphlets he published and distributed.[23]

During the Second World War, Jewish anthropologist, Earnest Hooton, laid out a plan to eradicate Germans through mass migration of non-European males, in order to breed German bloodlines out of existence.[24] The legacy of the Hooton Plan can be seen in Germany today, as government-funded websites and pamphlets have been produced to teach migrants how to have sex with German women. The images on the government-sponsored site depict brown men having sex with white women,

23 Theodore Kaufman. "WAR & PEACE: Slick Stuff." Time. October 23, 1939. content.time.com/time/magazine/article/0,9171,772239,00.html.

24 Mark Weber. "Germany must perish!" Institute for Historical Review. Accessed July 15, 2017. www.ihr.org/books/kaufman/perish.shtml. [http://archive.li/MBovU]

and provide information on how to have oral sex and sex with virgins.[25] Children all over the West are being indoctrinated to accept their eradication. In France for example, children are taught by state curriculum that migration is a "human right," "the essence of humanity," and that open borders are what have created our safe and prosperous nations.[26] Every instance of anti-white and miscegenation propaganda in TV, films, and advertisements is an expression of these same schemes. These plans that were laid out decades ago are the ideological groundwork for the United Nations' population replacement strategy.

The United Nations special representative for migration, Peter Sutherland, has said on more than one occasion that Europe needs to "undermine national homogeneity."[27]

Mass migration from the Third World was first justified to replace an aging population in Europe, despite the fact that for many years the media was telling Europeans and Americans not to have children due to overpopulation.[28] The idea was that if you allow millions of new people to come into Europe and work, they will pay taxes that will fund the social programs. Unfortunately it somehow happened that the majority of migrants to Europe and America go on welfare and do not pay taxes.[29] Once that the "migrants = new taxpayers" scam was up, the globalists simply

---

25 Oliver JJ. Lane. "Government Funded Website Teaches Migrants How To Have Sex... In 13 Different Languages" Breitbart. March 11, 2016. http://www.breitbart.com/london/2016/03/11/government-funded-website-teaches-migrants-how-to-have-sex/. [http://archive.li/9TfWZ]

26 Virginia Hale. "French Children Taught Migration Is a Human Right, Were All Africans." Breitbart. February 20, 2018. www.breitbart.com/london/2018/02/20/french-children-migration-right/. [http://archive.li/ox3yq]

27 Brian Wheeler. "EU should 'undermine national homogeneity' says UN migration chief" BBC News. June 21, 2012. http://www.bbc.com/news/uk-politics-18519395. [http://archive.li/LjoMO]

28 Oli Smith. "Merkel's open-door policy hits German economy as 99 percent of migrants STILL don't have a job" Express.co.uk. September 15, 2016. http://www.express.co.uk/news/world/710927/million-migrants-Germany-unemployed-Merkel-open-door-policy. [http://archive.li/7JwIZ]

29 Chris Tomlinson. "Fewer Than 500 of 163,000 Migrants Find Jobs In Sweden" Breitbart. June 01, 2016. http://www.breitbart.com/london/2016/06/01/less-500-163000-migrants-find-jobs-sweden/. [http://archive.li/M6X74]

came up with new reasons to justify mass migration, despite the fact that the immigrants are taking more out of the tax system than putting in, and by a large margin. Reports from Sweden and Germany show that the vast majority of migrants, over 80 percent, do not have jobs.[30] Most European nations will not even release the data out of fear of public outrage; given their silence, we can assume the employment rates for migrants in their nations are not much better.

Today we are being told by the media and Liberal politicians that we need to take in migrants as "refugees," despite the fact that again, the majority of these migrants are not fleeing any sort of persecution or war. Per Pew Research, over 70 percent of all migrants to Europe are men, 60 percent of which are young men, under the age of thirty-five.[31] Hardly war-torn families with women and children fleeing some sort of violent catastrophe. Hundreds of thousands of these "refugees" have traveled through a dozen stable countries to get to England, Germany, and France where the welfare benefits are more robust and the police allow them to run wild. They are simply coming for handouts. What was once justified as economic policy, is now being re-framed as "humanitarianism" and "human rights." The Liberal story continues to be re-written wherever necessary.

Europe and America cannot sustain their cultures and identities alongside waves of migrants from Africa and the Middle East. Liberals often cite low birth rates as a reason we "need" migration.[32] European and American families are being robbed of their tax dollars to pay the way for foreigners and to support their children, instead of being allowed to use our own hard earned money to support larger families of our own — and

30 Michelle Martin. "Only 13 percent of recent refugees in Germany have found work: survey" Reuters. November 15, 2016. http://www.reuters.com/article/us-europe-migrants-germany-survey-idUSKBN13A22F. [http://archive.li/xgUMW]

31 Phillip Connor. "Asylum seeker demography: Young and male" Pew Research Center's Global Attitudes Project. August 02, 2016. http://www.pewglobal.org/2016/08/02/4-asylum-seeker-demography-young-and-male/. [http://archive.li/KeR4z]

32 Laurens Cerulus. "Europe's (lack of) migration problem" POLITICO. December 28, 2016. http://www.politico.eu/article/europe-immigration-population-news-statistics-facts/. [http://archive.li/GygZy]

then our governments have the audacity to tell us that this is being done to promote population growth. So the answer to low birth rates is to totally replace us? Not incentivize reproduction in the native populations? Americans and Europeans are being subjected to an oppressive taxation, which forces many couples to delay having children or to have fewer children. Then, while the cost of living rises, we are forced to fund the families of people utterly foreign to us, people with the breeding habits of rodents. It is infuriating that nobody has called Liberals out on their maniacal proposition that the first world needs to stop having kids, so they can use their money instead support the people of Third World, who just pushing out more low-IQ spawns. The Liberal media and politicians keep forcing this agenda, while most of the world sleeps. This is the largest dysgenics experiment ever to be undertaken, the greatest conspiracy against an entire civilization that has ever been known.

The "low birth rate" argument is infuriating. Of course birth rates are low! They always are during times of social unrest, conflict, war, and invasion. And make no mistake, we are at war.

The idea of "out-breeding" the Third World is a self-fulfilling prophecy. There is a tremendous psychological burden on white families created by these hostile social conditions. Either consciously or subconsciously, people feel unsafe and unsure about bringing children into a hostile, anti-white, "multicultural" environment.

This is a concrete example of systemic racism Liberals often espouse, an actual and identifiable government policy that discriminates against the native populations of Europe and America, in favor of Saracen hordes. Indeed, the only systemic racism currently in existence is to be found in forcing whites to fund people that routinely attack us and abuse us in the nations our ancestors built. We can no longer stand for this level of organized violence against us.

It should also be said that it was never written anywhere that a nation's population must continue to grow each generation. This is indeed an obvious absurdity. Only unadorned ingenuity could assume that after the world's largest baby boom following World War Two, each generation following would grow even more. Birth rates are always suppressed during times of war and social unrest—as, indeed, in the present moment. If European and American nations were to expel all the invaders, were able to walk safely outside once again, and to spend their own money on their own families instead of giving it to their governments for the importation of hordes of mongrels, the birth rates just maybe would rise once more.

But even if they don't, will that be such a tragedy? Other nations, notably Japan, are not frantically bringing in foreigners by the boat load to replace their aging population; they understand that through all of human history, populations have grown and diminished. What's more, in Japan, the Japanese are seeing some changes to their quality of life as the population decreases. In the past fifty years, the average amount of living space that Japanese citizens have been able to afford in Tokyo has more than doubled.[33] The cost of living is declining, pollution will decrease, jobs will be more plentiful, wages will increase, and crime will be lower. What a *disaster* the Japanese are facing. If you've ever been on the freeway at rush hour, you've personally experienced why doubling the US population might not be so wonderful a proposition for our quality of life.

Let us not forget: the European Renaissance happened *after* the Black Death killed 30 percent-60 percent of the European population. Europe did not recover to pre-Plague levels for several hundred years, yet many experienced a higher quality of life after surviving the Plague. Perhaps a higher population is the very last thing we need in our nations.

This, of course, will not stop our globalist friends from using any excuse they can get their hands on. The United Nations Populations Division has released, on the UN website, reports espousing the "necessity" and "benefits" of what even the UN calls Replacement Migration. They are hiding their nefarious plans in plain sight. Kalergi, Hooton, Kaufman, The United Nations, The European Union — all espouse globalist plans to eliminate European and American identities and eventually the people. The very values that Europe and America were built upon pose a fundamental threat to the ruling elite's cosmopolitan dream of a mongrelized, cultureless, rootless horde, easily atomized, deracinated, manipulated, and conquered.

33 Steve Sailer. "Without immigration, Tokyo more than doubles housing space per person" The Unz Review. June 26, 2017. http://www.unz.com/isteve/without-immigration-tokyo-more-than-doubles-housing-space-per-person/. [http://archive.li/C7yS7]

They have used the excuse of aging populations, low birth rates, a struggling economy, and humanitarianism, to excuse our displacement. Every so often, the old excuses find their masks slipping off, and the Left has to invent a new reason we must accept millions of invaders. The most recent in this line of absurdities comes from German finance minister, Wolfgang Schäuble. He claims that closing European Union and German borders would lead to Europeans becoming inbred. He of course further claimed that "Muslims are an enrichment of our openness and our diversity."[34] He makes these proclamations without providing a single shred of evidence for either claim — probably because both claims are patently absurd. Europe has over 700 million people, Germany over eighty million; even in times of lower population numbers, inbreeding has never been a European issue. In fact, the places that have the highest rates of consanguinity, with some countries reaching levels of 50 percent inbreeding, are all North African and Arab nations. No other region on Earth has near the rate of consanguinity as Africa or the Middle East.[35]

I am not of the persuasion that we must censor claims of the enemies of our civilization that we must be replaced. Instead, I seek to embolden the men of my own stock, so that every time it is suggested that Europe must perish, we proudly proclaim that Europe and her people *must be eternal*!

The Myth Of Economic Benefits

The media of course loves the idea of our dispossession, and is now openly expressing their resentment of whites. *Bloomberg* published a shockingly racist article titled, "American Prosperity Depends on a Nonwhite

34 Harry Cockburn. "Closing EU borders will lead to inbreeding, German finance minister warns" The Independent. June 12, 2016. http://www.independent.co.uk/News/world/europe/closing-eu-borders-immigration-will-lead-to-incest-german-finance-minister-warns-a7077696.html. [http://archive.li/yEbLZ]

35 Dr. Michael Black. "Global Prevalence of consanguinity" Global prevalence Consanguinity. Accessed July 16, 2017. http://consang.net/index.php/Global_prevalence. [http://archive.li/vc79r]

Future."[36] From *Newsweek*, "America's Getting Less White, and That Will Save it."[37] According to the Left, the only way society will prosper is if it abolishes the white race which created it. These articles essentially argue the same tired points, that economic "growth" is predicated upon population growth, and the only way to save the country is for mass migration and miscegenation to take place. Evidently, this will save us from our otherwise inevitable demise, despite the fact that migrants use more welfare than native-born Americans, and have on average much lower IQs.

This Leftist argument that migrants "grow the economy," as seen yet again in articles such as, "Immigrants Are Makers, Not Takers," always involves a level of sophistry.[38] Although it is technically true, in strict terms, that additional people spending money augments the GDP, this ignores the high cost to native citizens.[39] Over half of migrant households in the US are on welfare.[40] The total cost of migration to US tax payers is around $300 billion per year.[41] Even including those migrants that are paying income taxes, migrants cause a total net loss in terms of taxation, meaning that the "economic growth" from migrants is being funded and subsidized by the native tax payers. The related argument that "immigrants

36 Noah Smith. "American Prosperity Depends on a Nonwhite Future" Bloomberg. May 24, 2017. https://www.bloomberg.com/view/articles/2017-05-24/american-prosperity-depends-on-a-nonwhite-future. [http://archive.li/SbMIR]

37 William H. Frey. "America's Getting Less White, and That Will Save It" Newsweek. December 06, 2014. http://www.newsweek.com/americas-getting-less-white-and-will-save-it-289862. [http://archive.li/EpcR8]

38 Marshall Fitz, Phillip Wogan, and Patrick Oakford. "Immigrants Are Makers, Not Takers" Center for American Progress. February 8, 2013. https://www.americanprogress.org/issues/immigration/news/2013/02/08/52377/immigrants-are-makers-not-takers/.

39 Steven A. Camarota. "The High Cost of Cheap Labor" CIS.org. August 25, 2004. https://cis.org/Report/High-Cost-Cheap-Labor. [http://archive.li/EgWel]

40 Steven A. Camarota. "Welfare Use by Immigrant and Native Households" Center for Immigration Studies. September 10, 2015. http://cis.org/Welfare-Use-Immigrant-Native-Households. [http://archive.li/5uouk]

41 Stephen Dinan. "Mass immigration costs government $296 billion a year, depresses wages" The Washington Times. September 21, 2016. http://www.washingtontimes.com/news/2016/sep/21/mass-immigration-costs-govt-296-billion-year-natio/. [http://archive.li/C3Czs]

do jobs natives will not," is also not supported by the data. There are nearly 500 civilian occupations; only six are occupied by a migrant majority, accounting for 1 percent of the workforce.[42]

In regard to work, an interesting study titled "Racial/Ethnic Differences in Non-Work at Work" was published in the National Bureau of Economic Research journal. The study investigated the time spent not working, while on the clock, of over 35,000 employees. The results of between-race analysis were statistically significant, finding that white men and women spend the *least* amount of their day not working. Asian men were the next group to waste the least time at work, followed by Asian women. Black women, followed by Hispanic women, then black men, and finally Hispanic men, spent the most time at work not working. The journal article notes, "These differences are robust to the inclusion of large numbers of demographic, industry, occupation, time and geographic controls. They do not vary by union status, public-private sector attachment, pay method or age; nor do they arise from the effects of equal-employment enforcement or geographic differences in racial/ethnic representation."[43] Across age, salary, skill level, geography, the results are the same. White people spend the most time working while at work.

Another fascinating study from 2007 investigated the link between workplace diversity and productivity over a six-year period. What they found was that as firm diversity increased, productivity decreased.[44]

National wealth, life satisfaction, and life expectancy all decline as the diversity of a nation increases.[45] In the United States, public trust and interpersonal trust have both steadily declined in relative proportion to how

42 Steven A. Camarota. "The Fiscal and Economic Impact of Immigration on the United States" CIS.org. May 17, 2013. https://cis.org/Testimony/Fiscal-and-Economic-Impact-Immigration-United-States. [http://archive.li/vCU4r]

43 Daniel Hamermesh, et al. "Racial/Ethnic Differences in Non-Work at Work." National Bureau of Economic Research, Jan. 2017, doi:10.3386/w23096.

44 Orlando C. Richard, et al. "The impact of racial diversity on intermediate and long-Term performance: The moderating role of environmental context." Strategic Management Journal, vol. 28, no. 12, Dec. 2007, pp. 1213–1233., doi:10.1002/smj.633.

45 "What Diverse Countries Really Look Like." The Alternative Hypothesis. November 30, 2016. thealternativehypothesis.org/index.php/2016/11/30/what-diverse-countries-really-look-like/. [http://archive.li/xsvah]

ethnically diverse the US has become. As mass migration increases, trust in society and between individuals declines. On a global scale, there is a very strong relationship between trust and GDP per capita; the nations with the highest amount of trust, consistently enjoy higher rates of GDP per capita.[46] The meaning is clear: as nations, cities, neighborhoods, and firms increase diversity, productivity, economic stability, and happiness all decline. Diversity is empirically proven to lower our quality of life, destroy trust, destroy social capital, cause less charitable contributions, cause us to be more atomized and deracinated, and even end our lives earlier.[47] By all measures, it is similarity and homogeneity, not diversity, that is our strength.

Despite the constant claims to the contrary, there is no evidence to suggest that per capita GDP is being raised by mass migration. Quite the opposite in fact. American citizens would be far better off if they were able to keep the several thousand dollars a year that they are forced to give toward the funding of migration. Each legal migrant household costs an average fiscal deficit of $4,300. On average, each of these households utilizes $4,300 dollars more in government services than it contributes.[48] That deficit of course is made up by native-born Americans — primarily, white Americans.

Moreover, a higher GDP does not inherently benefit Americans; it benefits the large corporations who desire cheap labor and more consumers. The health of a nation cannot be measured simply in GDP and stock indexes. We are more than an economy; we are people with a culture, history, tradition, and we have the right to exist, a right that is much more intrinsic than the "right" of Fortune 500 companies to earn a few dollars more. In truth, total GDP is an awful measure of quality of life. India,

46 Esteban Ortiz-Ospina and Max Roser. "Trust — Our World in Data." Our World in Data. Accessed July 15, 2017. ourworldindata.org/trust. [http://archive.li/uQmmF]

47 Jared Taylor. "September Diversity Destroys Trust." American Renaissance. September 2007. www.amren.com/archives/back-issues/september-2007/. [http://archive.li/qmvyU]

48 Jason Richwine and Robert Rector. "The Fiscal Cost of Unlawful Immigrants and Amnesty to the U.S. Taxpayer" The Heritage Foundation. May 06, 2013. http://www.heritage.org/immigration/report/the-fiscal-cost-unlawful-immigrants-and-amnesty-the-us-taxpayer. [http://archive.li/vOL81]

for example, has a higher aggregate GDP than Switzerland. China has a higher total GDP than Norway. The latter nations, meanwhile, have a higher *per capita* GDP, and a higher quality of life.[49]

The media narrative of the "hard working immigrant trying to make a better life in America while facing huge adversity" is laughable. They do nothing for native born Americans, other than cost us thousands of dollars per year. On average, immigration as a whole brings nothing but poverty for white families and a lower quality of life by virtue of more taxation, more crime, and destroyed social capital.

Weaponized Migration

As a direct result of Leftist open-border policies the West has experienced recent outbreaks of nearly eradicated diseases such as tuberculosis, measles, scarlet fever, even the bubonic plague, all of which have made a resurgence in the US and Europe.[50]

Europeans and Americans are being routinely subjected, sacrificed even, to violent massacres by foreign invaders. In the November 2015 attacks in Paris, 500 people were injured, 130 killed. In the Bataclan Theatre, eighty-nine hostages were mutilated and tortured before being killed. During the July 2016 truck attack in Nice, another ninety-eight lives were claimed, hundreds more injured. The December 2016 Christmas Market attack in Berlin, left twelve dead, dozens injured. Although the death toll has been horrid, the psychological effect on our people is more diffuse yet.

In Rotherham, England, there was a widespread organized rape gang. 1,400 or more women and children were raped and exploited by mostly Pakistani Muslim men. It went on for years, and there appears to have been quite a cover-up to keep the story from gaining widespread attention. Why? Because English authorities were worried that outrage might

49 Mark Venezia. "AP Flunks Economics 101." ImmigrationReform.com. February 28, 2018. immigrationreform.com/2018/02/28/ap-flunks-economics-101. [http://archive.li/d19Gh]

50 Michael Patrick Leahy. "Six Diseases Return To US as Migration Advocates Celebrate 'World Refugee Day'" Breitbart. June 19, 2016. http://www.breitbart.com/big-government/2016/06/19/diseases-thought-eradicated-world-refugee-day/. [http://archive.li/C8Sqk]

have been sparked from the news, which might have caused a rise in racism or intolerance against members of the Pakistani or Muslim communities. Similarly, the details about the torture and mutilation in the Bataclan Theatre were also suppressed by most media sources, so as to avoid giving a bad name to the Muslim community. The Judeo-Liberal media is more worried about giving offense than they are about the victims and the truth.[51] They are entirely complicit in these horrific crimes against our people. They are nothing but accomplices to the crimes against every girl who has been abused at the hands of foreign invaders, all the more contemptible because they are apparently more afraid of being called racists, than they are afraid of the rape and torture of young women.

Over 1,500 acid attacks have been reported in London alone over the past few years. Strangely, this never occurred before the advent of mass migration. The Leftist media chooses to ignore these attacks.[52] Europeans are being terrorized daily, and their governments have made it illegal for them to speak out. They have even made it illegal to fight back. Two fathers in the UK were able to track down the whereabouts of their daughters, who had been abducted by sex-trafficking gangs; when the two brave men arrived at the house where their daughters were being held, the police were called, who then promptly arrested — the fathers.[53]

Estimates from France indicate there are over 5,000 gang rapes in the country each year, mostly committed by African and Arab migrants.[54] At this point, living in Liberal-occupied multicultural France appears to be worse than living in German-occupied Paris.

---

51 Katerina Nikolas. "Muslim gang-rapes across Europe under-reported in press" Digital Journal. March 20, 2013. http://www.digitaljournal.com/article/346059. [http://archive.li/BLs72]

52 Saagar Enjeti. "1,500 Acid Attacks Hit London Since 2011" The Daily Caller. March 16, 2017. http://dailycaller.com/2017/03/16/1500-acid-attacks-hit-london-since-2011/. [http://archive.li/Zcdkj]

53 "Rotherham Dads Were Arrested after Tracking down Abusers." The Star. August 27, 2014. www.thestar.co.uk/news/rotherham-dads-were-arrested-after-tracking-down-abusers-1-6807187. [http://archive.is/6wxA1].

54 Katerina Nikolas. "Muslim gang-rapes across Europe under-reported in press" Digital Journal. March 20, 2013. http://www.digitaljournal.com/article/346059. [http://archive.li/BLs72]

The victims of organized rape gangs of Muslim, Arab, and African invaders are overwhelmingly white. There is, meanwhile, no known instance of white men and organizing gang raping enterprises in Europe. In England alone, it is estimated over one million women and children have been raped by migrants, primarily by Pakistani and Muslims rape gangs.[55] Although hard to believe at first, this has been going on since the 1980s — nearly forty years of terror. This is by definition genocidal rape, and should be declared as such. This should justify a declaration of war — but alas, the crimes are covered up and ignored, because the victims are white children. These are the victims of multiculturalism, Liberal tolerance, and politicians who believe that "diversity is our greatest strength." These crimes are nothing short of blood libel.

Under the guise of diversity, our people are being eradicated through population replacement and genocidal rape. *This is the Final Solution to the White Problem.* Wearing the mask of diversity and tolerance, they are killing us off — as most people sit around and watch.

After being on trial in the UK for a sex trafficking operation, a gang of men from Pakistan, Bangladesh, India, Iraq, Iran, and Turkey were found guilty of eighty-seven different offenses relating to sex crime and drug violations. The men used hard drugs to keep girls as young as thirteen sedated while they raped them for hours. During the trial, defendants commented that the police who arrested them "were racists," that "white women are good for only one thing — to be used like trash," and that the victims did not matter as they were "white trash."[56]

To add insult to injury, English legal analysts report that the Muslim and foreign men were actually given lighter sentences because their victims were all white. The presiding judges, fearing they might look "racist," gave the abusers lenient punishments. The gang members explicitly abducted white girls and women to sell, and only whites. Yet none of the trials nor

---

55 Dale Hurd. "'Easy Meat.' Britain's Muslim Rape Gang Cover-Up" CBN News. October 29, 2016. http://www1.cbn.com/cbnnews/world/2016/august/easy-meat-britains-muslim-rape-gang-cover-up. [http://archive.li/iUxqY]

56 Liam Deacon. "Grooming Gang: 'White Women Are Good for Only One Thing — for People Like Me to F*** and Use as Trash'" Breitbart. August 10, 2017. http://www.breitbart.com/london/2017/08/10/newcastle-groomers-white-women-are-trash-police-are-racist/. [http://archive.li/OkzAU]

sentencing reflected the racial targeting of whites.[57] There are laws against racial targeting in the UK, yet these were not applied: since the victims were white, they apparently do not matter. This is the same country that has arrested and jailed people for making "hateful comments" online about Muslims, a trend repeated in many parts of Europe. The Left now views Crime Think as more abhorrent a crime than gang rape.

Sweden has become a terrifying illustration of open-door politics. Even while I was writing these words, I kept seeing news reports of the gang rape of a young Swedish women being live-streamed on Facebook by three Afghan migrants. Most news sources simply labeled the rapist as "three men," or "three Swedish men." The video depicts the rape, and the foreign men laughing and jeering the entire time. For their crimes, the three Afghan men received only twenty-seven months, twelve months, and six months in prison.[58]

I have heard for sometime that Sweden had fallen far from their once safe and pristine past. I had no idea how severe it really was until I began researching further. Not only did I find startling statistics on rape and murder: much more troubling was the lengths to which the Swedish government has gone to keep this information a secret from its own people.

The story starts in the mid-1960s when Jewish migrants living in Sweden — David Schwarz and Inga Gottfarb, among others — began to lobby the Swedish government to become "multicultural." Within a decade the Swedish government unilaterally decided to embrace multiculturalism and open their doors to mass migration. The native Swedes were never asked their opinion. The majority of migrants have come from African and Middle Eastern countries. Over the last decade most migrants arrive from countries such as Algeria, Somalia, and Iraq, most of which claim refugee status and receive state welfare benefits.[59]

---

57 Zoie O'Brien. "Racist rapists handed lower sentences because their victims were WHITE" Express.co.uk. August 12, 2017. http://www.express.co.uk/news/uk/840325/Racism-Rape-victims-British-Newcastle. [http://archive.li/zwVNy]

58 Mclaughlin, Kelly. "Two Afghan migrants are jailed for up to two years for raping a woman in Sweden as their friend broadcasted it over Facebook Live" Daily Mail Online. April 25, 2017. Accessed July 15, 2017. http://www.dailymail.co.uk/news/article-4444016/Migrants-jailed-years-raping-woman-Sweden.html.

59 M. Eckehart. How Sweden Became Multicultural. Logik Forlag, 2017.

Something else happened over the last forty years in Sweden: rapes went from around 400 per year, to over 6,000 per year, an increase of over 1,400 percent. In the last forty years the Swedish population has increased from a little over 8,000,000, to just under 10,000,000, an increase of some 25 percent; one might expect crime to rise by a similar rate. Not in this case. Violent crimes have increase by 300 percent. The Swedish rape rate is now among the highest in the world.[60] As of 2002, 85 percent of those sentenced for rape were either foreign born, or second-generation migrants. There was a recent attempt to look at the latest crime data, but the Justice Minister of Sweden denied the request, stating there would be nothing to gain from a new inquiry.[61] [62]

Denmark, a close neighbor, and a nation with a more restrictive immigration policy, has taken in around a tenth of the foreign migrants that Sweden has. Denmark has a rape rate of 7.3 per 100,000 resident — not surprisingly, a fraction of Sweden's rape rate, which is nearing 60 per 100,000 people. The pattern could not be clearer: the more Third World vermin you allow into a nation, the higher the rates of crime and rape will fly.

The Swedish government describes itself as the "first feminist government in the world." Swedish officials and their official government website make it clear that they are endlessly committed to women's rights and equality. So committed in fact, they have worked tirelessly to ensure the women of Sweden reach parity, in terms rape rate, with women living in underdeveloped Third World nations. Sweden now has the highest rate of sexual assault in the Western world, with numbers pushing those of South Africa and Botswana.

During New Year's Eve celebrations in cities all over Germany, women were subjected to mass sexual assault and rape. In the city of Cologne, there were around 1,200 victims of rape and sexual assault in one night.

60 Ingrid Carlqvist and Lars Hedegaard. "Sweden: Rape Capital of the West." February 14, 2015. https://www.gatestoneinstitute.org/5195/sweden-rape. [http://archive.li/cRcwf]

61 Virginia Hale. "Sweden Blocks Request for Data on Crime and Immigration" Breitbart. January 18, 2017. http://www.breitbart.com/london/2017/01/18/sweden-blocks-data-crime-immigration/. [http://archive.li/WbBqi]

62 Ibid.

Police reports indicated that the perpetrators were large groups of men that were of Arab and North African decent.[63] The Leftist media in Germany once again tried to minimize reporting on the assaults until social outcry forced the news to into the light. Neither Cologne nor Rotherham is an isolated incident. Mass rapes, assaults, and sex trafficking have been found in hundreds of European cities, always at the hands of Arab and African invaders. Mass sexual assault is not uncommon in the parts of the world from which these devils come: this is the direct result of "cultural enrichment" policies and of political correctness. People do indeed bring their culture with them to new lands — for better and for worse.

In France, migrants celebrated the New Year by setting over 1,000 cars on fire. Most European news outlets insisted the festivities went well, forgetting to mention the rampant arson.[64] Perhaps burning cars is how they say "Happy New Year!" in Algeria.

"Cultural enrichment" policies are nothing more than orchestrated violence against our nations. The international Left has brought total war against Western civilization, and have been waging it with success for decades. Most of us still do not even know it has been declared.

Everywhere you look, you can see that Liberal policies lead to rape, death, poverty, and a loss of freedom. Mass migration is but one of the many weapons in the Liberal arsenal to undermine our values, traditions, and way of life. Liberals have cleverly manipulated citizens to feel a sense of collective guilt in order to burden the West with the worries of the entire world. They have manipulated policy and immigration to be weaponized against those of us who feel the Occident has a right to exist, to prosper, and to be secured for the future.

When political power is used as an instrument to lead a nation and its peoples towards peril, the only reasonable solution is rebellion. In fact, it becomes a moral imperative.

---

63 Gareth Davies. "Revealed: 1,200 women were sexually assaulted by 2,000 men in German cities on New Year's Eve" Daily Mail Online. July 11, 2016. http://www.dailymail.co.uk/news/article-3684302/1-200-German-women-sexually-assaulted-New-Year-s-Eve-Cologne-elsewhere.html. [http://archive.li/5b7My]

64 Henry Samuel. "Almost 1,000 cars torched around France on New Year's Eve but government insists it 'went particularly well'" The Telegraph. January 02, 2017. http://www.telegraph.co.uk/news/2017/01/02/almost-1000-cars-torched-around-france-new-years-eve-government/. [http://archive.li/JRVdB]

The Left began by telling the European peoples that their culture is not good enough. That everything which these peoples have contributed to society isn't enough. That they somehow need to be "culturally enriched" by migrants from the Third World. That the very group of people that created modern civilization as we know it, should learn to be more like the cultureless barbarians hailing from lands that still boast apostasy and blasphemy laws. Now we are being told that to oppose these acts of genocide makes one a Nazi, a bigot, a hater. We are being told that we are ignorant, uneducated, xenophobic, and uncultured, by a group of people who create nothing, produce nothing.

As if all of this were not enough, the Left now expects *us* to assimilate to *them*! Germany runs TV ads encouraging German woman to wear hijabs, and tells school aged girls to "dress modestly" so they do not provoke the "refugees" into raping them.[65]

Sadly, even Americans are experiencing the horrors of mass migration. In Idaho, a five year-old disabled girl was gang raped by three Muslim migrants. The judge presiding over the case, Thomas Borreson, issued a gag order so it would not gain widespread media attention, and presumably, much like Borreson's cowardly European counterparts, to protect the rapists.[66] Despite the fact that the migrant invaders pleaded guilty to the rape of the young, disabled girl, they received no jail time.[67] [68]

Where is the Leftist outrage? Where are all the feminists, who are usually so quick to blather on about "rape culture"? They should be pleased to know they are right: there is without any doubt a rape culture; it is

---

65 "Bavarian school warns girls should dress 'modestly,' due to Syrian refugees nearby" RT International. June 28, 2015. https://www.rt.com/news/270214-bavaria-muslim-school-clothes/. [http://archive.li/jGTbf]

66 Leo Hohman. "Idaho girl's refugee sex attackers walk free" WND. June 6, 2017. http://www.wnd.com/2017/06/news-blackout-on-refugee-boys-who-sexually-assaulted-idaho-girl/. [http://archive.li/1Kcni]

67 Pamela Geller. "Muslim migrant rapists of 5-year-old Idaho girl, get no jail time, JUDGE issues gag order on 'sentencing'" Geller Report. June 07, 2017. http://pamelageller.com/2017/06/no-justice-5-yearold-rape-victim-muslim-migrants.html/. [http://archive.li/N7jX0].

68 John Sowell. "Boys sentenced in sexual abuse of Twin Falls girl; family upset with punishment." Idaho Statesman. June 7, 2017. www.idahostatesman.com/news/state/idaho/article154650829.html.[http://archive.li/l5WsU].

currently the largest European import. Where are the proud Liberals protesting these savage rape gangs? Where is the call from the Left for the violence to end? Where are the Liberals, who love to claim that we must ban "assault" rifles for the sake of the children? Why are there no women's marches against the rape and molestation happening to children all over Europe and America?

Their silence has spoken volumes.

Though in truth, it's almost worse when they speak. The lying press is quick to tell us not to worry, that everything is going as planned. Jewish blogger David Rosenberg wrote an article for *Haaretz*, "Ignore the hysteria: Europe can live with terror."[69]

And what do those on the Left have to say for themselves and their policies when they *do* speak? Well, Sadiq Khan, London's first Muslim mayor, assured the world that terror attacks are "part and parcel of living in a big city," saying, "It is a reality I'm afraid that London, New York, other major cities around the world have got to be prepared for these sorts of things."[70] After yet another Muslim terror attack in London, Khan assured Londoners that despite increased amount of armed police there was "no need to be alarmed." London is turning into a war zone, but there is no reason for alarm. After all, according to Khan, this is how big cities are meant to function![71]

Former French Prime Minister Manual Valls, serving during the time of the Bastille Day terror truck attack in Nice, France, had this to say:

---

69 David Rosenberg. "Ignore the hysteria: Europe can live with terror" Haaretz.com. March 24, 2016. http://www.haaretz.com/opinion/.premium-1.710671. [http://archive.li/Wf5ao]

70 Gabriel Samuels. "Sadiq Khan: London mayor says being prepared for terror attacks 'part and parcel' of living in a major city" The Independent. September 22, 2016. http://www.independent.co.uk/news/uk/home-news/sadiq-khan-london-mayor-terrorism-attacks-part-and-parcel-major-cities-new-york-bombing-a7322846.html. [http://archive.li/4VHsd]

71 James Rothwell. "Donald Trump lashes out at Sadiq Khan over London terror attacks" The Telegraph. June 04, 2017. http://www.telegraph.co.uk/news/2017/06/04/donald-trump-lashes-sadiq-khan-london-terror-attacks/. [http://archive.li/NSjZE]

"Times have changed, and France is going to have to live with terrorism."[72] French President Emmanuel Macron, made it rather clear, after yet another shooting in Paris, that he has no intention of doing anything at all: "[terrorism] will be part of our daily lives the years to come."[73] During the November 2015 Paris attacks, Hillary Clinton was sure to remind us that "We're not at war with Islam or Muslims...we're at war with violent extremism."[74]

We are being betrayed. And for what? So that the global Left can feel good about its worthless values and utterly useless platitudes? The Left will evidently not be satisfied until we are unarmed, silenced, poor, our women and children raped. The-rank-and-file Leftist slugs are certainly mentally ill, about that there is no question. However, the hegemony of international global elites is evil to the core. These elites are operating out of pure hatred towards us. Figures like Tony Blair, Matteo Renzi, Manual Valls, Francois Hollande, Hillary Clinton, and Angela Merkel, have sought the total destruction of the Occident. Their policies and the outcomes of those policies make this vibrantly clear to anybody paying any attention whatsoever. They care not for the victims of Rotherham or Cologne. They care not for the Bataclan or the Christmas Market. They ignore the fact that they were elected to represent and protect their own people, not to give their nations away to savages from nations that still have blasphemy laws and honor killings. Millions of Europeans have been brutalized, raped, and murdered, all in the name of tolerance and diversity.

---

72 Jonah Bennett. "French Prime Minister On Nice Terror Attack: 'France Is Going To Have To Live With Terrorism'" The Daily Caller. July 15, 2016. http://dailycaller.com/2016/07/15/french-prime-minister-on-nice-terror-attack-france-is-going-to-have-to-live-with-terrorism/. [http://archive.li/rObum]

73 Jack Montgomery. "French Presidential Favourite Macron: Terrorism 'Part of Our Daily Lives for Years to Come' After Paris Shooting" Breitbart. April 21, 2017. http://www.breitbart.com/london/2017/04/21/macron-terrorism-part-daily-lives-years-paris-shooting/. [http://archive.li/Ktnit]

74 Ian Hanchett. "Hillary: 'We Are At War With Violent Extremism,' Refuses To Say 'Radical Islam'" Breitbart. November 14, 2015. http://www.breitbart.com/video/2015/11/14/hillary-we-are-at-war-with-violent-extremism-refuses-to-say-radical-islam/. [http://archive.li/Ej7CG]

The bloodshed will not stop until those responsible are removed from power.

For their transgressions against their own people, traitors Blair, Renzi, Valls, Hollande, Clinton, and Merkel, deserve nothing less than to be publicly tried for high treason. How much longer can we idly by while foreign men rape our children, mothers, wives, fiancées, and kill us? Pacifism is not the way in which we will cause the bloodshed to end. Cowardice and docility are the virtues of the enslaved and the conquered.

An article titled "Why the End of White Men is Actually Good for White Men," by Hugo Schwyzer, argues for all the benefits of whites becoming a minority in America.[75] This is but one example of the "white like me" phenomenon, in which those who claim to be advocating our interests are truly only interested in our demise.

Liberalism is clearly more of a fanatical religious cult than it is a political ideology. A cult that requires ritual human sacrifice and blood libel from time to time in order for its members to show their unyielding loyalty to the false gods of progress and tolerance. Liberals are mentally ill to a dangerous degree; their neurosis is now costing lives. Their never-ending crusade for diversity has lead to the rapes of over a million girls and women through Europe, women who will never be the same, some of whom are now pregnant with the children of their abusers. They had a right to grow up in their own homelands without being tortured. But because of the violently egalitarian Left insisting on the mass importation of Third World hordes, we have millions of girls and women that were robbed of their childhood, their freedom, and their happiness. We have families and friends that are struggling to pick up the pieces, fathers and brothers who are left feeling hopeless and powerless to protect them. History is repeating itself again.

Unless you plan to continue swimming through these Rivers of Blood, I suggest making some changes. Starting with the traitors.

---

75 Hugo Schwyzer. "Why the 'End' of White Men Is Actually Good for White Men" Jezebel. November 13, 2012. http://jezebel.com/5960099/why-the-end-of-white-men-is-good-for-actually-good-for-white-men. [http://archive.li/dg35a]

The Essence of America Lies Within Our Blood, Not Our Dirt

There is a pattern of thinking among Liberals the world over that suggests a nation is nothing more than its dirt and boundaries. Nothing more than the ground we walk upon, and the lines drawn in the sand. But America did not become great because of her dirt. The men and women who forged our nation did not stumble upon greatness. They sacrificed tremendously for it. American exceptionalism is the result of the careful study of thousands of years of civilizations that had risen and fallen like winter's wheat, revolting against the tyrannical monarchies in Europe, and taking a chance on an entirely new ideal. Our territory alone did not make us an unrivaled success. Our people did.

The Left evidently believes that you can take any person from anywhere in the world, drop him in America, and he will become an American. That he will spontaneously sprout American values and American traditions, and suddenly adopt an American way of life. Not too long ago a Siberian tiger cub was born in a zoo in Minnesota. That tiger is still a Siberian Tiger, not a Minnesotan tiger. People are like that too.

This false belief stems in part from Liberals themselves being so un-American, despite having been born here. Liberals claim to be global citizens, and as a result they are citizens of nowhere. They have no loyalty to any people. They are loyal to no motherland, no fatherland. They are only loyal to themselves.

Advocating for open borders and mass migration certainly accomplishes one thing: the undermining of the American people and values. Displacing the Third World population to Europe or America has only served to create a hostile environment for the host nation: hosts seldom benefit from their parasites. This does not create a more "diverse" environment; it creates a drain on our land and people, and in many cases, our freedom and safety. Liberals are actually creating a permanent underclass of people dependent upon the government, the majority of which are of course Democrat voters. But that is a core tenant of communism: to create a permanent group of people dependent upon their government for their each and every need.

To illustrate how absurd the Liberal magic dirt theory is, imagine for a moment this scenario. Suppose we could magically transport every citizen of Africa to the US. And suppose at the same time we magically transported every US citizen to Africa. Just the people are being moved, the buildings, infrastructure, and equipment all remain in each respective land.

What do you think would happen in ten years? My best guess is that the former USA would look like a scene from *Escape from New York*, and Africa would quickly become a world super power. The new America in the sub-Sahara would have extensive farming; all the animals currently endangered and facing extinction due to African poachers would be saved; Madagascar would be a top travel destination, with beautiful hotels on the beaches; and kindergartners would receive pet giraffes for their birthdays. Alas, there is no magic dirt.

If you want to help people advance in the world, you go and help them, educate them, aid them in the establishment of infrastructure, and teach them better means of food production. The present system is entirely unsustainable. Due to birth rates in the Third World, there will always be an infinity of Africans and Arabs waiting to flood our lands. The "migrant crisis" is a misnomer. There is only a crisis because we have forced mass migration and because we have subsidized the Third World, enabling unfettered population growth therein. Both of these policies need to end. The Left created this disaster, then labeled it a "crisis." We are living in a work of Liberal fiction.

Third World countries are poor, barbaric, corrupt, and backwards for the most simple of reasons: because the people in those countries are morally and intellectually poor, barbaric, corrupt, and backwards. By transplanting people from a Third World slum to the West, you're not helping them, you're not ushering in cultural diversity, you're simply importing those same barbaric views and practices into advanced civilizations at the grave expense of blood right citizens.

What Liberals do not seem to grasp is that America was not founded for them or people like them. There are places all over the world they can go to be with like-minded people. America was founded by and for revolutionaries. For those who did not want to be a part of a feudal system or to be ruled by a tyrant. This country was not forged to become a grotesque welfare state, it was founded so each man could be the master of his own destiny. If Liberals want to live in a "diverse" society, they can move anywhere in Africa, Asia, or South America. If they want to live in a nation full of Muslims, if they want to wear a hijab and be governed by Sharia law, they have around fifty countries they can chose from. If they want strict gun control, or no guns, they can go to Tunisia, Ethiopia, or Venezuela.

The Left often drones on about made-up problems such as "systemic racism" and "white-privilege," which are wholly unsupported by any data anywhere; if they want to live in a place where whites are a minority—guess what? There are well over 100 countries in which any white person can become an instant minority! If you do not believe in a well-armed society, if you are in favor of forcing others to pay for your way of life, if you are in favor of open borders, if you no longer want to live with those pesky white folk, and if you're not all that into rugged individualism and self-reliance—well, I think that's wonderful, and that you need to get out.

When Jewish Iraq-war proponent, Bill Kristol, called the term "America First" both vulgar and depressing, that was quite revealing.[76] If not America first, then *what*? Neoconservatives, Liberals, and virulent Left-wing organizations such as the Anti-Defamation League, who believe the term America First to be troublesome, worrying, and antisemitic, betray everything.[77] Liberals, neocons, and a myriad of influential organizations, have played their hand. They have let us know in no uncertain terms precisely how they feel: putting America and her citizens first does not coincide with their beliefs and agendas. When the ADL came out to condemn the use of America First and its message, they let everybody know that they never cared about the best interest of the American people. They showed where their true allegiance lies. And it was resoundingly *not*

76 Chris Buskirk. "Yes, America First" American Greatness. January 21, 2017. https://amgreatness.com/2017/01/21/yes-america-first/. [http://archive.li/LCKHx]

77 "ADL Urges Donald Trump to Reconsider "America First" in Foreign Policy Approach" Anti-Defamation League. April 28, 2016. https://www.adl.org/news/press-releases/adl-urges-donald-trump-to-reconsider-america-first-in-foreign-policy-approach. [http://archive.li/r6mCJ]

with us. If the term America First upsets you, in any way, no matter how slightly, then I suggest you take your subversive views elsewhere.

Of course, I defend the rights of people to hold a negative view of America First. You want Mexico first? Fine. Head south, hombre! Israel first? No problem: shalom! Anyone can hold the view that America should not be put first *anywhere but in America*. There are almost 200 other nations to choose from. Take your pick.

The problem is that men like myself don't have anywhere else to go. People like us do not believe in a large, overreaching government. We do not believe that our great nation is up for grabs and free for the taking. We do not plan to hand in our weapons anytime soon. Nor do we think anybody has any right to our property or freedom. Around 240 years ago or so, a small group of men came to a similar conclusion, and for that belief they declared war on the largest Empire the world had ever seen. Liberals need to remember where the came from—or rather, the swamp they slithered from: for they are the loyalists to the state. They are the "persons inimical to the liberties of America." They are the diametric opposition to freedom. And when their King was defeated, the Revolutionaries sent many of the loyalists packing. They didn't have to go home to England, but they couldn't stay here.

For us true Americans, us revolutionaries, transforming the foundation of America into something else is far more than succumbing to the false god of Liberal progress. It is an act of treason.

Immigrant *Rights*

According to Liberals, America's most central value is to admit millions and millions of foreigners who will never share any of our values. And so they waste no time in talking about the "fundamental right" of these foreigners to immigrate.

This is nothing new. Liberals have the bad habit of confusing what they merely *desire* with inalienable *rights*. The Left struggles in vain to discern the difference between what a man wants to happen, and what is owed to him. Liberals consider food, housing, clothing, education through college, healthcare, abortions, birth control, and immigration, all "basic human rights." This all sounds very nice, and sometimes I wish that I too lived in the delusional fairytale that Liberals occupy. The problem with the Liberal fantasy, of course, is that no one really has a right to anyone else's property. But the Liberals, through lies, litigation, and legislation, have been able to stomp on our true rights in favor of their delusional ones for quite some time. But even if immigration caused zero burdens on the host inhabitants of a nation, zero financial cost, zero crime increase, and zero unwanted effects, even *then* it still would not become an automatic right.

A nation can be viewed as an extension of the people's property, perhaps as an inheritance from our ancestors. And it is the right of our people to have a homeland, to keep our culture, to maintain our heritage, to protect our nation and descendants, and to prevent these things from being altered by foreign interlopers. If these people want to come here, they have to truly enrich us in some way.

But to say it again, per the Center for Immigration Studies, over 50 percent of immigrant households are using welfare. Even among immigrants that have been here for twenty or more years, the rate is still nearly 50 percent.[78] How could it possibly be argued that these migrants have the fundamental right, not only to our lands, but to our hard earned tax dollars? What benefits are there from endless Mexican, South American, African and the Middle Eastern migrants? How many more halal carts does New York City actually need? Any potential good that may come from immigration needs to outweigh the costs in terms of crime, violence, and welfare use. But the positive benefits we receive are not even remotely close to matching the negatives.

Right after the Liberal banality that "we are a nation of immigrants" comes the more recent platitude that "no human being is illegal." According to that principle, the world's seven billion human beings are all just Americans waiting to arrive. So as long as any or all of those seven billion manage to wash up on our shores, they become legal. This is evident, since *no* human being is illegal. But the insanity of this proposition does not even require indication.

If Liberals truly believe that "no human is illegal," I invite them to test that theory. Stop paying your property taxes, fail to renew your driver's

---

78 Steven A. Camarota. "Welfare Use by Immigrant and Native Households" Center for Immigration Studies. September 10, 2015. http://cis.org/Welfare-Use-Immigrant-Native-Households. [http://archive.li/5uouk]

license, and cut off your car insurance — then get back to me on how that works out.

This country is not for everybody. It never was. In fact, prior to The New Deal, a considerable number of immigrants returned to their home country.[79] Yet the destructive Left is absolutely hell-bent on giving away everything that our ancestors have struggled for. The American Revolution was not fought so that the entire Third World could flood our shores. The American Revolution was not fought so we could one day become an Islamic nation, or a majority Mexican nation. Neither Muslims nor Mexicans fought that American Revolution.

To be sure, I'm not entirely against the idea of immigration to the United States or Europe. I just simply believe immigration should be safe, legal, and rare. There should be no welfare available to migrants for any reason. Nor should migrants have voting rights until some time has passed — say, four or five generations. Granting people who have no connection of culture or birth to the nation the power to change the nation's laws is beyond irresponsible. The Left understands something very well that much of the Right still does not grasp: demographics are destiny. Each new invader makes the vote of the founding stock of our country that much more meaningless.

The Liberal view that all cultures are equal is appalling. They most emphatically are not. Nor are they necessarily compatible with each other. Sharia law, for instance, cannot be reconciled with the American Constitution, or with any of the European legal traditions. A 2015 Center for Security Policy poll of Muslim "Americans" found that over half of those surveyed, 51 percent, believe that in America, they should have the choice to be governed under Sharia, the law based upon the teachings of Islam.[80] That doesn't sound much like people wanting to assimilate to the American way.

---

79 Donna Przecha. "Immigrants Who Returned Home" Genealogy.com. Accessed July 14, 2017. http://www.genealogy.com/articles/research/96_donna.html. [http://archive.li/F6IzI]

80 "Poll of U.S. Muslims Reveals Ominous Levels Of Support For Islamic Supremacists' Doctrine of Shariah, Jihad" Center for Security Policy. June 23, 2015. https://www.centerforsecuritypolicy.org/2015/06/23/nationwide-poll-of-us-muslims-shows-thousands-support-shariah-jihad/. [http://archive.li/rQUv7]

Far more troubling is the fact that over 20 percent of all Muslims surveyed agreed that violence is a legitimate and just punishment for those who offend Islam. One-third of those surveyed believe that if there is a conflict between Sharia and the US Constitution, Sharia should be considered the supreme doctrine.[81]

The situation in Europe is even worse. In a Pew Research survey the question was asked; "Can Suicide Bombing of Civilian Targets to Defend Islam be Justified?" A shocking number of Muslims between the ages of eighteen to twenty-nine, which constitute a large portion of the recent migrants to Europe, answered that yes, civilian targets of suicide bombings is justified to defend Islam: 35 percent in Great Britain, 42 percent in France, 22 percent in Germany, and 29 percent in Spain. In the USA? 26 percent. Over a quarter of all Muslims surveyed under thirty years of age believe violence against civilians can be justified. There is no possible logical rebuttal from the Left. These are not the values that we believe in. These numbers represent the same people that the mainstream media refers to as "refugees" on a daily basis. This is the *tolerant religion of peace*. The title of the research document from Pew, by the way: "Muslim Americans: Middle Class and Mostly Mainstream."[82]

If more than a quarter of young Muslims are willing to admit that they believe the deaths of infidels are justified for insulting Islam, how many more are totally ambivalent about this question? What percent of those surveyed simply lied? How many of those surveyed fall under the social acceptability bias, the well-known psychological phenomena by which undesirable, negative, or stigmatized responses are nearly always under-reported in surveys?

I attended a large university during undergrad; in nearly every class there were at least two Muslims students. Walking between classes I would pass several Muslims on the walkways. Per the admission of Muslims in America, this means that each and every day, I was in near proximity to a person that would happily see me executed for insulting him or his cult. That should be somewhat disconcerting.

---

81 Ibid.

82 "Muslim Americans: Middle Class and Mostly Mainstream" Pew Research Center. May 22, 2007. http://www.pewresearch.org/2007/05/22/muslim-americans-middle-class-and-mostly-mainstream/. [http://archive.li/qT0hi]

Shouldn't these questions regarding whether violence and suicide bombings are reasonable reactions to insulting Islam, have been asked *before* the US made these people citizens? Wasting billions to kill terrorists hiding in caves somewhere in the Middle East seems rather absurd in light of the fact that there are evidently potential terrorists among us. They are already here and apparently have been "properly vetted." So well vetted, in fact, that they would not be troubled to see us dead for insulting their dogma.

It is already shocking that immigrants use welfare at nearly twice the rate of native born citizens. But from many countries like Somalia, first and second generation migrants are nearly entirely on welfare. There are at least ten nations, over 90 percent of whose first- and second-generation US migrants use welfare.[83] Of the migrants from Afghanistan, Iran, Iraq, Jordan, Kuwait, Lebanon, Saudi Arabia, Syria, Turkey, and Yemen, 91 percent receive food stamps, 73 percent Medicaid, and 68 percent cash welfare.[84] This not even to mention half a dozen other program benefits as well. Each person we resettle into the United States costs tax payers $64,000 for his first five years in our country. That rate is estimated to be around twelve times what it would cost to help resettle the same people in their own country or region.[85]

Think about that: Western nations could help *twelve times* the amount of people that they presently do by simply resettling them in the Middle East or in Africa, rather than in Europe or America. But this was never about helping people from the Third World. This was about further redistribution of wealth, about creating borderless nations, about ensuring that the hostile elite the world over could create a permanent underclass over

---

83 Steven A. Camarota. "Welfare Use by Immigrant and Native Households" Center for Immigration Studies. September 10, 2015. http://cis.org/Welfare-Use-Immigrant-Native-Households. [http://archive.li/5uouk]

84 Caroline May. "More Than 90 Percent of Middle Eastern Refugees on Food Stamps" Breitbart. September 10, 2015. http://www.breitbart.com/big-government/2015/09/10/more-than-90-percent-of-middle-eastern-refugees-on-food-stamps/. [http://archive.li/3csoi]

85 Steven A. Camarota. "The High Cost of Resettling Middle Eastern Refugees" Center for Immigration Studies. November 4, 2015. http://cis.org/High-Cost-of-Resettling-Middle-Eastern-Refugees. [http://archive.li/nj5Ia]

which they could rule with impunity. We are talking about a genocidal plot to eradicate the future of all white Europeans.

Over and over again while researching data for this book, I found myself staring at the facts in utter disbelief. I can only say, yet again, that this is madness. It is lunacy by any reasonable definition. But this is modern American policy as driven by the Left.

For a bit of comparison, in the US, 30 percent of native households are on some form of welfare. Asians use at the lowest rate at 21 percent, followed by whites at 23 percent, then blacks and Hispanics both at a 54 percent rate of use.[86] Just as there is a discrepancy among native household use, the variance is even larger among migrants. Those coming from South Asia use welfare programs at the lowest rate, at 17 percent. European migrants use at a rate of 26 percent (which includes those not native to Europe), East Asians a rate of 32 percent, South Americans a rate of 41 percent, Africans a rate of 48 percent, Caribbeans a rate of 51 percent, and those from Central America and Mexico at a rate of 73 percent.[87]

These are *legal immigrants*, mind you. We are cutting programs for the mentally retarded, mentally ill, disabled, and homeless all over the nation, yet we have $64,000 free change to dedicate to each single African we bring into this country instead of helping *our own*? This is abhorrent and morally vile. And it's up to us to end this insanity.

The Hart-Celler Act of 1965 needs repealed immediately, and the welfare needs cut off. Government tax money is meant to be used to protect its citizens and to protect their interests, not to be given haphazardly to those with no connection to the culture, no interest in contributing, and no desire to assimilate.

If we do not decide to take action and make the necessary decisions, the Left and their hordes will be deciding for us. England, France, Germany, Sweden, and even the US, are not serious countries anymore. If Charles Martel, Charlemagne, Richard the Lionhearted, or any of the US Founding Fathers were here, they would order all those responsible hanged.

---

86 F. Roger Delvin and Henry Wolff. "Welfare: Who's on It, Who's Not" American Renaissance. October 14, 2015. https://www.amren.com/features/2015/10/welfare-whos-on-it-whos-not/. [http://archive.li/UYqoJ]

87 Ibid.

We have given this whole multicultural thing the old college try. It has failed. Time to embrace something else. We *must* put the needs and well-being of our own people first, not those coming from places most of us cannot find on a map. If a nation cannot decide who to let in, from where, and in what numbers, it is not a nation at all. If a nation cannot protect its own borders without cries of racism and bigotry arising on every side, we are no longer dealing with a sovereign nation, but a piece of land that is up for grabs, and a population inviting other, strong peoples to conquer it.

We are not free until we have self-determination to preserve our cultures and homelands that our ancestors built for us.

Common Sense Border Control

The Left loves the idea of "common sense" gun control. How about taking the same approach to our crazy immigration policies? How about no welfare of any kind for at least thirty years after moving here? If you don't pay into the system, why should you get the benefits? And no voting privileges should be granted to new immigrants, either. After all, we wouldn't want "foreign interference" with our elections, would we?

In fact, what sense does it make to allow even a single migrant into the US until we have zero unemployment, zero national debt, and a clear and evident need of more people? Why, when native born Americans are out of work, would we bring in more people to compete against them for jobs? Why would we continue to spend nearly $300 billion per year on migrants, both legal and illegal, when we are already laboring under tremendous national debt and burdensome taxes? Keep in mind, that $300 billion did not start just last year. We have been plagued by mass migration for over half a century. Think of the world we could have built if we had used all of that money to better our own nation.

If you come to this country, you should be able to pay your own way, work, or have a sponsor. Enough of these handouts. America comprises 4.5 percent of the world's population, and only about half of Americans pay taxes. You can't reasonably ask 2 percent to 3 percent of the world population to pay for the remainder, without expecting some sort of breaking point to inevitably be reached.

When it comes right down to it, I do not even support so-called "high-skilled immigration." It does nothing but undermine "high-skilled" *US* workers, driving wages down for native born citizens. The high-skilled, highly educated workers from other countries can be of great service to their own homelands, helping their own people build a better civilization. We will do just fine without them, as we did for over 200 years.

I once heard a professor say that immigration is a racist construct, because the only difference between a legal migrant and a "mis-documented citizen" is a "piece of paper." Apart from the evident absurdity of this position, I found it troubling that this professor felt there should be no necessary "piece of paper" for immigrants. As an American citizen I cannot build a house, drive a car, get married, start a business, leave the country, come back into the country, or even work, without a "piece of paper." The government expects me to get permission before nearly every action I take in life, yet Liberals feel that holding foreign people to the same standard is somehow racist and unethical. There is a certain characteristically Liberal hypocrisy in clamoring for ever stricter background checks for American citizens who want to exercise their firearm rights, while simultaneously claiming that the mere vetting of migrants to the United States is racist and bigoted.

Of course, immigrants coming to America will find themselves right at home with this Liberal contradiction. They have little to no grasp of what made this country great. They vote for the same sort of communist and totalitarian policies that caused them to leave their home country in the first place.

Liberals seem to believe that this is a problem of "education." Imagine being so naïve that you think civilization and culture is something you can just up and teach people, or that migrants will somehow just "pick up" the our same values and morals and ways of life if they live long enough around us.

I happen to think almost precisely the contrary of that professor. A government that makes the conscious decision to open its borders is inherently illegitimate. The governments of Europe and the US are using the money that might spend to enforce our borders to fund the invasion of foreigners instead. At this point, there is no such thing as a *legal* migrant to the US or Europe. Legal migration is a globalist fiction. These are hostile invaders, illegitimate paperwork in hand, granted entry by illegitimate governments, permitted to live amongst us by illegitimate laws, who are colonizing our homelands and threatening our way of life.

An Open Mind with Closed Borders

"Open-mindedness" is one of the favored terms of especially older Liberals. But being open-minded does not mean blindly accepting every absurd ideology that comes your way, as Liberals do. People's beliefs and ideologies are not somehow exempt from critical scrutiny. Liberals believe that every warped and perverse ideology is somehow entirely equal to every other. But being truly open minded means you have some sort of objective norm. Some sort of basic moral principles. Some gold standard against which everything else is measured. And when a new idea comes your way, you can evaluate it thoughtfully, consider its logical outcomes, critique the underlying principles as well as the application of the idea in the real world, and make a value judgment in consequence. Liberals call this act of critical thinking judgmental and bigoted.

One can find examples of this Liberal acceptance of any random idea in practically every Liberal platitude and bumper sticker slogan: "Diversity is our greatest strength," "Muslims belong here," "Make America brown again," "We're a nation of immigrants," "Coexist," "Build bridges, not walls," "No human is illegal," and the like. These all might sound nice at first. But as we have seen, when you really evaluate each one against history, objective outcomes, and moral imperatives, they all fall apart.

The whole idea of this multiculturalism which is being forced upon us is absurd in its very premise. It reduces to the notion of immigration without assimilation, the idea of letting everybody into our nations according to literally no standards whatsoever. Moreover, the premise of multiculturalism is further flawed in the sense that it incorrectly assumes all cultures are equally good and valuable. But no one really believes this, and the proof is in the fact that there are certain parts of the world where not one of our precious Liberals would ever consider visiting, not to speak of living. Some cultures and people, are really quite awful. Others are incredible beyond words.

When you start out with an idea based on such massively flawed premises, it always goes downhill from there. In this case, there is a spectacular dumpster fire at the bottom of a long decline.

Liberals constantly push for more and more diversity. But at what point is a society sufficiently diverse? I've sent letters to several Liberal authors who have written articles calling for more diversity. I asked specifically what is the optimal number of halal carts in a city before they shut the hell up about being more "inclusive" and "diverse." How many women wearing exactly same black burka do we require to become officially "culturally enriched"? Is there a perfect ratio somewhere, some metric we can go by? Maybe the number of car burnings per night? Or perhaps once the rape rate increases by 800 percent? Strangely, I never did get a reply.

Immigrants from the Middle East and Africa have average IQs of eighty-five or lower. This is well below the US and European average.[88] It is absurd to expect them to benefit, or even to understand, our countries.

By nature, people prefer being with those like them. Nowhere on Earth has throwing groups of random people together turned out well in terms of crime, conflict, a sense of security, prosperity, culture, or any other value. History, as well as all relevant scientific studies and simple common sense itself, demonstrate this beyond any reasonable doubt.

America was built mostly by Europeans who were religiously and culturally Christian, with a Protestant work ethic. Muslims did not built America. Jews did not build America. Arabs did not build America. Mexicans did not build America. One never hears of the Islamic, African, Judaic, Hispanic or Arabian work ethic. America is not the result of mass migration from South America or Africa or from the Middle East. This is the hard truth. The Left, the open-minded Left, hates this truth so much that they are actively trying to change the racial and cultural fabric of our nation.

Countries all over Europe are seeing first-hand what happens when you try to "coexist" with groups of people that in truth want to dominate, not assimilate. The intolerable number of rapes and violent crime being inflicted upon native Europeans by migrant hordes is the result of our "building bridges, not walls." The truly open-minded will see this sooner

88 Richard Lynn and Tatu Vanhanen. IQ and global inequality. Augusta, GA: Washington Summit Publishers, 2006.

or later. The majority of Liberals, meanwhile, are little more than useful idiots who believe everything the Ministry of Truth tells them to believe in their blind worship of Big Brother. They are but pawns in the ongoing, often concealed, war between Globalism and Nationalism, perhaps more accurately, the crucible between Evil and Good.

End the Immigration Act of 1965

Even legal immigration ends in disaster.

Many countries through the world, like Mexico, have policies written into their constitutions to the effect that the demographics of the country are not to be changed. These countries fundamentally understand something that many still do not: if you replace the founding stock of a nation with an entirely different group of people, the nation itself becomes radically alien. Where Mexicans go, they will always build Mexico.

Will you accept becoming a minority in your own land, so long as it was effected legally? Are you alright feeling like a stranger in your own streets, even as the native English do now in the majority Muslim city of London? Are you comfortable with the idea that Europeans will have no homeland anywhere on Earth? We are the heirs to the Occident. The blood of those who built the West is in *our* veins, nobody else's.

Would it be acceptable to you if the immigration policy was changed, allowing not over a million migrants a year into the USA, but ten million per year? Fifty million? Supposing, of course, their paperwork was filled out properly, would you really permit an endless stream of people into our nation? Shall we keep pushing until we hit a billion or more, and the US is indistinguishable from any Third World nation? This is what everyone is really saying, who states that they are fine with immigration as long as it is done *legally*. As if bureaucratic correctness were somehow the saving grace of civilization.

What these people fail to understand is that Leftist politicians will continue to press the immigration limit higher and higher, even while making the paperwork easier and easier, to the point that an immigrant can just sign on the dotted line once he arrives to start collecting his welfare. If our immigration policy had not let in over fifty-nine million people in since 1965, the majority of which vote Democrat, the Democrat party could never come close to winning an election. They have totally lost the war of ideas, so they have shifted to the war of demographics. The Republicans that were voted in to stop them haven't even begun to realize the new tactic, or they know and quietly approve. They continued to allow it to happen: they voted for amnesty, and were happy cashing their checks from corporate sponsors that were in favor of more consumers and cheaper labor. The results of the 2016 election show that if any other group but whites had been a majority, Clinton would have won handily.[89] In fact, Democrats have not won the white majority vote even once in a presidential election since 1964.[90]

According to the Census Bureau, as of July 2015, the majority of US babies under one year old were racial or ethnically, non-white.[91] Just fifty short years since our gates were flung open, whites have gone from making up nearly 90 percent of the population, to being displaced in our own lands. Pew Research published an article titled "Explaining Why Minority Births Now Outnumber White Births."[92] In the article they neglected to mention rates of mass migration to the US and taxation patterns. They note that nearly 92 percent of all population growth is non-white. Not only is the majority of migration non-white, the taxation system is set

89 Dave Gilson. "These maps and charts show where Clinton's essential voters are" Mother Jones. November 01, 2016. http://www.motherjones.com/politics/2016/11/maps-presidential-election-race-gender-age/. [http://archive.li/oVVwn]

90 Stephen Nelson. "A List -- Why A Majority of Whites No Longer Vote Democratic at the Presidential Level" Daily Kos. March 6, 2013. https://www.dailykos.com/stories/2013/3/6/1192132/-A-List-Why-A-Majority-of-Whites-No-Longer-Vote-Democratic-at-the-Presidential-Level. [http://archive.li/WVMyr]

91 Kendra Yoshinaga and Bill Chappell. "Babies Of Color Are Now The Majority, Census Says" NPR. July 01, 2016. http://www.npr.org/sections/ed/2016/07/01/484325664/babies-of-color-are-now-the-majority-census-says. [http://archive.li/r7Npp]

92 Jeffrey S. Passel, Gretchen Livingston, and D'Vera Cohn. "Explaining Why Minority Births Now Outnumber White Births" Pew Research Center's Social & Demographic Trends Project. May 17, 2012. http://www.pewsocialtrends.org/2012/05/17/explaining-why-minority-births-now-outnumber-white-births/. [http://archive.li/5GcQQ]

up to force whites to support non-white families.[93] The budgetary impact of taxation revenue generated by each white person on average is $2,795. The budgetary impact of each Hispanic person on average in the US is -$7,298, and for blacks it is -$10,016 per person.[94] Meaning on average, it takes 3.5 whites to support one black person, and 2.5 whites to support one Hispanic. If both legal and illegal migration were ended, each US household would save an average of $3,000 per year in taxes. Migration quite literally makes us poorer.

Whites are having smaller families, in part because they cannot afford to have larger ones. Their money is being stolen by the government to give welfare payments to Hispanics, Muslims, and blacks, that as a result are able to have larger families through white money. The same holds true for migrants; they are a net negative, a drain on the system, and are nearly entirely funded by whites. I suppose this is another example our "privilege"; perhaps we can view this as an "enrichment tax." A better term yet would be White Slavery. Whites carry the fiscal burden and others use their money, all the while demanding ever more.

Anyone with his eyes open can see that this current paradigm is destined to collapse. It is wholly unsustainable. If the current migration trends are not stopped and reversed, Europeans will no longer have a homeland. Americans will no longer have a homeland. In fifty years, Mexico will still be a majority Mexican, and Somalia will still be a majority Somali, and Algeria will still be a majority Algerian. America, too, will be majority Mexican; France and Germany and Italy, too, will be majority Somali, Algerian, and Pakistani.

Europe is a near irrefutable argument for the horrors and pitfalls of mass, *legal*, migration. Europeans did not want their culture to become more like that in Africa or the Middle East; if they had, they would surely have moved to those places. The legal migrants have transformed Europe

93 F. Roger Delvin and Henry Wolff. "Welfare: Who's on It, Who's Not" American Renaissance. October 14, 2015. https://www.amren.com/features/2015/10/welfare-whos-on-it-whos-not/. [http://archive.li/UYqoJ]

94 Ryan Faulk. "Fiscal Impact of Whites, Blacks and Hispanics" The Alternative Hypothesis. May 11, 2016. http://thealternativehypothesis.org/index.php/2016/05/11/fiscal-impact-of-whites-blacks-and-hispanics/. [http://archive.li/b7zRw]

into something it is not, and I do not see a single shred of evidence suggesting that the rise in crime, welfare use, and mosques are in any way improving Europe, or the lives of Europeans.

London, in which the native British are a minority, is a case in point. Men who grew up in London, fought to save London, no longer recognize the city they once called home. Parts of London now have more mosques than churches, more halal markets than fish & chips shops. A dozen pubs are closing a week, and churches nearly as often. This all happened through *legal immigration*. Londoners are being legally dispossessed in their own homeland. The same is happening all over the West. Washington D.C. is now a white minority, Paris will soon be as well. All through "legal" migration. Think of the absurdity. White nations, white capital cities, without a white majority, in many of our largest cities. Imagine going to Tokyo or Seoul, and seeing more brown hordes than Japanese or Korean people.

Imagine being homesick for a place that no longer exists. Wanting to visit somewhere that looks like a distant memory that you can almost recall, but now feels totally unknown. We are facing a sort of collective Paris Syndrome.

Besides flooding the streets with foreign invaders, European governments have also enacted strict gun laws and eroded the freedom of speech. In order to facilitate mass migration and the replacement of the native people, it is first necessary to ensure that they are defenseless, unable to publicly oppose the policies that so clearly work against them. Merely twenty years after enacting strict firearm regulation in the UK following the Dunblane massacre, UK police are now kicking in people's doors for posting "hate speech" online. They make it illegal to speak out and defend ourselves even as they drop the hammer. Silenced and disarmed through laws, impoverished by the diversity tax, and forced to live with violent savages that brutalize them — these are all the trappings of a total occupation government run by a hostile alien clique.

The same thing will happen to America and the rest of Europe, make no mistake. America is great because of the values and ideals it was founded upon, and the people that intend to carry on those rich traditions — the children of those who created the nation. Migrants that do not share those same values will simply use our democratic process to undermine nearly 250 years of our culture, and thousands of years of culture in

European nations. They will change their host nation to align with their own worldviews. They should not be allowed to subvert and corrupt our way of life, turning our nations into hollow shells, mere shadows, of what they once were.

The Liberal narrative continually harps on how "minorities" all over the planet need our help. But Americans and Europeans *are* the minority. There are 7 billion humans on Earth, and fewer than one billion are of European descent. Referring to non-whites as a "minority" group, even in majority white nations, is nothing but a lie, a tactic of psychological manipulation. It is nothing but a clever way to trick the unquestioning masses into accepting mass migration, population replacement, and their own dispossession, in the form of the decimation of the founding stock of their nations, and the evisceration of the white race itself.

We have been the most tolerant and welcoming group of people in the entirety of human history. No non-white people has ever welcomed populations so different from them, housed them, fed them, educated them, all while simultaneously being called racists and attacked for our very hospitality and kindness. When we finally decide this has gone too far, when we finally say "enough," the entire world will shudder under our collective footsteps.

Demographics Are Destiny

Based on the results of the latest Human Development Index indications, the United Nations has announced that by the year 2030, Sweden will become a Third World country.[95] While Sweden continues to decline, the neighboring nations, which have not taken in millions of migrants, are still doing relatively well.

Switzerland — not part of the European Union — heavily regulates both foreign immigration and travel. Not surprisingly, Switzerland enjoys one of the lowest crime rates on the planet. Switzerland also has far lower

95 "Sweden to become a Third World Country by 2030, according to UN" Speisa. Accessed July 15, 2017. http://speisa.com/modules/articles/index.php/item.454/sweden-to-become-a-third-world-country-by-2030-according-to-un.html. [https://archive.li/21b3k]

taxes, no massive welfare program, and the freedom to own firearms. Sweden, meanwhile, has a Global Terrorism Index rating *fourteen* times higher than that of Switzerland.[96]

These differences are not coincidental. They are the direct result of each nation's laws and politics. You cannot have a First World nation with a Third World population.

California was once a state Republicans could and did win in presidential elections. Due to migration and amnesty, it's likely it will remain a Liberal Democratic stronghold from here on out. With Florida, Texas, and other southern states receiving more migration, they too will soon be lost to the invading hordes, while the Mexican border creeps ever northward.

Historic battleground states in the US are being flooded with wave after wave of migrants from the Middle East and Africa, the majority of which will vote Democrat, as demonstrated by all relevant statistics. If this isn't stopped, swing states, and historic Republican strongholds, will all turn Democrat. Not because the Liberals were able to convince the native population that their party policies are better for the citizens, but because they were able to continue importing foreign voters, individuals dependent on the massive welfare state that Democrats will promise to continue.

Liberals politicians have made a Faustian deal in regard to immigration. They are literally destroying our civilizations, and forcing tax payers to fund the destruction, in order to gain more power. And the Liberal proles that vote for these goblin-faced wretches are too dense, ill, and gullible to see it. They are sold the lie of diversity as a strength, and they vote with their fragile emotions, no matter the cost.

In a very interesting Pew research poll regarding government policy, the question "Would you prefer a smaller government with fewer services or a bigger government with more services?" was asked. Only 27 percent of white Americans were in favor of larger government. Over 71 percent of Hispanic and 59 percent black citizens supported a larger government with more services.[97] Who could possibly be surprised by this? Blacks and

96 "Terrorism Index 2016—Vision of Humanity" Vision of Humanity. Accessed July 15, 2017. http://visionofhumanity.org/indexes/terrorism-index/.

97 "General opinions about the federal government" Pew Research Center for the People and the Press. November 23, 2015. http://www.people-press.

Hispanics use welfare programs at twice the rate of whites and Asians. They want more governments services, while whites are forced to fund their ineptitude. In 2014, whites paid 76 percent of individual taxes for the year.[98]

The demographic voting trends in the 2016 US election show why the Left is so desperately trying to replace white Europeans in our own lands. Exit polls and election maps revealed how the results would have turned out if the white vote was excluded: Clinton would have won all fifty states.[99] No matter how you split the white demographic, by sex or education, without them, Clinton wins.[100] No matter how you split the *non*-white vote, Clinton wins. White people, especially white men, were the single vanguard to block Clinton in her quest for the White House. Which is exactly why white men are a despised out-group to the Left. Soon after the election, white women joined the ranks, becoming the latest target of the vitriolic Left:

> White women, own up to it: You're the reason Hillary Clinton lost — *Chicago Tribune*[101]

---

org/2015/11/23/2-general-opinions-about-the-federal-government/. [http://archive.li/wLWRO]

98 Ryan Faulk. "Fiscal Impact of Whites, Blacks and Hispanics" The Alternative Hypothesis. May 11, 2016. http://thealternativehypothesis.org/index.php/2016/05/11/fiscal-impact-of-whites-blacks-and-hispanics/. [http://archive.li/b7zRw]

99 Dave Gilson. "These maps and charts show where Clinton's essential voters are" Mother Jones. November 01, 2016. http://www.motherjones.com/politics/2016/11/maps-presidential-election-race-gender-age/. [http://archive.li/oVVwn]

100 Jon Huang, Samuel Jacoby, Michael Strickland, and K.K. Rebecca Lai. "Election 2016: Exit Polls" The New York Times. November 08, 2016. https://www.nytimes.com/interactive/2016/11/08/us/politics/election-exit-polls.html. [http://archive.li/0qJst]

101 Dahleen Glanton. "White women, own up to it: You're the reason Hillary Clinton lost" Chicago Tribune. November 18, 2016. http://www.chicagotribune.com/news/columnists/glanton/ct-white-women-glanton-20161118-column.html. [https://archive.li/bSa40]

> White Women Helped Elect Donald Trump — *The New York Times*[102]

> White Women Sold Out the Sisterhood and the World by Voting for Trump — *Slate*[103]

> Blame white women for country's failure to shatter glass ceiling — *NY Daily News*[104]

Once the demographics shift beyond the tipping point, there is no going back. The majority of all non-whites are in favor of open borders, hate speech laws, firearm restriction, censorship, heavier taxation, and a larger government. Once they have the ability to outvote whites entirely, our nation will never be the same again.

Mass migration is indeed a problem. But the hordes have always been outside our walls, and we must not forget the gates were opened from within. Those who caused the invasions are the root of the problem. The eternal Left and the hostile international clique have always been the strangers within our gates.

If We Go, So Shall Western Civilization

Republican Congressman Steve King of Iowa has been attacked by the media and on social media with accusations of being a racist and white supremacist. The allegations came immediately after King commended Dutch politician Geert Wilders for his stance on immigration to Europe.

---

102 Katie Rogers. "White Women Helped Elect Donald Trump" The New York Times. November 09, 2016. https://www.nytimes.com/2016/12/01/us/politics/white-women-helped-elect-donald-trump.html. [http://archive.li/1gwZl]

103 L.V. Anderson. "White Women Sold Out the Sisterhood and the World by Voting for Trump" Slate Magazine. November 09, 2016. http://www.slate.com/blogs/xx_factor/2016/11/09/white_women_sold_out_the_sisterhood_and_the_world_by_voting_for_trump.html. [https://archive.li/mxqsS]

104 Leonard Greene. "Blame white women for country's failure to shatter glass ceiling" NY Daily News. November 09, 2016. http://www.nydailynews.com/news/election/blame-white-women-country-failure-shatter-glass-ceiling-article-1.2866025. [http://archive.li/Q2AX7]

King wrote that Wilders understands the importance of culture and demographics as they relate to the destiny of a nation, stating that we cannot restore our civilizations with people from foreign lands or with other people's children.[105] What King and Wilders are saying is exactly what I have been writing: that the most important and irreplaceable aspect of a nation will forever be its people. If you replace the population of a nation with the population of a foreign nation, the original nation ceases to exist.

Other people and their children cannot carry on our cultures, this is fundamentally true for all cultures. If all the Japanese all were vanish into thin air one day, then a bunch of Texans all moved to Japan, Japanese culture would cease to exist. It would thus be replaced by Texan culture. Because culture is not transmitted merely via the land on which you walk. People create and maintain a culture, for better or for worse.

America is a nation united by culture and history. It was never intended to be some doss-house for the world's indigent. America is not just some random ideal that anybody can claim as theirs, even while they recreate the nation in their image. The "ideal" of the American experiment was to grant the highest power to the individual, to his self-reliance, to his freedom. America for this reason is the homeland to the natives of the land, and the children of the people who built this nation. It belongs by right to no one else.

A nation is not some abstract set of ideals. A nation is the people who built it, and their descendants that carry on their blood and traditions. Western values, and American values, are not things that can be taught, or learned. They are the physical manifestation of the blood that flows through our veins, thus they can never be recreated by others. All the cultures that Europeans have built can only be understood as the physical manifestations of our DNA. "Ourselves and our posterity," written in the Preamble of the Constitution, surely never meant just any of the planet's billions of dwellers.

105 Philip Bump. "Rep. Steve King warns that 'our civilization' can't be restored with 'somebody else's babies'" The Washington Post. March 12, 2017. https://www.washingtonpost.com/news/politics/wp/2017/03/12/rep-steve-king-warns-that-our-civilization-cant-be-restored-with-somebody-elses-babies/. [https://archive.li/DEVWh]

In fact, for the majority of our nation's history, immigration was limited by a quota or national original formula, which heavily favored Europeans, and ensured the nation would not shift in demographics away from the people who built this country. For over 100 years, US naturalization was limited to "free white persons … of good character." Until 1965, all immigration acts were specifically designed to maintain the WASP, European Christian culture of the country. The national origin quota must be restored to preserve the Western tradition of our nation.

The provision that "good character" was required meant that we could turn away those with views that were in clear opposition to our own. This idea of having two political parties, one which constantly undermines us, is relatively new; our nation was designed by white nationalists to avoid these type of problems. Had we been able to grant citizenship as it was intended, we would not have people advocating to take away our gun rights, property rights, and assailing our freedom of speech. The Founders of this nation anticipated the very issue we are facing today, over 240 years ago. They knew the dangers of letting people into our nation with views too radically different from our rightful ideals. The Founders of this nation would have never granted citizenship to purple-haired Gender Studies majors, to any strain of communists, to welfare tourists, or to those seeking to undermine our rights.

Being American is not just a legal label. This is about having the bravery to fight for freedom at every turn and over every hill. This is about having the blood of revolutionaries in your veins, the bones of renegades deep within you, and a wild heart. Self-reliance is the essence of American identity. Taking pride in your heritage, having an understanding not only your past, but of why America was a beacon of light in the darkness of tyranny and oppression. There are people that were born in this fair land, that are faithfully un-American. There are people who come here that have no reason to be in this land. After the Revolution, many of the Tories and loyalists were expelled from the newly created nation. The Revolutionaries knew people like them had no place here any longer. This sentiment is as true today as it ever was. Half of our nation is in favor of gun restrictions, in favor of the welfare state, in favor of laws limiting speech, in favor of open borders, and in favor heavy taxation. Fully half of our Nation has no business in a country founded by men who were willing to pay quite literally any price to be free from an overreaching government.

Speaker Paul Ryan claimed in an interview that cutting Muslim migration is un-American, and "not who we are."[106] To the contrary, that is *precisely* who we are. The Immigration Act of 1907, signed by Teddy Roosevelt, prohibited "polygamists, or persons who admit their belief in the practice of polygamy," from immigrating to the US, effectively prohibiting any Muslim from entering the United States.

During a State of the Union address in 1905, Theodore Roosevelt said there was a need "to keep out all immigrants who will not make good American citizens." He would later write that Muslims "are the enemies of civilization," and that "The civilization of Europe, America and Australia exists today at all only because of the victories of civilized man over the enemies of civilization." Teddy Roosevelt praised Charles Martel for fighting off the hordes of Muslim conquerors, noting that without Martel's actions and bravely, Christianity would have vanished, and Europe would have been conquered.[107] [108]

In Federalist Paper No. 2, John Jay wrote that a unified and homogeneous people, not diversity, will create a strong nation:

> With equal pleasure I have as often taken notice that Providence has been pleased to give this one connected country to one united people — a people descended from the same ancestors, speaking the same language, professing the same religion, attached to the same principles of government, very similar in their manners and customs, and who, by their joint counsels, arms, and efforts, fighting side by side throughout a long and bloody war,

106 Jay Newton-Small. "Speaker Paul Ryan Condemns Donald Trump's Ban on Muslims" Time. December 08, 2015. http://time.com/4140558/paul-ryan-donald-trump-muslims/. [http://archive.li/MNJKU]

107 Daniel Greenfield. "When Teddy Roosevelt Banned Muslims from America" Frontpage Mag. August 18, 2016. http://www.frontpagemag.com/fpm/263879/when-teddy-roosevelt-banned-muslims-america-daniel-greenfield. [https://archive.li/OsLRH]

108 Theodore Roosevelt. Fear God and Take Your Own Part. Hardpress Publishing, 2012.

> have nobly established their general Liberty and Independence. This country and this people seem to have been made for each other.[109]

In the same year that Teddy Roosevelt signed the Immigration Act of 1907, he spoke about immigration and becoming American:

> In the first place, we should insist that if the immigrant who comes here in good faith becomes an American and assimilates himself to us, he shall be treated on an exact equality with everyone else, for it is an outrage to discriminate against any such man because of creed, or birthplace, or origin. But this is predicated upon the person's becoming in every facet an American, and nothing but an American ... There can be no divided allegiance here. Any man who says he is an American, but something else also, isn't an American at all. We have room for but one flag, the American flag ... We have room for but one language here, and that is the English language ... and we have room for but one sole loyalty and that is a loyalty to the American people.[110]

Migrants are supposed to integrate; we are not supposed to tolerate their norms and values, no matter what these might be. If migrants expect their new nation to change the laws, customs, and culture to accommodate them, in any way, even the slightest, they need to go back to wherever they came from.

Liberals are engaging in a nefarious ship of Theseus experiment, replacing Europeans and Americans with Third World hordes in some hope they can by some miracle become similar to us and carry on our cultures.

If just anybody can become an American, then it is entirely meaningless to be an American. The American experiment is truly the last bastion of freedom on Earth; America itself was nothing less than an appeal to heaven. Those of us who are patriots, dreamers, revolutionaries, and still

---

109 John Jay. "The Federalists Papers No. 2" Congress.gov. Accessed July 15, 2017. https://www.congress.gov/resources/display/content/The Federalist Papers#TheFederalistPapers-2.

110 "Broken Borders: Teddy Roosevelt's words to live by" CNN. March 27, 2006. http://www.cnn.com/2006/US/03/27/quote.roosevelt/. [http://archive.li/LcXKN]

wild at heart, have nowhere else we can go. This fair land is the final frontier. And it belongs to no one but us.

Flowers for Europe

I can't quite recall when I began to concern myself with the politics of Europe. There was certainly a time in my life where I was rather indifferent to anything happening beyond my own little sorrows. At some point, years ago, I began to feel a kinship towards the people of Europe. At first I was mostly interested in the shared culture and values of my own ancestry. Then I began to be more concerned with their well-being, at about the same time I felt a growing concern for my own American kin. I had always felt this to some extent, but not to the same degree.

Through the study of culture and politics, I noticed similar trends materializing. I was continually lead to see the sickness and rot of Liberalism causing our civilizations to decay, everywhere in the West. Every destructive Liberal policy that was plaguing Europe arose eventually in the US, as well. The Leftist cabal has been able to advance their agenda more aggressively in Europe — but America is not far behind.

I feel a profound despair for the peoples of Europe, many of whom, election after election, vote for the Right-wing and nationalists candidates in a desperate hope for a change of course. They have had their voices silenced, they are unarmed, and now, because of the Liberal disease, and the import of mongrel hordes, their vote has been nullified. Their countries are being destroyed, their families victimized, all while their "leaders" tell them to enjoy their demise and revel in the Kali Yuga.

Liberal leaders in America routinely praise the policies of Europe. Hillary Clinton extols Angel Merkel,[111] and Barack Obama lauds Australia and the UK for their firearm restrictions.[112] While the European Left is turning Europe into South Africa, the US Left desires the same for us.

111 Nolan D. McCaskill. "In swipe at Trump, Clinton names Merkel as her favorite world leader" POLITICO. September 29, 2016. http://www.politico.com/story/2016/09/hillary-clinton-angela-merkel-228926. [https://archive.li/eegkt]

112 Josh Butler. "Obama Praised Australia's Gun Laws After Oregon Shooting" Huffington Post Australia. October 2, 2015. http://www.huffingtonpost.com.

The current state of geopolitical affairs reminds me a lot of the classic novel, *Flowers for Algernon.*[113] Europe is much like Algernon, the mouse. America, meanwhile, is reminiscent of Charlie Gordon. The "fatal flaw" of course being the ideology and political projects of the international Left.

I can relate to Charlie on a profound level. Desperately trying to hold on and salvage something, anything, from his fleeting soiree with brilliance. I too am grasping for something that can be preserved from the collapse of our culture.

Just as Algernon and Charlie were inextricably bound, so too are we with Europe, through the sickness known as Liberalism. The sickness has already turned much of Europe into hell on Earth, while we watch the demise. I feel like Charlie, watching the slow, inevitable demise of his little mouse friend, Algernon. Knowing I might be next.

Although the story of Algernon and Charlie provides a stunning allegory for the way we can look to Europe to see the future of unfettered Liberalism, we still have time to change the path we're on. But we are swiftly running out of that time, and anyone who wants to know what lies ahead for us if we do not change course should look to Africa.

Mugabe, the president of Zimbabwe, declared that none of the people who have participated in the ethnic cleansing of whites in what was formally Rhodesia, none of those responsible for the torture, rape, and murder of white farmers, will be prosecuted.[114] South African whites are similarly being ethnically cleansed in a state-sponsored genocide. The president of South Africa, Ramaphosa, has vowed to confiscate white land without compensation, and the government has begun the process to amend its constitution to do so "legally."[115] White settlers have been farming that land for over 400 years; the land was settled, not stolen. None of

---

au/2015/10/02/obama-australia-gun-law_n_8230240.html. [http://archive.li/0QSVc]

113 Daniel Keyes. Flowers for Algernon. Harcourt; 1st edition, 1966.

114 Conor Gaffey. "Robert Mugabe says that the killers of Zimbabwe's white farmers will not be prosecuted" August 16, 2017. http://www.newsweek.com/zimbabwe-president-robert-mugabe-white-farmers-651326. [https://archive.li/NcN8k]

115 "New South African president wants to seize land from white farmers without compensation." RT International. February 22, 2018. www.rt.com/business/419543-south-africa-land-compensation-whites/. [https://archive.li/NJuEa]

that matters now that blacks have control of the government. Another South African politician, Julius Malema, praised the land confiscation plans; he even platforms on removing all whites from political office, and proposes to continue "cutting the throat of whiteness." Malema added, "We are not going to listen to any Britain, we are not going to listen to European Parliament, we are not going to listen to UN — we are going to listen to the people of South Africa."[116]

Our story does not have to end in despair and ruin. With their perverse meanderings, Liberals have led us right to the edge. With our backs against the wall, time running out, and little left to lose, there has never been a finer moment to take it all back. I won't have time to place flowers on any graves, or to attend the requiem mass. I'll be raging against the dying light. Working through the night to preserve our Promethean flame.

Their game is up. And the fire is rising.

Killing a Culture

Hordes of Third World migrants are stopping Europeans and Americans from enjoying the society our ancestors created and passed down to us. Our very cultures are being assaulted from every side. What's worse, Leftist politicians sit idly by, refusing even to utter the word "terrorism." They refer to terrorist attacks as knife attacks, machete attacks, gun attacks, car attacks, train attacks, bus attacks, truck attacks — anything to avoid calling a spade a spade. And even more afraid to identify the terrorists themselves.

When the Berlin Christmas Market was attacked killing twelve, leaving dozens more injured, that was an attack directly on German culture. The French were celebrating Bastille Day when dozens were murdered and hundreds injured. The message could not be clearer. Migrants are not interested in assimilation. They are interested in turning Europe into

116 Julian Robinson. "'We are cutting the throat of whiteness': South Africa politician vows to target white mayor as he praises plan to hand land to black people and vows: 'Angry white people can go to hell.'" Daily Mail Online. March 6, 2018. www.dailymail.co.uk/news/article-5460177/S-Africa-firebrand-Malema-launches-bid-presidency.html. [http://archive.li/yX05b]

Muslim nations and creating an environment in which native Europeans can no longer participate in their long held traditions.

Liberals claim this is about freedom to migrate to and from whatever country you please. What about the freedom of the European peoples not to have their taxes stripped from them to fund violence against them? What about the freedom of the children to grow up in their own country without having their dreams shattered by tragedy? Or what about the freedom to leave your house without fear? A recent study in France reports that 60 percent of French people do not feel safe anywhere outside of their homes due to the amount of terror and crime.[117] Similar studies in Sweden and Germany revealed that half of all women are afraid to leave the house after dark, and feel unsafe in their own neighborhoods.[118] [119]

Obama, while rigidly refusing to condemn Muslim migrants for the violence they commit, was quick to remind us of the violence during the Crusades against Muslims committed by Christians in the name of Christ.[120] Either nobody told Obama what caused the Crusades, or else he knew, and was betting on most people not being aware of what brought Pope Urban II to finally decide that enough was enough.

Before the launch of the First Crusade, Muslims seized Constantinople, they attacked Rome, they invaded Spain, Italy, and France. In the lands they conquered, Muslims raped, enslaved, and murdered the native

---

117 Virginia Hale. "Six out of 10 People in France 'Don't Feel Safe Anywhere'" Breitbart. March 17, 2017. http://www.breitbart.com/london/2017/03/17/six-ten-france-dont-feel-safe-anywhere/. [https://archive.li/HZ75H]

118 Donna Rachel Edmunds. "Half Of German Women Feel Unsafe In Their Own Neighbourhoods" Breitbart. January 09, 2017. http://www.breitbart.com/london/2017/01/09/half-german-women-feel-unsafe-neighbourhoods/. [http://archive.li/gijRx]

119 Oliver JJ. Lane. "Scared Sweden: Almost Half Of Women 'Afraid' To Be Out After Dark In Europe's Rape Capital" Breitbart. March 04, 2016. http://www.breitbart.com/london/2016/03/04/scared-sweden-almost-half-of-women-afraid-to-be-out-after-dark-in-europes-rape-capital/. [http://archive.li/LqrsJ]

120 Juliet Eilperin. "Critics pounce as Obama again shows he isn't easy on America" The Washington Post. February 05, 2015. https://www.washingtonpost.com/politics/obamas-speech-at-prayer-breakfast-called-offensive-to-christians/2015/02/05/6a15a240-ad50-11e4-ad71-7b9eba0f87d6_story.html. [http://archive.li/J7ZA9]

inhabitants, all in the name of Islam. Over half of Christendom had been sacked and pillaged, for nearly four centuries, before the First Crusade was launched.[121] Finally, after centuries, the European Christians put the invaders to fire and sword. Yet somehow modern Leftists ignore that crucial bit in the timeline of history. They not only want to place the blame of the Crusades solely on Christian shoulders, they also want to somehow use conflicts from 1,000 years ago as justification for the victimization of modern Europeans at the hands of Muslims.

Nearly as pathetic as the reactions of Left-wing politicians is the media portrayal of the attacks. Migrants kill 100 people, and the first thing the media worries about is protecting the migrants from any potential hate crime and Islamophobia. The media claims terrorism never has anything to do with Islam or migration; if you deny this claim, you are instantly deemed a racist. Everybody changes their social media photo to one with a flag of whatever country was attacked, along with a self-gratifying post that says "Pray for [insert recent victimized city here]." And then they proceed to change absolutely nothing, and wait for the next slaughter. Rinse. And repeat.

Germany's Interior Ministry, which oversees a myriad of responsibilities, from civil protection to displaced persons and government administration, released a recent study of crime. The Ministry found that while asylum seekers and illegal migrants make up only 2.5 percent of the population, they accounted for 5.7 percent of total crime, and were strongly overrepresented in every type of crime as compared to native Germans.[122] Non-German migrants committed nearly half of all theft, a quarter of assaults, and over a third of all robberies. If all non-German invaders were deported today, crime would drop by a third.[123] German news outlets had been focusing instead on the "extreme rise" in Right wing hate

121 Dan McLaughlin. "A Timeline of Islamic Expansion In The Dark Ages" RedState. May 22, 2013. http://www.redstate.com/dan_mclaughlin/2013/05/22/a-timeline-of-islamic-expansion-in-the-dark-ages/. [http://archive.is/0nUz7]

122 Raheem Kassam and Chris Tomlinson. "Report: Migrants Committing Disproportionately High Crime In Germany, Media/Govt Focus on 'Far Right' Thought Crimes" Breitbart. May 23, 2016. http://www.breitbart.com/london/2016/05/23/germany-registers-surge-crimes-right-wing-radicals/. [http://archive.li/L6Kwz]

123 Ibid.

crimes, citing that in 2015 there had been 1,485 instances of Right-wing hate crimes against migrants — most of which, incidentally, were "hate speech" or vandalism crimes.[124] Meanwhile, the Ministry report shows over 400,000 crimes were committed by migrants the same year, which the lying press mostly ignored, as it was not conducive to their narrative.[125] Here's a taste of what the German press doesn't want its citizens to know:

> On Christmas Eve, a homeless man was set on fire in a Berlin train station by seven "refugees."[126]
>
> In the small town of Neuenhaus, Germany, a Somali "refugee" broke into an elderly care home, raped two disabled men, before he murdered one of the victim's wife.[127]
>
> Vienna, on New Year's Eve a woman was abducted from a bar, and gang raped for hours by a family of nine Iraqi "refugees."[128]
>
> An elderly woman, visiting the grave of her sister early one Sunday morning was raped in the cemetery by an African "refugee."[129]

---

124 "Rightwing violence surges in Germany" The Guardian. May 23, 2016. https://www.theguardian.com/world/2016/may/23/germany-rightwing-violence-surges-asylum-seekers. [http://archive.li/m3kBG]

125 Ibid.

126 "Berlin migrants on trial for fire attack on homeless man" BBC News. May 09, 2017. http://www.bbc.com/news/world-europe-39855824. [http://archive.li/koV52]

127 Gareth Davies. "Somalian asylum seeker 'rapes two elderly disabled men in a care home before murdering one of the victims' wives' in Germany" Daily Mail Online. April 03, 2017. http://www.dailymail.co.uk/news/article-4374836/Somalian-asylum-seeker-rapes-two-elderly-disabled-men.html. [http://archive.li/MZLG8]

128 Allan Hall. "Family of nine Iraqi asylum seekers 'gang-raped drunk woman in Austria for two hours as she pleaded "No, I don't want this" after luring her from her friends on New Year's Eve'" Daily Mail Online. February 23, 2017. http://www.dailymail.co.uk/news/article-4248492/Family-Iraqi-asylum-seekers-gang-raped-drunk-woman.html. [http://archive.li/sZ3XI]

129 Nick Enoch. "Eritrean refugee 'rapes a 79-year-old woman in a CEMETERY in Germany while she was visiting her sister's grave'" Daily Mail Online. July

> During a camping trip outside of Bonn, Germany, a "refugee" from Ghana took a young woman by machete, and raped her in front of her boyfriend.[130]

This is by no means an exhaustive list of crimes, but a sample of daily occurrences. Germans are not able to enjoy a holiday or camping trip without being terrorized by invaders.

These stories rarely make headlines throughout the Leftist-controlled media in Europe. The American press never bothers to cover them either. They instead focus on the *real* threat of Right-wing hate crimes and the rise of Islamophobia, and antisemitism. If there really is a rise in "Islamophobia" and "antisemitism," it seems it would be a normal reaction to the amount of terror and crime we are being subjected to through mass migration of Muslims and forced cultural enrichment policies that are heavily promoted by Jews in Europe and the US.[131]

The same theme has been repeated for centuries, since the early Muslim conquest under Muhammad in the 7th century A.D. *Hijrah*, the proper term for the spread of Islam through land conquest, is what we are seeing now.[132] The European Union Parliament Chief, Antonio Tajani, has stated that within the next ten years, thirty million new "refugees" will come from Africa alone into Europe.[133] Tajani then went on to declare Europeans could prevent the flood of tens of millions of Muslim men into

---

27, 2016. http://www.dailymail.co.uk/news/article-3710209/Eritrean-refugee-rapes-79-year-old-woman-cemetery-visiting-sister-s-grave.html. [http://archive.li/ddH5s]

130 Alan Hall. "Boyfriend forced to watch as refugee rapes his girlfriend at knife-point during camping trip in Germany" Daily Mail Online. April 09, 2017. http://www.dailymail.co.uk/news/article-4395310/Boyfriend-forced-watch-refugee-rapes-girlfriend.html. [http://archive.li/HhMGZ]

131 Kevin MacDonald. " Jewish Involvement in Shaping American Immigration Policy, 1881-1965: A Historical Review." Population and Environment: A Journal of Interdisciplinary Studies, vol. 19, no. 4, Mar. 1998, pp. 295–356.

132 Robert Spencer. "The Hijrah Into Europe" Frontpage Mag. September 04, 2015. http://www.frontpagemag.com/fpm/260019/hijrah-europe-robert-spencer. [http://archive.li/MJEis]

133 "30mn Africans may come to Europe within next 10 years — EU parliament chief" RT International. March 29, 2017. https://www.rt.com/news/382706-african-migrants-millions-europe/. [http://archive.li/CDYqv]

their nations if they invest billions of dollars into Africa to create a more sustainable environments for them. This is what people are being paid to do at Immigration Summits: threaten their citizens with the invasion of tens of millions of foreigners if they do not pay enormous sums of money to fund the teeming Third World population, which makes this invasion possible to begin with. Not only is the *Hijrah* clearly happening, we are being betrayed by the people who are supposed to be fighting *for* us, as they are evidently more interested in creating a managerial state and eradicating our people. At some point, these politicians will need to be removed from power.

Development Minister Gerd Müller of Germany claims that over 100 million African migrants will come to Europe as "economic and climate refugees" in coming years. Chancellor Angela Merkel's response was to give away hundreds of millions in tax-payer dollars to help fund migrants coming to Europe.[134]

Politicians in Europe and America use migrants to terrorize and solidify their power. Migrants are little more than the bottom stones of their great pyramid scheme. As long as migrants need welfare, the governments can continue to tax the native citizens, print money, and pretend the economy is growing, all while eradicating us.

What we are seeing is nothing but weaponized migration. Liberals use these barbarians as of the tools of psychological warfare, an effort to keep the population scared and controlled, so that they will accept whatever it is the politicians want from them. Whether it be in the form of higher taxes or the creation of a surveillance police state, the terror and crime waves that result from mass migration greatly benefit the political elite. When the media and leaders of the Left tell us after every terrorist attack that "diversity is still our strength" and that we must deal with this new "way of life," they are desensitizing society to the violence and the abnormality of dysfunction, ushering in a state of conditioned helplessness and apathy. And in true SPLC and ADL fashion, they claim that anyone who has the wild idea that once Muslims become a majority in Western nations, they

134 Jacob Bojesson. "Germany Says 100 Million African Refugees Could Head North" The Daily Caller. June 18, 2017. http://dailycaller.com/2017/06/18/germany-says-100-million-african-refugees-could-head-north/. [http://archive.li/PAwAv]

might seek to fundamentally change the legal system and culture to reflect their own, must be a bigoted anti-Muslim conspiracy theorist.[135] [136]

Speaking of the idea that a Muslim majority might become radically intolerant of other religions and peoples — I wonder where anyone might get such a ridiculous notion? Maybe because that's precisely what Muslims have done in over 50 different countries over the last 1,400 years? Muslim politicians in Canada have passed laws to make it illegal to criticize Islam or Muslims.[137] The majority of Muslims in American and Europe openly admit to wanting to be governed Sharia law. But all of these historical examples and modern examples are evidently nothing but the conspiracy theory ravings of racist lunatics. I'm glad we have the SPLC and ADL doing tireless propaganda work to clear these little misunderstandings up for us.

During a visit to Europe, the Dalai Lama remarked there were too many "refugees" coming into Europe. He went on to say refugees should be admitted into Europe only temporarily. "Germany cannot become an Arab country. Germany is Germany," the Dalai Lama stated.[138] Perhaps the Dalai Lama, too, is a Nazi. Or maybe decades of solitary meditation in exile in the Himalayan mountains have given the Dalai Lama a somewhat keener understanding of geopolitics than that possessed by most Liberals.

Poland and Hungary were threatened with sanctions from the European Union after they refused to accept more migrants into their nation. To which the Polish Interior Minister Mariusz Błaszczak replied that taking more migrants would be "much worse" than any EU sanctions.

---

135 "Anti-Muslim Ideology" Southern Poverty Law Center. Accessed July 16, 2017. https://www.splcenter.org/fighting-hate/extremist-files/ideology/anti-muslim.

136 "Anti-Muslim Bigotry" Anti-Defamation League. Accessed July 16, 2017. https://www.adl.org/education/resources/backgrounders/anti-muslim-bigotry.

137 Ryan Maloney. "M-103: Anti-Islamophobia Motion Easily Passes House Of Commons" HuffPost Canada. March 23, 2017. http://www.huffingtonpost.ca/2017/03/23/m-103-anti-islamophobia-motion-house-passes_n_15567120.html. [http://archive.li/tC0Po]

138 "Dalai Lama says Europe has accepted 'too many' refugees" RT International. May 31, 2016. https://www.rt.com/news/344983-dalai-lama-refugee-crisis/. [http://archive.li/k689y]

Minister Błaszczak cited the current change in demographics as being responsible for the meteoric rise in crime and terror throughout Europe.[139]

Polish Prime Minister Beata Szydło remarked that it is impossible not to see how the rise of terrorism in Europe is linked directly to migration policy.[140] Poland has a lower Global Terrorism Index rating than any other European Union nation. This is not a coincidence. It is the direct result of leaders like Błaszczak and Szydło at the helm.

Interestingly enough, Poland is experiencing a baby boom, with over 400,000 children expected to be born in the next year, a seven year high. Perhaps this is connected in some inexplicable way to the fact that the Polish government decided to use its tax dollars to give back to those of their own people who choose to start families, instead of giving them away to invaders.[141]

The Center for Strategic and International Studies tracks global terror incidents over the world. Since 2012, Poland has had zero attacks, Switzerland, two.[142] These two nations look out for the best interests of their people, and it shows.[143]

While researching European nations, comparing and contrasting policies to outcomes, I couldn't help but wonder—is this how Charles Dickens felt while writing *A Tale of Two Cities*? How could it be that two

---

139 Virginia Hale. "Poland Says Taking Migrants 'Much Worse' Than EU Sanctions" Breitbart. May 17, 2017. http://www.breitbart.com/london/2017/05/17/poland-migrants-worse-sanctions-eu-threatens-june-deadline/. [http://archive.li/XEwjB]

140 Harriet Agerholm. "Polish PM: London terror attack is about Britain's refugee policy" The Independent. March 24, 2017. http://www.independent.co.uk/news/world/europe/polish-prime-minister-london-terror-attack-szydlo-uk-refugee-policy-britain-immigration-a7648391.html. [http://archive.li/m4U9m]

141 Silvia Elena Ionita. "Poland is experiencing a baby boom" New Europe. March 17, 2017. https://www.neweurope.eu/article/poland-experiencing-baby-boom/. [http://archive.li/E6Tpv]

142 "Global Terrorist Attacks 2012—2015" CSIS. Accessed July 16, 2017. https://csis.carto.com/builder/60931f8e-9bcb-11e6-98fa-0e05a8b3e3d7/embed.

143 Rachel Marsden. "Why does terrorism spare Switzerland" Chicago Tribune. March 21, 2017. http://www.chicagotribune.com/news/columnists/sns-201703211400--tms--amvoicesctnav-b20170321-20170321-column.html. [http://archive.li/UKOzU]

countries, so close in proximity and culture, are worlds apart in quality of life? People in one country are afraid to leave their houses, and in the next country, they enjoy low crime, no terrorism, and a higher quality of life. Given the shocking discrepancy here, why is it so difficult for people to see the destruction Leftists policies have wrought?

We are told over and over again that the shifts in demographics, culture, and terrorism are unavoidable. Barack Obama, during an NPR interview, said the demographic shifts in the US are inevitable, and that this is going to be "a browner country."[144] French Prime Minister Emmanuel Macron proclaimed that mass migration is unstoppable, inevitable, and that Europeans "must get used to mass immigration."[145]

Leftist news organizations around the planet agree. Headlines such as "Mass Immigration Is Unstoppable,"[146] "Cities urged to 'embrace new reality' of mass migration,"[147] "Mass EU migration into Britain is actually good news for UK economy,"[148] and "UK needs more immigrants to avoid Brexit catastrophe,"[149] are but a few examples of a wider trend.

---

144 Justin Caruso. "Obama: It's 'Inevitable' That America Is Getting 'Browner'" The Daily Caller. December 19, 2016. http://dailycaller.com/2016/12/19/obama-its-inevitable-that-america-is-getting-browner-video/. [http://archive.li/sDJVa]

145 Belinda Robinson. "Emmanuel Macron: Europe faces 'unstoppable mass migration' says French PM hopeful" Express.co.uk. February 26, 2017. http://www.express.co.uk/news/world/772288/Emmanuel-Macron-Europe-faces-unstoppable-mass-migration-says-French-PM-hopeful. [http://archive.li/fgV7Q]

146 Donna Rachel Edmunds. "Financial Times: Mass Immigration Is Unstoppable" Breitbart. January 12, 2016. http://www.breitbart.com/london/2016/01/12/financial-times-mass-immigration-is-here-to-stay-we-should-learn-to-accept-it/. [http://archive.li/k4h8x]

147 Sophie Hares. "Cities urged to 'embrace new reality' of mass migration" Thomson Reuters. May 11, 2017. http://news.trust.org/item/20170511113358-bgt2e/. [http://archive.li/7gKIe]

148 Alan Travis. "Mass EU migration into Britain is actually good news for UK economy" The Guardian. February 18, 2016. https://www.theguardian.com/uk news/2016/feb/18/mass-eu-migration-into-britain-is-actually-good-news-for-uk-economy. [http://archive.li/uVvZ1]

149 Patrick Wintour. "UK needs more immigrants to 'avoid Brexit catastrophe'" The Guardian. May 19, 2017. https://www.theguardian.com/uk-news/2017/may/19/

Why? Why are politicians all over the Western world pretending changing demographics and heightened terrorism are somehow absolutely fated? But the reason should be clear. These changes are in fact entirely intentional, and driven by the same policy these very politicians created. Beirut was once called the Paris of the East. Now Paris has become the Karachi of the West. This did not *have* to *happen*; it was intended to happen. The very people that go on TV to assure us time and time again that nothing can be done to alter our course, are the same who are actively guiding it. When they exhort us to tolerance, what they mean is, "Please be calm and tolerant while we murder your civilization."

The largest city in the world is Tokyo. Japan has seen years with a Global Terrorism Index of precisely *zero*. Japan routinely has a terror index among the lowest in the world.[150] Japan: the country with the largest city in the world, immense population density, and no worries of terrorism. Could it be a coincidence that Japan takes in no refugees, no asylum seekers, no economic migrants, and enforces very strict immigration policies? Japanese politicians are *not* telling the Japanese people that they are going to be a minority in their own homeland in a few short decades. Japanese officials are *not* telling them they must learn to live with the rapes, car burnings, kidnappings, murders, and terror attacks. So why are we allowing it to happen in Europe and the United States?

The political positions of Japanese leaders would be called "radical" and "extremist," and the leaders themselves "supremacists" and "Right-wingers" by our media, if they were in any Western nation. Japanese Prime Minister Shinzo Abe had this to say about migrants in Japan: "As an issue of demography, I would say that before accepting immigrants or refugees we need to have more activities by women, by elderly people and we must raise the birth rate. There are many things that we should do before accepting immigrants."[151] Which is exactly the same sentiment politicians all over Europe and America *should* be adopting.

---

uk-needs-more-immigrants-to-avoid-brexit-catastrophe. [http://archive.li/517hM]

150 "Japan Terrorism Index." Trading Economics. Accessed May 27, 2018. https://tradingeconomics.com/japan/terrorism-index. [http://archive.is/184y1]

151 "Japan not taking in refugees; says it must look after its citizens first" Fox News. September 30, 2015. http://www.foxnews.com/world/2015/09/30/

Governments should not be in the business of global welfare or the business of pathological altruism. They should be concerned only with the welfare and safety of their own people. But I wonder if our elected leaders even view us as their own tribe? It somehow seems they are far more akin to the Bolsheviks, who had a deep disdain for Orthodox Russians and Ukrainians. In fact—they might just be the exact same group as those who lead the Bolshevik party long ago.

Once the demographic shift tips the scales too far, it's over. Western civilization as we know it will be erased. Thousands of years of work, washed away. Why? So some of *our* people can feel good about being "inclusive"? Once we are the minority in our own homelands, we will never be able to win another election. Every official will be interested in what blacks, Hispanics, and Muslims want: restrictions of free speech, more welfare, open borders, mass migration, and their warped ways of life, forced upon us.

In Germany alone, the Muslim population is projected to quadruple by 2020 according to the Gatestone Institute. During a discussion of the open border policies of Germany and the EU, German politician Walter Lübcke told native German citizens that if they do not like the policies, or the newly arriving hordes of Muslims, they are "free to leave Germany."[152]

Not only is it now illegal to speak out against mass migration all over Europe, government officials are telling people to leave their own homelands if they do not enjoy the "cultural enrichment." But to go *where*? Muslims already have over fifty nations in which they are a majority. Where is a German to go once his country has transformed into a Muslim nation? Where are Americans to go, when we too become strangers in our own lands? The sentiments of Walter Lübcke are becoming increasingly common, even in the US. Liberals want open borders and amnesty, Hillary wants to increase the amount of legal "refugees" to the US by tenfold. Signs reading "deport racists"—meaning, of course, anybody who disagrees with mass migration—are to be found at every Liberal protest

---

japan-not-taking-in-refugees-says-it-must-look-after-its-citizens-first.html. [http://archive.li/4SZWT]

152 Kern Soeren. "Germans Opposed to Mass Migration are "Free to Leave" Gatestone Institute. November 24, 2015. https://www.gatestoneinstitute.org/6944/germans-oppose-mass-migration. [http://archive.li/XpUun]

in the US. The Left is literally telling us that if we disagree with them ruining our countries, we should be forced to leave.

Once Texas and Arizona are entirely Mexican, and Ohio, Idaho, and Missouri have been overrun with Somalis, then what? We will never be able to win even an election again. Just as London is now a Muslim city, with a Muslim leader, we too will be displaced in our own lands by foreign invaders.

What do you think will happen to free speech and our gun rights? Hillary Clinton wanted to make it legal to be able to sue firearm and ammunition manufactures for any "misuse." Once that happens, firearm and ammunition companies will be sued out of business until none are left. This is what the majority of blacks, Hispanics, Asians, Arabs, and Jews, voted for in 2016. Muslims all over Europe have already been able to enact laws that make it illegal to criticize their mass migration, or their religion. The majority of Muslims, blacks, and Hispanics — who knows why — support expansion of our systems of welfare. What do you think will happen when these groups have become so large that they can begin to outvote us? Do you think they are going to somehow wake up one day and decide to start acting like *Americans*? Not a chance. They will continue to advocate for "hate speech" laws so we can be imprisoned for offending them, they will vote for politicians who will disarm us, who will and tax us heavily, so they can have more government services coddling them.

A study by Pew on gun rights and gun control found that 73 percent of blacks and 69 percent of Hispanics report considering controlling gun ownership to be more important than protecting the rights of Americans to own guns. 42 percent of whites, meanwhile, agreed that controlling gun ownership was more important than the right to own. 78 percent of Democrats, as compared to only 18 percent of Republicans, felt controlling gun ownership was more important than the rights of Americans to own guns.[153] Quantifiable data proves that the majority of blacks and Hispanics would prefer to have laws that illegalize "offensive"

153 "Opinions on Gun Policy and the 2016 Campaign" Pew Research Center for the People and the Press. August 26, 2016. http://www.people-press.org/2016/08/26/opinions-on-gun-policy-and-the-2016-campaign/. [http://archive.li/W0wFN]

statements.[154] Research also shows that over half of blacks, Hispanics, Muslims, and white Democrats are in favor of laws to ban "hate speech" and "offensive statements."[155] The US Constitution and Bill of Rights will not survive a non-white majority. Within a few decades — maybe more, maybe less — whites will be a demographic minority in the US Those first two amendments are just that, amendments. A quick civics reminder: it only takes two-thirds of Congress and thirty-eight states to eviscerate either (or both) of our most cherished rights.

The Bill of Rights was ratified in 1791. A year before that, the Naturalization Act was passed, limiting US citizenship to free white persons. Limitations on who could become an American came *before* the US ratified the rights we take for granted; we should not forget this lesson in chronology. A white nation is a predicate to such expansive freedoms. To deny this, and to believe that we should not be concerned with the fact that the Mexican border creeps ever northward, is to play a very dangerous game — a game in which we bet the future of our civilization against the misguided hope that we can convince an alien race to somehow become "just like us." We simply cannot have a high trust society with either non-whites or with too much diversity. Asians are generally seen as the "model minority," and I have spoken highly of them throughout this book; however they still do not make for great Americans. Asians are really great at being Asian. They build nice nations, they take care of their own, they commit little crime, and use little welfare. However, as a whole in the US, Asians support larger governments, firearm restrictions, migration, and they vote majority Left-wing as a diaspora population. Asians may be "model citizens," but they are not good *Americans.*

The Liberal plan is incredibly simple. Outnumber us, and then vote "legally" to erode our rights. I'll never forget nor forgive these transgressions against us or their attempted *coup d'état* in November of 2016. I will never forget their gloating as they were closing in on my people like a

154 Sean Last. "Political Ideology in America by Race" The Alternative Hypothesis. April 28, 2016. http://thealternativehypothesis.org/index.php/2016/04/28/political-ideology-in-america-by-race/. [http://archive.li/BIo6L]

155 Peter Moore. "Half of Democrats support a ban on hate speech" YouGov. May 20, 2015. https://today.yougov.com/news/2015/05/20/hate-speech/. [http://archive.li/KKrgL]

pack of hungry cannibals. Do you think when we lose our nations to these people, our history will remain? Once we are total minorities in our own homelands, do you think the mongrel hordes will preserve our legacy? Or that even the physical artifacts of our civilization will be saved?

Non-white students across American universities are already requesting Shakespeare be banned, as his writing is not "diverse" enough; English literature, they say, is dominated too much by white male authors. They add helpfully that white, male, authors create a "hostile" environments for students of color.[156] Universities are already teaching revisionist history of the West without the Westerners. University courses like "Islam in the United States" tell the "story" of how Muslims were an essential part of shaping America, starting from the 1500s.[157]

We are already seeing historical monuments across the entire nation being removed or destroyed for being "racist" and "offensive."[158] [159] The ones that remain are frequently defaced; historic monuments have been covered in graffiti including tolerant, multicultural statements like "die whites die."[160] They will not be stopping at Confederate statues either. That is merely the beginning. While our culture is being destroyed, the Left,

156 Alison Flood. "Yale English students call for end of focus on white male writers" The Guardian. June 01, 2016. https://www.theguardian.com/books/2016/jun/01/yale-english-students-call-for-end-of-focus-on-white-male-writers. [http://archive.li/dtBcE]

157 Amanda Tidwell. "New Ohio State course extols Muslims' role in America from its founding to present day" The College Fix. February 03, 2017. https://www.thecollegefix.com/post/31030/. [http://archive.li/qU9R9]

158 Ilya Somin. "The case for taking down Confederate monuments" The Washington Post. May 17, 2017. https://www.washingtonpost.com/news/volokh-conspiracy/wp/2017/05/17/the-case-for-taking-down-confederate-monuments/. [http://archive.li/7xNwX]

159 Jess Bidgood, et al. "Confederate Monuments Are Coming Down Across the Country. Here's a List." The New York Times. August 16, 2017. www.nytimes.com/interactive/2017/08/16/us/confederate-monuments-removed.html. [http://archive.li/53GRi]

160 John Binder. "'Die Whites Die': Anti-Trump Rioters Vandalize NOLA Monuments" Breitbart. November 10, 2016. http://www.breitbart.com/texas/2016/11/10/die-whites-die-anti-trump-rioters-vandalize-nola-monuments/. [http://archive.li/rHJud]

and the likes of the SPLC, support it entirely.[161] They want to erase us. Turn us into exiles in our own homelands. But our history is more important than their pathetic feelings.

Although I have forwarded many arguments and dispelled many lies regarding the economic and moral justifications of replacement migration, ultimately, none of this matters. There are entire neighborhoods and entire cities all over the US and throughout Europe that look and feel entirely alien. These foreign enclaves share nothing in common with our memories of these places in our once great lands. There is no amount of money, no moral imperative, no humanitarian cause, that can outweigh the loss of our homelands. For once they are lost to the hands of hostile alien tribes, they are lost forever. Our roots will be severed and we will be forced to live our remaining days in exile, in the very lands our ancestors once created, defended, and passed down to their posterity — to *us*.

More monuments will be torn down; cities and roads will be renamed. As sure as Tsaritsyn was changed to Stalingrad, and Saint Petersburg renamed to Leningrad, we too will be erased from our own history. Everything the Left deems undesirable will be razed if it is not stopped. The Liberals will continue until every remnant of our culture and existence is removed. And with our heritage and history eradicated, it will be as if we never existed at all.

At Oxford University, students are demanding that the statue of Cecil Rhodes be taken down, as he represents British imperialism. King's College London is removing portraits of many of the founders of the university after complaints arose that they were too white. The portraits of men who founded the university will be replaced with non-whites and women.[162] A professor at the University of Iowa claims that the white marble used

161 "Send a letter: It's time to take down Confederate monuments." Southern Poverty Law Center. Accessed August 26, 2017. www.splcenter.org/news/2017/08/15/send-letter-its-time-take-down-confederate-monuments.

162 Luke Mintz and Harry Yorke. "Top UK university to swap portraits of bearded white scholars with wall of diversity" The Telegraph. July 14, 2017. http://www.telegraph.co.uk/education/2017/07/14/top-uk-university-replaces-busts-portraits-bearded-white-scholars/. [http://archive.li/twhZm]

in many famous sculptures, such as Michelangelo's *Pietà*, contributes to white supremacy.[163]

None of this will be surprising to students of history. After conquering a land, foreign invaders destroy the previous history and culture, and all remnants of the people who were once there. ISIS has destroyed art, shrines, temples, and monuments in every territory they have conquered.[164] Just as the Bolsheviks did in Russia after torturing and slaughtering the Romanovs. Just as the Left wing of Spain desecrated the nation during the Red Terror through the Spanish Civil War, before Franco secured the nation. And just as Maoists destroyed cultural relics all throughout China.

Blowing up Mount Rushmore, razing historic buildings, or painting over the Sistine Chapel because they lack diversity and were created by white men, will surely be an aspiration for the Left sooner or later. Their desire to destroy everything beautiful and their hatred for us are both illimitable. A day will come when destroying Gothic cathedrals, marble sculptures, and high culture art, will too fall in their hateful sights. This was never about racism; this is an assault on art and beauty. On all the things our beloved ancestors created and left for us to enjoy. The Left is filled with chaos and ugliness, and so they naturally hate our kind for being everything they are not. They hate us for being everything they could never become.

I have heard students in college classes complaining that there were "too many old white guys" in text books, and that they need to be made more diverse. Articles such as "The Unbearable Whiteness of History," express the same sentiment.[165] What happens on university campuses is the canary in the coalmine.

Europe, too, is on the forefront of these changes. The situation in Europe is so grave that Europeans are no longer able to enjoy a holiday, a

---

163 Dan Jackson. "Prof: 'white marble' in artwork contributes to white supremacy" Campus Reform. June 08, 2017. http://www.campusreform.org/?ID=9285. [http://archive.li/dj3gV]

164 Sturt Manning. "Why ISIS destroys antiquities" CNN. March 0, 2015. http://www.cnn.com/2015/03/06/opinions/manning-isis-antiquities/index.html. [http://archive.li/ChijA]

165 Jendella Benson. "The unbearable whiteness of history" Media Diversified. January 27, 2017. https://mediadiversified.org/2017/01/27/the-unbearable-whiteness-of-history/. [http://archive.li/rNzB7]

concert, a night out, without fear of Muslim violence. Islam is no longer allowing Europeans to carry on their cultures and pass their traditions on to their children. Our homelands are under siege. It is not our tradition to act with haste, but it is even further from our heritage to lay down our weapons and allow the hordes to overwhelm and dominate us.

It is not in our nature to sit around and wait to be conquered. The ancient Greeks staved off the invading Persians, defending all of Europe. The Romans did not submit to the Carthaginian Empire — they fought three brutal wars to protect Europe. When the Huns marched through the Catalaunian Plains, did the Romans and the Visigoths lay down their weapons? They never dreamed of such a thing. And when the Ottomans laid siege to the gates of Vienna, were they met with signs reading "Refugees welcome!"? They were greeted as any invader should be — by shield and sword.

The health and future of Western civilization is inextricably tied to us, the descendants of those who built these magnificent civilizations. No group of people can continue the rich history and culture of Western civilization, except for the descendants of those who built it. The once great Rome fell because it allowed invaders into Roman homelands. When Rome was no longer able to protect its borders, mass migration from the barbarians followed. Government corruption, wasteful spending, and a diluted currency all accelerated the decline of the great empire.[166] Finally, a loss of traditional values among Romans, combined with an apathetic indifference towards their demise. It's all been done before; you can see it all through history and in literature. The parallels are haunting.

T.S. Elliot was right. *This is the way the world ends. Not with a bang. But a whimper.*

If they kill the West, destroy our homelands, dispossess our people; if they tell us to "be tolerant" and to "not look back in anger" when our

166 Evan Andrews. "8 Reasons Why Rome Fell" History.com. January 14, 2014. http://www.history.com/news/history-lists/8-reasons-why-rome-fell. [http://archive.li/JBTgA]

children are murdered and raped;[167] if they label us as "Nazis" for wanting to protect our people from gang rapes, abuse, extortion, and terror — then what do we have left? If the Occident crumbles, nothing will remain for us to fight for. We will become a generation of revenge. In that moment, their advice will be sound. I will agree: at such a point, we should not be looking back in anger — we should be looking forward. With steady eyes, voices low, and hate in our hearts. Once there's nothing left to save, once our civilization lies in ruin, we will having nothing left to lose. And then there will be no reason to not send them all straight to hell as we ascend to Valhalla.

Without hatred for everything that threatens what we love, love itself becomes a worthless cliché for cowards and degenerates.

We are at a crossroads unlike anything we have seen in centuries. When my children and grandchildren ask me what happened to our once great civilizations, I'm not going to tell them with shame in my eyes that I did nothing. Because I was too afraid of losing a few friends and too afraid of being called racist and xenophobic by the Liberal hordes. I'll be able to tell them I sacrificed part of my youth fighting to rein our culture back from its death throes.

When they ask me why such brutality was necessary, I'll tell them about Rotherham, the Christmas market, the Bataclan, of Reagan Tokes, Pat Mahaney, and about little Reese Bowman. And I will not forget to tell them of the deranged criminal vermin who ensured these atrocities would to take place.

The Left is taunting us. Mocking us. Daring us even. We gave the Left and migrants alike every opportunity to live peacefully in the lands that our ancestors built. They have mistaken our kindness for weakness and they have used it as an opportunity to abuse us. We have been icy, willing to wait. When we finally decide the Left has taken this too far, there will be no going back. The global Left has been waging a total war on us for nearly 100 years, and we are just now waking up. The hour is late, the night is dark, but all is not yet lost. Either we decide that enough is enough, and

167 Frances Perraudin and Josh Halliday. "Don't Look Back in Anger becomes symbol of Manchester's spirit" The Guardian. May 25, 2017. https://www.theguardian.com/uk-news/2017/may/25/dont-look-back-in-anger-becomes-symbol-of-manchester-spirit. [http://archive.li/y6cGY]

secure our nations for the future of our people. Or like Nero, we watch it burn down around us. What we do in the next few years will echo through eternity. Those echoes will either haunt us, or define us. If we fail, if we must leave the scene of history. Let us shake this history to the core so that generations of our enemies will speak of the horror and rage of the last white men.

> If I had but one bullet and were faced by both an enemy and a traitor, I would let the traitor have it. — Corneliu Zelea Codreanu

Manifestations of the Liberal illness: Mass Migration

All arguments Liberals use to promote migration are full of lies. The data they present is a lie concealing a lie. Liberals hide and omit the information about migrant welfare use and crime, or distort the data to make it invisible.

We've seen the Liberal outrage when we try to limit migration and travel. In America they shut down airports and rioted over proposed travel limitations for a handful of nations.

When presented with all the data in terms of crime and welfare use, Liberals still hold steadfast to their view that every person on planet Earth deserves to come to our nations, that every last human being somehow belongs in the West. Mass migration is turning Europe into a Chernobylian wasteland. Sweden is set to become a Third World nation. America will become an extension of Mexico. Islamic expansion will consume the majority of the European Union. Like Sweden, the rest of Europe and the US is also only a generation at most away from sliding into Third World conditions. Yet Liberals refuse to take account of any of this. They still shrilly claim that "diversity is our greatest strength."

Unjustified feelings of victimization are seen in illegals and Liberals alike. Liberals feel it is their right to give our nations away. They appeal to marginal cases of Right-wing violence and take that as justification for their stance of moral righteousness, as if they are saving the people from some sort of persecution, even as they themselves are the true persecutors.

Tremendous self-guilt and self-hatred is seen here. American and European Leftists are claiming they have no culture, that they need Third World savages to "enrich" them. Of all symptoms of Liberal pathology, self-hatred and ethnomasochism is the most frightening due to the havoc it wreaks.

Nobody is born hating their own race. It is learned. It has become institutionalized in every university social science class, throughout the press, and in the entertainment industry. Imagine hating yourself and your own people so much, that you would happily participate in the demise of your own culture and nation. That is what it means to be a Liberal today.

The desire for power, control, and dominance is revealed in the destruction of our culture, the removal of our statues, art, and history. It was not the Arabs, Mexicans, Africans, or Muslims who opened our borders to hordes of migrants. It was not the invaders who promoted Marxism, oppressive governments, feminism, abortion, and pornography. It was the Left who constantly attacked our rights of expression and to maintain arms. It was the Left who expanded the welfare state, and it was the Left who involved us in nearly every major war we have been entangled in throughout recent decades. It was not the invaders who opened our gates. We can forget: the gates were opened from within.

Liberal idealism is based on their hatred for themselves and their own people, a hatred so deep that they would gladly doom their children to lives of terror and abuse. Have all the massacres not been enough? Have the sex slavery rings of young girls in Rotherham and a hundred other European cities not been enough? Has the meteoric rise in rapes not been enough? Is there a point at which Liberals realize their ideals are not working? Or is their hated for their own people so great they will not stop until the last white people are hunted down and killed or sold as sex slaves?

The Left is showing no signs of stopping the madness. It appears we are going to have to put an end to this for them. Once and for all.

From Cluster I we see symptoms 1, 2, 3, and 5. In cluster II symptoms all symptoms are observed.

Cluster I

1. Deceitfulness, indicated by repeated lying, grand exaggerations, or omission of contrary information, with the purpose to advance their chosen narrative and discrediting others.

2. Irritability or aggressiveness towards anybody that questions or opposes their views. Coupled with the inability to recognize they own hypocrisy, double standards, and doublethink.

3. Inability to adjust views when presented with information contrary to their own beliefs.

4. Frequent projections of their own traits onto others.

5. Difficulty in dealing with a loss of control or power, or a strong desire for control and power.

Cluster II

6. Appeals to altered and redefined definitions of words, or relies on fictitious terms for argumentation.

7. Consistent feelings of having been victimized or wronged, without any actual harm being done. Seen also as playing the victim after attacking others.

8. Intense sense of righteousness or moral superiority.

9. The inability to recognize the negative outcomes of their own actions. Often placing the blame on others.

10. Intense guilt or self-hatred, often manifests as hatred towards one's larger group identity.

Act III:

Winning the War

I

Revolution 2016

Liberals still don't get it. They honestly believe that the 2016 election was won by "hate, fear, racism, sexism, homophobia, xenophobia" — the list goes on *ad infinitum*. Liberals still can't figure out why they lost. They *actually* believe racism and sexism defeated them.

In truth, quotations from Hillary Clinton such as, "My dream is a hemispheric common market, with open trade and open borders," defeated them.[1] Hillary telling people she will continue on with the policies that have already cost hundreds of thousands of jobs, defeated them. Liberal values no longer resonate with Americans, who wish to see their lives and communities revitalized. Liberals are ever concerned with efforts toward globalization and increased mass migration, while they turn their backs on the very people they are elected to serve. Liberals were defeated by their own manipulations and failures.

The stakes of the 2016 election could not have been higher. Had Trump not won, the Supreme Court would have been stacked with young, deranged Liberals, blanket amnesty would have been granted, mass migration to the US would have been given a cocktail of steroids and cocaine, and we would be taxed to fund it all. An unambiguously Left

1 Ben Wolfgang. "Clinton admitted she's for 'open borders' in paid, private speech: WikiLeaks" The Washington Times. October 08, 2016. http://www.washingtontimes.com/news/2016/oct/8/hillary-clinton-dreams-open-borders-leaked-speech-/. [http://archive.li/aGKRv]

Supreme Court could have paved the way for firearms manufacturers to be sued out of existence by holding them liable each time one person shot another. The election of Donald Trump may very well have saved, among other things, the Second Amendment.

Had the election gone differently, a Leftist Congress might have tried to make that worthless poem on the base of the Statue of Liberty an official Amendment, or removed any sort of limitation at all on the number of migrants that would be allowed to flood our nation each year. Firearms would now be restricted, censorship would be the norm, hate speech laws would be enacted, and taxation would become increasingly oppressive. An entire horror novel could be written about the "what ifs." It's fair to say that this was a close one.

There is a local electronics store I stop by every few months. I like the manager and they usually have what I'm looking for. I stopped by one evening on my way home after noticing a 50 percent-off sale sign out front. As I pulled into the parking lot I realized that the sale was a going out of business sale. I noticed the store manager outside taking a photo of the storefront. The sun was setting behind the store on the crisp autumn evening — rather symbolic now that I'm looking back. As I approached to say hello, I noticed his eyes were heavy and blurred. I didn't say much; he didn't seem to be in the talkative mood. I made my purchase, sat in the parking lot for a few moments, then drove home.

I thought a lot about that scene the rest of the night. I truly felt for him. I'm not sure if he was saddened by the store closing that he had spent so many years working. If it marked the end of an era in his life. If he was anxious and feeling uncertain about what he would do now. He might already have a better job lined up. He might be wondering how he'll pay rent. I really have no idea.

What I do know is that there have been millions of people just like him all over the country, facing similar struggles, similar thoughts, and similar uncertainties. There are small towns all over the nation that have been utterly devastated by businesses closing or moving overseas. Once vibrant and lovely towns have become barren wastelands, devoid of all hope.

That night, I thought about a summer I spent exploring New England. While visiting Maine, I passed through Freeport, home of L.L. Bean.

Freeport is not a particularly large town in size or population, yet it was striking in terms of its spirit. Shops and restaurants were bustling, sidewalks were filled with people enjoying the day. Freeport had an entirely different atmosphere than so many other small towns I've visited across the nation. There was one main difference: people in Freeport had a place to work. There was a vibrant economy, and despite the small size, there was opportunity to be found. Companies like L.L. Bean are not simply providing jobs and income for their workers. They give hope, a sense of purpose and opportunity.

Donald Trump seems to understand this on some deep, almost instinctual level. During many speeches, President Trump declared his campaign and presidency would be about three things: "Jobs, jobs, and jobs." That resonated profoundly with the millions of Americans affected by awful trade agreements, open-border policies, and greed. The Left is out of touch with reality, and further out of touch with what made America great. They do not seem to grasp that by simply having an opportunity, a chance, lives can be transformed. Families can be invigorated. Entire communities can thrive.

Hillary campaigned on ideals opposite to these principles.

I've traveled all over the country. And I've seen the places that were once brilliant little communities, that have been totally hollowed out through a loss of jobs and shattered economic opportunity. Throughout the election campaign I had the feeling that Donald Trump had also seen something similar, had spent time talking to the people who face these difficulties day by day. They didn't want a handout or another government program, they only wanted a chance.

Liberals are still clinging to "how qualified" Clinton was. And how "ignorant" Trump and his supporters are. I am still an entirely unaware of what "qualifications" the Left was speaking of. Hillary is the wife of a former President, and used those political connections to become a Senator and Secretary of State. Almost without exception, every single thing Hillary has been involved in has turned into a scandal or a disaster of some sort. Her "qualifications" appear to be little more than having caused so much destruction and manipulation that people finally lost track of the reasons she's so unfit. Even so, the election was far more important than the transgressions of Clinton.

Indeed, what the global Left fails to grasp is that the 2016 election had almost nothing to do with Hillary Clinton and Donald Trump. Don't get me wrong, Donald Trump was possibly the only man who could have taken on the Democrats, the establishment Republicans, the media, the special interest groups, the globalists, the entertainment industry, and the social media all together, and *still* won. But the election was larger than Trump, too. The election went beyond Left and Right. This election was about nationalism verse globalism, truth verses lies. In a sense, it was almost the manifestation of the eternal conflict between good and evil.

When Donald Trump proclaimed, "We're going to start saying Merry Christmas again," the Left did not understand the significance of that phrase. And why would they? Their religion is that of totalitarian Liberalism, they believe in nothing higher than their own egos. For many of us, it was a welcomed sign. It had actually been years since somebody in a store or market had said "Merry Christmas" to me. Always "happy holidays," all through December. I do not live or shop in areas with an abundance of people that do not celebrate Christmas. Nor do I remotely look like I might celebrate any other holiday in December. Nor did the people saying "happy holidays" appear to celebrate anything other than Christmas. 92 percent of Americans celebrate Christmas; why did we as a society decide that those 8 percent matter so much, that we wouldn't want to burden them with *our* traditions? How absurd and ethnomasochistic. Any society that would tolerate this sort of subversion is hardly a society worth saving. This is the tyranny of political correctness: a small group of hostile foreigners can come into our nation, and tell us how we are supposed to behave and how we are supposed to celebrate our own traditions. For many Americans, myself included, December 2016 was the first time, in a long time, that people in stores said what they *should* have been saying all along: Merry Christmas.

All of these small actions by Donald Trump added up to something tremendous. And Liberals don't see it. They are perfectly happy living in a society that shuns their own traditions, that sacrifices their own holidays to the false god of "inclusion." If saying Merry Christmas is mortally offensive to any person or group, I'm sure we can raise the money to fund their repatriation.

The leaked emails proved that the media and the Democratic National Committee work together to shape a simply deceptive narrative. A vote for Hillary was the same as a vote for the hostile global elite that constantly undermines our interest and sovereignty. This election was not about two personalities: it was about keeping the experiment that is America out of the hands of tyrants.

The election was a revolt against globalist policies, against open borders, against a loss of rights, a total rejection of the Liberal narrative, and outright denial of their "progress." The 2016 election was the start of a revolution.

The 2016 election was a total rejection of Liberals telling us that every little thing we do or believe is racist, xenophobic, and offensive. There is nothing at all wrong with preserving a nation, or with fighting the regressive Left and Cultural Marxism. Arrogant Liberals claim to be well educated, but I've realized they know nothing of global politics, nor have they ever read any of the texts that inspired the American Revolution. They have a shallow and narrow view, shaped by distortions. The depth of their political understanding generally lies a few pages within *The Communist Manifesto*, and with what the TV tells them to believe.

Their time is over. We are rejecting their degenerate culture, we are rejecting the false gods of tolerance and egalitarianism, we are rejecting the tyranny of political correctness and social justice.

We are tired their "safe space" culture, their obsession with herding invaders into our homeland, insisting they belong here as if they built the nation. All while our tax dollars are stolen to fund this attempt to replace us and to make us exiles in our own lands. We are tired of the Left policing our thoughts and our language, tired of their unilateral decision that certain words are "problematic" and "harmful."

This election was the outright rejection of the constant multiculturalism, the rampant degeneracy, and the insolence of the lying press.

The Left did not realize that it was their own arrogance and feigned superiority that brought this down on them. They seem to have learned nothing. They certainly have not learned that the constant lecturing from the media, the news, and "celebrities" (read: court jesters), is no longer welcome. Nobody cares if during yet *another* self-congratulatory, séance of self-polluting Liberal "entertainers," everyone moans about how the *indispensable* "Hollywood, foreigners, and the press are so vilified." In fact, I'm rather certain most of us would gladly deport the entire lot of them, save for perhaps Mel Gibson, Christopher Nolan, and a handful of others. The film industry, as with the entertainment industry as a whole, has been a stunning heap of rubbish for years, with one or two gleaming exceptions scattered through the abyss that is modern "art." Yet if we kick out Hollywood, foreigners, and the press, all we'll have left is football, they tell us.[2] If I had to trade all of Hollywood, foreigners, and the press, for a sport I almost never even watch anyway, I would gladly make the deal.

Films were once used to entertain, to enlighten, to tell a story. Now they are mostly propagandist garbage. The Left lost because they are so out of touch with reality, so self-absorbed, so arrogant, that they honestly forgot how little they matter to us. Not only do they not matter, we have become tired of listening to anything that comes out of their lying, insolent mouths. We are tired of being lectured by Hillary, Obama, Bernie, our peers at school, work, and professors, for our "privilege" and our differing views.

This is only the beginning of Americans rejecting their safe space culture, their obsession with allowing invaders into this nation, their welfare state, and their total war on our most fundamental values.

After losing, the Left has rioted, sought re-counts, made threats to Electors, and threatened and initiated violence against their political foes; and now, some are seeking impeachment. Al Green and Maxine Waters, for instance, are two members of Congress that have been very vocal about their goal to impeach President Trump.[3] [4] Had two white members of Congress sought the impeachment of Barack Obama, I have no doubt

2 Christie D'Zurilla and Jessica Roy. "Meryl Streep: Without 'vilified' Hollywood, there'd be nothing but football and MMA" Los Angeles Times. January 08, 2017. http://www.latimes.com/entertainment/la-et-golden-globes-2017-live-hollywood-s-president-meryl-streep-1483933196-htmlstory.html.

3 Miranda Green. "Congressman calls for Trump's impeachment" CNN. May 17, 2017. http://www.cnn.com/2017/05/17/politics/al-green-impeachment-call/index.html. [http://archive.li/m8bLa]

4 Vanessa Williams. "'Auntie Maxine' and the quest for impeachment" The Washington Post. May 01, 2017. https://www.washingtonpost.com/politics/auntie-maxine-and-the-quest-for-impeachment/2017/04/29/38a26816-2476-11e7-a1b3-faff0034e2de_story.html. [http://archive.li/Nvr6R]

they would have been immediately denounced as racists. When two black members of Congress incessantly attack President Trump, they are lauded as heroes. When Jewish congressman Steven Cohen introduced articles of impeachment, nobody thought of the ethnic dynamic at play.[5] Yet when any Jewish person is criticized, no matter how legitimate the critique may be, it is immediately dismissed as antisemitism. But if we lived in a white supremacist society, would whites really be the only people who could be attacked regularly with impunity?

The Left is engaging in sedition. It is subverting the political will of the American people. Millions of men and women supported Trump because they wanted something different. Because they wanted another path. A path that only Donald Trump even had the courage to *speak* of. If the Left had their way, had stopped Electors from voting for Trump, or if they are successful in ousting Trump from office, what message would that send? What would it say to the millions of people that rejected the dogma of political correctness? The people that no longer want to participate in the globalist scheme of domination and demographic replacement? The people that want sovereign borders and lower taxes, that want to defend those inalienable rights that the Left so rabidly despises?

What choice would remain to us, if the Left renders our votes worthless? What the Left still fails to grasp is that this isn't about *them* anymore. This is about patriots taking our country back. And this might never be about *them* again. If they still insist on trying to destroy and rebuild the country in their wicked image, our backs will be against the wall.

The days and weeks after the election I constantly heard from my Liberal classmates, the news, and social media, about how afraid they were following Trump's (and, I might add, America's) triumph. *The Huffington Post* ran the article, "It's Not 'Melodramatic' To Fear For Our Safety After This Election. This is real."[6] According to a November 2016 Gallup Poll

5 Emily Tillett. "Rep. Steve Cohen introduces articles of impeachment against Trump." CBS News. November 15, 2017. www.cbsnews.com/news/rep-steve-cohen-introduces-new-articles-of-impeachment-against-trump/. [http://archive.li/ntIZZ]

6 Jenavieve Hatch. "It's Not 'Melodramatic' To Fear For Our Safety After This Election" The Huffington Post. November 10, 2016. http://www.huffingtonpost.com/entry/its-not-melodramatic-to-fear-for-our-safety-after-this-election_us_5823831ce4b0d9ce6fc08f1c. [http://archive.li/TjFoW]

that asked people to describe the emotions they had been feeling, 76 percent of Clinton voters reported feeling afraid, 66 percent devastated, and 58 percent angry.[7]

Many articles were published with sniveling claims of antisemitism, citing fake hate crimes.[8] I heard that Muslims all over my campus and all over the country were afraid to wear their hijabs in public. Liberals all over my campus were in tears the day after the election. Many were so grief stricken and scared they did not even come to class until the following week. They were genuinely afraid. They still are.

And they should be.

Deep down they know this election was a reaction to their sick behavior. It was the reaction of people like me, who are tired of seeing dozens of women in hijabs anywhere I go, foreigners that my tax dollars go to feed and house. Tired of my tax dollars paying for the murder of babies. Tired of being told I'm uneducated and ignorant because I do not blindly accept a warped Leftist ideology. This is the reaction when you call people like me a racist merely for asking *why*—why 85 percent of interracial crime involves blacks attacking whites, why nearly 100 percent of interracial rapes are white women being raped by non-whites.

The Left had a good ride. But they pushed too far this time by trying to anoint Commissar Clinton. Their violence, censorship, endless migration, and insolence has more than worn out its welcome.

They deserve no empathy. They have constantly attacked us, chipping away at our rights. They have abused us for years, calling us bigots, uneducated, ignorant, saying we "cling to our guns and religion." And for the first time in a very long time, we have finally said "enough."

The Liberal proles, politicians, and media spoke of the "flyover states" and "the rust belt," with the same sort of unmitigated disdain with which the

7 Jim Norman. "Trump Victory Surprises Americans; Four in 10 Afraid" Gallup. November 11, 2016. http://www.gallup.com/poll/197375/trump-victory-surprises-americans-four-afraid.aspx. [http://archive.li/zN1Cm]

8 Charlie Allenson. "Being a Jew in Trump's America." The Huffington Post. March 16, 2017. www.huffingtonpost.com/entry/being-a-jew-in-trumps-america_us_58cab208e4b07112b6472b50. [http://archive.li/6hmjl]

Bolsheviks talked about the Kulaks prior to exterminating them. They displayed an open air of superiority, hostility, and haughty contempt for us. Yet they were still somehow shocked when we wouldn't give their Chosen One the presidency. They were still shocked that we had the audacity, the *nerve*, to refuse to hand our country over to them.

Hillary said that the NRA, gun owners, and Republicans are her *enemies*. And now the losing Left wants quarter from us? After declaring war on our way of life?

Liberals have been terrified of losing their power. Much of their fear comes from knowing, deep down, that they are guilty of so many crimes against us and our people. For years, Liberals have been stepping on the snake and poking the bear; what they are really afraid of is a well deserved retaliation. On some primordial level, they know that their transgressions merit righteous retribution.

Throughout this book I have repeatedly asked the rhetorical questions: What if the roles were reversed? What if the Right was instituting laws that would fine and imprison people for "hate speech" against white people, or speaking out against Right-wing views? How would the Left feel if every time they went to hear a speech at a university, they were violently attacked by Right-wing hordes? How would the Left feel if every single time a cop killed a white man, we burned cities to the ground? Or if every last time one of them raped or killed one of us, we destroyed their neighborhoods?

And what if one day, instead of merely asking "what if," we turned the tables on the Left? That is the reason they are terrified.

In a sense I understand their fear. Historically, our level of organized violence surpasses all others. Our kind is not easily moved. It took 400 years of Islamic terror before the Crusades were launched. American colonists endured years of provocations from the King and Parliament before they finally grabbed their rifles. But when we finally move — when we finally say enough is enough, the entire world trembles.

The Left recognizes all of this. Now that we have seen the unmasked disdain the Left has for us, we can never let them win. If they were ever to gain power again, they would do everything possible to ensure we never have another chance to save our nation.

This much, at least, is clear: the debate is over. The last appeal to reason has been made. The lines have been drawn. We will not win this war by being silent, peaceful, docile, compromising, and diplomatic. Those who take no sides will be forgotten — or perhaps remembered as history's most despicable cowards. The situation is desperate; the coming times require formidable men with hardened hearts. Those with unflinching eyes and an unyielding resolve will be the iron guard through the long night, so keep your lamps burning. It's time to burn the ships. The reality we face is grim. There will be no second chances. And if we are to fail, let us fail while daring greatly. Let us dance into the fire with pride in our hearts, not scurrying off the ship like a pack of rats. If we are to finally be overwhelmed, let us go down as the greatest generation of Europeans, the last legionnaires raging against the dying light.

And if we succeed? Those of us who chose to ride the tiger will have statues built of us in the squares of our revived cities and towns. Which way, Western man? Our finest hour awaits.

11

Tomorrow We Live

Reclaiming our birthright and securing the future requires a number of things, including first of all the dismantling of the perverse state that has been created through corrupt Liberal principles. The Left has been remarkably successful at infiltrating and controlling nearly every aspect of society; they long ago mastered the long march through the institutions. Despite their institutional stronghold, despite their endless propaganda through the mainstream media, despite their flooding our nations with more interlopers and invaders, we are still staving off their hordes. Now is our last chance to wreak total havoc on their century-long insurrection.

Every single institution they have infiltrated needs razed. Everything they control needs gutted. Every position they have taken needs stripped.

Our previous efforts to stop the Left have failed. Despite maintaining a strong number of Republican seats in American government, our elected officials have done nothing but cower before the Left. Almost 100 years after The New Deal, Republicans have almost completely failed to rein in the welfare state. The so-called "Right-wing" was unable to stop or even to repeal the disastrous 1965 Immigration Act, or Lyndon Johnson's Great Society; in truth, it has not even made an adequate attempt in this direction. I'm not sure if the elected Republicans are the world's greatest cowards, the world's greatest idiots, or the world's greatest betrayers. Nearly all of them remind me of Emmanuel Goldstein from *1984*: controlled opposition to give the illusion of a free choice. Do Republicans exist merely to make us *think* we have some say in this grand scheme? Clearly, modern conservatism and the Grand Old Party are insufficient to win this war. If the mainstream Republicans will not take their gloves off and help us win, they need to be replaced with those who are not interested in being part of a managerial state, not interested in what foreign interlopers have to say, and not interested in bowing obsequiously to the Left at every turn.

Sadly, that appears to be a dying breed of nobility, nearly extinct. But I still have a glimmer of faith.

Modern conservatism as a political project is entirely worthless. What have these conservatives been able to conserve? They have not been able to conserve our tax dollars, our borders, our soldiers' lives, the lives lost from the opioid epidemic, our culture — nothing. They were not even able to "conserve" a safe bathroom for children. To be a "conservative" in this day and age has become laughable.

The cowardly eunuchs who still wear the name "conservatives" have been utterly useless in stopping the Leftist onslaught. Mass migration is out of control, taxation is more oppressive than ever, infrastructure is crumbling before our eyes, people need jobs — and these "conservatives" have been sitting around doing nothing. The fight needs to be taken to the Left, on their turf. We cannot just wait around and then, at the eleventh hour suddenly awaken to try to stop them.

This will take some difficult decisions, and our conservatives have clearly shown that they do not have the stomach. This will take men with hardened hearts. We must finally realize that there is *no* true Right-wing party in the US. This fight is between the real Right on the one hand and the Leftist cabal which has enveloped the majority of the Republican party on the other. If it were up to me, I would be at the border myself, riding in a Jeep with a rifle at my side, or dragging the architects of all the conflicts from Vietnam to the Iraq war out of their homes in the middle of the night to face a true court of law. Those who wish to spill our blood and treasure to fight wars for the vaguest of reasons are guilty of treason and must be brought to justice.

Until somebody is willing to face the grim reality of what must be done, we are sitting ducks.

The lying press has been seen without its mask. The American people are waking up to who is standing behind the curtain. Mainstream media *is* fake news. Its makers lie, manipulate, manufacture stories, edit film and audio to present a totally fabricated reality. We must act in consequence. Find independent sources. Stop letting them feed you rubbish. Turn off the TV. Find journalists that aren't on the payroll of the five or six conglomerates that control the narrative. There are some amazing nationalist and dissident writers, journalists, podcasts, shows, and documentary makers. Seek them out. It'll be worth your time.

The media oligopoly needs shattering. Five or six companies controlling nearly all information is a disaster for freedom of expression and the freedom of press. There is no "free" radio anymore — not when one company owns the majority of radio stations across the country. Trust-busting and media regulation need to make a resurgence, so that the American people can once again have access to reliable information.

Read banned and "beyond the pale" books. Things that have been blacklisted by box stores and large online retailers are often a good place to start. They aren't as bad as what they would have you believe; on the contrary, censorship these days is almost a recommendation. Find the most far-out book you can, and give it a shot. The more that the mainstream bourgeois and the Left despises them, the better they are. Trust me. And read old books too. Things you don't come across often — the books written by the men who built civilization, not those by the ones trying to tear it down.

Learn as much as you can. American education has become a joke. Instead of teaching the propaganda conspiracy theory of white privilege to young and impressionable children, the school system should be inspiring the next generation. We have an education system that spends an entire year teaching nothing but the Holocaust, told exclusively from the Jewish perspective, and the Atlantic Slave Trade in order to peddle white guilt. This is done, of course, by design. The "architect" of the Common Core Initiative is David Coleman, whose Jewish values, belief system, and upbringing all influenced Common Core standards, which are adopted by schools the nation over. "Very few people in America today are having a bigger influence on what kids are learning than David Coleman."[1]

1 Joy Resmovits. "David Coleman, the Most Influential Education Figure You've Never Heard Of." The Forward. August 25, 2013. https://forward.com/culture/182587/david-coleman-the-most-influential-education-figur/. [http://archive.is/vYcOp].

Coleman was one of *Times*' 100 most influential people in the world in 2013.[2] It is no accident that the United States Holocaust Memorial Museum makes recommendations to Common Core reading.[3] *Night* by Elie Wiesel is forced upon children from a very early age, *The Diary of Anne Frank* comes shortly thereafter alongside *The Book Thief*, followed by Wiesel's lecture, "Hope, Despair and Memory."[4] Currently, ten US states have laws that mandate Holocaust education in schools.[5]

American children of European stock are graduating high school with a far better grasp of recent Jewish history than of their own. Children are taught all about the Atlantic Slave Trade, shown *Amistad* and *Roots*, but never learn of their own European ancestors being sold into slavery and sex trafficking by Arab and Jewish slavers to other Middle Easterners.[6] These educational trends have wrought an unprecedented level of discord and obfuscation. The entire education system needs rebuilding from the ground up.

Instead of using Rothenberg's *White Privilege: Essential Readings on the Other Side of Racism* as a textbook, schools and universities should be using Taylor's *White Identity* and Kemp's *March of the Titans: A History of the White Race* to educate our children — to inspire them, to show them the proud and heroic traditions of their ancestors, as should be the proper role of a people's education.

---

2 Jeb Bush. "The 2013 TIME 100." Time. April 18, 2013. time100.time.com/2013/04/18/time-100/slide/david-coleman/. [http://archive.li/zCmqo]

3 "Common Core Reading Standards." United States Holocaust Memorial Museum. Accessed April 20, 2018. https://www.ushmm.org/educators/lesson-plans/redefining-how-we-teach-propaganda/standards [https://archive.is/di0Ws].

4 Alan Singer. "Common Core and the Holocaust." The Huffington Post. March 14, 2014. www.huffingtonpost.com/alan-singer/common-core-holocaust_b_4964319.html. [https://archive.is/XE5L3].

5 "Push by Catholic Educator Makes Holocaust Studies Mandatory in Kentucky Schools" Jewish Telegraphic Agency. March 26, 2018. https://www.jta.org/2018/03/26/news-opinion/push-catholic-educator-makes-holocaust-studies-mandatory-kentucky-schools.

6 Mikhail Kizilov. "Slaves, Money Lenders, and Prisoner Guards: The Jews and the Trade in Slaves and Captives in the Crimean Khanate." Journal of Jewish Studies, vol. 58, no. 2, Jan. 2007, pp. 189–210., doi:10.18647/2730/jjs-2007.

> Since it is so likely that children will meet cruel enemies, let them at least have heard of brave knights and heroic courage. Otherwise you are making their destiny not brighter but darker.
>
> —C.S. Lewis

So far as immigration policy goes, the Hart-Celler Act should have never even been introduced to Congress. It's clear that Emanuel Celler and those involved introduced the bill with hostile motives and bad intentions. That 1965 Immigration Act didn't just open the flood gates to mass migration, it tore those gates from their hinges. As a result of the Act, we have virtually no limitations on migration. It doesn't matter where people are from, what their skills are or their education (if any) or if they will need welfare immediately upon arriving. There are virtually no standards to becoming an American at this point. None.

To make matters worse, subversive organizations, such as the Hebrew Immigration Aid Society (HIAS), receive federal tax dollars to go get migrants in their home countries, bring them to the US, and "resettle" them here. HIAS and similar organization have brought in countless invaders, and we have paid to introduce them into our communities.[7] A majority of course are on welfare, costing $64,000 house and feed for their first few years in the US. This is not only unsustainable, it is entirely unconscionable. Between the Hart-Celler Immigration Act and non-government organizations, the Left is insuring that America will eventually reach a billion inhabitants, most of which will be non-white. It will up to us to repeal the Immigration Act of 1965, and to let HIAS know how little we appreciate their efforts to replace us, and the abuse of our tax dollars these efforts have entailed.

These so called "migrant crises" are all Liberal fiction, propaganda narratives, and they will never end. The African and Arab population is growing without limit, with no signs of slowing down, and every indication of exploding in the coming decades. There will always be hordes of

7 Aaron Klein. "U.S. Funded Group Behind Rabbis Urging Refugee Intake" Breitbart. December 03, 2015. http://www.breitbart.com/immigration/2015/12/03/exclusive-state-department-un-funded-group-behind-1000-rabbis-urging-u-s-refugee-intake/. [http://archive.li/JKfsY]

foreigners pressing on our borders, just as there always have been. There should be no Western plan to handle this "crisis," either, other than steady men armed to the teeth standing our borders. It is not *our* problem if certain groups spend more time reproducing than they do working or farming to feed their families. Expecting the West to feed and house the world is criminally unfair. The welfare state is being expanded globally before our eyes while many politicians throughout Europe and America tell us there is nothing we can do, that it is inevitable, and we must foot the bill.

Really? Nothing we can do? If you gave me a few good men, some trucks, and a few rifles, I could stop the invaders from storming our gates tonight. It wouldn't take much. I guarantee it.

Foreign aid needs to be ended, and the borders closed. Taking in endless numbers of needy or greedy migrants is suicidal while we are trying ourselves to recover. Migration should be completely abolished until every single American that wants to work has a job, and until the national debt is zero. Our current system shamelessly puts Americans last, behind every single person that makes it to our shores and across our borders. There is no moral justification for this. We must first secure the well-being of Americans before even considering what foreign governments or peoples might need.

Birthright citizenship needs to be ended. It is an absurd concept to begin with — this wild notion that a Mexican kid born in Texas after his nine-month pregnant mom jumped the border, is every bit as much an American, and deserves the same vote and the same rights, as somebody whose family fought in the Revolution. 300,000 or more anchor babies are born in the US each year, accounting for around 10 percent of all births. They are able to receive government services and vote when they come of age. They have no connection to us and will only vote for those who promise open borders and amnesty. Their allegiance will always lie with their own people, not ours. This is perhaps the one thing we could stand to learn from them.

All welfare to migrants must be ended, and all illegals deported. Migrants presently on welfare must be given a choice: get off welfare and get a job, or have their citizenship stripped and deported. Those who live with illegals should be held accountable for aiding and abetting them, and either jailed or deported right along side them. After all, we wouldn't want to separate families.

Many of those who have been granted citizenship have made it abundantly clear that they hate us. Repatriation programs and incentives should be awarded to all those willing to go back to their rightful homelands. Due to the net drain on the tax payers represented by their presence here, every single person, man, woman, and child, that has come to the US post-1965 should be offered a one-time payout to renounce their citizenship, leave, and never come back. *We* will save money in the long run, and *they* will finally be able to live among their own, as they so evidently desire.

Dual citizens should not be eligible to hold any sort of public office, or to vote in our elections. They have somewhere else they can always go if our nation becomes uninhabitable to them for whatever reason. They will therefore vote for their personal interests, which very often will not correspond to those of our own citizens, for they have no necessary stake in this nation or loyalty to our people.

The wall needs to be built, and needs to be visible from outer space; that must be the measure of our resolve. All amnesty must be ended. The idea of thinking we can continue to have a fundamentally American nation with the population demographics of Mexico and South America is a fantasy not based in reality. California amnesty did not secure Republican votes, it simply turned California into a state that Republicans will never win again. Once we are a minority and can no longer win elections, the nation will turn into another hell hole like Mexico or any given South American nation. The misguided hope that somehow, someday, foreigners will become American is an absurdity that sooner or later will cost us our country. Even after several generations, most non-whites still vote Left. They always will. They are not going to somehow decide that low taxation, smaller government, free speech, and less welfare, is in their best interest. Not when over half of them are benefiting from those government services.

The civic nationalist types that place misguided hope in the idea that the majority of non-whites will somehow be won over to the Right are living in a fantasy world. They are soft globalists without even realizing it. The same is true of those who support so called "legal" immigration; they are still doing nothing but supporting open-border mass migration and population replacement. The only difference is that their plan will delay the demise of the West by a mere decade or two. In an effort to be inoffensive and inclusive, they are risking everything they hold dear. Their sky castles will come crashing down on their heads, sooner even than they could imagine.

Civic nationalists promote the image of America as a melting pot in which non-whites somehow simultaneously retain their ethnic identities and act in a way befitting this country and its history. They have the bizarre idea that the Founding Fathers mutually pledged their "lives, fortunes, and sacred honor" to each other to create a "homeland for all." They therefore explicitly reject the Founding Fathers view of what it means to be an American, as well as nearly 175 years of law that limited immigration to white Europeans.

Here is the end result of their civic nationalism: white families paying a third of their income in taxes, so we can feed, house, clothe, and "educate" a family of seven Somalis, which will have twice the voting power as the white family that is funding them. Civic nationalism is the ideology that Africans flying into JFK airport, picked up by their HIAS representative, and driven to their newly furnished apartment, are just as American as the descendants of a family that came here on a fifty-day boat ride from England with a few pence in their pockets.

One of the most foundational tasks of all governments everywhere for as long as governments have existed has been to secure and maintain borders. The once great Western Roman Empire, spanning continents and centuries, fell, not because of a superior rival, nor through total war, as so many others have: Rome fell as a result of the barbarians she herself let pass through her gates.

There is an absurdity creeping around this topic. A sort of dramatic irony lurking in the shadows, an irony I was never able to put into words. Never, that is, until I happened to stumble upon a documentary about strife in Africa, which showed me something incredible — African warlords, with sixty year-old AK-47s, that are able to secure informal territorial borders, while the most well-funded military in human history cannot stop low-skilled Mexicans from invading the USA. Anyone who believes that this is anything other than a deliberate policy decision is deluding himself.

The US government as well as the governments of Europe are *choosing* not to enforce our borders. They are *choosing* to use our tax dollars to help fund the invasion. This raises several questions: What does our military actually defend, other than the government's ability to mendaciously and malevolently replace the founding stock of the nation? What do our "leaders" really care for us, for the citizens, and what can we do about it? And how would a foreign occupation look any different than what we are presently experiencing? Men swarming a country, securing territory, installing their own people as government officials, murdering and raping the native population, and looting coffers—*every aspect* of our present "immigration policy" mirrors invasion by a hostile army, rather than a rational policy choice made by people with the concerns of their citizens in mind.

The reason African warlords with sixty year-old AK-47s are able to maintain territorial borders is quite simple: *will*. They are not afraid to use those rifles. The cost of protecting our borders, whatever it may be, is less than the cost of being subjected to millions of crimes, being subjected to rape, murder, drug epidemics, and supporting a de facto invasion via welfare. Perhaps our government and the majority of our fellow citizens do not see this war for what this really is. But we should begin to act according to the reality of our situation.

Many have remarked that my view is hyperbolic or extreme. I disagree. You cannot save your nation from destruction by thrusting your head under the sand while your nation is overrun by adversaries, whom your leaders happily usher in.

Due to unnatural and hostile demographic shifts, mass-deportations should be the norm to expel the invaders. When we are facing down our demographic demise, in our own homelands, nothing should be off the table. If loading them up in cattle cars by gun-point is necessary, so be it. If using force against invaders as they run across the border is what it will take to send a message that this land is not up for grabs, fine.

The hordes of migrants and their children, along with the vast majority of non-white US citizens, do not care at all about liberty or the foundations of our nation. They come here as welfare tourists. They are mere paper citizens. They come for benefits and handouts acting from an entirely selfish paradigm, without fail. They do nothing but drag us down. We do not need them, we never have. They are nothing but the albatross around our necks, who keep us from what truly matters — achieving Imperium.

In the 2016 president election, we only won because of the white vote. Without that, our country would have been lost. Over 70 percent of blacks, Hispanics, Asians, Jews, and Muslims voted for Clinton.[8] They voted, that is to say, for fundamentally un-American policies. They voted for gun control, hate speech laws, open borders, mass migration, amnesty, more taxation, and a bigger government. They all voted directly against our interests. Against our values. Against the Western tradition.

Since 1965, fifty-nine *million* migrants have come to the US (not counting the children they have once here), dragging the white population from nearly 90 percent to nearly 60 percent in only half a century. There will be a projected 441 million residents of the US in 2065, up from the 324 million currently. Of those 117 million new "Americans," 103 million will be due to non-white mass migration. Sometime around 2040, whites will drop below 50 percent of the population, ensuring that the election of somebody running a campaign based on *our* interests, will never happen again.[9]

White America is the last vanguard against the Liberal cataclysm looming large on the horizon. The last bastion standing in the way of the mongrel hordes upon us. Without us, there will be nothing left but an apocalyptic future in which the darkness of the Third World covers the Earth.

We have an intrinsic right to maintain our own homelands and our own culture, without either of these precious heirlooms being altered by foreign invaders.

All international organizations are inherently dangerous to our individual liberties and the sovereignty of our nations. NATO, the United

---

8 Jon Huang, Samuel Jacoby, Michael Strickland, and K.K. Rebecca Lai. "Election 2016: Exit Polls" The New York Times. November 08, 2016. https://www.nytimes.com/interactive/2016/11/08/us/politics/election-exit-polls.html. [http://archive.li/0qJst]

9 "Modern Immigration Wave Brings 59 Million to U.S., Driving Population Growth and Change Through 2065" Pew Research Center's Hispanic Trends Project. September 28, 2015. http://www.pewhispanic.org/2015/09/28/modern-immigration-wave-brings-59-million-to-u-s-driving-population-growth-and-change-through-2065/. [http://archive.li/GN67z]

Nations, the European Union, Paris Climate Accords — all of them are totalitarian tools to facilitate globalism. Together, they siphon billions of tax dollars from us, giving us nothing in return but misery, debt, and the loss of our rights. The highest power in the land shall be granted to the people, not some unelected cabal of men running the planet from the shadows. The US must depart from all such organizations, and seek their abolishment.

All domestic organizations engaging in sedition need dismantled. The Anti-Defamation League and Southern Poverty Law Center both work with law enforcement and politicians. This is a radical miscarriage of justice and a case of textbook subversion. Both groups are supremacist in nature, and they are far from partisan; they mislead, lie, and create far more hatred than they have ever stopped. Both organizations seek to forward their agenda, influence public policy, attack their enemies, all while collecting tens of millions of dollars in the process. Both organizations collect mountains of data on US citizens; the ADL has been found illegally spying on American citizens, and both have harassed people personally for their political views. They both seek the firing, blacklisting, and defamation of people they disagree with.[10] The ADL and SPLC are well-funded political terrorist organizations. Nothing more. Not a single person working for either of these organizations is American. Not one.

The ADL and SPLC spend more time ghost-hunting "white supremacists" than they do focusing on the groups that are actually damaging property, rioting, attacking, and murdering people. Groups like this have no place in our society.

When we speak of returning to our roots and reviving the American and European spirit, it may sound grandiose. People seem to think we are merely selling a dream, something out in the void with no real meaning. But we can look back on our history we can find specific moments that marked striking deviations from the path that we needed to be on.

Even if you never questioned the specifics of how we might find our way home, you always knew something was wrong. You could feel it in

10 Richard C. Paddock. "New Details of Extensive ADL Spy Operation Emerge : Inquiry: Transcripts reveal nearly 40 years of espionage by a man who infiltrated political groups." Los Angeles Times. April 13, 1993. articles.latimes.com/1993-04-13/news/mn-22383_1_spy-operation/2. [http://archive.li/S8czd]

your bones. Something about this "new" America bothered you, something was never quite right. "Like a splinter in your mind, driving you mad." That splinter is the persistent feeling that we've been sold out, that we are being replaced; it is the feeling of a paradise lost.

America was great first and foremost because of the tremendous freedoms we enjoyed. And although we still have greater freedoms in relative terms than most other nations of the world, we are a long way from home. Ending the income tax, property taxes, the National Firearms Act, the National Security Agency, and the Immigration Act of 1965 would be a great start.

Gun rights should be restored to the point that, unless you're prohibited from buying a firearm, you should be able to legally carry and travel with a firearm. There should be no government-required permission-slip to exercise your fundamental rights. Peaceable journey laws should be the rule, not the exception.

I've often been mocked by Liberals with the sneering question, "When was America *ever* great?" They would often throw in something along the lines of, "What, do you want to go back to when you could own slaves and beat your wife?"

No. I'm not interested in owning anybody, nor beating anybody either. I just want my country back, the way it was meant to be. Before the government spied on us, before a third of our income was stripped away annually, before we were reduced to serfs on our own land, before we were forced to fund the arrival of migrants that will never assimilate, and have neither the capacity nor the intention to carry on our culture.

I would like to see politicians act more like Teddy Roosevelt and Andrew Jackson in their strong attitude towards large banks, corporations, and foreigners. Mine is more of an economic third position, with the aim of benefiting the people in a nation, rather than corporate and foreign interests. I would like to see openly nationalist, isolationist, and protectionist policies from our leaders. If companies want to use foreign sweatshop labor to make fatter profits or bring in foreign workers on H-1B visas, they should be forced to show cause or face high tariffs. Our economy is not a true "free market" anyway; we have a mixed economy, and that mix of governmental involvement should always lean towards protection, not fatter profits. After all, the fundamental purpose of a government, the reason governments have ever been formed, is to protect its citizens.

Big tech corporations that silence people under terms and conditions should be regulated by federal legislation, as should companies engaging in communication services. You cannot be denied access to electricity or phone service due to ideology; you should not be censored online either. The US government should indeed step in to ensure we are able to speak freely when a hostile clique is actively stifling our thoughts. When a handful of private companies can control who has a voice and who does not, we no longer have freedom of speech in practice, only in theory.[11]

There is a cyber-oligarchy in place, consisting of social media platforms, search engines, web hosting services, and internet service providers; these together can control practically the entire realm of information access for the majority of internet users. If they choose to de-platform a person or ideology, it can be done within hours — as we have seen. A small clique of technocrats are able to entirely dismantle freedom of speech in practice, and only allow what they deem to be approved speech to be seen and heard. Social media and the internet form the new public forum; they should be treated as such.

Those who argue these companies have the "right" to censor whomever they wish are arguing in very bad faith. Private companies are subjected to thousands of federal regulations as is. There is moreover a tremendous legal precedent for actions as invasive as eminent domain and regulatory takings, all justified as "public use." Light-touch legislation to guarantee digital equal access based on political ideology is arguably less extreme than the legal favoritism of current protected classes under the Civil Rights Act, and far less restrictive than what people are told they can and cannot do with their own private homes and property under the Fair Housing Act. There is also already a body of case law that supports the notion that public forums, although owned privately, should be compelled to allow lawful speech on their premises.[12]

---

11 Josh Smith. Transcript of "Shall Not Censor" interview with Josh Smith. 2017. (On file with author.)

12 James D. Barger. "Extending Speech Rights into Virtual Worlds." The SciTech Lawyer, vol. 7, no. 1, 2010, pp. 18–22.

Tech companies in concert with the ADL have been suspending, banning, and demonetizing Right-wing content solely for political gain. They manipulate search results as well as "trending" topics, all in a conscious effort to warp the political discourse. The danger this poses is clear and present.

Terms of service should not be used to prohibit Americans from saying totally legal things, just because it might hurt somebody's feelings or go against the hegemonic status quo.

Soon, people are going to be denied the most basic of rights by companies claiming that obscure "terms of services" were violated. Under current federal civil rights law, a grocery store cannot deny you service for being of a certain race or sexual orientation. But they can deny you service for being Right-wing. It has already been suggested that banks should prohibit customers from buying firearms with their debit or credit cards, as a way to curb gun sales.[13] What happens when merchant banks decide to close accounts for those having the wrong views, as PayPal has already done? Or when gas stations and grocery store chains decide not to sell to anybody on a blacklist of political dissidents? These questions, among others, show glaring problems in the "free market," when that market is run by elements hostile to the founding stock of our nation. Anybody who does not participate in the destruction of the West is seen as a pariah; soon, they will be excommunicated entirely.

We need an American Renaissance. Society has been progressing further into degenerate filth and the effects are becoming clear. Never in human history have we had such easy access to food, such easy access to information, such opportunity. Yet what have recent generations become? The first to live shorter, less healthful lives than their parents. Despite having constant, year-round access to fresh fruit, meats, and vegetables; despite being relatively richer than almost any other in history; despite having more information at its fingertips than has ever been contained in any single physical library, my generation has become wretched and pathetic. Internet access gives us the ability to search through the entirety of human accomplishment and knowledge, thousands of years of writings

---

13 Andrew Ross Sorkin. "How Banks Could Control Gun Sales If Washington Won't." The New York Times. February 19, 2018. https://www.nytimes.com/2018/02/19/business/banks-gun-sales.html. [http://archive.li/XFmR9]

in our pockets. Is my generation the most intelligent or well-informed in consequence? No. It uses that unparalleled power to become addicted to pornography, to waste precious time in elaborate virtual Skinner boxes, scrolling endlessly through mindless social media sites. Never in history has any group of people squandered so many beautiful days.

This is the result of Liberalism, the ideology that seeks to make us all equal, ensuring that everybody gets a trophy. This is the result of the modern feminism that seeks to undermine masculine traits and destroy the family unit. This is big pharmacy drugging up an entire generation of boys merely for acting like boys. This is the single-mother generation, the welfare generation, the collectivist generation. The generation of obesity, porn, and video games. Will that be our legacy? Surely it will — if we continue down this dark and decadent path.

Although we have a lot to change in terms of policy, it must all begin with each single American. Be proud of your heritage and your culture. I encourage you to learn more about who you are and where you are from. Learn the language of your great grandparents. Find the European town your ancestors came from and go visit it if you can. If not, read about it. Learn to cook some of the old family recipes. Read about your culture and ancestry. Read about the Wright Brothers and their unwavering sister, Katherine. Read about the Revolutionaries, the dissidents, the thought criminals of years gone by. Learn about the people who changed the world for the better. Discover where you came from; it will help you understand where you're going. We have become rootless in our own lands. Find your way home again.

Take care of yourself. The CDC reports that 80 percent of Americans do not get enough exercise.[14] According to Bankrate, over 60 percent of Americans have less $500 in savings, and far more in personal debt than in savings.[15] Get out more, save your money, pay off debt, and take care of

14 Ryan Jaslow. "CDC: 80 percent of American adults don't get recommended exercise" CBS News. May 03, 2013. http://www.cbsnews.com/news/cdc-80-percent-of-american-adults-dont-get-recommended-exercise/. [http://archive.li/LzJ41]

15 Kristin Wong. "Most Americans Lack Reserve Cash to Cover $500 Emergency: Survey" NBC News. January 08, 2016. http://www.nbcnews.com/business/personal-finance/most-americans-lack-reserve-cash-cover-500-emergency-survey-n493096. [http://archive.li/T856O]

each other. Eat rice and fish if it'll help you escape the bondage of usury or improve your health. If we are healthy and free, in body and in mind, we cannot be controlled. Help your family, your parents, your friends, and neighbors along these same lines. Encourage each other, pay off debt, save, and exercise together. Work towards common goals.

Travel the country if you can. See for yourself how beautiful and how splendid our nation truly is. Visit places you've always dreamt of seeing, and find places you never knew existed along the way. If you do it right, you won't come back the same as when you left.

Explore your community. Meet some new people. Take that yoga class, or music lessons, or whatever it is. Learn about the local history of the place where you live. Find a new local bar or restaurant or shop you never knew existed. Do something — anything — other than the regularly scheduled programming. Do something to wake yourself up.

Live your life in such a way, that you will not find yourself one day looking back on your life and wishing you hadn't taken so many beautiful days for granted — days just like this one.

And read more. But don't believe everything you read. Question everything. I'm not even asking you to believe *me*. Check my sources, see for yourself.

Remember — the System needs us to be poor, sick, and unlearned. The entire basis of their power is predicated upon *our* weakness, not *their* strength. Free yourself from financial strain, from a sedentary life, and free your mind.

> The free man is a warrior. — Friedrich Nietzsche

Perhaps most importantly — tell the truth. To the forked-tongue liars among us, the truth is as Holy water cast on demons. The truth is an elegant weapon; it is the one and only silver bullet needed to expel the golem army which is rising up even now, enchanted by their lies.

All is not yet lost. There is still time to change the road we are on. The hour is late, and the night is dark. But all it not yet lost. A light still flickers — if only we choose to fan the Promethean flames of the Occident.

Never lose hope. And never despair. Do not give in to culturally transmitted malaise and hopeless nihilism, as is so easy to do with the odds stacked against us, as they presently are. Never forget what a small, dedicated group of men can achieve. It only takes a handful of brave souls to change the world. In fact, it's the only thing that ever has.

There would be no Europe or America today if not for small bands of men coming together against seemingly insurmountable odds and proclaiming in the face of looming disaster that tomorrow, we shall live yet, and more boldly still than ever before.

III

Beyond Left & Right

In the dystopian science fiction film *The Matrix*, a young boy helps Neo realize the fundamental truth that "There is no spoon." In the same sense that there is no spoon, there is no need for party politics or political debates. I've come to realize there is no Left and no Right. There is only the truth.

It took writing an entire book for me to see that I was not merely attacking the Left or the fake "conservative" Right. Nor was I supporting the true Right. I was seeking only the truth. Looking for some objective high ground in this postmodern flood. And upon coming as close as I could reach towards an objective reality, I found that, beyond a certain point, there were no more politics. If two people look on the reality of what is happening daily in our societies and come to different conclusions about it, they both cannot be correct. Only one, or neither, has epistemologically realized knowledge. The other must be either lying or deranged. What the mainstream, hegemonic culture, calls a "Far Right" ideology, is at heart, in its social and political principles, little more than truths that are becoming increasingly evident.

There was a lot of talk, before the 2016 election, between the election and inauguration, and after, about "healing the divide." This is no surprise; the US experienced a very personal, drawn-out election. The social mood slowly decayed from innocuous folly, to nervous tension, to rampant hatred, all before a single ballot was cast. It makes sense that many people were interested in bringing Americans back together. For many saw the election as a soft civil war, and never has this country forgotten the horror of civil war.

However, I do not see this as an era of post-civil-war reconstruction. Nor do I see a possibility of attaining any reasonable compromise. Both the American and European Left and Right do not simply want different things; they do not merely have somewhat varying goals. They are fundamentally different cultures. Their dispute goes far beyond them, far beyond Left and Right. It even goes beyond Nationalism and Globalism. What we have entered is a battle over the truth. And certain factions have declared they will fight to their last breath in order to hide that truth, because the vast web of lies they have spent almost a century weaving is the unique trap by which we might be captured and enslaved.

Indeed, the post-election is less an era of reconstruction, than it is a period akin to the removal of the Loyalists following American Revolution. I did not see the election as a civil war, I saw it as more of a revolution — or at least the start of one.

The divide between the Left and Right can never and will never be healed. We cannot compromise. Nor should we. The Left has made it clear: they want our money, they want our guns, they want us controlled, and they want dissenters dead in mass graves in snowy forests. In such a case as this reconciliation is literally impossible. When *we* say we do not want any more migration, and *they* say we need to let in another half a million male "refugees" next year, the "compromise" falls at a quarter of a million coming next year, and the year after that, and the year after that — and sooner or later, *they* win.

When *we* say we do not want to be taxed, that we want to be able to own our homes without paying rent to the government for eternity, *they* say they need more tax dollars to pay for an endless refugee "crises" or global warming or any other number of schemes. They always have a new cause or scam that requires our money. The "compromise" will be temporarily lowering tax rates by a percent or two, while we are still effectively slave laborers and feudalistic serfs.

When the 1965 Immigration Act was passed, America was 90 percent of European descent; the Left passed the Act while lying through its teeth that this legislation would not change the fundamental demographics of the nation. Now, they cheer and applaud the demographic projections that show every single European population on Earth becoming a minority in its own homeland, within this very century.

Germans were not even able to enjoy a Christmas market this past Christmas season without being murdered, or having the market shut down, or living anxious under the continual threat of these things. This is the natural result of the Liberal lie that migration will not change our culture: we are left with a shadow of our former nations.

The international Left-wing clique cannot be compromised with or negotiated with. They have launched a total war on our way of life, our fundamental values; compromise means demise.

Stop trying to find a middle road with them or to get them to like you or to discover some mutual ground with them. Liberals want us dead. No one but the suicidal and the insane try to make peace with their mortal enemies. They will never care about you. They are monsters. And they will never relent nor give us any respite, until better men force them to do so. Nobody in the history of Western civilization has been able to vote his way out of this kind of quagmire. Reasoning with them, voting against them, hoping they might be persuaded to change their minds, is not a plan.

The difference between us and them is not merely political or ideological. We are of fundamentally different ilk. The differences are irreconcilable and their hate against us is illimitable.

It is impossible to bargain with extremists; but Liberals are extremists. They will anchor their propositions on entirely unrealistic expectations, then adjust down to a smaller victory, but a victory nonetheless. As fundamental a psychological trick as this is, most of the people we have elected to fend off the Liberals still haven't caught on. Reasoning with extremists does not work; becoming extreme in our own convictions is our only hope.

Liberals would rather live under a globalist government ruled by an international clique than under a sovereign and nationalist regime. The Left has made it clear they want a global state with no borders, in which everything is "equally" divided and the collective is always put before the individual. How can we compromise with this line of thinking? According to *our* values, the international Left is the world's foremost problem.

The US was designed as a Constitutional Republic, and not a democratic majority rule, because those who created our nation understood the perils of direct democracy. The majority of people will inevitably vote to take away rights from the minority in order to achieve some egalitarian dream. Those who oppose the egalitarian dream are of course sent to the Gulag. We tend to forget how soon social democracy devolves into social totalitarianism.

In the book *Democracy: The God That Failed*, economist and philosopher Hans-Hermann Hoppe wrote about the inherent conflict that arises between collectivists and those that wish to maintain individual liberties and private ownership. He concludes that egalitarianism is simply incompatible with freedom. If you wish to have a society that values individual liberty and private property, those seeking to undermine those values either through voting to take away your rights, or any government which actively does take away your rights, need to be physically removed from society.

He writes,

> Egalitarianism, in every form and shape, is incompatible with the idea of private property. Private property implies exclusivity, inequality, and difference. And cultural relativism is incompatible with the fundamental — indeed foundational — fact of families and intergenerational kinship relations. Families and kinship relations imply cultural absolutism.
>
> One may say innumerable things and promote almost any idea under the sun, but naturally no one is permitted to advocate ideas contrary to the very covenant of preserving and protecting private property, such as democracy and communism. There can be no tolerance toward democrats and communists in a libertarian social order. They will have to be physically separated and removed from society.[16]

Those who support communism, or any of its variations, even communism masquerading as democracy, are implicitly, or explicitly if they are versed in history, supporting our physical demise. There is no way around

16 Hans-Hermann Hoppe. Democracy — the god that failed: the economics and politics of monarchy, democracy, and natural order. New Brunswick, NJ: Transaction Publ., 2007.

this fact. More mass murders, famine, disease, and death have been directly and indirectly caused by communism than by any other ideology in the history of the world. Those who espouse the same principles, no matter how shrouded or veiled these principles might be, deserve no place in our society. Do not take them lightly: the useful idiots are as dangerous as the very elected officials who are leading our people to ruin. They are all actively seeking our demise. More, those marching in the streets to silence us and disarm us are engaging in sedition. They should not be granted rights they do not fundamentally believe in. People using their free speech in an effort to take *our* right to free speech through "hate speech" laws highlights the failures of Liberalism and Libertarianism. We simply cannot coexist with these people. Simply wanting to be left alone is not an effective strategy. They will never leave you alone. They will always seek more taxation, more mass migration, more infringements, more gun control, more censorship. All I ever wanted was to be left alone. But at a certain point I realized there would be no peace until the warmongers and war-bringers among us were dealt with.

There is no more time to waste tolerating subversive entities that seek to destroy the West. Our enemies, the enemies of Western civilization, are tribal, very well-organized, and extremely efficient. We must be the same if we are to win.

Viktor Orbán was right: "We are fighting an enemy that is different from us. Not open, but hiding; not straightforward but crafty; not honest but base; not national but international; does not believe in working but speculates with money; does not have its own homeland but feels it owns the whole world."[17]

The mere act of advocating for policies that would restrict the fundamental rights specified in the Bill of Rights should be considered treason against the American people. Until we get serious about this, and politicians are physically removed from office who seek to open our borders, to silence us, to endanger us and our futures, the Left will continue to launch

---

17 Shaun Walker. "Hungarian Leader Says Europe Is Now 'under Invasion' by Migrants" The Guardian. March 15, 2018. https://www.theguardian.com/world/2018/mar/15/hungarian-leader-says-europe-is-now-under-invasion-by-migrants. [http://archive.is/cVohU].

assault after assault against us. Sitting around and playing gate keeper does not work when our worst enemies have already entered.

Gun control, mass migration, censorship, taxation might not all appear to be directly related, but they are. They are united under the same goal of ensuring the white European people are silenced, defenseless, poor, and replaceable, devoid of any recourse against the onslaught of the global Left. Throughout history, the silencing, extortion, disarmament, and displacement of a people were always the first steps towards genocide. Our enemies are preparing to turn the Occident into one gargantuan communist prison camp, if not a Rhodesian nightmare.

As long as Liberals exist in a society, they will not rest until they have found a way to limit individual liberties in favor of the collective. They will try to outvote us, and when that doesn't work they will import more people to vote with them, and when that doesn't work they will do whatever is necessary to gain power once more and limit our freedoms. We have seen this all before; we will see it again. But sooner or later, it will be too late to go back.

Hate speech laws are an example. The Left all over Europe has achieved such laws, and those in the US are hungering for them. At essence, a society that enacts hate speech laws is smothering the value of truth. The idea of hate speech indicates that the potential for somebody to be offended is such a priority that society would prefer to deprive another of his liberty, and lock him in a cage, than so much as risk that he might hurt another person's feelings, or bring the truth to light. That the mere utterance of certain words is justification for ruining a life.

Taxation and firearm bans are further examples. Taxing personal income means depriving a person of their labor. It means stealing their time and effort. Property taxes create a state of feudalism. The theft of time and property are advocated by the Left, which "democratically" grants the State the power to imprison a man or to execute him if he resists. Firearm restrictions fall within the same frame: if you do not comply with the will of those who voted against you, they will have the State come and give you a choice of prison or execution. Every time a Liberal votes for another tax, another restriction, another needless law, he is saying that if you do not comply, he will gladly have the State force you to submit to his will. Under no circumstances should a system like this be allowed to exist. For the logical conclusion of wanting to take away property or rights of a person, is to have that desire enforced through violence.

The call for amnesty, mass migration, and open borders, should not be viewed as Liberal expressing their opinions on immigration, but rather as Liberals betraying their desire for our dispossession. This should be viewed as their almost open planning of a hostile invasion, a coup, and our eventual genocide. The stakes are far higher than what they would have you believe: this is not about "immigration policy," this is about whether or not we continue to exist as a race of people.

Nobody censors the far Left. They are able to freely espouse views that would lead to our demise as a people. It's time we not only give the Left a taste of their own medicine, but force fed them the entire bottle. If they are going to openly press for our demise with such insolence, they should be treated as the hostile invasive species that they are.

The Left has been abundantly clear that they will cheer our death as a victory, simply because we have the wrong political views (or in many cases the wrong skin color). They are fighting to destroy everything we have ever held dear. They do nothing but destroy and tear down. We are fighting to preserve everything that is good and beautiful in this world. They bring chaos and destruction. As the men against time, we fight for order and clarity.

After the American Revolution, thousands of those who remained loyal to the King were given a choice; they didn't have to go home to England, but they couldn't stay here. As the remaining British soldiers were leaving American cities, many Loyalists went back with them. Many others went to live in Canada, as they were no longer welcome in the United States after they had demonstrated where their loyalty truly lay.[18] Our forefathers recognized the truth of this simple fact: that those who wish to subvert an order, because they fundamentally do not agree with it, will continue with their subversion until they are removed or disenfranchised. But the entire Liberal platform is one of subversion and oppression.

Throughout history there have been certain groups that build civilizations and certain groups that destroy them. It is well within our rights to

18 "What Happened To British Loyalists After The Revolutionary War" NPR. July 03, 2015. http://www.npr.org/2015/07/03/419824333/what-happened-to-british-loyalists-after-the-revolutionary-war. [http://archive.li/anprg]

expel everybody and anybody that works towards the destruction of our civilization and the demise of our people. We will not know peace until we do so.

The people who are burning our civilization, the criminal lunatics that seek our demise — they have names. They have jobs. They have families. They have addresses. They should know their days of impunity are coming to an end. In truth, they should be afraid of the Right. They have been attacking our kind for years, generations even. Comeuppance is due. If I were them, I wouldn't be so worried about "white privilege"; I would be far more concerned about looming white Imperium.

Fin

I was, and still am, a simple man. Once upon a time I was not all that interested in politics. Certainly not interested enough to dedicate so much time to writing a treatise on the subject. I have simple interests. I like to ride my road bicycle on the wooded trail near my home, an old railroad line turned into a bicycle path, then stay out to watch the sunsets from the same spot. I like to spend time with my family; it's not a big family, but they are my only connection to the past. And I like to spend time with the few close friends I have, the majority of whom I've known most of my life.

It wasn't that I had changed; it was the world around me that was changing. I watched it happen in Europe rather abruptly, with the States following suit. The change was not for the better. We moved away from our proud traditions and long-held ideals. The further we moved from them, the closer we moved towards something dark and horrifying. Something hardly recognizable. No place I wanted to call home.

> Tradition is not the worship of ashes but the preservation of fire. — Gustav Mahler

I have been made political by the time in which I live. I'm more of a radical traditionalist, searching for the truth as if it were some high relic of a bygone era. The ideas I have written in this book are merely the logical conclusions to which I have arrived after thoroughly examining the evidence, after the countless hours I have spent trying to find my way out of the postmodern maze. And I find that, after writing a political critique and treatise, I am still not interested in politics. I'm interested in something far grander. I am thinking toward our future as a people, toward what we could become.

I am interested in ending the hopeless nihilism and impersonal atomization that is so prevalent among our people. I am interested in moving beyond this era and working towards building a lasting legacy for ourselves and our posterity. Something that will live on far beyond our years.

I've grown weary of our consumerist, materialistic, deracinated, preplanned obsolescence, our asphalt culture, in which we pave over everything in order to make way for the next box and chain stores, the next hollow sub-division rented by hollow people. Instead of every city beginning to look the same, I would love a culture that favored small businesses and master craftsman again, and helped them thrive. I've grown tired of conspicuous consumerism and empty materialism that has been replacing our traditional values — this "lifestyle" which encourages our people not to aspire to be more, but to have more.

I dream of an architectural revival. A revenge of Classicalism. An American Renaissance. And a return to aesthetics. Where we once again build cities to last for generations, cities magnificent for their beauty, rather than their size, which even in ruin and remnants would surpass all others.

I am weary of the foodstuffs and prolefeed. The media trash that keeps being piled higher. The bread and circuses. We have become so decadent we seem no longer even to mind our own enslavement and dispossession. How soon we have forgotten "that man does not live on bread alone"!

I am interested in finding the way back to our roots.

> Everyone needs beauty as well as bread, places to play in and pray in where nature may heal and cheer and give strength to body and soul alike. — John Muir, 1869

We are being wildly dispossessed in our own homeland. Imagine being homesick for a place that no longer exists: I've come across few thoughts to be as depressing as this. Eventually the desire to return home, to our roots, will beckon. If we do not act now, we will have nowhere to turn when it does.

Revitalizing our nation means recovering the inner strength and spirit of the American people. The greatness of this nation lies within each of us. Through our own struggle, diligence, endurance, and defiance, will we rise again. If there was ever a greater torch to take up than in the fight for our history, our civilization, and our people, I have yet to find it.

So take care of yourself. Take care of your family, your community, your culture, your neighbors, your environment, and the creatures we share this planet with. It is all connected. I don't know how exactly, but I know we are all born of the same stars, and wander under the same sun.

> Be radical, have principles, be absolute, be that which the bourgeoisie calls an extremist: give yourself without counting or calculating, don't accept what they call "the reality of life" and act in such a way that you won't be accepted by that kind of "life," never abandon the principle of struggle.[19]

This is beyond Left and Right. This is about good and evil. Those seeking our destruction, and those of us fighting for survival. Many Liberals might be decent people in some ways. They seem to want to help animals, protect the environment, and help people, things I can appreciate. However, the policies which they favor are so destructive, so harmful, so massively insane, it becomes hard to see any good at all in them. They are causing the genocidal rape of young girls and women all over Europe, they are extorting us via taxation, they are fighting to take away our rights, they are causing tens of thousands of lives to be lost through open border policies, destroying social capital, turning our homelands into trash heaps, and spitting in the face of the matchless heritage of the West. The say they want to help those down on their luck, the homeless — yet the Arab and African migrants they welcome set fire to homeless people in train stations. They

19 Koenraad Elst. *Return of the Swastika: Hate and Hysteria versus Hindu Sanity.* Arktos. 2015.

support animal welfare — yet the migrants they welcome torture and dismember small kittens, snap the necks of swans, and cook dogs alive in our homelands.[20] [21] The followers of Liberalism are nothing but useful idiots, willing apparatchiks, to the internationalists and the globalists, who are men without any redeeming characteristics whatsoever. In a way, I feel bad for them. They have been infected and corrupted by a foreign ideology, a mind-virus. They have lost their way.

I don't think anything could be written more accurately describing the current metapolitical and cultural divide than what was said already in 1776:

> When in the course of human events, it becomes necessary for one people to dissolve the political bands which have connected them with another, and to assume among the powers of the earth, the separate and equal station to which the Laws of Nature and of Nature's God entitle them, a decent respect to the opinions of mankind requires that they should declare the causes which impel them to the separation.

We are the guardians of the weak, the defenseless, the small; we are the custodians of nature. We should act as such. Children and women are being raped. Animals abused, bred to have muscular dystrophy and subjected to horrific experiments, living out a miserable existence in small cages. All of this, including the barbaric practice of Kosher and Halal slaughter, have no place in the West. It must all be expelled, and with haste.

While the Left continues to attack my virtues, and to defame me as some hate-filled monster, I ask simply: is it hateful that I want to restore a sense of calm and inner peace to my fellow men? Is it xenophobic if I want to end mass migration in order to ensure the safety of my people?

---

20 Selwyn Duke. "Kittens' Guts Ripped Out: Heinous Cruelty to Animals in Muslim "No-go Zone"" The New American. June 16, 2017. https://www.thenewamerican.com/world-news/item/26271-kittens-guts-ripped-out-heinous-cruelty-to-animals-in-muslim-no-go-zone. [http://archive.is/h5RuT].

21 Thomas D. Williams. "Culture Shock: Italians Aghast as Immigrants Barbecue Dog at Welcome Center" Breitbart. February 16, 2018. http://www.breitbart.com/london/2018/02/16/culture-shock-italians-aghast-as-immigrants-barbecue-dog-at-welcome-center/. [http://archive.li/5eVCZ].

Is it bigoted if I want Americans to feel a sense of pride and purpose in their lives? Is it vile of me to want humanity to live more harmoniously with nature? To want to end animal mills, factory farming, trapping, along with the reckless, wasteful, and barbaric animal testing? Am I a "science denier" because I see the horrors of a vivisection which produces no justifiable results? That I see the practice as barbaric sadism hiding under the guise of "education, science, and progress"?

Is it sexist of me to see the rape rates increasing and to want to hold those responsible accountable for their crimes? And I ask, is it hateful to want to expel the Judeo-Liberal-Marxist decadence, filth, and degeneracy which deteriorates the values that built this nation? Is it hateful of me to notice the misery brought on by Liberalism, and to want to see it vanquished, in all the masks it wears?

If those things make me a xenophobic, bigoted, ignorant, barbaric, sexists, hate-filled monster, then I will gladly accept the honor of those charges on behalf of my people.

And even if the Left is correct, even if my people are all racist, drunken, ignorant, and white trash — they are still my people. I still love them and I will still fight for them. I'm not as concerned with what they are today. But what I know they can become tomorrow.

I dream of what we could achieve if we were not wasting our time staving off Liberal assaults and barbarian hordes. The stars could have been ours had they not held us back at every turn. The Left has been given long arrears to make good. And now, long overdue, with our eyes level and straight, we will take back everything that is rightfully ours.

This is our great war. Before us lies one of two paths and one of two paths alone: either our extinction — or the dawn of a magnificent era. The Occident isn't going to save itself. It will need our bravery. Our people need us, now more than ever. This new era of nationalism we embark upon entails perhaps the greatest struggle that has ever been undertaken. This is a rescue mission. They are trying to take everything from us, everything we have ever held dear. We must decide if we are going to continue heaping up our own funeral pyre, or if we are going to emblazon the world with this flame. As night falls upon us, we must always remember, only those who step into the darkness will see the stars.

Our nations are worth the sacrifice. Our civilization is worth fighting for. Our people are worth any struggle. Because in the end, they will be our greatest legacy.

In the end, it was this simple realization which led me to sit down and to write the book that the reader is now concluding. I could not sit idly by any longer and watch the flames of my people's spirit being smothered by rootless politicians, deracinated masses, an insolent press, and maniacal Leftists. I really didn't know what to do. This country and the West as a whole needed another awaking, like that which was once brought by the Renaissance and the Age of Enlightenment.

I thought a long time about every great revolution the world has known. But I kept looking in all the wrong places. I was too focused on the specifics, thinking about the individual incitements, and who played what role in overthrowing whom. I needed to step back and look at the grand scheme. Every great revolution started much earlier.

The American Revolution did not start because the king taxed paper products; it did not start by tossing tea into a harbor; nor was is started with that rifle shot at North Bridge. The American Revolution started many years before, when those who would later become the fearless Revolutionaries first read the works of Locke, Voltaire, and Rousseau. As with every revolution, it started with one man's dream for a better world. A vision written down, followed by an appeal to heaven.

These are the steps I have chosen to follow in. Nothing could be more humbling and more bracing, than to be standing on this hallowed ground with those who came before me. There could be no higher honor, or greater privilege, than the opportunity to struggle for my people. For our own people will always be the most precious possession we have. I have no doubt that these are the times that try men's souls. It is ours now to prove ourselves. We are the children of men who looked longingly into the heavens and dreamed of something greater. We are the men among the ruins. The men against time.

We are the last of a dying breed — or perhaps, the first of a new one.

Technical Appendix: The Cure for Liberalism

There is no known cure. Treatment may help.

Experimental treatments involving high-altitude rotorcraft therapy proved wildly successful for a brief period circa 1973.[1] [2]

1 Jonathan Franklin. "Chilean army admits 120 thrown into sea" The Guardian. January 08, 2001. https://www.theguardian.com/world/2001/jan/09/chile.pinochet. [http://archive.li/a3O6t]

2 "General Pinochet's statement in full" BBC News. November 08, 1998. http://news.bbc.co.uk/2/hi/uk_news/209742.stm. [http://archive.li/3MoH]

Index

E

Y

Z

OTHER BOOKS PUBLISHED BY ARKTOS

Sri Dharma Pravartaka Acharya	*The Dharma Manifesto*
Joakim Andersen	*Rising from the Ruins: The Right of the 21st Century*
Alain de Benoist	*Beyond Human Rights*
	Carl Schmitt Today
	The Indo-Europeans
	Manifesto for a European Renaissance
	On the Brink of the Abyss
	The Problem of Democracy
	Runes and the Origins of Writing
	View from the Right (vol. 1–3)
Arthur Moeller van den Bruck	*Germany's Third Empire*
Matt Battaglioli	*The Consequences of Equality*
Kerry Bolton	*Revolution from Above*
	Yockey: A Fascist Odyssey
Isac Boman	*Money Power*
Ricardo Duchesne	*Faustian Man in a Multicultural Age*
Alexander Dugin	*Ethnos and Society*
	Eurasian Mission: An Introduction to Neo-Eurasianism
	The Fourth Political Theory
	Last War of the World-Island
	Putin vs Putin
	The Rise of the Fourth Political Theory
Mark Dyal	*Hated and Proud*
Koenraad Elst	*Return of the Swastika*

OTHER BOOKS PUBLISHED BY ARKTOS

Julius Evola	*The Bow and the Club*
	Fascism Viewed from the Right
	A Handbook for Right-Wing Youth
	Metaphysics of War
	The Myth of the Blood
	Notes on the Third Reich
	The Path of Cinnabar
	Recognitions
	A Traditionalist Confronts Fascism
Guillaume Faye	*Archeofuturism*
	Archeofuturism 2.0
	The Colonisation of Europe
	Convergence of Catastrophes
	A Global Coup
	Sex and Deviance
	Understanding Islam
	Why We Fight
Daniel S. Forrest	*Suprahumanism*
Andrew Fraser	*Dissident Dispatches*
	The WASP Question
Génération Identitaire	*We are Generation Identity*
Paul Gottfried	*War and Democracy*
Porus Homi Havewala	*The Saga of the Aryan Race*
Lars Holger Holm	*Hiding in Broad Daylight*
	Homo Maximus
	Incidents of Travel in Latin America
	The Owls of Afrasiab
Alexander Jacob	*De Naturae Natura*

OTHER BOOKS PUBLISHED BY ARKTOS

Jason Reza Jorjani	*Prometheus and Atlas* *World State of Emergency*
Roderick Kaine	*Smart and SeXy*
Peter King	*Here and Now* *Keeping Things Close*
Ludwig Klages	*The Biocentric Worldview* *Cosmogonic Reflections*
Pierre Krebs	*Fighting for the Essence*
Stephen Pax Leonard	*Travels in Cultural Nihilism*
Pentti Linkola	*Can Life Prevail?*
H. P. Lovecraft	*The Conservative*
Charles Maurras	*The Future of the Intelligentsia & For a French Awakening*
Michael O'Meara	*Guillaume Faye and the Battle of Europe* *New Culture, New Right*
Brian Anse Patrick	*The NRA and the Media* *Rise of the Anti-Media* *The Ten Commandments of Propaganda* *Zombology*
Tito Perdue	*The Bent Pyramid* *Morning Crafts* *Philip* *William's House* (vol. 1–4)
Raido	*A Handbook of Traditional Living*
Steven J. Rosen	*The Agni and the Ecstasy* *The Jedi in the Lotus*

OTHER BOOKS PUBLISHED BY ARKTOS

Richard Rudgley	*Barbarians* *Essential Substances* *Wildest Dreams*
Ernst von Salomon	*It Cannot Be Stormed* *The Outlaws*
Sri Sri Ravi Shankar	*Celebrating Silence* *Know Your Child* *Management Mantras* *Patanjali Yoga Sutras* *Secrets of Relationships*
George T. Shaw (ed.)	*A Fair Hearing: The Alt-Right in the Words of Its Members and Leaders*
Oswald Spengler	*Man and Technics*
Tomislav Sunic	*Against Democracy and Equality* *Homo Americanus* *Postmortem Report* *Titans are in Town*
Hans-Jürgen Syberberg	*On the Fortunes and Misfortunes of Art in Post-War Germany*
Abir Taha	*Defining Terrorism: The End of Double Standards* *The Epic of Arya* (2nd ed.) *Nietzsche's Coming God, or the Redemption of the Divine* *Verses of Light*
Bal Gangadhar Tilak	*The Arctic Home in the Vedas*
Dominique Venner	*For a Positive Critique* *The Shock of History*
Markus Willinger	*A Europe of Nations* *Generation Identity*

41753757R00264

Made in the USA
Columbia, SC
15 December 2018